A

DIGEST OF LAWS

RELATING TO THE

CITY OF PHILADELPHIA,

FROM ITS

Territorial Extension, by Act of Assembly, approved February 2d, 1854, until the close of the Session of the Legislature in 1865.

WITH AN APPENDIX CONTAINING THE CHARTERS OF THE

VARIOUS PASSENGER RAILWAYS,

WHICH ARE SUBJECT TO THE CONTROL OF THE

COUNCILS OF PHILADELPHIA,

AND OF THE LAWS AND ORDINANCES THERETO.

PREPARED UNDER THE SUPERVISION OF THE

Law Department of the City of Philadelphia.

1865.

PHILADELPHIA:
KING & BAIRD, PRINTERS, 607 SANSOM STREET.
1865.

PREFATORY NOTE.

In every case in which there is italization in a section, the words italicised are inserted because such is the legal effect of the Act of March 21st, 1861, (P. L. 165,) usually known as the Act abolishing the Spring Election.

INDEX.

INCORPORATION OF THE CITY.

LEGISLATIVE POWERS OF THE CITY.

WARDS.

MAYOR OF PHILADELPHIA.

SOLICITOR OF PHILADELPHIA.

CITY TREASURER.

CITY CONTROLLER.

CITY COMMISSIONERS.

ASSESSORS.

BOARD OF REVISION.

RECEIVER OF TAXES, AND TAXES.

SCHOOL DIRECTORS AND CONTROLLERS.

ALDERMEN.

CONSTABLES.

COMMISSIONERS AND SUPERVISORS OF HIGHWAYS.

SURVEYORS AND SURVEYS.

BUILDING INSPECTORS AND BUILDINGS.

BOARD OF HEALTH.

BIRTHS—MARRIAGES—DEATHS.

BOARD OF GUARDIANS OF THE POOR.

INSPECTORS OF COUNTY PRISONS.

ELECTION DIVISIONS.

ELECTIONS AND ELECTION OFFICERS.

PORT WARDENS.

DELAWARE AVENUE.

INCOMPATIBLE OFFICES.

LEGISLATION OF 1862.

LEGISLATION OF 1863.

SESSION OF 1864

INDEX TO PASSENGER RAILWAYS.

SESSION OF 1865.

SESSION OF 1865.

A DIGEST OF THE LAWS

RELATIVE TO THE

CITY OF PHILADELPHIA

INCORPORATION OF THE CITY.

SECTION 1. That the corporate name of the Mayor, Aldermen and Citizens of Philadelphia, shall be changed to "The City of Philadelphia," and the boundaries of the said city shall be extended so as to embrace the whole of the territory of the county of Philadelphia, and all the powers of the said corporation, as enlarged and modified by this act, shall be exercised and have effect within the said county and over the inhabitants thereof.

SEC. 2. All the right, title, and interest of the several townships, districts, and other municipal corporations mentioned in this act, of, in, and to all the lands, tenements, hereditaments, bridges, ferries, railroads, wharves, market stalls, landings, landing places, water works, gas works, buildings, easements, and franchises, of, in, and to all goods, chattels, moneys, effects, debts, dues, demands, amercements, fees, perquisites, rights, incomes, bonds, obligations, judgments, liens, actions, and rights of action, books, accounts, and vouchers, and of, in, and to, all other property and estates whatsoever and wheresoever, belonging to any or either of them, be and they are hereby vested in the city of Philadelphia, to take effect on the first organization of the City Councils. *Provided*, That all the estates and incomes now held in trust by the county (present city) and each of the townships, districts, and other municipal corporations united by this act, shall be held by the city of Philadelphia, upon, and for the same uses, trusts, limitations, charities and conditions, as the same are now held by the said corporations respectively.

SEC. 3. That all bonds, contracts and obligations heretofore executed, judgments entered, claims filed, and suits now pending in the name of any department of said city, formerly having had a corporate existence, are declared to

1. Act of Feb. 2, 1854, Sec. 1, P. L. 21.
2. Ibid. Sec. 38, P. L. 40.
3. Act of April 21, 1855, Sec. 11, P. L. 264.

be good and valid and to inure to the use of the city; but no such department shall be taken to have had since the passage of the act to which this is a supplement, a separate corporate existence, and hereafter all suits growing out of their transactions, and all claims to be filed for removing nuisances, together with all bonds, contracts and obligations, hereafter to be entered into or received by the said department, shall be in the name of the city of Philadelphia, and that all indentures of apprenticeship by the Guardians of the Poor of the said city shall be executed in the name of the said city; and the assent of the said city thereto, and to all contracts, bonds, and obligations, entered into by any of the said departments, shall be evidenced by the signatures of the President and Secretary of such department affixed thereto.

SEC. 4. That all laws providing for the appointment of tax collectors within the said city of Philadelphia, and all other laws altered or supplied by this act, are hereby repealed. *Provided, however,* That the city of Philadelphia shall have and possess all and every, the full power, right and authority to collect all the debts, demands and property of all and every kind transferred to and vested in the said city by virtue of this act, as if the corporations hereby dissolved were not extinct, and all suits to be brought therefor shall be in the name of the city of Philadelphia, as if the same had been originally vested in the said city.

Suits against the city now pending.

SEC. 5. That all suits now pending against any department of the city of Philadelphia, formerly having had a corporate existence, may be prosecuted with the same force and effect as if such corporation were still in existence, and the said city shall be liable in the same manner and form as such corporation might or would be if still existing.

Power of Councils to extend the the operation of laws in force to other parts of the new city.

SEC. 6. That all acts of the Legislature not inconsistent with this act, now in force, shall continue in operation within the limits of the county, city, district, borough or township in which they are now operative, under the authority of the City Councils, courts and officers created by this act or permitted to continue as consistent therewith, until such acts shall be altered or repealed by the Legislature. *Provided,* That the City Councils shall have power by ordinance to extend the operation of laws now in force within the city, police or municipal districts, to other parts, or over the whole of the enlarged limits, and to declare what laws have become obsolete by this act, or the extension as aforesaid of other laws.(*a*) All ordinances of the present

4. Act of Feb. 2, 1854, Sec. 43, P. L. 43.
5. Act of May 16, 1857, Sec. 1, P. L. 548.
6. Act of Feb. 2, 1854, Sec. 44, P. L. 43.

(*a*) As this would seem to be a delegation by the Legislature of their franchise to enact laws, it would be inoperative if applied. Parker *v.* Commonwealth 6 Barr, 507.

city of Philadelphia and other municipalities within the county of Philadelphia, shall continue in force within the limits of said city and municipalities respectively, until repealed by said Councils, and no longer; and said Councils in enacting new ordinances may make such distinction between the built and rural portions of the new city as they may deem required by circumstances. It shall be the duty of Councils to cause the laws and ordinances of said city, as they shall be framed and adopted under this act, to be published for the information of the citizens, and to present copies thereof to the Executive, the State Library, and each member of the present Legislature and the Legislature to convene next after the publication, and to make applications for such further legislation as shall thereupon be found necessary.

Ordinances to be published.

To apply further legislation.

SEC. 7. That the county of Philadelphia shall continue to be one of the counties of this Commonwealth, and all county officers not superseded by this act, shall continue in office, and continue to be elected and voted for at the places of election provided for by this act, as in other respects now provided by law, and be denominated officers of the county of Philadelphia; and all courts shall continue therein to exercise the jurisdiction and powers now conferred upon them by the Constitution and laws of this Commonwealth, and the Councils of said city and the officers thereof, shall exercise all the powers and authorities of the superseded County Commissioners and County Board, and Commissioners of Sinking Fund, and of other officers, not inconsistent with this act, in such way and manner as by this act is, or by the City Councils may be, established.

County of Philadelphia.

County officers not superseded to continue in office.

LEGISLATIVE POWER OF THE CITY.

SECTION 8. That the legislative powers of the said city shall be vested in two bodies, to be called the Select and Common Councils; the Select Council shall consist of one member from each ward, who shall have the same qualifications as are required by the Constitution of this Commonwealth for members of the Senate, and shall be elected as follows:

SEC. 9. That hereafter each ward of the City of Philadelphia shall have one member of Select Council, who shall serve for three years from the first day of January next succeding his election, and that one-third of Select Council shall be chosen each year; the qualified voters, on the second Tuesday of October, 1861, of the 1st, 3d, 5th, and 7th wards shall each elect a member of Select Council to

Election of members of Select Council.

7. Act of Feb. 2, 1854, Sec. 41, P. L. 39.
8. Ibid. Sec. 4, P. L. 21.
9. Act of March 21, 1861, Sec. 5, P. L. 165.

serve for one year; of the 9th, 11th, 13th, and 15th wards shall elect each a member of Select Council to serve for two years; of the 17th, 19th, 21st, and 23d wards shall elect each a member of Select Council to serve for three years. And the qualified voters, on the second Tuesday of October, 1862, of the 2d, 4th, 6th, and 8th wards shall elect each a member of Select Council to serve for one year; of the 10th, 12th, 14th, and 16th wards shall elect each a member of Select Council to serve for two years; and of the 18th, 20th, 22d, and 24th wards shall elect each a member of Select Council to serve for three years.

SEC. 10. That in case of a vacancy occurring in the Select Council by death, resignation, or otherwise, and such vacancy taking place during the first year of the term, the qualified voters of such ward shall, at the annual election in May succeeding such vacancy, elect one person duly qualified to serve for one year.

SEC. 11. The members of the Common Council shall have the same qualifications as are required by the Constitution of this Commonwealth for members of the House of Representatives, and shall be elected as follows, to wit:

Election of members of Common Council.

Sec. 12. That each ward of the City of Philadelphia shall have a member of Common Council for each two thousand of taxable inhabitants that it shall contain according to the list of taxables for the preceding year, who shall serve for two years from the first day of January succeeding their election, except those who shall be first elected under the provisions hereof, who shall draw by lot from a list prepared by the clerk, whether their terms shall be for one year or for two years, and thereafter the members shall be elected for two years, and the terms of the present members of Councils of Philadelphia shall continue until their successors shall be elected and qualified to take their seats; and the newly elected members shall meet in the Council Chambers and be qualified on the first Monday of January, at 10 o'clock in the forenoon, of each year, at which hour the terms of their predecessors shall expire. (*b*)

SEC. 13. And it shall be the duty of the Sheriff of the County of Philadelphia, in his proclamation for every municipal election, * * * to state the number of members of the Common Council which the qualified voters of each of the said wards shall be entitled to elect as aforesaid.

SEC. 14. *Provided,* That no member of the State Legis-

---

10. Act of March 30, 1858, Sec. 1, P. L. 183.
11. Act of Feb. 2, 1854, Sec. 4, P. L. 21.
12. Act of March 21, 1861, Sec. 6, P. L. 165.
13. Act of Feb. 2, 1854, Sec. 2, P. L. 21.
14. Ibid. Sec. 4, P. L. 21.

(*b*) Under the provisions of this, there is a representation in Common Council for the year 1862 of 47

lature, nor any one holding office or employment from or under the State at the time of said election, shall be eligible as a member of said Councils; nor shall any member of said Councils, during the term for which he shall be elected, hold any office or employment herein created or provided for of a municipal character. Disqualification clause.

SEC. 15. That the members of the Select and Common Councils shall meet at the City Hall, in said city, and shall then and there organize in separate chambers; the members of each Council shall each be sworn or affirmed to support the Constitution of the United States and of the Commonwealth of Pennsylvania, and that they will discharge the duties of their office with fidelity; each Council shall elect a President and such other officers as may be deemed necessary for the tranaction of business, and shall keep a journal of its proceedings, which shall at all times be open to public inspection. Organization of Councils, oath of office, elect a President and other officers.

SEC. 16. That upon the first organization of the Councils provided for in the preceding section, the City of Philadelphia, as established by this act, shall be vested with all the powers, rights, privileges, and immunities, incident to a municipal corporation, and necessary for the proper government of the same, and those of the present corporation of the Mayor, Aldermen and Citizens of Philadelphia; and upon the said organization of Councils, and upon proclamation made by the Mayor by direction of the said City Councils, fixing a day therefor not exceeding sixty days after the first Tuesday in July then next, all the powers, rights, privileges, and immunities possessed and enjoyed by the following corporations respectively, and of all officers under them, to wit: the Commissioners and inhabitants of the district of Southwark; the Commissioners and inhabitants of the incorporated district of the Northern Liberties; the Commissioners and inhabitants of the Kensington district; the Commissioners and inhabitants of the district of Spring Garden; the Commissioners and inhabitants of the district of Moyamensing; the Commissioners and inhabitants of the district of Penn; the Commissioners and inhabitants of the district of Richmond, in the County of Philadelphia, and of the districts of West Philadelphia and Belmont, of the boroughs of Manayunk, Germantown, Frankford, White Hall, Bridesburg, and Aramingo, and of the townships of Passyunk, Kingsessing, Blockley, Roxborough, Germantown, Bristol, Oxford, Lower Dublin, Moreland, Byberry, Northern Liberties, Delaware and Penn; also of the Board of Police and of the Police District; the present Mayor and Councilmen of the City of Philadelphia; the Commissioners of the County of Philadelphia; the

---

15. Act of Feb. 2, 1854, Sec. 5, P. L. 21.
16. Ibid. Sec. 6, P. L. 24.

Treasurer and Auditors thereof; the County Board; the Commissioners of the Sinking Fund, and Supervisors of townships, shall cease and terminate, except so much thereof as may be necessary to enable the City of Philadelphia, as established by this act, to collect the outstanding debts, and make a full and complete settlement thereof: *Provided,* That all Treasurers, Police and other officers, of the aforesaid, corporations, county and townships, shall continue to discharge the duties of their respective offices until superseded or dismissed by the authority of the City of Philadelphia, and be accountable as officers holding office under said city, and shall account for all moneys in their hands through the auditor, and make payment to the Treasurer of said city: *And Provided,* That no corporation hereby superseded, or whose estate may by force of this act be vested in the city of Philadelphia or the present Council of the corporation of the Mayor, Aldermen and Citizens of Philadelphia, shall, at any time after the passage of this act, contract any loan or debt other than for the ordinary supplies, repairs and payment of labor and salaries.

Power to organize a Police department, and a Fire department.

SEC. 17. That the Select and Common Councils of the city of Philadelphia shall be and they are hereby authorized and directed to organize a police department in and for the said city, and may organize, if necessary a fire department, subordinate to or independent of that of police, and to make, ordain and establish all needful laws and ordinances for the regulation thereof, and for the preservation of the public peace, the suppression of riots and disturbances, and for the extinguishment of fires and the protection of property thereat, and for this purpose the said Councils shall be and hereby are vested with ample power and authority in the premises.

Power to appoint heads of departments.

SEC. 18. That the powers conferred by law on the Police Board of the Police District, shall be exercised by the City Councils. They shall fix the whole number of supervisors of highways, policemen and watchmen, for the service of the whole city. * * * * The Councils shall in joint meeting, and by *viva voce* vote, appoint all the heads of departments not elective, and shall provide by ordinance for the appointments of clerks and officers, except the Mayor's clerk, who shall be appointed by the Mayor, and the Marshal's clerk, who shall be appointed by the Marshal —all of whom shall serve for such periods as may be fixed by ordinance subject to dismissal by the appointing power or superior officer, as such ordinance may provide. The head of each department shall nominate, and by and with the advice and consent of the Select Council, appoint the clerks and officers in his department. The Mayor shall

---

17. Act of Feb. 2, 1854, Sec. 42, P. L. 43.
18. Ibid. Sec. 9. P. L. 27.

nominate, and by and with the advice and consent of the Select Council, appoint the policemen and watchmen.

Policemen may receive rewards.

SEC. 19. That all policemen shall be allowed, with the permission of the Mayor, to receive any rewards or gratuities which may be offered them by persons or institutions who may consider themselves benefited by their extra services: *Provided*, The same shall not have been asked for or promised before the service was rendered to them personally

Policemen not to serve civil process.

SEC. 20. That hereafter it shall not be lawful for any police officer of the City of Philadelphia to perform any service in civil suits*.

Power to establish departments.

SEC. 21. That it shall be the duty of City Councils to provide by ordinance for the establishment and regulation of all the departments indicated by this act and other laws in force in said city, under the proper heads, and with the necessary clerks, officers, and assistants, to wit: For law, police, finance, surveys, highways, health, water, gas, fire, the poor, the city property and the public grounds, and such others as may from time to time be needful; and, through the Mayor and proper committees, the said Councils shall maintain a supervision of each department, whether corporate or otherwise, and over the Inspectors of the County Prison, for the exposure and correction of all evils and abuses, and for that purpose may require the production of and inspect all books and papers, and the attendance of witnesses by subpœna, and examine them under oath or affirmation; but no member or members of Council, whether as a committee or otherwise, shall make any disbursement of corporate moneys, nor audit the accounts thereof, nor perform any other executive duty whatever.

Councilmen not to perform executive duty.

Power to fix duties of others.

SEC. 22. That the City Councils shall fix the compensation and prescribe the duties of all officers of said city in such manner as to carry out the purposes of this act and as the welfare of said city may require, not inconsistent with the laws and Constitution of this Commonwealth and of the United States. Whenever any elective officer of said city shall die, or become incapable of fulfilling the duties of his office, his place, except where other provision is made for filling the vacancy, shall be filled by a joint vote of the City Councils, until the next city election and the qualifications of a successor in the office. *Provided*, That such vacancy shall exist at least thirty days before the next city election, otherwise such vacancy shall be filled at the next election thereafter.

To fill vacancies.

19. Act of April 21, 1855, Sec. 23, P. L. 264.
20. Act of May 13, 1856, Sec. 28, P. L. 567.
21. Act of Feb. 2, 1854, Sec. 50, P. L. 43.
22. Ibid. Sec. 46, P. L. 43.

(*c*) Except to serve writs of summons and capias for the violation of all criminal and penal acts and ordinances issued by the mayor or police aldermen.—Sec. 123

Salaries of elected officers not to be increased during term.

SEC. 23. That no salary of any officer to be elected according to the provisions of this act, by the qualified voters of the city hereby incorporated, shall be increased or reduced by an act or ordinance to take effect during the term for which he shall have been elected; and in all cases where the salary of any officer shall not be fixed by law, it shall be fixed by Councils. *Provided*, That it shall not be lawful for Councils, at any time, to pass an ordinance or by other means provide for the payment of any money in the shape of per diem pay or compensation of any kind, for services rendered by them in their capacity as councilmen, or members of committees emanating from Councils.

Councilmen to have no compensation.

Power to remove officers for cause.

SEC. 24. That the officers elected by the qualified voters under this act shall be subject to removal from office under impeachment for misdemeanor in office, or other sufficient cause, on charges to be preferred by the Common Council and tried by the Select Council in manner prescribed by the Constitution and laws of this Commonwealth as to the impeachment by the House of Representatives and trial thereof by the Senate. All officers shall be subject to removal for sufficient cause, in such manner as Councils may determine.

Power to pave and lay water pipes.

SEC. 25. That it may be prescribed by ordinance that paving of streets, except at the intersections thereof, and of footways, and laying of water pipes within the limits of the city, shall be done at the expense of the owners of the ground in front whereof such work shall be done, and liens may be filed by the said city for the same as is now practiced and allowed by law.

Charges for municipal work.

SEC. 26. The charges for culverts and pipes shall be at not exceeding the following rates per lineal foot, according to the fronts of the owners, to wit: For water pipes, seventy-five cents, making the usual allowance for corner lots; for culverts, seventy-five cents; and for street paving, one dollar per square yard, and all extra or further charge, and for intersections, shall be paid out of the general taxation. (*d*)

Repeal of power to charge for culverts.

SEC. 27. That so much of the Act of April 21, 1855, or of any other Act of Assembly as authorizes the city of Philadelphia to levy a tax or charge for constructing culverts upon the property fronting upon the street so culverted,

---

23. Act of Feb. 2, 1854, Sec. 47, P. L. 43.
24. Ibid. Sec. 45, P. L. 43.
25. Ibid. Sec. 40, P. L. 43.
26. Act of April 21, 1855, Sec. 8, P. L. 264.
27. Act of May 1, 1861, Sec. 1, P. L. 639.

(*d*) Under this act the city had power to construct culverts within the boundaries of the former municipalities of the county, and to file liens therefor against the lots fronting thereon. City *v.* Tryon, 11 Casey, 401, (Decided in 1860.) But not within the limits of the city, as they existed before the Act of February 2, 1854. City *v.* Greble, 2 Wright, 339, (Decided in 1861.)

be and the same is hereby repealed, and the expenses of the construction of culverts shall be paid out of the general taxation. *Provided,* That nothing in this act shall be so construed as to interfere with the Councils of the city of Philadelphia passing such ordinances as they deem expedient relative to inlets opening from private property into such culverts.

Power to clean docks.

SEC. 28. That the City Councils of Philadelphia shall have authority, by ordinance, to direct owners of docks and wharf property to clean their docks after certain notification by the proper officer of the city government, with power, in case of refusal or neglect on the part of any parties thus notified, to cleanse such docks, and to enter liens against the surrounding property for its respective proportion of the expense attending such work.

SEC. 29. That it shall be lawful for the councils of said city to provide, by ordinance, for the cleaning of the docks on the Delaware and Schuylkill front of said city, and to require the owners of wharves and piers, which surround such docks, to cleanse the same; and after thirty days' default from the service of notice on them to perform said duty, it shall be lawful for the city to do said work, and to apportion the expenses thereof among the owners of the wharves, and piers adjoining, in proportion to the extent of their wharves, having the privilege or use of such docks, and to collect the same by filing liens therefor and process thereupon, as in case of claims for paving: *Provided,* That no dock shall be cleansed to a greater depth than the natural bed of the river.

Power to construct bridges.

SEC. 30. That it shall be lawful for said city to construct any bridges that may be necessary to carry any street or highway at the proper grade across any ravine or stream therein: *Provided,* That nothing herein contained shall relieve Councils from the duty of constructing a bridge over the Schuylkill at Chestnut street, as directed by law.

Power to purchase plank and turnpike roads.

SEC. 31. That whenever it shall become necessary in the progress of the building improvements of said city, to grade, curb, bridge, culvert, or pave any of the highways used as turnpikes or plank roads, it shall be lawful for Councils to agree for the relinquishment of such parts thereof, as may be required from time to time; and if the parties cannot agree, to obtain a jury view upon such parts to assess the damage the company owing the franchise may sustain by the city using the same for said purposes; such jury to be appointed, three by the Court of Quarter Sessions of Philadelphia county, and three by such court in the next adjoining county to which such road leads; and

---

28. Act of April 22, 1858, Sec. 1, P. L. 449.
29. Act of May 13, 1856, Sec. 12, P. L. 567.
30. Act of April 21, 1855, Sec. 8, P. L. 264.
31. Ibid. Sec. 9, P. L. 264.

such viewers shall take into consideration whether such turnpike or plank road company shall have occupied a previous public highway or ground purchased by the company: *Provided*, That no contract shall be entered into by the Board of Commissioners of Highways unless previously confirmed by the concurrent action of Councils.

Power to provide for the inspection of leaf tobacco.

SEC. 32. That it shall and may be lawful for the Councils of Philadelphia to enact an ordinance providing for the inspection of leaf tobacco, of domestic growth, received at that port, to be sold by sample, for establishing the fee for charges for inspection and sampling, and storage, and imposing penalties for any violation of the same.

Power to aid the House of Correction.

SEC. 33. That the said Councils may provide for the payment of the expenses incurred for the plans, estimates, and other necessary purposes, by the Board of Managers of the House of Correction and Employment for the city of Philadelphia, upon the production by said Board, of the proper accounts and vouchers therefor.

Power to change the site of Chestnut street bridge.

SEC. 34. That the Councils of the city of Philadelphia are hereby authorized and required to erect, or cause to be erected, over the river Schuylkill, at either Chestnut, Walnut or Spruce street, as they may deem most expedient, in the said city, the bridge authorized and required to be located at or near Chestnut street, by "An act to authorize the erection of free bridges over the river Schuylkill," approved the 27th day of March, A. D. 1852.

Power to order streets on public plans to be opened.

SEC. 35. That whenever Councils shall deem the public exigency to demand it, they may order, by ordinance, any street, laid upon any of the public plans of the city, to be opened, giving three months notice thereof to the owner, whereupon any of the owners whose ground will be taken by such street may forthwith petition the Court of Quarter Sessions for viewers to assess the damages which such owners may sustain by the opening of such street; and if the same be not paid within one year, may sue the said city for the recovery thereof: *Provided*, That security shall be given by said city to the owner for the payment of such damages before his ground shall be actually taken, and the city may indemnify the persons entering such security; and no proceedings to assess the damages on any street on such plan shall lapse by the delay of a year in paying such damages; it shall be lawful for Councils to institute an inquiry as to persons benefited by the opening of any new street, and to withhold appropriation for the opening of the same until the persons found to be benefited shall have contributed according to the benefit to be

---

32. Act of April 21, 1855, Sec. 18, P. L. 264.
33. Ibid. Sec. 29, P. L. 265.
34. Act of May 16, 1855, Sec. 3, P. L. 549.
35. Act of April 21, 1855, Sec. 7, P. L. 264.

derived therefrom towards the damages awarded to the owners whose ground will be taken therefor; but in no instance shall the contribution exceed the damages awarded for the ground taken.(*e*)

Power of Councils in the payment of road damages.

SEC. 36. That whenever Councils shall order any street upon the plan of said city to be opened or widened, no damages therefor shall be paid unless first assessed by a jury and approved by the Court of Quarter Sessions, in accordance with the general road laws of the Commonwealth: *Provided,* That Councils may in all cases, whether the proceedings to open any street shall have been commenced in Councils or in the ordinary course before the Court, refuse to appropriate for the opening of any street, until the owners or citizens to be benefited shall have contributed the whole or any part thereof, as Councils may have determined to be just, and in such case such street shall not be actually opened, nor any security which may have been taken for the damages be responsible therefor.

Duty of road juries, and the power of Councils relative to their awards.

SEC. 37. That it shall be the duty of juries selected to assess damages for the opening, widening, or vacating roads or streets within the said city, to ascertain and report to the court, first, what damages the parties claiming the same are entitled to, and second, to assess and apportion the same among and against such owners of land as shall be benefited by such opening, widening, or vacating any such road or street; and when such report shall be affirmed by the court upon notice to all such parties, and the damages paid or secured by the parties among and against whom it shall be so assessed and apportioned, the Chief Commis-

---

(*e*) If Councils order a street to be opened under this act, and the damages are assessed upon the city of Philadelphia, the city is liable to suit, one year after the confirmation of the award, whether the city takes possession of the ground or not, and is also liable to interest on the award. City *v.* Dickson, 2 Wright, 247, and City *v.* Dyer, 5 Wright, 463. The opinion of J. Allison, (which was affirmed in Souer *v.* City, 11 Casey, 231,) on this act may be of use, he says: "no interference with the ordinary procedure, which is by petition of persons owning property on or near the line of the street designed to be opened was intended; and application for this purpose can only be successful, when the court becomes satisfied that the improvements of the neighborhood requires such street to be thrown open for public use. The Act of 1855, is intended only for special cases requiring immediate or speedy action, as they may from time to time arise, and are to be considered only as exceptions to the general rule; for Councils are only empowered to direct a street to be opened when in their judgment the public *exigency* demands it. An exigency of this nature contemplates the existence of a state of facts, where there is an urgent want or need; a pressing necessity for the opening of a street or road; a case which demands immediate action and which cannot, without prejudice to the interests of the public, be subjected to the delay incident to the usual course of petition to the Court of Quarter Sessions. It is true that the Councils are made the exclusive judges of the existence of the public exigency, which demands the throwing open of a street to common use, and when they have decided that a case is one proper for their affirmative action there is no review of that decision here or elsewhere."

36. Act of May 13, 1856, Sec. 18, P. L. 567.
37. Act of April 21, 1858, Sec. 6, P. L. 385.

sioner of Highways shall proceed to open, widen, or vacate such road or street accordingly: *Provided, however,* That it shall be lawful for Councils, when in their judgment the public interest shall require it, to provide for the payment of such damages out of the City Treasury: *And further provided,* That two-thirds of the members of Councils present at the passage of such ordinance consent thereto, and the yeas and nays on the passage thereof shall be entered on the Journals.

Power to organize a Home Guard.

SEC. 38. That the Councils of Philadelphia for the defence of said city and the protection of life and property therein, are hereby empowered to create and organize a Home Guard which shall consist of such companies and regiments of volunteer soldiers as are now or may be organized for the defence of the said city: *Provided,* The same shall not exceed 10,000 men.(*f*)

Mayor to appoint commander.

SEC. 39. That the Mayor of Philadelphia, by and with the advice of the Select Council, shall appoint an officer with the rank of brigadier-general in the volunteer militia of this Commonwealth, who shall be commissioned as such by the Governor, and shall command the Home Guard organized in pursuance to the provisions of this act, and who shall hold and execute the duties of said office until his successor elected as hereinafter determined shall be qualified to perform the duties thereof.

Election of commander.

SEC. 40. That on the second Monday of September, one thousand eight hundred and sixty-one, an election shall be held by the Home Guard, according to the mode established for elections for the office of Brigadier-General, by the general militia laws of this Commonwealth, and the person so elected when confirmed by the Select Council, and commissioned by the Governor, shall enter upon the duties of the office of commander of the Home Guard, on or after the second Monday of October, one thousand eight hundred and sixty-one, and shall hold and execute the duties of said office for the term of five years, from the said second Monday of October, one thousand eight hundred and sixty-one, if the said Home Guard shall so long continue to exist. If the said Home Guard shall exist for a longer term than five years, elections for the commander of said Home Guard, shall be held every five years after the first election shall be held, or oftener if vacancies shall occur.

SEC. 41. That the Home Guard hereby established shall be a part of the militia of this Commonwealth, and shall be composed of white male residents of the City of Philadelphia, above the age of eighteen years, who shall enrol themselves for the performance of military duty in the defence

38. Act of May 16, 1861, Sec. 1, P. L. 762. 39. Ibid. Sec. 2, P. L. 762.
40. Ibid. Sec. 3, P. L. 762. 41. Ibid. Sec. 4, P. L. 762.

(*f*) The Councils of Philadelphia, by ordinance approved May 23d, 1861, constituted the Home Guards, which this act contemplates.

of the said city, and the officers thereof shall be elected or appointed as provided for by officers of like grade in the general militia laws of this Commonwealth, and shall be commissioned by the Governor; and the commander, officers, and members thereof shall be liable to be tried for misconduct by court martial as is provided for by the militia laws of this State.

SEC. 42. That the commander of the Home Guard shall command the same and shall promote the efficiency and discipline thereof by proper regulation, which shall be subjected to the approval of the Councils of Philadelphia; and, when required by the Mayor of said city, he shall order out the whole or any part of said Guard for the preservation of the public peace and the defence of the city, and during the existence of the said Guard shall determine the style of the uniform: *Provided,* Uniformity of color shall be preserved in each regiment respectively, the equipment and arming thereof and the division of the same into corps of infantry, cavalry, artillery or otherwise.

Members of Home Guard to be sworn.

SEC. 43 That every member of the Home Guard shall, on being enrolled, be duly sworn or affirmed to support the Constitution of the United States and of the State of Pennsylvania, to defend the City of Philadelphia, when called upon so to do, and to obey the orders of his superior officers, so long as he shall be a member thereof, but nothing in this act shall be construed to exempt any of the members of the Home Guard between the ages of eighteen and forty-five from military service, either under the laws of this Commonwealth or of the United States, and that the said Home Guard, or any portion thereof, shall be subjected to the requisition of the State or General Government at any time: *Provided,* That nothing in this act shall be so construed as to require the State to furnished, equip or pay said Home Guard, except when called into the service of the State by the Governor.

Power to erect a bridge over the river Schuylkill at South street.

SEC. 44. That it shall be lawful for the Select and Common Councils of the City of Philadelphia, and they are hereby authorized, as soon as practicable, to erect or cause to be erected, a good and substantial bridge over the river Schuylkill at or opposite to South street, which bridge shall be constructed upon such piers or abutments as to afford at all times a clear or uninterrupted passage for the water of the said river, equal at least in area to that now existing at the Permanent Bridge over the Schuylkill at High or Market street, the cost of said bridge not to exceed two hundred and fifty thousand dollars, which shall be provided for by a loan to be raised as hereinafter directed; and the said bridge

---

42. Act of May 16, 1861, Sec. 5, P. L. 762.
43. Ibid. Sec. 6, P. L. 763.
44. Passed over veto, May, 1861, Sec. 1, P L. 714.

when erected shall at all times hereafter be a free bridge, and no toll shall be charged for passing the same, and shall belong to, and be lighted, watched, superintended and kept in repair, and from time to time be altered, remodeled, or renewed if necessary, at the proper cost and charges of the City of Philadelphia, who shall have power to make such rules and regulations as may be necessary for the preservation of said bridge.

To create a loan therefor.

SEC. 45. That the said Select and Common Councils of the City of Philadelphia, are hereby authorized to create a loan for the purpose aforesaid, not to exceed the sum of two hundred and fifty thousand dollars, negotiable at not less than its par value, and payable in forty years at the rate of six per cent. per annum, and the certificates thereof shall pass by delivery as in case of negotiable paper: *Provided*, That no certificates shall be issued for a less sum than one hundred dollars.

SEC. 46. That it shall and may be lawful for the said Select and Common Councils to occupy, build upon, and alter, so much of any public landing or road as may be requisite for the erection of said bridge.

Whereas, By an Act of Assembly, passed February twenty-seventh, one thousand seven hundred and ninety-seven, Cohocksink creek in the then township of the Northern Liberties, and county of Philadelphia, from the mouth thereof to the bridge on the road leading to Frankford, was declared a public highway, forty feet in width for the passage of all kinds of vessels and rafts which can float therein; and by an Act passed April sixteenth, one thousand eight hundred and twenty-nine, the said creek, of the width aforesaid, from the said bridge up to Sixth street, was also declared a public highway, and authority given to the municipal commissioners to erect a culvert along the same:

And whereas, Upon the survey and plan of the said township of the Northern Liberties, made in pursuance of an Act of Assembly, passed April seventeenth, one thousand seven hundred and ninety-five, duly confirmed and recorded according to law, a canal was laid out along the several courses of the said creek, from the mouth thereof to Front street, and the canal constructed in conformity with said plan; and divers attempts have been made, as well at the expense of the owners of adjacent lots as by the public, to keep the canal in such order as to answer the end originally intended, but it has been found by experience that the expense of cleaning the same, and keeping it in such order, is vastly greater than all the public or private benefits resulting from the landings thereon; and by reason of the filth and rubbish which are carried by the rains into the said canal, the same is nearly filled up, and has become a grievious

---

45. Passed over veto, May, 1861, Sec. 2, P. L. 714. 46. Ibid. Sec. 3, P. L. 714.

nuisance, dangerous to the health of the inhabitants, and requires a speedy remedy:

And whereas, By the act of March sixteenth, one thousand eight hundred and nineteen, incorporating the district of the Northern Liberties, it was declared that no law, ordinance or regulation shall ever be made to annul or alter the lines of any street, lane, alley or road, or the courses and degrees of descent, or the distances from the lines of such streets, lanes, alleys or roads, or of the gutters, water courses and common sewers within the said district, as the same has been surveyed, regulated and fixed by the said Act of April seventeenth, one thousand seven hundred and ninety-five; therefore,

Power to culvert in the late district of Northern Liberties.

SEC. 47. *Be it enacted, etc.*, That the Select and Common Councils of the City of Philadelphia be and they are hereby authorized to cause a re-survey to be made of those parts of the late district of the Northern Liberties and Kensington, lying contiguous to Cohocksink creek, east of Front street, and lay out so many new streets, and extend such of the streets already established within the same, as in their judgment will be necessary to accommodate the inhabitants with convenient ways and passages, laying the same out, at or as near to right angles with each other as the nature of the place and a reasonable conformity to the streets already established will admit, and to establish and fix the grade of the streets so laid out or extended, and if need require, to revise and change the grade of the streets already established, and connecting with such new streets; and the said streets so laid out or extended, the plan thereof being first approved by the said Councils, shall be recorded, and the streets opened in the manner now provided by law in the city of Philadelphia; and the said Councils shall continue the culvert intended to drain Cohocksink creek, by the shortest practicable course, from Front street, along the said creek or canal, and any of the streets hereby authorized to be laid out or already established, into the river Delaware; and upon the completion of the said culvert, and opening the streets so laid out or extended, the said Councils are further authorized to fill up the said creek or canal to the proper grade, and declare vacated such parts of it west of Delaware Avenue as may not be occupied by the said culvert, or made a part of any of the streets so laid out, in such manner and at such times as they may deem expedient: *Provided*, That if the said Councils decide to construct said culvert on Laurel street, the owners of property on said street shall be exempt from the usual charges for culverts, under the acts of Assembly; and that so much of any existing law or Act of Assembly as may conflict with the provisions of this act be and they are hereby repealed.

47. Act of Feb. 12, 1861, Sec. 1, P. L. 42.

WARDS.

SEC. 48. That the said city shall be divided into wards, as follows:

First Ward.—That part thereof bounded as follows: beginning at Wharton street and the river Delaware; thence along Wharton street to the Passyunk road; thence along the Passyunk road to Little Washington street; thence along Washington to Broad street; thence along Broad street to South street; thence along South street to the river Schuylkill; thence along the river Schuylkill to its junction with the river Delaware; thence along the river Delaware to the place of beginning, together with League Island.

Second Ward.—That part thereof lying between Broad street and the river Delaware, and between the lines of the aforesaid First Ward and Christian street.

Third Ward.—That part thereof lying between Broad street and the river Delaware, and between Christian street on the south, and Fitzwater, German, Mead, and Catharine streets on the north.

Fourth Ward.—That part thereof lying between Broad street and the river Delaware, and between the north line of aforesaid Third ward and South street.

Fifth Ward.—That part thereof lying between Seventh street and the river Delaware, and between South street and Chestnut street. including Windmill Island.

Sixth Ward.—That part thereof lying between Seventh street and the river Delaware, and between Chestnut street and Vine street.

Seventh Ward.—That part thereof lying between Seventh street and the river Schuylkill, and between South street and Spruce street.

Eighth Ward.—That part thereof lying between Seventh street and the river Schuylkill, and between Spruce street and Chestnut street.

Ninth Ward.—That part thereof lying between Seventh street and the river Schuylkill, and between Chestnut street and Arch street.

Tenth Ward.—That part thereof lying between Seventh street and the river Schuylkill, and between Arch street and Vine street.

Eleventh Ward.—That part thereof lying between Third street and the river Delaware, and between Vine street and Poplar street.

Twelfth Ward.—That part thereof lying between Sixth street and Third street, and between Vine street and Poplar street.

---

48. Act of Feb. 2, 1854, Sec. 2, P. L. 2[illegible].

Thirteenth Ward.—That part thereof lying between Sixth street and Tenth street, and between Vine street and Poplar street.

Fourteenth Ward.—That part thereof lying between Tenth street and Broad street, and between Vine street and Poplar street.

Fifteenth Ward.—That part thereof lying between Broad street and the river Schuylkill, and between Vine street and Poplar street.

Sixteenth Ward.—That part thereof bounded as follows: beginning at Maiden street and the river Delaware; thence along Maiden street to the Frankford Road; thence along the Frankford Road to Franklin avenue; thence along Franklin avenue to Sixth street; thence along Sixth street to Poplar street; thence along Poplar street to the river Delaware; thence along the river Delaware to the place of beginning.

Seventeenth Ward.—That part thereof bounded on the north by Oxford street, on the east by the Frankford Road, on the south by Franklin avenue, and on the west by Sixth street.

Eighteenth Ward.—That part thereof bounded as follows: beginning at Maiden street and the Delaware river; thence along Maiden street to the Frankford Road; thence along the Frankford Road to Norris street; thence along Norris street to the river Delaware; thence along the river Delaware to the place of beginning.

Nineteenth Ward.—That part thereof bounded as follows: beginning at Norris street and the Delaware river; thence along Norris street to the Frankford Road; thence along the Frankford Road to Oxford street; thence along Oxford street to Sixth street; thence along Sixth street to Lehigh avenue; thence along Lehigh Avenue to the Frankford Road; thence along the Frankford Road to Westmoreland street; thence along Westmoreland street to the Point road; thence along the Point road to the northeast boundary of the district of Richmond; thence along the same to the river Delaware; thence along the river Delaware to the place of beginning.

Twentieth Ward.—That part thereof bounded as follows; beginning at Poplar street and the river Schuylkill; thence along the said Poplar street to Sixth street; thence along the said Sixth street to Susquehanna avenue; thence along the said Susquehanna avenue to Eleventh street; thence along the said Eleventh street to Montgomery street; thence along the said Montgomery street to the river Schuylkill; thence along the same to the place of beginning.

Twenty-first Ward.—That part thereof lying within the present bounds of the borough of Manayunk and the townships of Roxborough and Penn; and the southern boundary thereof, shall be as follows; beginning at Montgomery street and the river Schuylkill; thence along Montgomery street to Eleventh street; thence along Eleventh street to Susquehanna avenue; thence along Susquehanna avenue to the Germantown Road.

Twenty-second Ward.—The part thereof lying within the present bounds of the townships of Germantown and Bristol, and the borough of Germantown.

Twenty-third Ward.—That part thereof including all the remainder of the present county of Philadelphia, east of the river Schuylkill.

Twenty-fourth Ward.—That part of the county of Philadelphia lying west of the river Schuylkill.

Provided, That whenever a street, road, avenue, or river is named as a boundary in this section, the centre thereof shall be understood.

SEC. 49. *Twenty-fifth Ward.*—That all those certain parts of the Nineteenth and Twenty-third Wards of the City of Philadelphia included and contained within the following boundaries, shall hereafter constitute and form the Twenty-fifth Ward of the said City, to wit: Beginning at a point on the Delaware river at a point where Lehigh avenue would intersect said river if continued in a right line; thence to the eastern termination of said Lehigh avenue; thence along Lehigh avenue to Germantown avenue to the line of the Twenty-second Ward; thence along said line to the Frankford creek; thence along Frankford creek to the Delaware river to the place of beginning.

Members of Council for 25th Ward.

SEC. 50. The qualified voters of the said Twenty-fifth Ward shall at the next election, elect one member of Select Council who shall serve for two years, and also one member of Common Council, who shall serve for two years, and shall thereafter elect members of Councils as now provided by law.

School Directors of 25th Ward.

SEC. 51. The qualified voters of the Twenty-fifth Ward shall, at the next election, vote for nine citizens to serve as School Directors, and the twelve persons having the highest vote shall be elected, four of whom shall serve for one year, four for two years and four for three years, and at every annual election thereafter the qualified voters of said ward shall vote for three citizens of said ward to serve as School Directors, and the four persons having the highest vote shall be elected to serve for three years.

School Directors of the 23d and 19th Wards.

SEC. 52. The qualified voters of the Nineteenth and Twenty-third Wards shall at the next election, elect School Directors to fill any vacancies in the several Boards of School Directors of said wards, caused by the passage of this act.

---

49. Act of April 12, 1861, Sec. 1, P. L. 293.
50. Ibid. Sec. 2, P. L. 293.
51. Ibid. Sec. 3, P. L. 293.
52. Ibid. Sec. 4, P. L. 293.

SEC. 53. The qualified voters of the Twenty-fifth Ward shall, at the next election, elect one Assessor who, in conjunction with the Assessors now resident in the said ward, shall act as Assessors of the same until the last day of December, 1862.

Assessor of the 25th Ward.

SEC. 54. The Aldermen and Constables of the Nineteenth, Twenty-third, and Twenty-fifth Wards, shall be elected according to existing laws.

Alderman and Constables of 25th Ward.

SEC. 55. All acts of Assembly in conflict with the provisions of this act be, and the same are hereby repealed.

MAYOR OF PHILADELPHIA.

SEC. 56. That the qualified voters of the city of Philadelphia shall, *on the Second Tuesday of October*, 1862, *and every third year thereafter*, elect one person to serve as Mayor of the said city, by a plurality of votes, and in case of a tie, the Councils shall order a new election. He shall serve for *three* years, and until his successor shall be elected and duly qualified. He shall be at least thirty years of age, a citizen of the United States, and have resided seven years next preceding his election within this Commonwealth, and the last two years thereof in the said city. He shall take the usual oath of office, in the presence of the Councils, to be administered by one of the judges of the courts in said city, at twelve o'clock, noon, *on the first Monday of January, next succeeding his election:* besides the powers otherwise conferred by law, he shall have the like power and authority as the Sheriff of the county of Philadelphia now has for the suppression of any riot, disturbance, and violation of law, and shall exercise the authority of making the requisition for the commanding officer of the military, in lieu of the Marshal of Police as now authorized by law, and of dismissing all police officers * * * * for failure in the discharge of duty. It shall be the Mayor's duty to communicate to Councils, at least once a year, and oftener if deemed expedient, a general statement of the condition of the city in relation to its government, finances, and improvements; to recommend the adoption of all such measures as he may deem expedient for the security, health, cleanliness, improvement, and welfare of the city; to be vigilant and active in causing the laws and ordinances of the city to be duly executed; for which purpose * * * all policemen and watchmen shall obey his orders, and make a report to him when acting under his orders, and he shall exercise a constant supervision and control over the conduct of all subordinate officers, receive and examine all complaints preferred

Election of the Mayor.

His qualifications.

His duties and powers.

53. Act of April 12, 1861, Sec. 5, P. L. 293.
54. Ibid. Sec. 6, P. L. 293.
55. Ibid. Sec. 7, P. L. 293.
56. Act of Feb. 2, 1854, Sec. 7, P. L. 21.

against them, and generally perform all such duties as may be prescribed by the laws and ordinances of said city and of this Commonwealth; and he may call special meetings of the Councils whenever any public emergency may require. Every ordinance which shall have passed both Councils shall be presented to the Mayor. If he approve, he shall sign it; but if he shall not approve, he shall return it with his objection to the Council in which it originated, which shall proceed to reconsider it. If, after such reconsideration, two-thirds of that Council shall agree to pass the ordinance, it shall be sent, with the objections, to the other Council, by which likewise it shall be reconsidered, and if approved by two-thirds of that Council also, it shall be a binding ordinance. In such case the votes of both Councils shall be determined by yeas and nays, and the names of the members voting shall be entered on the journals. Every ordinance which the Mayor shall not so return within fifteen days, shall take effect as if it had been approved. The Mayor may approve ordinances in vacations of Councils, and may call special meetings of Councils to reconsider ordinances which he does not approve, on three days' notice to each member. In case of his temporary absence or inability to act, the Councils shall appoint a Mayor to serve until he shall resume the duties of his office; and whenever a vacancy shall occur in the office of Mayor, by death or otherwise, it shall be the duty of the Select and Common Councils, in joint meeting, forthwith to elect, *viva voce*, a person qualified as aforesaid, to serve as Mayor, who shall continue in office until the Tuesday succeeding the next city election, and until his successor shall have been duly elected and qualified. The Mayor shall receive a salary, to be fixed by Councils, which shall not be increased nor diminished during the term for which he shall have been elected. The police officers, policemen and watchmen, shall receive the compensations to be fixed by ordinance of said Councils.

Power of Marshal of Police vested in him.

SEC. 57. That after the term of the present Marshal of Police shall expire by limitation or death, the office shall cease, and all the powers in him vested, not subordinate to the Mayor, shall thereupon become vested in the Mayor, and all his duties subordinate to the Mayor shall be performed by a Chief of Police, to be appointed by the Mayor, with the approval of the Select Council, subject to be dismissed by him, who shall receive such salary and perform such further duties as may be prescribed by ordinance.

Power of a committing Magistrate vested in him.

SEC. 58. That so much of the act entitled "A Further Supplement to the Act consolidating the City of Philadelphia," approved the thirteenth day of May, Anno Domini

---

57. Act of May 13, 1856, Sec. 1, P. L. 567.
58. Act of March 28, 1860, Sec. 1, P. L. 318.

one thousand eight hundred and fifty-six, as prohibits the Mayor of the City of Philadelphia from sitting as a committing magistrate, be and the same is hereby repealed, and the said Mayor shall have all the jurisdiction and power of a committing magistrate throughout the said city.

Power to appoint a committing magistrate.

SEC. 59. It shall be lawful for the Mayor at pleasure to appoint any one of the aldermen of the said city to sit as a committing magistrate at the police station, adjoining the office of the Mayor, and such alderman shall thereupon lawfully have and exercise such jurisdiction thereat, and warrants issued by the Mayor may be made returnable before him, and the compensation of the said alderman for such services shall be at the rate of one thousand dollars per annum. *Provided,* That said compensation be paid out of the fines, forfeitures, penalties, costs, and fees to be received at the said police station, and a statement shall be made under oath to the City Controller, on the first Monday of January, April, July, and October, in each year, of the entire amount of the said fines, forfeitures, penalties, costs, and fees, and payment thereout of the said compensation, the balance shall be paid into the City Treasury.

SOLICITOR OF PHILADELPHIA.

SEC. 60. That the Select and Common Councils shall establish a law office, in which shall be deposited and preserved all patents, deeds, wills, leases, mortgages and other assurances of title, together with all contracts, bonds, notes, official bonds, books and other evidences of debt belonging to the said city, and all other papers which the said City Councils may direct. The qualified voters of said city shall, on the *second Tuesday of October*, 1862, and every *third* year thereafter, elect one person learned in the law, to act as Solicitor of said city, whose duties shall be prescribed by ordinance, and who shall be allowed to employ such number of assistants as Councils may prescribe. The said Solicitor shall hold his office for the term of *three* years from the *first day of January next succeeding his election*, and until his successor shall be duly qualified.

CITY TREASURER.

Election of City Treasurer.

SEC. 61. That the qualified voters of the said city shall, on the *second Tuesday of October* 1861, and on the *second Tuesday of October* in every second year thereafter, elect a City Treasurer to serve for two years from the *first day of January* next succeeding such election. He shall give bond to the city, conditioned for the faithful performance of his duty, in such amount as the City Councils shall direct, and

His duties.

59. Act of March, 28, 1860, Sec. 2, P. L. 318.
60. Act of Feb. 2, 1854, Sec. 15, P. L. 31.
61. Ibid. Sec. 10, P. L. 28.

shall, before he enters upon his office, take and subscribe an oath or affirmation, honestly to keep an account for all public moneys and property entrusted to his care; and if such Treasurer shall knowingly violate said oath, he shall be deemed guilty of perjury, and on conviction thereof in the proper court, be sentenced to undergo solitary imprisonment at hard labor in the Eastern Penitentiary, for the term of not less than one nor more than ten years. Any vacancy in said office shall be filled by the City Councils, by *viva voce* vote in joint meeting. No money shall be drawn from the treasury of the city, except the same shall have been previously appropriated by Councils to the purpose for which it is drawn; the accounts to be kept by the said City Treasury shall exhibit all the receipts and all the expenditures of the city in an intelligible manner, in the form of accounts current, in which the particulars of each item of charge and discharge shall fully and precisely appear. Any citizen may, on the payment of a fee of twelve and a half cents, to be paid to the City Treasurer for the use of the city, inspect the said accounts; and for a further fee of fifty cents, and one cent per line of ten words, to be paid for the use of the city, the Treasurer shall, on request of any citizen, furnish a transcript of any part thereof. It shall be the duty of the Councils of the said city to provide, and said Treasurer to pay, on or before the 25th day of July, 1856, and in each year thereafter, into the treasury of the State, the amount of the State tax assessed within the limits of the said city, deducting all allowances made by law; and said Treasurer elected as aforesaid shall, before he enters upon the office, give bond, with sureties to be approved by the judges of the Court of Common Pleas of Philadelphia county, in such sum as they shall direct, conditioned for the safe keeping of and accounting for all moneys received by him for the use of the State; the said Treasurer shall keep the public moneys in such place and manner as the City Councils shall direct, and shall verify his cash account at least once every week, to the satisfaction of a standing committee of Councils: and upon the affidavit of a majority of such committee of any default therein, the said Treasurer shall be suspended from office until the further action of Councils; and the Court of Common Pleas of Philadelphia county shall, upon said affidavit and cause shown, forthwith issue a writ of sequestration to the sheriff of the county against such defaulter, for the amount of such default, to be levied of all his property, estate and effects, in favor of said city, which writ shall be a lien thereon from the issuing thereof, with a clause of attachment contained therein, directing the sheriff to arrest the body of such defaulter, to answer the said charge on a day certain, on which day the said court shall inquire of the premises and enter judgement thereon as

His accounts to be verified weekly.

may be just, or in their discretion award an issue to try the disputed facts; and if the said court upon such hearing shall be satisfied that there is probable cause to believe that such Treasurer has committed the crime of perjury as mentioned in this section, it shall be their duty to commit him for trial at the next Court of Quarter Sessions of said county.

City Treasurer to account quarterly with the State Treasurer.

SEC. 62. That the Treasurer of the city of Philadelphia, and all County and City Treasurers, every Recorder of Deeds, Register of Wills, Prothonotary, Clerk of the Court of Quarter Sessions, and Clerk of the Orphans' Court in the Commonwealth, shall, on the first Monday of July next, and quarterly thereafter, or oftener if required by the State Treasurer, pay into the treasury, or such place of deposit as said State Treasurer shall designate, to the credit of the Commonwealth, the whole amount of money received during the period preceding said payments; and shall furnish to the State Treasurer, statements, under proper heads, designating the source from which the money was received; and said officers shall file and settle quarterly accounts in the office of the Auditor-General, as now required by law. Upon the settlement of said quarterly accounts, if it appear that the receipts shall not have been paid as directed by this section, any officer so offending shall forfeit his fees and commissions on the whole amount of money collected during the quarter; in every case where a balance due the Commonwealth shall remain unpaid for a period of ten days after such quarterly settlement, suit shall be commenced against such delinquent and his sureties, as is provided in case of defaulting officers.

CITY CONTROLLER.

Election and duties.

SEC. 63. That the qualified voters of said city shall, on the *second Tuesday in October*, 1862, and on the *second Tuesday in October* in every *third* year thereafter, elect a City Controller, to serve for the term of *three* years, from the *first day of January* next, succeeding his election. He shall, before entering upon his office, take and subscribe an oath or affirmation, faithfully to discharge the duties thereof; and if he shall knowingly violate said oath or affirmation, he shall be subject to the same penalty as is provided by the tenth section of this act in regard to the City Treasurer. It shall be the duty of the said City Controller to scrutinize, audit and publish, in two or more newspapers, annually, verified by his oath or affirmation, the public accounts of the said city, and of the trusts in their care, exhibiting all the receipts and expenditures of the city, the sources from which the revenues and funds are derived, and in what

---

62. Act of May 18, 1857, Sec. 79, P. L. 570.
63. Act of Feb. 2, 1854, Sec. 12, P. L. 30.

manner the same have been disbursed, each account to be accompanied by a statement in detail, in separate columns, of the several appropriations made by the City Councils, the amount drawn on each appropriation, and the balance standing to the debit or credit of each such appropriation. He shall countersign all warrants on the City Treasurer, and shall not suffer any appropriation made by the City Councils to be overdrawn, and shall perform all the duties now enjoined by law on the County Auditors. He shall superintend the fical concerns of the city, in such manner, and make reports thereon at such times, as shall be prescribed by ordinance.

Keep separate accounts for specific items.

SEC. 64. That the City Controller shall be and he is hereby required to keep separate accounts for each specific or separate item of appropriation made by City Councils to each and every department of the city, and shall require all warrants to state particularly against which of said items the said warrant is drawn; and he shall at no time permit any one of the items of appropriation to be overdrawn, or the appropriation for one item of expenses to be drawn upon for any other purpose by any one of the departments than that for which the appropriation was specifically made; he shall upon receiving a bill or warrant from any one of the departments proceed immediately to examine the same, and if the said bill or warrants contain an item for which no appropriation has been made, or the appropriation for which is exhausted, or to which, from any other cause, he cannot give his approval, it shall be his duty, immediately, to inform such department, and the warrant therefor shall not be issued unless by special authority from the City Councils.

SEC. 65. That it shall be the duty of the Controller of said city, upon the death, resignation, removal or expiration of the term of office, of officers and persons who, by law or ordinance, may be authorized to receive or pay city moneys, make contracts, or draw warrants on the treasury, to audit and examine the accounts and official acts of such officer, and if such officer shall be found to be indebted or liable to said city, a copy of the report of said Controller shall be filed in the office of the Court of Common Pleas of said city, and a writ of *scire facias* may be issued thereon, and the City Councils shall have full power and authority to prescribe by ordinance the mode and means by which the said Controller shall exercise the duty hereby enjoined, and the officers and persons whose accounts and official acts shall be so audited and examined. And whenever the writ of *scire facias* herein authorized shall issue, it shall be lawful to file with the præcipe therefor a copy of the official bonds of such defendant, and the writ of *scire facias* shall contain

---

64. Act of May 13, 1856, Sec. 30, P. L. 573.
65. Act of April 21, 1858, Sec. 7, P. L. 387.

a clause warning the surety or sureties, or the executors or administrators of such surety or sureties, to appear and make defence, and the judgment in such proceedings may be entered against all the parties named in said writ.(*d*)

CITY COMMISSIONERS.

Powers and duties.

SECTION 66. That the qualified voters of the said city shall on the *second Tuesday in October*, 1861, and annually thereafter, elect one person for City Commissioner to serve for three years from the *first day of January* next, succeeding his election. The City Commissioners, under the direction and control of the City Councils, shall be charged with all duties relating to assessors and to assessments, to the selection and drawing of jurors, and to elections and election officers, that are now performed by the County Commissioners, and all other duties now performed by the Commissioners of the County, not otherwise provided for in this act. They shall, together with the City Treasurer and Receiver of Taxes, perform the duties of a County Board of Revision, according to the laws in force in other counties of this Commonwealth, and hear the appeals of the tax-payers. And they shall correct all irregularities in valuation, both as respects individual cases and wards, and complete the same before the end of the year in which the valuations shall be made for the tax of the succeeding year. If, in equalizing the valuation of the property in the several wards, an addition of ten per centum be made to the returns of the Assessor for any ward, twenty freeholders of such ward may, by writing, filed within ten days, take an appeal from such decisions to the Councils, whose decision thereon shall be final.

With City Treasurer and Receiver of Taxes to perform duties of a County Board of Revision

To equalize valuation of taxes.

City Commissioners to take no part in the opening of streets.

SEC. 67. That the City Commissioners shall disburse no moneys, nor make any contracts for public works or highways, nor take any part in the opening of streets, or the assessment of the damages therefor, but notice of the meetings of all viewers to lay out, open or vacate any street or highway, or assess damages therefor, shall be served at the law department of the city, and the solicitor or assistant shall represent and protect the interests of the city in relation to all road matters, and countersign every order granted by the Court of Quarter Sessions, for the payment of road damages, and keep a register of all damages confirmed by the court, and of orders countersigned, which shall not be countersigned or paid until an appropriation therefor be made by Councils.

---

66. Act of Feb. 2, 1854, Sec. 13, P. L. 30.
67. Act of May 13, 1856, Sec. 4, P. L. 567.
(*d*) The proceedings indicated by this act are unnecessarily tedious. The better way is to execute a warrant with the official bond; and if there should be default, an execution can issue at once to collect the money without leave, suggestion or scire facias. McCann *v.* Farley, 2 Casey, 173. City *v.* Lamb. (Decided by J. Read, March, 1859.)

How warrants for jurors, officers of Courts, &c., to be drawn.

SEC. 68. That the City Commissioners shall draw no warrants upon the city treasury for the payment of the fees of jurors, viewers, witnesses, or officers of the courts, without a certificate of the Prothonotary or Clerk of the court, countersigned by one of the Judges of the court in which the duty or service was performed, that the same is correct to the best of his belief, nor shall any warrant be drawn for jury or witness fees, in favor of any person but the juror or witness entitled to such fees.

To give bond and not to exceed appropriations.

SEC. 69. That the City Commissioners of the said city hereafter chosen, shall, before entering upon the duties of their office give bond in such amount, and with such sureties as shall be approved by Councils, for the faithful performance of the duties of the said office, and that no debt shall be contracted, or warrant drawn against the city by said Commissioners, except for purposes legally authorized, and not to exceed the appropriation therefor made by Councils. (g)

ASSESSORS.

Election of Assessors.

SEC. 70. That on the *second Tuesday of October*, 1862, and in every third year thereafter, the qualified voters of each ward of the City of Philadelphia shall elect the same number of Assessors in the same manner as they are now by law required to elect, who shall do and perform the duties and receive the same compensation as is now provided by existing laws.

How vacancies filled.

SEC. 71. That in case of the removal of any assessor by death, resignation or otherwise, the vacancy thus occurring shall be filled by the City Commissioners, by appointment, until the ensuing municipal election, at which time the qualified electors of the ward where such vacancy occurred, shall elect a person to fill said unexpired term.

SEC. 72. That all laws or parts of laws of this Commonwealth, inconsistent with the provisions of this act, are hereby repealed, so far as it relates to the city of Philadelphia.

Two assessors for each Ward, with certain exceptions.

SEC. 73. That the qualified voters of each ward of the said city shall elect two Assessors, who shall have and possess the qualifications that members of the Senate are required to possess, who being duly qualified, shall do and perform within their respective wards all the duties that the usages and laws of this Commonwealth now enjoin upon

---

68. Act of May 3, 1856, Sec. 5, P. L. 262.
69. Act of April 21, 1858, Sec. 4, P. L. 386.
70. Act of March 26, 1859, Sec. 1, P. L. 262.
71. Ibid. Sec. 2, P. L. 567.
72. Ibid. Sec. 3, P. L. 262.
73. Act of Feb. 2, 1854, Sec. 17, P. L. 33.

(g) By ordinance of May 11, 1858, (page 200,) the amount of the bond under this act was fixed at $10,000.

Assessors and Assistant Assessors. *Provided,* That the qualified voters residing within the limits of the townships of Byberry, Moreland, Delaware, Lower Dublin and Oxford, in the Twenty-third Ward, shall in like manner elect two Assessors; and the qualified voters of the remaining portions of said ward shall in like manner elect two Assessors. And at all elections of such Assessors each voter shall vote for one Assessor, and the two candidates having the highest number of votes shall be elected. The City Commissioners shall, immediately after such election, in each year, issue their precept to the said Assessors of the respective wards, requiring them to make out and return, within such time as the said Commissioners shall designate, not later than the first day of September following a just and perfect list, in such form as the Commissioners shall direct, of all the taxable persons residing within their wards respectively, and all property taxable, and exempt by law, with a just valuation of the same; and whenever the Assessors of any ward cannot agree upon the valuation of any property, the City Commissioner senior in office shall be umpire, and decide. The office of Assistant Assessors within the said city is hereby abolished. The duty of making extra assessments, now enjoined by law upon the officers of election, shall be exclusively performed by the Assessors. The Assessors of each ward shall meet for that purpose, in their respective wards, on the thirteenth day prior to the second Tuesday of October, annually, and continue their sessions from one to ten o'clock, P. M., each day for three successive juridical days, and public notice of the time and place thereof shall be given by the City Commissioners, in two or more daily newspapers of the said city, ten day prior thereto. Each Assessor shall return the names of one-half of the number of jurors within his ward, required for each year, and the precept of the City Commissioners to the Assessors shall conform to this provision. Any Assessor who shall receive any reward for returning or omitting to return the name of any person to serve as juror, any person who shall offer or give such reward, shall forfeit the sum of one hundred dollars to the said city, to be recovered before any alderman. Each assessor shall receive an annual sum in lieu of all other compensation, to wit: for the year ending May, Anno Domini 1856, and for every third year thereafter, the sum of four hundred dollars, and for all other years the sum of three hundred dollars per annum.

Extra assessments.

Compensation.

SEC. 74. That on the *second Tuesday of October*, 1862, and as often thereafter as the law requires, the qualified voters of the first, second, third, fourth, ninth and tenth divisions of the Nineteenth Ward, of the City of Philadelphie, shall elect two Assessors, and the qualified electors of

Certain divisions in the 19th Ward to elect assessors.

74. Act of April 11, 1859, Sec. 1, P. L. 503.

the fifth, sixth, seventh and eighth election divisions of said ward, shall elect two Assessors of like qualifications, and in the same manner, and to perform the same duties as is provided in regard to assessors in the seventeenth section of a further supplement to an act, entitled "An Act to incorporate the City of Philadelphia," approved the second day of February, Anno Domini one thousand eight hundred and fifty-four: *Provided*, That if, at any time, the Councils of Philadelphia shall change the election divisions of said ward they shall designate which of said divisions shall elect the Assessor as aforesaid.

Certain divisions in the 21st Ward to elect assessors.

SEC. 75. That on the *second Tuesday of October*, 1862, and as often thereafter as the law requires, the qualified voters of that part of the Twenty-first Ward, in the city of Philadelphia, comprising the first and second election divisions thereof, shall elect two Assessors, and the qualified electors of the remaining portions of said ward, shall also elect two Assessors of the like qualifications, and in the same manner, and to perform the same duties as is provided in regard to Assessors in the seventeenth section of a further supplement to an act entitled " An Act to incorporate the City of Philadelphia," approved the second day of February, Anno Domini one thousand eight hundred and fifty-four; *Provided* That if, at any time, the Councils of the City of Philadelphia, shall change the election divisions of said ward, they shall designate which of said divisions shall elect the Assessors as aforesaid.

Duties of assessors.

SEC. 76. That the books for assessment shall be furnished to the assessors by the fifteenth day of May in each year, from the said department, and any assessor who shall not have completed and returned his assessment by the fifteenth day of August following, shall forfeit his compensation and surrender his books, to be finished by the board of revision. It shall be the duty of the Assessors to mark opposite every property used for agricultural purposes the word " rural," and on every property so returned there shall be assessed or collected but two-thirds the rate for city tax that shall be assessed on other real estate in the city : *Provided,* That any error in such return in this respect shall be corrected by the Board of Revision or appeal. The Assessor of each ward shall make out an alphabetical list, with the names, occupations and residences of all the taxables of each division of the ward, to be returned to the City Commissioners, with the assessment-book to be used for election purposes, for which they shall receive four dollars for each division book.

SEC. 77. That the assessors of the several wards of the

---

75. Act of April 11, 1859, Sec. 2, P. L. 503.
76. Act of May 13, 1856, Sec. 6, P. L. 568.
77. Act of May 16, 1855, Sec. 2, P. L. 549.

city of Philadelphia, shall, at the same time they make the assessments required by law, ascertain the dimensions or quantity of each lot or piece of ground assessed, and return the same with their assessment, to the City Commissioners, as provided by law, and whenever the said return shall not be sufficiently certain to enable the Receiver of Taxes properly to describe any lot or piece of ground against which he is about to proceed for the recovery of registered taxes, it shall be the duty of the Surveyor of the district in which said lot or piece of ground is situated, to furnish the said Receiver with an accurate measurement thereof, together with a precise description of its locality.

Ascertain the dimensions of each lot of ground.

SEC. 78. That it be the duty of the several Assessors of the city of Philadelphia to ascertain, by strict inquiry, the proper orthography of the name of each taxable person within his ward, the exact number of his place of residence, together with his present occupation, profession or business, and to state, plainly written, all such particulars in his assessment list.

Duty to ascertain the name of each taxable.

SEC. 79. That from and after the expiration of the terms of the present Assessors of the twenty-fourth ward of said city, the said ward shall be divided into two assessment districts, the first of which shall be all that portion of said ward lying north of Market street on West Chester road, and the other shall be all that part of said ward south of Market street or West Chester road; and the qualified electors of each of said districts hereby created, shall, at the next election for assessors, elect the same number of assessors as required by the Act to which this is a supplement.

Division of 24th Ward into two assessment districts.

BOARD OF REVISION.(k)

SEC. 80. That the County Board of revision shall commence the discharge of its duties on the first Monday of September in each year, taking into consideration each assessment, and shall complete the same within six weeks; and the County Board of appeals shall commence the hearing of appeals on the third Monday of October, and proceed to hear the tax-payers of the several wards in succession, until the same be closed, not exceeding six weeks: *Provided*, That no change shall be made in the valuation of real estate, in other than the triennial year, except in cases of destruction by fire or flood, or of improvements made, and that only by a majority of the Board. The City Commissioners, or head of the department, shall make the

Duties of Board.

78. Act of April 13, 1859, Sec. 1, P. L. 595.
79. Act of March 16, 1861, Sec. 1, P. L. 147.
80. Act of May 13, 1856, Sec. 7, P. L. 567.

(k) The City Commissioner, Receiver of Taxes, and City Treasurer, constitute the Board of Revision in the present city. (Section 66.)

return required by law to the State Treasurer, for the Board of Revenue Commissioners, by the first Monday of February of the year when such Revenue Commissioners shall meet, after all allowances shall have been made on the appeals.

Oath of office.

SEC. 81. That hereafter it shall and may be lawful for the several Prothonotaries of the Courts of Common Pleas of this Commonwealth, or any of the Associate Judges thereof, to administer to the Board of Revision the oath of office now required by law to be taken before the Presidents of the said Courts of Common Pleas.

RECEIVER OF TAXES, AND TAXES.

SEC. 82. That the qualified voters of said city shall, on *second Tuesday of October*, 1862, and biennially thereafter, elect one person who shall be denominated Receiver of Taxes, to serve for two years *from the second Monday succeeding the 15th of January next following his election.*(*l*) He shall give bond and be sworn or affirmed to perform his duty in like manner as the City Treasurer. He shall collect and receive all taxes and public assessments payable and receiveable within the limits of the said city, and for that purpose shall have and exercise all the powers conferred by law in that behalf, and shall have assistance of the necessary clerks to afford proper facilities to all citizens to pay their taxes at all business hours of the day. It shall be the duty of the City Commissioners to place the duplicates of taxes in the possession of the said Receiver of Taxes as early as practicable in the year for which the taxes shall be assessed. And the said Receiver shall make allowance to all tax payers who shall pay their taxes in the year for which they are assessed, at the rate of twelve per cent. per annum from the date of payment until the end of such year.(*m*) All taxes remaining unpaid on the 1st of January in each year, shall continue a lien upon the real estate upon which they are levied in like manner as if registered in the County Commissioner's office under existing laws. In case legal proceedings are commenced, there shall be an additional charge of five per centum upon all sums; and the Receiver of Taxes shall render each day to the City Controller an account of each item of his receipts, and daily

Allowance to tax payers.

Taxes to be liened.

Extra charge.

---

81. Act of Feb. 11, 1859, Sec. 1, P. L. 37.
82. Act of Feb. 2, 1854, Sec. 11, P. L. 28.

(*l*) As the Receiver of Taxes collects on the taxes of the current year until the 15th of January in the year succeeding, it was thought proper to continue him, as herein provided, beyond the first of the year, otherwise the incoming Receiver would collect fifteen days on the book upon which a twelve months' collection was had. This provision allows therefore each Receiver to settle his own books.

(*m*) The allowance to tax payers has been changed by the Act of April 17, 1861, (Sec. 102,) which confers upon Councils the power to fix any allowance which by them may be deemed expedient.

pay the same into the city treasury; * * * * and the Aldermen in every ward shall be authorized and required at all times to receive the personal taxes of persons resident therein, for which purpose they shall each be furnished with a tax list of such taxes as early in the year as they can be made out, and not later than the first of June in each year, and such aldermen shall receive therefor ten per centum for receiving and paying over such taxes, which they shall at least do once in each month, to the Receiver of Taxes or his agent. And each of said Aldermen shall, under the penalty of one hundred dollars to the said city, be in attendance at his office for the purpose of receiving the same on the day of any election. The said Receiver shall, immediately after the first day of December, annually, give public notice in at least four of the public newspapers of said city for ten days, to all persons who shall have omitted to pay their taxes, to pay them before the first day of January, and that if not paid by that time, a warrant will issue to collect the same; and it shall be the duty of the Receiver to issue his warrant after the fifteenth day of said month of January, directed to any constable of said city or county, commanding him to levy said taxes, with all charges accrued thereon; of any goods or chattels of the delinquent wheresoever found, and to make sale thereof after advertisement, as in cases of distress for rent, which warrant shall be returnable within thirty days. To pay over daily to City Treasurer.

Provided, That if any person against whom such taxes shall have been assessed shall make affidavit that he did not own the premises for which such taxes were assessed at the time they accrued and became a lien thereon, the said taxes shall be collected of the true owner thereof, or by proceedings to sell the premises by execution. And the said Receiver of Taxes shall furnish certificates of all taxes and claims which are a lien on real estate, and receive therefor twenty-five cents for each certificate and five cents for each lien and claim certified.

SEC. 83. That as soon as the City Commissioners shall place the duplicates of taxes in the hands of the Receiver, he shall cause his clerks to make out bills against the tax payers, so that all persons indebted for taxes may have their bills by the first day of July in each year, and the same to be delivered at a cost not exceeding one cent for all persons served within two miles of the office, and one and a-half cents for all more distant, for making such delivery, the expense whereof shall be charged to the city: *Provided*, That all properties owned by one person, or belonging to any one estate in any one ward, shall be included in the same bill. Duty to make out tax bills as soon as he receives duplicates.

SEC. 84. That it shall not be lawful for the Receiver of

83. Act of April 21, 1855, Sec. 14, P. L. 264. 84. Ibid. Sec. 15, P. L. 264.

Warrants against delinquent tax payers.

Taxes to place any warrant against delinquent tax payers into the hands of any constable until such constable shall have given security, by bond and warrant, with two sufficient sureties, to the satisfaction of the Court of Quarter Sessions, in the sum of five thousand dollars, nor have in the hands of any constable at any one time warrants for a greater amount of taxes than the amount of such bond; and such constable shall make report and payment of all his collections on such warrants at least once in every week, after they shall have been issued to him. And all taxes unpaid on the first day of January after the year for which they were assessed, shall bear interest until paid, besides the commissions thereon for collection.

To give general notice of non-payment of taxes.

SEC. 85. That the Receiver of Taxes shall, on the first Mondays of October, November, and December, give a general notice to all taxpayers, three times in three newspapers, to pay the taxes then due; and that if not paid before the first day of the following January, interest will thereafter be charged thereon, and that the names of all delinquent tax payers will then be published according to law, and the names of the delinquent tax payers, when published, shall be alphabetically arranged for the several wards.

To pay daily into the city treasury.

SEC. 86. That the Receiver of Taxes of the City of Philadelphia shall collect, and hereafter daily pay into the city treasury all State taxes by him collected. The City of Philadelphia shall pay over all State taxes collected and paid into the city treasury before the twenty-fifth day of July in each year, and receive therefor the five per cent. allowed by law, and one per cent. for the commission of collection, but no allowance for the then uncollected State tax, unless the city shall advance the same by the said date, in which case the city may borrow the amount of such residue of the current year's State tax: *Provided*, That the loans therefor be all payable within the year, and the whole of the State taxes for the year for which they accrued, shall be paid into the State treasury by the twenty-fifth of January next thereafter. The city shall allow the tax payers for the State tax five per cent. on all sums paid before the twenty-fifth of July of the year when due, and nothing if paid thereafter.

List of delinquent tax payers to be published if the valuation exceeds $100.

SEC. 87. That all laws or parts of laws now in force, requiring the Receiver of Taxes in the city of Philadelphia, to publish the names of all delinquent tax payers, shall be so construed as to apply to the taxes upon real estate in the said city of Philadelphia, and upon personal property only when the assessed valuation of the latter shall amount to or exceed one hundred dollars.

---

85. Act of May 13, 1856, Sec. 8, P. L. 573.
86. Ibid. Sec. 9, P. L. 573
87. Ibid. Sec. 2, P. L. 489.

SEC. 88 That the Receiver of Taxes of said city shall be charged by the City Controller, with the amount of the duplicates for each ward placed in his hands by the City Commissioners for State and city taxes, and that in the month of January annually, the said Receiver shall, in books to be called "The Register of Unpaid Taxes on Real Estate," register all unpaid taxes (except occupation taxes) of the preceding year, and the said taxes are hereby declared to be a lien on all real estate in accordance with the provisions of the act of third February, one thousand eight hundred and twenty-four, entitled "An Act relating to taxes on certain real estate in the City and County of Philadelphia," and the said Receiver shall issue his warrants for the collection of said taxes as now provided for by law, and the said warrants and bills of taxes uncollected in the hands of said constables, shall be returned by them to the Receiver of Taxes in the month of January every two years succeeding the year for which said taxes were levied, or sooner if the said Receiver shall require the same; and the said Receiver of Taxes shall place in the hands of the City Solicitor a list of all registered taxes unpaid in the month of January every two years succeeding the year for which such taxes were levied, and furnish to the said Solicitor, bills for said taxes, and he shall enforce payment thereof by sale of the real estate upon which the said taxes are a lien; and the said Solicitor shall pay to the said Receiver all moneys collected by him for taxes by the sale of such real estate, monthly, and the said Receiver shall enter satisfaction therefor on the register books. The City Controller shall immediately after the expiration of the term of office of the Receiver of Taxes, audit his accounts, and make allowance for uncollected taxes, and all real estate sold by order of the Orphans' Court, if returned to and confirmed by the said Court, shall be certified to the Receiver of Taxes by the Prothonotary of said Court, and all real estate sold by order of the Court of Common Pleas, or any other Court, (except sold by the Sheriff,) if returned to said Court or Courts, and confirmed by said Court or Courts, shall be certified to the Receiver of Taxes by the Prothonotary of said Court. General regulations.

SEC. 89. That the Receiver of Taxes for the City of Philadelphia be and he is hereby authorized and directed to refund all State and City taxes that may have been paid to and collected by him on duplicate and erroneous assessments, to the person or persons who may have so erroneously paid the same; all amounts to be refunded out of the taxes collected in the respective wards, and in the respective years in which said errors occurred: *Provided, however,* That proper vouchers of allowance of such errors by the City Com- Taxes collected on erroneous assessments to be refunded. Vouchers to be furnished.

88. Act of April 21, 1858, Sec. 2, P. L. 385.
89. Act of March 30, 1859, Sec. 1, P. L. 303.

missioners of said city shall be first furnished to the said Receiver of Taxes: *And Provided further*, That the lien of the taxes on the real estate wrongfully paid shall not have been discharged by a judicial sale, or otherwise.

Power to appoint solicitor, who shall have commissions.

SEC. 90. That all the powers and authority conferred on the Treasurer of the county of Philadelphia by the third and fourth sections of an Act entitled "An Act vacating part of old Master street, or Master lane, in Penn Township, in the County of Philadelphia, and for other purposes," passed the sixteenth day of April, one thousand eight hundred and forty-five, are hereby conferred on the Receiver of Taxes of the city of Philadelphia: *Provided, however*, That all suits or proceedings that may be instituted, and liens filed for registered taxes, in pursuance of this Act, or any Act of Assembly, shall be in the name of the city of Philadelphia; any act or acts hereby altered or supplied, or that are inconsistent herewith, be and the same are hereby repealed. (*p*)

List of taxables.

SEC. 91. That the list of taxables, directed in the second section of the Act to which this is a supplement, to be lodged with the Sheriff by the Receiver of Taxes of the city of Philadelphia, be so lodged before the tenth day of November next, and before the same day and month in every year thereafter.

Councils to levy tax.

SEC. 92. And the said City Councils shall fix the rate and levy all the taxes now authorized by law within the limits of said city and county, except the State tax, and direct the amount to be applied and paid by the City Treasurer to health, school, poor, city, and other purposes, according to law. The said taxes shall be voted so as to show how much is raised for said objects respectively; they shall be collected and accounted for to the Treasurer as one city and county tax The said tax, and all State taxes accruing within said city limits, shall be paid to the Receiver of Taxes, and all allowance made by law for the collection and prompt payment of the State tax shall accrue to the city treasury for the use of the city. *Provided*, That the said City Councils shall so discriminate in laying said city taxes as not to impose upon the rural portions those expenses which belong exclusive to the built portions of the said city; for which purpose the assessors shall distinguish in their returns what properties are within agricultural or rural sections, not having the benefit of lighting, watching, and other expenditures for purposes exclusively belonging to built portions

All taxes to be paid to the Receiver of Taxes.

Allowance for State tax to accrue to the city.

City Councils to discriminate as regards the rural districts in laying tax.

90. Act of April 12, 1859, Sec. 1, P. L. 543.
91. Act of April 13, 1859, Sec. 2, P. L. 595.
92. Act of Feb. 2, 1854, Sec. 39, P. L. 40.

(*p*) The act of 1845, (P. L. 496,) conferred upon the Treasurer of the County of Philadelphia the power to employ counsel to enforce the payment of regis tered taxes, who should be entitled to a commission of five per cent. [illegible] collected by him. Under the Act of 1859, the Receiver of taxes app[illegible] sel and the registered taxes were then taken from the Law Depart[illegible] City, where they were collected without any commission.

of said city; and all lands within agricultural or rural districts, used for the purpose of cultivation or farming, shall be assessed as farm land.

Councils not to impose taxes upon rural portions of the city, for police, watchmen, lighting and paving and cleaning streets.

SEC. 93. The councils shall not impose taxes upon rural portions of the city, for police and watchmen, for lighting and paving, and cleaning streets, and shall make an allowance therefor of at least one-third of the whole city tax in favor of such section, and any greater rate than aforesaid assessed or paid for the present year shall be remitted or refunded.

Certain marsh or meadow land subject only to one-half the tax on real estate.

SEC. 94. That on and after the passage of this Act, all meadow, or marsh or meadow land situated in the Twenty-fourth Ward, city of Philadelphia, and assessed as marsh or meadow land, and paying, besides the usual city taxes, a further tax for keeping up and in repair the banks on said land, shall only be liable to pay one-half the rate of tax levied on real estate in said city for city purposes.

Real property of railroad corporations subject to taxation.

SEC. 95. That the offices, depots, car houses, and other real property of railroad corporations situated in said city, the superstructure of the road and water stations only excepted, are and hereafter shall be subjected to taxation, by ordinances, for city purposes.

SEC. 96. That all owners of meadows or other farming lands in the rural portions of the twenty-fourth Ward, city of Philadelphia, who paid the full rate of city tax levied by the said city on real estate, in the years one thousand eight hundred and fifty-five and one thousand eight hundred and fifty-six, are hereby entitled to the amount of difference between the city and the rural rate; and upon presentation of their tax bills so paid, or by such proof of payment as may be required by and to the Receiver of Taxes for the city of Philadelphia, be and he is hereby authorized and directed to refund said amount of difference out of any city tax collected for this ward. Any act or acts hereby altered or supplied, or that are inconsistent herewith, be and the same are hereby repealed.

Receiver of Taxes to appoint and may discharge collectors.

SEC. 97. That the Receiver of Taxes shall appoint the requisite number of collectors of the taxes due from delinquent tax payers for the several wards, and shall not be confined to constables in making his selections; and he may at pleasure discharge such Collectors; and the Receiver of Taxes shall have all the authority and the same power to proceed against and enforce collection of all moneys received by any collector, and by any Sheriff for State or city taxes, which either or both of the County Commissioners and County Treasurer of any county of this State have, or

Mode of enforcing collection of money received by collectors and sheriff.

---

93. Act of April 21, 1855, Sec. 12, P. L. 264.
94. Act of April 16, 1858, Sec. 1, P. L. 318.
95. Act of April 21, 1858, Sec. 1, P. L. 385.
96. Act of March 2, 1861, Sec. 1, P. L. 87.
97. Act of April 9, 1861, Sec. 1, P. L. 286.

Sheriff to make a monthly statement, &c.

has, to enforce the payment over of any county tax collected by such officer; the Sheriff shall make a monthly settlement, and in default thereof, may be ruled to pay such taxes into court, and shall pay the expenses incurred thereby.

Powers and duties of collectors.

SEC. 98. That the collectors appointed by the Receiver of Taxes shall have all the powers to collect the taxes under their warrants conferred by the laws of the city of Philadelphia, which the collectors of any county have under the warrants of the County Commissioners of any county, against any delinquent tax-payer, or tenant of such tax-payer, and shall perform the same duties and be subject to the like penalties for any default; no warrant shall issue to them to collect any taxes until after the fifteenth day of the month of January succeeding the year for which such taxes were laid; and all collectors shall make return of all taxes against any parcel of real estate which he may not have collected before the thirty-first day of December, of the same year, which shall forthwith be placed in the hands of the proper solicitor for suit and collection by him; such collectors shall make weekly returns of their collections to the Receiver of Taxes, and in default thereof shall be discharged as defaulters.

Commissions and charges to be made by delinquent tax payers.

SEC. 99. That there shall be the following commissions and charges paid by the delinquent tax-payers, and no other, or more, and any demand and collection of other or greater charges, shall subject the party receiving the same to the like penalties, to be in the like manner recoverable as the Sheriff is liable to for the like offence, that is to say, a commission of five per cent. to be paid and received by the Receiver of Taxes; and the following shall be paid to and received by the collectors, upon warrants placed in their hands, for their own compensation, and the collectors shall collect no commission for the Receiver or city; on all sums over ten dollars due from one tax-payer, five per cent. on all sums so due; between five and not over ten dollars in amount, ten per cent.; on sums between one and not over five dollars, fifteen per cent.; on sums not over one dollar, twenty per cent.; and the following fees, to wit: seventy-

Distresses.

five cents for the warrant and three cents a mile circular measurement to be but once charged from such delinquent; and in case of a distress or distresses and sale made, the same fees which are provided by the fee bill to be paid to constables in Philadelphia, where distress shall be made for rents; no distress shall be made by any collector until he

Notice to be served.

shall have served a printed notice upon the delinquent or tenant, or some adult member of his family, stating that if the amount be not paid within thirty days, distress will be made therefor and for the costs, giving the amount of such costs, nor until after such time has expired.

---

98. Act of April 9, 1861, Sec. 2, P. L. 286. 99. Ibid., Sec. 3, P. L. 286.

SEC. 100. That if taxes be paid into the Receiver's office after the bills have passed into and remain in the hands of the collector, the Receiver shall collect the same costs which would have been then payable to the collector, if the money had been received by him, and shall pay them over to the collector.

Costs in certain cases to be collected and paid by receiver to collector.

SEC. 101. That all taxes in default on the same real estate, filed in the same Court, shall be collected in one suit; and no sale of real estate shall be made by the city for taxes, unless the property will bring enough to pay all the taxes in arrear to the State and city; but the sale shall be stayed, unless the said city shall purchase the same, which they shall have power to do, and hold the same, for redemption by the owner, as provided by law; and the same shall not become irredeemable in the city, until six months' previous previous notice thereof shall be published by the City Solicitor, in manner required by law in respect to suits intended to be brought for registered taxes; and after the period of redemption shall have expired, the city shall expose the same to public sale, after such notice as is required in respect to Orphans' Court sales. [In all cases of registered taxes, municipal claims, assessments for removing nuisances, or other charge by the city assessed on real estate, the advertising required, before suit brought, shall be in two newspapers, once a week, for six weeks, with such brevity of description that the charges therefor shall not exceed one dollar and fifty cents for each property; and no sale shall take place for any such claims, taxes, or assessments, except on the second Mondays of May and November.](*o*)

Suits and sales.

Notice.

Times of sale.

SEC. 102. That there shall be an allowance to all payers of taxes, who shall pay the same in the year for which they are assessed, as follows: five per cent. if paid on or before the first day of April; four per cent. if paid on or before the first day of June; two per cent. if paid on or before the first day of July. If paid after the first day of July, and on or before the first day of September, no deduction shall be made; if paid after the first day of September and on or before the first day of October an addition of two per cent, shall be added to and payable on the same, and if not paid until after the first day of October then an addition of five per cent. shall be added to and payable on the same, and the Councils of Philadelphia shall have the power to allow any other per centage for the payment of taxes, or add any other penalty for their non-payment during the current year. *Provided, however*, That the provisions of this act shall

Allowance for the payment of taxes during the year for which they are assessed, and the penalty for non-payment.

---

100. Act of April 9, 1861, Sec. 4, P. L. 286.
101. Ibid. Sec. 5, P. L. 286.
102. Act of April 17, 1861, Sec. 1, P. L. 354.

(*o*) The portion of this section in brackets has been repealed by act of January 31, 1862. [See Sec. 313.]

not be construed to apply to the tax levied and assessed in the year 1861. *And provided,* That the provisions of the 6th section of the act, approved May 1, 1852, entitled An act relative to the District of West Philadelphia, be and the same is hereby repealed.(*p*)

RECEIVER of TAXES for TWENTY-THIRD Ward. (*q*)

Receiver of Taxes of 23d Ward.

SEC. 103. That the Receiver of Taxes of the City of Philadelphia shall appoint one suitable person who shall serve for two years, and every two years thereafter shall appoint one suitable person to serve for the same time as Receiver of Taxes of the Twenty-third Ward of the City of Philadelphia, who shall be furnished with duplicate books of the assessment of said Ward at the same time that the books are furnished to the General Receiver by the Commissioners.

His bond.

SEC. 104. That the said Ward Receiver shall give bond to the city with good and sufficient security in the sum of ten thousand dollars, for the faithful collecting and paying over to the General Receiver of Taxes all money so received, accompanied by a list of the parties so paying, the amount of valuation, with the amount of city and State taxes so paid, opposite to each name, once in every week during the current year for which said tax shall have been levied.

Location of office.

SEC. 105. That the said Ward Receiver shall be a citizen of the Twenty-third Ward, and shall have an office conveniently located in said ward, and it shall be his duty to keep said office open during business hours, for the purpose of receiving the taxes of persons wishing to pay the same; and the said Ward Receiver shall receive from the City Treasurer, by warrant, drawn by the General Tax Receiver, as compensation for his services, the rate and amount of one and a half per centum of all moneys received by him during the current year for which the same shall have been levied, in lieu of the salary now paid to the clerk of the Twenty-third Ward in the General Receiver's Office, whom this Ward Receiver is to supersede.

Compensation.

SEC. 106. That the Receiver so appointed shall enter

103. Act of May 3, 1860, Sec. 1, P. L. 757.
104. Ibid. Sec. 2, P. L. 757.
105. Ibid. Sec. 3, P. L. 757.
106. Ibid. Sec. 4, P. L. 758.

(*p*) This last proviso has nothing apparently to do with allowances to tax-payers. It is in P. Laws, p. 509, and reads thus:

"That all certificates of loan of the Pennsylvania Railroad Company, shall be subject to taxation for state purposes only, as is now provided by law, in the case of certificates of loan received by said company, in payment of subscriptions to its capital stock, made by municipal corporations."

(*q*) The powers of the Receiver of Taxes *appointed* under this act, do not exclude the Receiver of Taxes elected by the qualified voters from collecting taxes in the 23d Ward. It is only the appointment of a subordinate officer.

upon the duties of his office at the same time as the General Receiver of Taxes elect shall enter upon the duties of his office, and shall be accountable to the General Receiver, for all taxes received by him, as provided in section third. When to enter upon his duties.

SEC. 107. That the said Ward Receiver shall collect all the delinquent taxes of said ward, but shall receive no compensation from the city for the collection of the same, but shall charge and receive from each such delinquent the rate and amount of five per cent. on all such tax, and seventy-five cents on each bill, and no more, except in case of distress for the collection of the same; then he shall be allowed to charge, in addition to the above, the same costs as are allowed to the Constable of said city in cases of distress for rent, et cetera; he shall be allowed to charge the rate of three cents per mile, circular measurement, to be but once charged to each delinquent; and any greater charge in any case than above recited, shall be considered a misdemeanor, and shall be punished in like manner as is provided for in the case of the Sheriff for a like offence; and the said Receiver shall have all the powers now vested in the collectors of delinquent taxes of the City of Philadelphia, but no distress shall be made in any case until he shall have served a printed notice upon the delinquent or tenant, or some adult member of his family, stating that if the amount be not paid within thirty days, distress will be made therefor and for the costs, giving the amount of such tax and costs, nor until after such time has expired. Charges. Misdemeanor. Notice of distress, when served.

SEC. 108. That if taxes be paid into the office of the General Receiver after the bills have passed into and remain in the hands of said Ward Receiver, the General Receiver shall collect the same costs which would have been then payable to the Ward Receiver if the money had been received by him, and shall pay them over to the said Ward Receiver, and the General Receiver shall pay to the said Ward Receiver fifty cents, by draft on the Treasurer, for every case where he shall have reported the proof of a tax having been paid or discharged by judicial sale, and which had not been entered upon the Receiver's books or registry of taxes as having been paid; and whenever said Ward Receiver shall ascertain the true owner of a vacant lot to be a different person than the person in whose name the assessment was made, he shall receive the sum of fifty cents, by draft on the Treasurer, as provided for the proof of a tax having been paid, and the General Receiver shall cause such alteration to be made on the books in his office. Taxes, bills, and costs, between ward receiver and general receiver

SEC. 109. That all laws, or parts of laws, inconsistent with this act, be and the same are hereby repealed.

107. Act of May 3, 1860, Sec. 5, P. L. 758.
108. Ibid. Sec. 6, P. L. 758.
109. Ibid. Sec. 7, P. L. 758.

SCHOOL DIRECTORS AND CONTROLLERS.

Election of School Directors.

SEC, 110. *That on the second Tuesday in October*, 1861, the qualified voters of each of the wards shall elect four citizens of like qualifications as members of the Senate to serve as Directors of Public School for three years, * * * * Each qualified voter shall vote for three Directors, and the four highest shall be elected. *Provided*, That the qualified voters within the Twenty-first, * * * * * Twenty-third and Twenty-fourth Wards shall elect, in the same election districts as heretofore, the number of School Directors as are now by law allowed, except the territory included in the boroughs of Frankford and Whitehall, which shall be separated from the township of Oxford in the election of School Directors. And the qualified voters of the said boroughs of Frankford and Whitehall shall elect three Directors of the Public Schools; and the qualified voters of the township of Oxford shall elect three Directors; and the qualified voters in the territory included within the bounds of the township of the unincorporated Northern Liberties and the boroughs of Armingo and Bridesburg, shall elect three Directors of the Public Schools.

22d Ward.

SEC. 110*a*. That the 20th section of the Act of February 2d, 1854, is amended to entitle the qualified voters of the Twenty-second Ward to elect twelve citizens, qualified to serve as members of the Senate. * * * Four of whom shall be elected to serve for one year, four for two years, four for three years as Directors of the Public Schools; said Directors to be elected at the next election held for city offices, and annually thereafter the qualified voters of the Twenty-second Ward shall elect four citizens of like qualifications to serve as Directors of Public Schools for three years.

SEC. 111. That for Public School purposes, each ward shall constitute a school section and the Board of Controllers shall have full power to apportion the school houses and distribute the duties of the Directors of the schools to and for all or any of the wards of the city in such manner as the Board of Controllers shall direct. The Directors of each section shall meet and organize on the first Monday in July next, succeeding their election; and upon such organization shall have and possess all the power, rights, privileges and immunities that shall then be by law or otherwise vested in the School Directors of the several sections of the first school district; and from and after such organization, all the rights, privileges and immunities of the School Directors last named shall cease and terminate, and all laws of this Commonwealth regulating and

---

110. Act of Feb. 2, 1854, Sec. 20, P. L. 33.
110*a*. Act of May 1, 1861, Sec. 1, P. L. 675.
111. Act of Feb. 2, 1854, Sec. 21, P. L. 33.

governing the School Directors last named shall cease to operate with regard to them, but shall continue in full force and operation for regulating and governing the School Directors elected and organized in accordance with the provisions of this act. In case of any vacancy occurring in either of the sectional boards of School Directors by death, resignation or otherwise, such vacancy shall be filled by the remaining directors of the ward wherein such vacancy exists, and the Director chosen to fill such vacancy being promptly qualified, shall continue to serve for and during the time the Director whose vacancy he fills could have served, and no longer. Vacancies how filled.

SEC. 112. That, hereafter, in case of any vacancy occurring in the Directors of any sectional School Board in the City of Philadelphia, it shall and may be lawful for the remaining directors of said sectional board to fill the same; and the person so chosen, to fill said vacancy shall serve until the next municipal election, at which time the qualified voters of the district in which said vacancy shall have occurred shall elect a Director for the unexpired term of such School Director. Vacancies how filled.

SEC. 113. That School directors in the first school district of Pennsylvania, elected in the wards of said district, shall reside in the wards for which they are elected; and a removal from the ward shall cause a vacancy in the said board, which shall be filled by the said board in which such vacancy occurs, except in the twenty-first, twenty-second, twenty-third, and twenty-fourth sections where all vacancies shall hereafter be filled by the remaining Directors within the election Districts in which such vacancies occur. School Directors to reside in the ward for which they are elected.

SEC. 114. That it shall be lawful for the City Councils by ordinance, to provide for the payment of the Secretaries of the several sections in the said first school district: *Provided*, That no more than fifty dollars per annum shall be appropriated or paid to each of said officers, and warrants therefor shall be drawn in such manner as by said ordinance may be directed. Salaries of secretaries.

SEC. 115. That the School Directors of each ward of the city of Philadelphia for the ensuing year shall, on the third Tuesday of June, of each and every year, elect one of their own number a Controller to serve for one year, and shall give him a certificate of such election; the Controllers thus elected shall each be sworn or affirmed that he will discharge the duties of the office of Controller of Public Schools with fidelity to the best of his ability, and they shall enter upon the duties of their office on the first Monday in July next succeeding their election. The Controllers elected in the Election of a controller.

112. Act of April 12, 1859, Sec. 1, P. L. 604.
113. Act of May 20, 1857, Sec. 1, P. L. 617
114. Act of April 16, 1857, Sec. 1, P. L. 221.
115. Act of February 2, 1854, Sec. 22, P. L. 33.

year 1854, shall meet at ten o'clock A. M., on the first Monday in July of that year, in the room of the Controllers of Public Schools in the city of Philadelphia, and shall then and there organize themselves into a Board and shall elect a president and such other officers as they may deem necessary, to serve for the term of one year; and upon such organization shall have the name and style of the Controllers of Public Schools of the First School District of Pennsylvania. And on the first Monday of July, in each year thereafter, the Controllers shall meet as aforesaid, and shall take the oath of office and enter upon the duties thereof. The President and other officers of the Board shall be elected on the first Monday in July.

Qualifications for controller of schools.

SEC. 116. That no person shall be eligible as a Controller of Public Schools in the First School District of this Commonwealth, unless he shall have the qualification to serve as a member of the State Senate.

Property vested in city.

SEC. 117. That immediately upon the organization of the said Board of Controllers, all property, real and personal, all trusts and trust funds, and all estate, rights, privileges and immunities whatsoever that are, or shall be by law or otherwise vested in, owned, possessed or enjoyed by, or that in any wise appertain to the Corporation created by the Act of Assembly passed April 16, A. D. 1845, entitled An Act relating to the Controllers of the Public Schools of the City and County of Philadelphia, subject to all the trusts, conditions and liabilities now legally applicable thereto, and all sums of money due, payable to or received by the Board of Controllers, shall be paid into the city treasury, and all sums expended by or for the purposes of the Board of Controllers, shall be paid by the City Treasurer upon orders drawn under appropriations regularly made by Councils.

ALDERMEN.

Two aldermen for each ward

SEC. 118. That there shall be two Aldermen in each of the wards of the city of Philadelphia; these Aldermen and Justices of the Peace who are in office at the time of the passage of this act, shall continue to reside and hold their offices within the limits of the ward, township or borough in which they were originally elected. In any ward of the said city where there shall be more than two Aldermen or Justices of the Peace residing and holding their offices at the time of the passage of this act, the number thereof shall be reduced to two as their commissions shall respectively expire, unless the qualified voters of such ward shall vote to increase the number thereof. The Aldermen of the said city shall be elected in each ward by the qualified voters

116. Act of May 13, 1856, Sec. 29, P. L. 567.
117. Act of Feb. 2, 1854, Sec. 23, P. L. 33.
118. Ibid. Sec. 24, P. L. 35.

thereof, on the SECOND TUESDAY OF OCTOBER, in accordance with the provisions of the Act of Assembly of June 21, A. D. 1839, entitled "An Act providing for the election of Aldermen and Justices of the Peace," and the Acts supplementary thereto. It shall be lawful for Councils to designate and appoint as many of the Aldermen of the said city as the public welfare may require, to be police or committing magistrates, who shall receive such compensation as Councils may provide and pay, and it shall not be lawful for any Alderman in said city to take fees in criminal cases but nothing herein contained shall be taken to impair the powers or diminish the duty of any and all Aldermen and Constables to be conservators of the peace, and to execute the criminal laws of the Commonwealth: *Provided*, That nothing herein contained shall be so construed as to prohibit any Alderman now in commission from becoming a candidate for election in that office.

Police magistrates.

SEC. 119. That so much of the twenty-fourth section of the act, entitled "A further supplement to an act, entitled 'An Act to incorporate the City of Philadelphia,' passed February second, one thousand eight hundred and fifty-four," as declares that there shall be but two Aldermen in each of the wards of the City of Philadelphia, is hereby repealed, so far as the same relates to the Twenty-first, Twenty-second, Twenty-third and Twenty-fourth Wards of said city.

Aldermen in 21st, 22d, 23d and 24th Wards.

SEC. 120. That if in any ward the term of any Alderman or Justice of the Peace shall expire between any two municipal elections, and there shall not be more than one Alderman or Justice of the Peace holding over, it shall and may be lawful for the qualified voters of said ward, at the Constables' election next preceding the expiration of such term, to elect one qualified person to act as Alderman, although the term of the one whose place he is to fill shall not have expired: *Provided*, That this section shall only apply in such cases where the term so to be filled shall expire within seven months next after the election, when such successor may be elected.

Vacancies.

SEC. 121. That it was the true intent and meaning of the Legislature in and by the twenty-fourth section of the act consolidating the several districts of the County of Philadelphia, and such is hereby declared to be the construction thereof, that the Aldermen in commission at the time of the passage of said act, should be Aldermen of and for the wards established therein, and should reside and hold their said office in such wards for the unexpired term of their commissions.

Construction of prior acts

---

119. Act of April 18, 1855, Sec. 1, P. L. 254.
120. Ibid. Sec. 2, P. L. 254.
121. Ibid. Sec. 3, P. L. 254.

Collection of taxes by aldermen.

SEC. 122. That it shall and may be lawful for any Alderman authorized to collect taxes, to appoint a clerk to attend in his office to collect taxes on election days or when from sickness or other cause, such Alderman cannot attend; the Alderman and his securities to be answerable for all taxes collected by such clerk, and the Alderman so appointing a clerk, shall not be liable for any penalty for not attending in his office on election days to receive taxes.

Increase of aldermen.

SEC. 123. That whenever the voters of any ward shall require by a majority of votes an additional Alderman, at any general or municipal election, such voters may vote for such additional Alderman at the succeeding municipal election, who shall thereupon be duly commissioned as such Alderman. It shall be lawful for any Alderman or Justice of the Peace, or Constable in said city, to receive fees in criminal or penal cases, but said costs and penalties shall be paid over to the City Treasurer monthly, under like penalties as in the payment of taxes. It shall be the duty of police officers to serve writs of summons and capias, for the violation of all penal and criminal acts and ordinances issued by the Mayor or Police Aldermen, within the City of Philadelphia, the costs for which shall be received and paid into the treasury as aforesaid.

Fines to be paid into the City Treasury.

SEC. 124. That all sum or sums of money accruing to and being in the hands of any Alderman or other officer, arising from the violation of any ordinance, forfeited recognizance, or for any other violation of law, shall be returned to and paid over to the City Treasurer on the first of each and every month; and any such Alderman or other officer neglecting or refusing to make return, and pay over as aforesaid, shall be deemed guilty of a misdemeanor in office, and be proceeded against in like manner as for other misdemeanors.

General provisions.

SEC. 125. That in lieu of the report now required to be made to the City Treasurer, the Aldermen of the said city shall on the first of every month, submit to the Controllers a statement, under oath, of all fines, penalties, costs, and sum or sums of money whatever, received by them and payable to the said city, and shall forthwith pay over to the City Treasurer the amount certified by the Controller to be in their hands and payable, and for this purpose the Controller may require the production of their books and dockets; and no warrant for the payment of the salary of any Alderman as police magistrate, shall be countersigned by the Controller, unless the receipt of the City Treasurer for the moneys so certified to be due by him for the period for which said salary is payable, shall be first produced and exhibited, and

---

122. Act of April 18, 1855, Sec. 4, P. L. 254.
123. Act of April 21, 1855, Sec. 25, P. L. 264.
124. Ibid. Sec. 27, P. L. 264.
125. Act of May 13, 1856, Sec. 21, P. L. 573.

any Alderman failing to comply with the provisions of this section, shall be punishable in the manner provided in the preceding section.

SEC. 126. That it shall be the duty of the Controller and Treasurer of the city, within the first five days of each month, to report to the City Solicitor every person who has been delinquent in rendering his account, or making payment of any moneys, fines, or costs, payable to the City Treasurer, and of the City Solicitor forthwith to proceed to make collection of the same, and otherwise to enforce the law against the delinquent.

SEC. 127. That so much of the twenty-fourth section of the Act of the General Assembly of this Commonwealth, approved on the second day of February, Anno Domini one thousand eight hundred and fifty-four, the twenty-fifth section of the Act approved on the twenty-first day of April, Anno Domini one thousand eight hundred and fifty-five, and the twentieth section of the Act approved on the thirteenth day of May, Anno Domini one thousand eight hundred and fifty-six, as prohibits Aldermen and Constables from receiving fees in criminal or penal cases, or requires them to submit a statement of the costs or fees so received, to the Controller, and to pay over the same to the City Treasurer; and also the entire Act, entitled "An Act relative to Aldermen and Constables in the city of Philadelphia," approved on the fifth day of April, Anno Domini one thousand eight hundred and fifty-eight, be and the same are hereby repealed: *Provided*, That nothing herein contained shall be so construed as to repeal or alter any law requiring police or committing magistrates in the said city to submit to the Controller a statement of all the fines, penalties and costs received by them in virtue of their offices as such, and to pay the same over to the City Treasurer. Repeal of prior laws.

SEC. 128. That Aldermen in and for the city of Philadelphia in place of those whose commission will expire previous to the time of holding the general election in October of the present year, and also of those whose commissions will expire in the year 1862, respectively, shall be elected at the time of holding the general election on the second Tuesday of October, 1861. And thereafter the election of Aldermen shall take place on the second Tuesday of October, annually, to fill the place of those whose commissions will expire previous to the next succeeding general election. Commissions to be issued to the said Aldermen under existing laws as to such as shall be elected in place of those whose commissions had expired at the time of the election in the present year, and as to such who shall be elected in General pre visions to prevent vacancies.

---

126. Act of May 13, 1856, Sec. 22, P. L. 573.
127. Act of March 1, 1859, Sec. 1, P. L. 89.
128. Act of March 21, 1861, Sec. 7, P. L. 165.

the place of those whose commissions expire before the then next succeeding October election, so as to take effect at the expiration of the respective commissions so terminating until the year 1864, and thereafter on the first day of January succeeding the election.

CONSTABLES.

Election of Constables. SEC. 129. On the *second Tuesday in October*, in each year, the qualified voters of each ward of the city of Philadelphia shall elect two Constables; they shall be qualified as the laws of this Commonwealth require such officers to be, and shall, upon entering the requisite security, be commissioned by the Court of Quarter Sessions of the county of Philadelphia; they shall be under and subject to the same legal penalties, to do and perform all duties that the usages and laws of this Commonwealth enjoin upon such officers: *Provided*, That the qualified voters within the Twenty-first, Twenty-second, Twenty-third, and Twenty-fourth Wards shall elect the same number of Constables as are now by law allowed: and the Constables in said wards shall be elected by separate districts, each district embracing the qualified voters of said wards respectively residing within the bounds of the present districts for electing Constables, in like manner as if this Act had not been passed.

Duties. SEC. 130. That every Alderman or Constable who shall not have made report and payment over to the Receiver of Taxes of all taxes received by him for each successive month after he shall have received any taxes or warrants to collect taxes, shall be proceeded against as is provided by law in respect to delinquent tax collectors, under the Act of the twenty-eighth of February, one thousand eight hundred and thirty-five, a supplement to the Act relating to county rates, &c., except that the certificate therein required to be filed by the County Commissioners shall be filed by the Receiver of Taxes, the Treasurer and Controller of the City of Philadelphia, or a majority of them.

Duties. SEC. 131. That any Alderman or Constable who shall have made default on the payment over of any taxes collected by him, as required by law, shall cease to be authorized to receive any more taxes, and notice thereof shall be published by the Receiver of Taxes in three daily papers three times; nor shall he be capable of drawing any salary or other dues from the city until he shall have fully paid up the amount of his collections. It shall be lawful for the Receiver of Taxes to administer oaths and affirmations to all persons who may be authorized or required to make oath or affirmation in relation to the collection of taxes or other revenue payable to said Receiver.

---

129. Act of Feb. 2, 1854, Sec. 26, P. L. 35.
130. Act of April 21, 1855, Sec. 16, P. L. 264.
131. Ibid. Sec. 17, P. L. 264.

SEC. 132. That at the next election for Constables in said ward, the qualified electors of said ward shall elect six citizens to serve as Constables, for the same term as the other Constables of said city. Election of Constables for 24th Ward.

SEC. 133. That the term of service of the Constables of the several wards of the city of Philadelphia, be and is hereby extended to two years; said Constables to be elected on the first Tuesday in May, A. D. eighteen hundred and fifty-eight; and in case of vacancy by death, resignation or otherwise, the vacancy so occurring shall be filled at the first annual election in May thereafter; and the person so elected shall be required to enter security and be duly commissioned by the Court of Quarter Sessions, in accordance with the provisions of existing laws: *Provided*, That the provisions of this Act shall not extend or apply to the Twenty-first, Twenty-second, Twenty-third and Twenty-fourth Wards of said city. Term of service of Constables extended to two years.

SEC. 134. That the qualified voters of each ward shall elect as many Constables as they have Aldermen, and whenever, by a vote of the qualified citizens, they shall increase the number of Aldermen, the number of Constables shall also be increased: *Provided*, That this Act shall not apply to the Twenty-first, Twenty-second, Twenty-third and Twenty-fourth Wards of said city. Aldermen and Constables to be of equal number.

COMMISSIONERS AND SUPERVISORS OF HIGHWAYS.

SEC. 135. That the City Councils shall annually nominate, and the Mayor shall, as hereinbefore provided, appoint the requisite number of Supervisors of streets and roads for the different wards, who shall be under the direction and accountable to the Commissioners of Highways, who shall be appointed by the said Councils annually, and whose numbers and duties shall be prescribed by ordinance. City Councils to nominate Supervisors, and Mayor to appoint.

SEC. 136. That the Chief Commissioner of Highways and the Commissioners of Highways shall constitute a Board, of which the Chief Commissioner shall be President, for the transaction of all business relative to highways, under the ordinance of Councils creating the Department of Highways, or any ordinance that Councils may hereafter pass; and said Board shall, at the expiration of the terms of office of the present Supervisors, recommend to the Mayor, three suitable persons in each Supervisor's District, from whom the Mayor shall appoint one person to act as Supervisor. Board of Highway Commissioners created. To recommend Supervisors.

SEC. 137. That the Chief Commissioner of Highways of

132. Act of March 16, 1861, Sec. 2, P. L. 147.
133. Act of March 25, 1858, Sec. 1, P. L. 163.
134. Act of March 30, 1858, Sec. 1, P. L. 185.
135. Act of Feb. 2, 1854, Sec. 14, P. L. 30.
136. Act of April 21, 1855, Sec. 24, P. L. 264.
137. Act of May 1, 1857, Sec. 2, P. L. 376.

Chief Commissioners to open 52d street.

the city of Philadelphia be and he is hereby directed to open and make passable Fifty-second street, as laid down on said plan of the first section of the survey of Kingsessing, from Darby avenue to Baltimore avenue; and also said Fifty-second street, as laid down on the plan of the first section of the survey of Blockley, from said Baltimore avenue to Market street; the damages to property owners (if any there be) to be assessed and paid as is by law provided.

SURVEYS AND SURVEYORS.

Survey Districts.

SEC. 138. That so much of the twenty-seventh section of the Act of Assembly, approved February second, one thousand eight hundred and fifty-four, as declares that the Surveyors shall continue in office during good behavior, be and the same is hereby repealed; and that the said city of Philadelphia shall be divided into twelve Survey Districts, as follows: In District One shall be the First Ward west of Broad street; in District Two shall be the residue of the First Ward, the Second and Third Wards; in District Three shall be the Fourth, Fifth, Seventh, Eighth, Ninth and Tenth Wards; in District Four, the Thirteenth, Fourteenth, and Fifteenth Wards; in District Five, the Sixth, Eleventh, Twelfth, Sixteenth, and Seventeenth Wards; in District Six, the Eighteenth and Nineteenth Wards; in District Seven, the Twentieth Ward; in District Eight, the Twenty-first Ward; in District Nine, the Twenty-second Ward; in District Ten, the Twenty-third Ward; in District Eleven, the Twenty-fourth Ward, north of Market street; and District Twelve, the Twenty-fourth Ward, south of Market street; and on the first Tuesday in May, one thousand eight hundred and fifty-five, the qualified voters of each of said districts shall elect one citizen, who shall have had five years' experience and skill in his profession, to serve as Surveyor and Regulator of said district for five years; and whenever a vacancy shall occur in said Board by resignation, death, expiration of term of service, or otherwise, it shall be filled at the next municipal election for the aforesaid term of five years, and in the meantime by said Board.

Election of Surveyors.

3d survey district.

SEC. 139. That the Sixth Ward of the City of Philadelphia, from and after the passage of this act, shall form part of and be included in the third Survey District of the said city, any law or parts of laws to the contrary notwithstanding.

1st survey district.

SEC. 140. That hereafter the first Survey District shall be composed of all that part of the city west of Passyunk road, and Broad street east of the river Schuylkill, and south by South street.

---

138. Act of April 21, 1855, Sec. 3, P. L. 264.
139. Act of April 3, 1860, Sec. 1, P. L. 622.
140. Act of May 13, 1856, Sec. 16, P. L. 568.

SEC. 141. That the said twelve Surveyors shall constitute the Board of Surveyors, and the Chief Surveyors, and Engineer, shall serve for five years, and shall receive a salary of three thousand dollars for all services by him to be performed, and each District Surveyor a salary of five hundred dollars for keeping the public record of surveys, and performing all services as a member of said Board, and such fees as has been usual or shall be established by ordinance. All the public plans of town plots in the office of the Clerk of the Court of Quarter Sessions and of the Recorder of Deeds, shall be deposited in the office of the Board of Surveyors, subject to the public inspection without charge. It shall be the duty of Councils, under the supervision of the President of said Board, to cause to be completed by the District Surveyors, in sections, from time to time, a survey and plans of the city plot not already surveyed, according to the provisions of the laws under which the late district of Spring Garden was surveyed;(*r*) one copy of which plans, when approved by the Court, shall be filed in the office of said Board, and the other in the office of the proper District Surveyor, and in like manner and with like approval, existing plans may be revised and altered: *Provided*, That the plans made under existing contracts shall be approved by said Board before being returned to Court for confirmation, and that no ground shall be taken for public use, under this act, without compensation as provided by law. The said Board of Surveyors, under the direction of Councils, shall have authority to alter the lines and regulate the grades of any street or streets which may have been laid out upon any of the public plans or otherwise, but not opened, subject to the exception and approval of the Court of Quarter Sessions, as in the case where the plans are originally submitted for approval and confirmation.

Surveyors to constitute a Board, and elect a president, who shall be the Chief Surveyor. Salaries of Chief and District Surveyors. All plans, &c., to be deposited in the office of the Board of Surveyors. Councils under supervision of President of Board of Surveyors to have completed surveys, and plans, of the city plot not already surveyed. Plans to be approved by the Court, and filed in the office of the Board. No ground to be taken for public use, without compensation. Board of Surveyors, under direction of Councils, authorized to alter the lines and regulate the grades of any street or streets not yet opened.

SEC. 142. And such number of said Surveyors and Regulators shall be organized into a board under a head for such purposes relating to surveys, the planning of the city, the building of bridges, the construction of sewers, and grading of highways, as Councils may declare by ordinance: which Board may hear by appeal, and, if neither party before a hearing shall have appealed to court, shall finally decide upon all questions of party lines, the position

To be organized into a Board.

141. Act of April 21, 1855, Sec. 4, P. L. 264.
142. Act of Feb. 2, 1854, Sec. 27, P. L. 27.

(*r*) The District of Spring Garden was surveyed under the provisions of the 18th Section of an act approved March 22, 1813, (P. L. 142,) which provides that "at least thirty days previous notice shall be given in at least two of the public newspapers published in the City of Philadelphia, and by hand-bills posted up in at least ten of the most public places, that on a certain day appointed by the Court, the Court of Quarter Sessions will hear any objections that may be made thereto by any freeholder, and stating where the said plans are deposited for inspection.

and thickness of party walls, of the condemnation thereof for insufficiency, and of the proper structure of new buildings and the party walls thereof, so as to secure the safety and health of the citizens, under the statutes in force in said city: *Provided*, That nothing herein contained shall alter or interfere with any survey or regulation made or directed to be made under the several laws of this Commonwealth of any portion of the county of Philadelphia, but the same shall be completed, or if already confirmed, shall remain unalterable, as therein provided, unless said alterations shall be ordered by a resolution of said Councils, and approved by the Court of Quarter Sessions, upon public notice previously given for the space of thirty days in at least two of the daily newspapers of the said city, until otherwise provided by ordinance: *And provided further*, That in any alteration that may be made of the regulations of any portion of the city, in conformity with the provisions of this section, whereby damage may ensue to private property, compensation shall be made for such damage, to be ascertained and paid by law, as in case of damage for opening streets. All official acts and proceedings of the Surveyors and Regulators shall be returned to the head of said Board, to remain in his office, from which certified copies shall be made and furnished on request, in the same manner and for the same compensation as copies are furnished from the land department of this Commonwealth.

Surveys already made not altered.

Except by resolution of Councils, &c.

Compensation for damage.

Official acts, &c., to remain at office.

Copies, how furnished.

SEC. 143. Whenever a vacancy by limitation or otherwise shall occur in the office of President of the Board of Surveyors, the Chief Engineer and Surveyor to fill that office, shall be elected by the Councils of said city, by *viva voce* vote, in joint meeting, to serve for five years. The said Chief Engineer and Surveyor shall be a citizen who shall have had five years previous practical experience as a civil engineer, and be sworn or affirmed before the Mayor to the truth thereof, and that he will perform his duties with fidelity, and file the certificates thereof in the law department. He shall be president of and a member of the Board of Surveyors, and as the head of the department of surveys, perform all the duties imposed on him by law or ordinance. Each District Surveyor shall have three years experience in the business of regulating and surveying, after having completed his apprenticeship and become of lawful age, and make oath or affirmation of such fact, and to perform his duties with fidelity, and file his certificate as aforesaid.

Chief Engineer and Surveyor, how elected.

Qualifications.

District Surveyor.

SEC. 144. That it shall be lawful, and is hereby made the duty of Councils, by ordinance, to regulate the survey department, to take security from and prescribe the duties

---

143. Act of May 13, 1856, Sec. 13, P. L. 568.
144. Act of May 13, 1856, Sec. 14, P. L. 568.

of the District Surveyors, the books and records they shall keep, and returns they shall make to the Board of Surveys: also, what records and surveys shall be deposited in the office of the Board of Surveys: and prescribe the duties, powers and services to be performed by the Chief Engineer and Surveyor, and each member of said Board of Surveys, and establish all needful regulations for said Board of Surveys and District Surveyors, and their offices and records, and to the use thereof by the citizens.

Councils to provide for regulation of survey department

SEC. 145. That should any District Surveyor and Regulator refuse to comply with any of the regulations of the Department of Surveys, or prove to be unskilful and incompetent to the performance of his duties, a majority of said Board of Surveys may, on the representations of at least six citizens, examine into the charge made against such Surveyor; and if they find just cause, may petition the Court of Quarter Sessions of the County of Philadelphia for his removal; and if said court shall be satisfied of the truth of the allegation of the petition, such Surveyor and Regulator, shall be dismissed, and another Surveyor and Regulator shall, on the recommendation of such Board of Surveys, be appointed by the court to hold the appointment, and perform all the duties of the office until the next municipal election.

Removal of surveyors and regulators.

Vacancies

SEC. 146. That the Chief Engineer and Surveyor of the City of Philadelphia be and he is hereby authorized and directed to revise and change the grades of the streets laid out in the Twenty-fourth Ward of said city, north of Market street, the Lancaster turnpike, and south of Bridge street, and east of late Sixth, now Thirty-fifth street, so as to conform in as great a degree as he shall deem advisable, to the natural grade or surface of the ground; the said revised survey shall be confirmed by the Board of Surveys, and be approved by the Court of Quarter Sessions, in the manner now provided by law: *Provided*, That no alteration shall be made in the grades of Market street, Lancaster turnpike, Bridge street, and Sixth street, now Thirty-fifth street, as aforesaid; and the commissioners for the survey of the plan of Blockley shall proceed to cause the same to be completed and approved by the Court, in manner provided by law before said township was embraced in the City of Philadelphia.

Re-survey of the grade of the streets in 24th Ward authorized.

SEC. 147. That the plan of the survey and regulation of the first section of Kingsessing, as made by the Surveyor of the twelfth district of the City of Philadelphia, and approved by the Chief Engineer and Surveyor, one copy of which plan is now on file in the office of the Board of Sur-

1st section of Kingsessing.

---

145. Act of May 13, 1856, Sec. 15, P. L. 568.
146. Ibid. Sec. 19, P. L. 568.
147. Act of May 1, 1857, Sec. 1, P. L. 376.

veyors, and a duplicate thereof in the office of said Surveyor of the twelfth district, be and the same is hereby confirmed, and the streets, lines, heights, and grades marked and designated on said plains are hereby fixed and established; and the Department of Surveys of the City of Philadelphia is hereby authorized and directed to have the remaining portion of Kingsessing (except the meadow land) completed without unnecessary delay, in strict accordance with the plan hereby confirmed.

Act relative to survey of Blockley, repealed.

SEC. 148. That so much of the eighteenth section of an Act of Assembly, entitled, "A further supplement to the Act consolidating the City of Philadelphia," approved May 13, 1856, as provides that the commissioners for the survey of the plan of Blockley, appointed under an Act of Assembly entitled, "An Act to change the name of the Borough of West Philadelphia to the District of West Philadelphia, and relative to the District of Kensington and Richmond, in the county of Philadelphia," approved April 3, 1851, shall cause the same to be completed and approved by the Court, in the manner provided by law before the said township was embraced in the City of Philadelphia, be and the same is hereby repealed, and the duties of said commissioners shall forthwith cease and determine: *Provided,* That nothing herein contained shall affect any contract made for the survey of any portion thereof, prior to the first day of January, A. D. 1857, but the said contract shall be carried out under the supervision and subject to the control of the Board of Surveys of said city, and paid for in the manner provided for general surveys of said city.

Duties of commissioners to cease. Proviso.

Duties of Board of Surveys.

Railroads extending into the City to submit their plans, etc., to the Board of Surveyors.

SEC. 149. That hereafter no railroad company, whose road does or shall terminate within the City of the Philadelphia, shall have the right or power to locate and construct that part of said road which shall extend within the limits of said city, without first submitting the plans and surveys thereof, exhibiting the grades and routes, to the Board of Surveys of said city, who shall have the power to conform the same, as far as may be practicable, to the general plan and regulations of said city, as adopted at that time, and all charters authorizing the construction of any railroad within said city shall be taken to be subject to the above restriction: *Provided,* That this shall not be construed to apply to any railroad already graded or laid with rails in said city, unless the route or grade thereof shall be altered.

Repeal of certain survey commissions.

SEC. 150. That section fifteen of an Act of Assembly entitled, "An Act relating to certain State roads and other purposes," approved May 3, 1832, and sections four to six

148. Act of May 13, 1857, Sec. 1, P. L. 489.
149. Act of April 21, 1855, Sec. 10, P. L. 264.
150. Act of May 1, 1861, Sec. 1, P. L. 565.

inclusive, with ten, twelve, and thirteen, of an Act entitled, "An Act relative to certain streets in the District of Moyamensing, Kensington, Penn," &c., approved March 29, 1850, sections six and seven of an Act entitled, "An Act to revise the levels and grades of streets in Southwark and Moyamensing," &c., approved May 15, 1850, and section twenty-eight of an Act entitled, "An Act to incorporate the Butler Coal Company, &c., and relative to the survey of Passyunk Township," approved April 18, 1853, be and the same are hereby repealed, and the duties of Commissioners and Surveyors therein noted shall forthwith cease and determine; and henceforth the surveys therein specified and provided for shall be prosecuted only by the direction of the Select and Common Councils of the City of Philadelphia, under the supervision and direction of the Department of Surveys of said city. (s)

12th section of Blockley confirmed.

SEC. 151. That the plan of the twelfth section of the survey of Blockley, as approved by the Board of Surveyors of the city of Philadelphia, being plan No. 19, on file in the office of the Department of Surveys of said city, be, and the same is hereby confirmed, and the streets and avenues all fixed and established as they are marked and located on said plan.

Public Plan No. 42 confirmed.

SEC. 152. That the plan of the revised grade regulation of Market street and vicinity, in the Twenty-fourth Ward of the city of Philadelphia, bounded by Arch street on the north, York street on the south, the river Schuylkill on the east, and Crammond street on the west, prepared in compliance with resolution of Select and Common Councils, approved March twenty-third, one thousand eight hundred and fifty-nine, and approved by the Board of Surveyors, at their stated meeting of December nineteenth, one thousand eight hundred and fifty-nine, be and the same is hereby confirmed, and all the heights and grades marked thereon established; said plan being on file as No. 42, in the Department of Surveys of the city of Philadelphia.

BUILDINGS AND BUILDING INSPECTORS.

Act appointing two Building Inspectors repealed.

SEC. 153. That so much of the Act to which this is a supplement, as provides that the Judges of the Court of Common Pleas of the city and county of Philadelphia shall appoint two Building Inspectors, be and the same is hereby repealed; and, in the month of May, one thousand eight hundred and fifty-eight, or as soon thereafter as possible, the Judges of the Court of Common Pleas shall appoint one

151. Act of May 1, 1861, Sec. 1, P. L. 430.
152. Act of March 21, 1861, Sec. 1, P. L. 167.
153. Act of April 13, 1858, Sec. 1, P. L. 244.

(s) This was passed in compliance with a Resolution approved March 24, 1859.

Inspectors to be appointed by Courts and City Councils.

person, and the Judges of the Supreme Court of this State shall appoint one person, and the Select and Common Councils of the city of Philadelphia shall elect jointly, on the third Thursday in April, Anno Domini one thousand eight hundred and fifty-eight, one person, who shall possess all the qualifications provided in the Act to which this is a supplement, who shall perform all the duties and be subject to all the penalties now imposed by law upon the Building Inspectors of said city; said Building Inspectors shall hold their office for three years from the first Monday in July, one thousand eight hundred and fifty-eight, or until their successors are duly appointed and qualified: *Provided*, That the Court of Common Pleas shall not appoint until the first day of June, Anno Domini one thousand eight hundred and fifty-nine, and the Inspector of the First District, as now divided, shall continue in office until the expiration of the term for which he was appointed.

Duties of.

Term of office.

Salary.

SEC. 154. That the said Inspectors so appointed shall be paid an annual salary of two thousand dollars each.

SEC. 155. That all laws or parts of laws inconsistent with the provisions of this Act, be and the same are hereby repealed.

Term of office.

SEC. 156. Said Inspectors shall be suitable persons of experience and skill, each of whom shall have served a regular apprenticeship to the house-carpentering or brick-laying business, and afterward, been engaged, for at least seven years in working in or carrying on such business, to be Inspectors of Buildings in the city of Philadelphia, for the term of two years next succeeding their appointment, and until their successors shall be appointed and qualified; and in case of a vacancy by death, resignation, removal, or otherwise, the said Judges shall appoint another person or persons of like qualification, who shall perform all the duties, have all the rights, and be subject to all the penalties and provisions of this Act, for the remainder of the term so vacated.

Vacancies.

Oath of office.

SEC. 157. That every such Inspector, before he enters upon the duties of his office, shall be required to take and subscribe, before some person authorized by law to administer the same, the following oath or affirmation: I do solemnly and sincerely swear or affirm (as the case may be,) that I am duly qualified, as required by section first, to act as Inspecter of Buildings, and that I will faithfully, impartially and truly execute and perform the duties of an Inspector of Buildings in the city of Philadelphia, and see that the buildings inspected by me are built as required by the laws of the Commonwealth, according to the best of my

154. Act of April 13, 1858, Sec. 2, P. L. 244.
155. Ibid Sec. 3, P. L. 244.
156. Act of May 7, 1855, Sec. 1, P. L. 466.
157. Ibid. Sec. 2, P. L. 466.

judgment and abilities; which said oath or affirmation shall be reduced to writing and filed in the office of the Prothonotary of the Court of Common Pleas of said city and county, and shall be entered on the record in said office; every such person shall, moreover, before entering on the duties of his office, execute a bond to the Commonwealth in the sum of ten thousand dollars, with one or more sureties, to be approved by said Court or by two of the Judges thereof in vacation, conditioned for the faithful performance of the duties imposed upon him by law, which bond shall be for the use of any or all persons who may be aggrieved by the acts or neglect of such Inspector.

To keep an office.

SEC. 158. That the said Inspector shall keep an office as nearly central as may be, (notice of which shall be given by advertisement in three daily newspapers, not less than three times,) where shall be filed all applications for permits, and where notices may be left requiring the Inspector of the proper district to visit and inspect any building which may be in progress of erection or construction; and if such Inspector shall fail or neglect to attend within thirty-six hours after notice left for that purpose, he shall forfeit and pay to the owner or owners, contractor or contractors, the sum of twenty dollars for each and every day he shall so fail or neglect to attend, beyond the thirty-six hours aforesaid, which said penalty shall be recoverable in any action of debt before any alderman or justice of the peace of said city.

Building Inspection Districts.

SEC. 159. That the said Inspectors as soon as may be after their apointment, shall meet and divide the city into two districts,(*t*) as nearly equal as may be, (excluding therefrom the rural portions of said city, and to each of the said Inspectors shall be allotted one of the said districts, and he shall visit and inspect, as provided for in the fifth section, all the houses or buildings in progress of erection, construction, or alteration, in his district; they shall have power to appoint one or more deputies, to assist them in the performance of their duties, and the same to remove at pleasure, who shall possess the like qualifications, and take and subscribe the like oath or affirmation to perform the duties of Deputy Inspector as are prescribed in the first and second sections of this act, in relation to the Inspectors, which shall

---

158. Act of May 7, 1855, Sec. 3, P. L. 466.
159. Ibid Sec. 4, P. L. 466.

(*t*) The City of Philadelphia has been divided into three Districts: The 1st, includes all that portion of the City of Philadelphia, south from the south side of Chestnut Street, together with the Falls of Schuylkill and Manayunk. The 2d, includes all that portion of the City, from the north side of Chestnut Street, to the south side of Coates Street, together with West Philadelphia. The 3d, includes all that portion of the City, from the north side of Coates Street, including Germantown, Frankford, Bridesburg, Chestnut Hill; and excepting the Falls of Schuylkill and Manayunk.

in like manner be filed in said Court, and entered on the records thereof; the said Deputy or Deputies shall be paid by the Inspector for whom they shall officiate, and shall be accountable to him for the faithful discharge of his or their duties; and said Inspector shall be responsible for his or their acts, in the same manner as if done by him personally.

General duties to inspect buildings in process of erection.

SEC. 160. That it shall be the duty of every Inspector appointed under the provisions of this act, to visit and inspect each or any house or houses, building or buildings, which may be in the course of erection, construction, or alteration within the limits of his district, either by himself or by his Deputy, and to see that such house or houses, building or buildings, are being erected, constructed, or altered, according to the provisions of this act, and all acts and ordinances in force in said city, and in manner adapted for the security thereof against fires and the safety of the occupants; that the materials used are suitable for the purpose, and that the work is done in a substantial and workmanlike manner, and is of sufficient strength and solidity to answer the purpose for which it is designed; and before the foundations are laid he shall examine the trenches dug for the same, and be fully satisfied that the soil or substratum is sufficient for the structure, or at least the best that can be obtained; and should the nature of the soil be such, and the work of sufficient magnitude as to require piling, flagging, or logging, the same shall be done: *Provided*, That it may be deemed necessary by the Board of Inspectors; that his visits and inspection shall be repeated from time to time during the erection, construction or alteration of such house or houses, building or buildings, until all the walls shall have been completed and the same enclosed, when his duties shall terminate; he shall, on application for that purpose, furnish the owner or owners, contractor or contractors, his certificate that the said house or building is in all respects conformable to law, and properly constructed, for which certificate he shall receive a fee of fifteen cents.

Permits to be issued.

SEC. 161. That when any person or persons shall be desirous of erecting, constructing, or altering any house or building, he or they shall make application at the office of the Inspectors of Buildings for a permit for that purpose, and he or they shall be required to furnish a written statement of the proposed location, the dimensions and manner of construction of the proposed buildings or edifice, together with the different stories and the cornice, and the materials to be used in such house or building, and in addition to any fee or fees he or they are now or may be hereafter required to pay, he or they shall pay for such permit the sum of three dollars, for the inspection of each or any building not ex-

160. Act of May 7, 1855, Sec. 5, P. L. 466.
161. Ibid., Sec. 6, P. L. 466.

ceeding thirty feet in height and eighteen feet in width, nor covering more than sixteen hundred square feet of ground; the sum of five dollars for the inspection of each or any building over eighteen feet in width, not exceeding thirty feet in height, nor covering more than two thousand square feet of ground; and the further sum of one dollar in addition for each story above thirty feet in height; and the like sum for each additional one thousand square feet of ground covered by such house or building, which said sum or sums, and all other fees received by them, shall be paid by the Inspectors into the city treasury monthly; and the said Inspectors shall be paid an annual salary of three thousand dollars each.

Alteration of buildings subject to inspectors

SEC. 162. That from and after the first day of June, Anno Domini one thousand eight hundred and fifty-five, it shall not be lawful for any person or persons to erect, construct or build, or cause to be erected, constructed or built, any brick, iron, granite, marble or stone house, or building, or any house or building composed partly of brick, iron, granite, marble or stone, or to alter any such building, so as to make it substantially a new building, unless the same shall have been inspected, from time to time, by one of the Inspectors of Buildings, or one or more of the deputies, and a certificate furnished by him, that the said house or building is properly constructed, and in all respects safe and secure; and should any Inspector award such certificate to any person or persons for any house or building not constructed according to the provisions of this act, the bond given by such Inspector shall be declared to be forfeited, and the whole principal sum therein named shall become due and payable, and such Inspector shall be forthwith dismissed from office by the said Court, and the vacancy thus created filled under the provisions of this act, and the said principal sum shall be collected by due process of law, and the same held to the use of any person or persons, either in an individual or corporate capacity, who may be injured or sustain any damage thereby.

Thickness of walls.

SEC. 163. That the thickness of the walls of all buildings hereafter erected, constructed, built or altered in the city of Philadelphia, (excluding therefrom the rural portions of said city,) shall be as follows, to wit: In all buildings hereafter to be erected, constructed, built or altered, with a front of not more than sixteen feet, and not more than thirty-five feet high, the cellar or foundation walls shall be not less than sixteen inches in thickness, the party walls not less than nine inches, and the front walls not less than nine inches; in all buildings with a front of not less than sixteen and not more than twenty feet, and not more than

162. Act of May 7, 1855, Sec. 7, P. L. 466.
163. Ibid. Sec. 8, P. L. 466.

forty-five feet high, the foundation or cellar walls shall not be less than eighteen inches in thickness, the party walls not less than thirteen inches, and the front walls not less than thirteen inches in thickness; in all buildings with a front of not less than twenty nor more than twenty-eight feet, and not more than fifty-five feet high, the foundation or cellar walls shall not be less than twenty inches in thickness, the party walls not less than thirteen inches, and the front walls not less than eighteen inches to the height of the first story, and thirteen inches the remainder of the height; in all buildings with a front of more than twenty-eight feet, and not more than sixty-five feet high, the foundation or cellar walls shall not be less than twenty-four inches in thickness, the party walls not less than eighteen to the height of the first story, and thirteen inches the remainder of the height, and the front walls twenty-eight in the cellar, twenty-two inches to the height of the first story, and seventeen inches the remainder of the height; and whenever any builder, owner or contractor, may construct or erect any building to a greater height than those above specified, the increased thickness of the walls shall be determined by the Board of Inspectors: *Provided*, That any lot of the width of sixteen feet or less, shall not be encumbered with more than nine inches of the stone wall, or more than four and a half inches of the brick wall; nor in any case shall any party wall be placed on the adjoining lot more than ten inches for the stone wall, or more than six and a half inches for the brick wall: *And provided further*, That in any case where the proposed building is to be used for a storehouse, the party or division walls shall not be less than thirteen inches the full height thereof.

Wooden girders and supports prohibited.

SEC. 164. That it shall not be lawful for any person or persons to erect, construct, or build any rear wall, or any party or division wall between two or more houses or buildings, upon any wooden girder or rafter, or to support any such rear, party or division wall by any wooden support whatever; it shall be the duty of any or all persons erecting, constructing or altering any house or building, to build the party or division wall to at least the height of ten inches above the line of the roof of such house or building; such party or division wall to be covered by stone or metal, so as effectually to prevent the connection of the roofing or wooden cornice of any two or more houses or buildings; and the said builder or builders shall be entitled to compensation for such portion of said wall, as is now provided for; nor shall it be lawful for any person or persons to build any wooden joist, rafter, beam or girder in any chimney or flue whatever, in any such house or building.

SEC. 165. That if any person or persons, whether owner

164. Act of May 7, 1855, Sec. 9. P. L. 466.
165. Ibid. Sec. 10, P. L. 466.

or owners, contractor or contractors, shall erect, construct, build or alter, so as to make it substantially a new building, any house or building within said city as hereinbefore designated, without first obtaining a permit from the office of the Inspectors of Buildings, shall forfeit and pay the sum of one hundred dollars, for each and every offence; and if any person or persons as aforesaid, shall proceed to complete any such building, without having the same inspected as required, or shall fail or neglect to have the walls thereof built or constructed of the thickness required by, or otherwise comply with, the provisions of this act, he or they so offending, shall forfeit and pay the sum of one hundred dollars for each and every offence, and the further sum of one hundred dollars for each and every calendar month that the said house or building shall be suffered to remain without the necessary inspection, and the procuring the proper certificate; which said several sums shall be recoverable as debts are now by law recoverable; and if upon any inspection, it shall appear to the inspector, or his deputy, that such house or building is being erected or constructed, in violence of any of the provisions of this act, the Inspector shall forthwith notify the owner or owners, contractor or contractors, of such violation; a notice thereof being given to any person employed upon such house or building, shall, in all cases, be taken and deemed sufficient; and if, after such notice, the said parties, or either or any of them, shall proceed in the said erection or construction of such house or building, on petition, an affidavit o the facts having first been filed by the Inspector, setting forth the said violation particularly, it shall and may be lawful for the Court of Common Pleas, or one of the judges thereof in vacation, to forthwith issue an injunction, restraining such person or persons from the further progress of said work, until the facts of the case shall have been investigated and determined; and if it shall appear to the said Court, upon such investigation, that such house or building is not, in all respects, conformable to the provisions of this Act, in addition to the penalty hereinbefore designated, said Courts shall issue an injunction to restrain the continuance and to remove so much of the said house or building as may be decreed by the court, within such time as the court may appoint. Penalties.

SEC. 166. That the said Inspectors shall have the power to direct and require provision to be made, in relation to counter-arching over openings in the walls of buildings, to be used for public or for manufacturing purposes, to direct what means of access shall be provided, and the method of swinging of the doors in such buildings, the construction and method of fastening wooden cornices, and such other Power to direct counter-arching.

166. Act of May 7, 1855, Sec. 11, P. L. 466.

regulations as they may deem necessary not inconsistent with the provisions of this Act.

No building to be erected on a street less than twenty feet in width.

SEC. 167. That no new dwelling-house or other building within said city, shall front upon any street, alley, or court which shall be of less width than twenty feet, or without being made to recede so that such street, alley or court shall be of that width, the buildings on each side equally exceeding; the damage for which widening shall be assessed and paid to the owner in manner provided by law in case of opening new streets. Every new dwelling-house shall also have an open space attached to it in the rear or at the side, equal to at least twelve feet square; and no building of any kind shall be permitted to be erected on any street, court or alley hereafter to be laid out, or if laid out and wholly unimproved by brick or stone buildings before the passage of this Act, of a less width than twenty-five feet; and every builder or owner who shall hereafter build otherwise than as aforesaid, shall pay to the said city one hundred dollars, to be recovered with costs as debts of that amount may by law be recovered, and shall also be restrained by injunction, from so building, or if having so built after the passage of this Act, from the continuance of such building contrary to the requirements of this Act, and shall pay all the expenses of such alterations which the Court may decree to be made. It shall be the duty of the Commissioners of highways(*u*) to give notice to the City Solicitor of all violations of this Act, and if the building be made to conform thereto on notice, without suit, one-half the fine shall be abated.

Steam engines to be inspected.

SEC. 168. That no steam engine shall be erected in said City without the inspection and approval of an Inspector as aforesaid, for the security and safety of the inhabitants, under the penalties hereinbefore prescribed, in respect to buildings constructed contrary to this act, and if built in connection with any wooden or brick-paned building, or in other dangerous manner, contrary to the permit or direction of such Inspector, the same shall be altered or removed according to the decree of the said Court.

SEC. 169. That in all cases where any building or engine shall be constructed, altered or continued contrary to any law or ordinance in force in the city of Philadelphia, and the owner shall be resident without the State or beyond the reach of the process of said Court, it may be served upon the agent or tenant of the owner, and advertised as provided by law in respect to absent owners in proceedings in partition; and thereupon all further proceedings may be

---

167. Act of April 21, 1855, Sec. 6, P. L. 264.
168. Act of May 7, 1855, Sec. 12, P. L. 466.
169. Ibid. Sec. 13, P. L. 466.

(*u*) The City Solicitor will proceed, upon information given by Inspec under their general duties they should see that this section is not disobe

had as required by law, for the alteration or removal of such building or engine.

SEC. 170. That if the owners shall not comply with the decree of the Court within the time limited by the Court therefor, the Court shall decree the same to be done by the Sheriff of the County, under the supervision of one of the Inspectors, and to collect the expenses thereof of the owner, with ten per cent. thereon, to be paid into the City Treasury, besides costs of suit, as in equity cases.

Fees and penalties reduced.

SEC. 171. That the Inspectors' fees shall be reduced one-third below the rate fixed in the act to which this is a supplement, and the penalties therein imposed shall be reduced fifty per centum below the amount therein fixed, and be also applicable to any violation of the provisions of this supplement.

Thickness of walls regulated.

SEC. 172. That the eighth section of said act shall be taken and construed to require the walls of buildings (dwellings) to be of the thickness therein required, when of respective heights therein specified, without any reference whatsoever to the fronts or widths of said buildings.

Division walls regulated. Wooden girders allowed. Privies. Chimneys. Joists.

SEC. 173. That no party or division wall shall be built upon a wooden girder except in the case of a party alley wall, where the alley shall not exceed four feet in width. And the act to which this is a supplement shall not be taken to prohibit wooden girders over piazzas, or any opening not exceeding six feet. All privy-wells or other wells or cess-pools near buildings coming within the provisions of said acts, shall be securely arched or covered with stone. Every chimney shaft of such buildings shall be carried up in brick or other incombustible material, to a height of not less than three feet above the junction of any part thereof with the roof. And the trenches for the foundation walls shall be at least three inches below the surface of the cellar floor, and the ends of all joists of adjoining buildings shall be separated by an interposed brick, and grouted with mortar.

Dangerous walls to be inspected.

SEC. 174. That it shall be lawful and is hereby made the duty of the Building Inspectors to inspect all walls and supports of buildings deemed dangerous, on the written request of any two citizens, upon giving forty-eight hours' written notice of such intended visit to the owner thereof or his agent, and if the same be found insufficient or dangerous, to order the removal or such alteration thereof as they may deem necessary for safety: *Provided*, That the owner may appeal within three days by writing to the Board of Surveys, when a majority of a quorum thereof shall speedily decide the matter as prescribed by the twenty-seventh section of the

---

170. Act of May 7, 1855, Sec. 14, P. L. 466.
171. Act of April 11, 1856, Sec. 1, P. L. 319.
172. Ibid. Sec. 2, P. L. 319.
173. Ibid. Sec. 3, P. L. 319.
174. Ibid. Sec. 4, P. L. 319.

act consolidating the city of Philadelphia, and if the decision of the said Inspectors be against the sufficiency, or Surveyors shall be against the sufficiency of the walls or supports, the owner thereof shall forthwith comply with the decision given, and pay to the Inspector a fee of four dollars, and in case of appeal to the President of the Board of Survey, ten dollars for the use of the city. And if such owner makes default in complying with any decision so given, he may be compelled thereto as provided by the act to which this a supplement.

Inspectors to examine party walls.

SEC. 175. That it shall be the duty of the Inspectors of Buildings of the City of Philadelphia, upon the application of any person or persons about to erect on his or their lot or lots of ground any new building or buildings, according to the provisions of the Act of the first day of May, Anno Domini one thousand eight hundred and fifty five, entitled "An Act to provide for the regulation and inspection of buildings," to examine all such party or division walls upon or adjoining said lot of ground, and which shall have been erected prior thereto, and if deemed and adjudged by them to be insufficient and unfit for the purpose of such new building about to be erected, such party or division walls shall be removed and taken down by the last builder; the cost and expense of which removal, together with the cost and expense of the new wall or walls to be erected in lieu thereof, shall be borne and paid exclusively by him: *Provided nevertheless*, That an appeal from the decision of the Building Inspectors may be had to the Board of Surveyors in conformity with the provisions of an act, entitled "An Act to provide for the better regulation of buildings in the city of Philadelphia," approved May seventh, Anno Domini one thousand eight hundred and fifty-five; and in settlement of their accounts the said Inspectors shall file in the Court of Common Pleas of said city, on the first day of June annually hereafter, a full statement of their receipts and expenditures, which accounts shall be audited by said court, and on their order, the balance, if any, found to be in the hands of said Inspectors, shall be by them paid into the city treasury for the use of the said city; and all acts or parts of acts inconsistent with or contrary to the provisions of this act, be and the same is hereby repealed

Expenses of removal, by whom borne.

Appeal to Board of Surveyors.

BOARD OF HEALTH.

Abolishment of the elective Board of Health.

SEC. 176. The present Board of Health of the city and port of Philadelphia, as constituted and organized by and under an act for establishing a Health Office, and to secure the port of Philadelphia from the introduction of pestilential and contagious diseases, and for other purposes, passed

175. Act of May 20, 1857, Sec. 1, P. L. 590.
176. Act of April 7, 1859, Sec. 4, P. L. 400.

January 29, Anno Domini one thousand eight hundred and eighteen, and an act entitled "A further supplement to the act entitled 'An Act to incorporate the city of Philadelphia,' passed February second, Anno Domini one thousand eight hundred and fifty-four," shall be abolished, and shall cease and determine from and after the first Monday in July next, Anno Domini one thousand eight hundred and fifty-nine; and all laws and parts of laws providing for the organization of said Board, as now established, and under and by virtue of which said Board of Health is now constituted, by the election of its members by the qualified electors of the several wards of the city of Philadelphia, shall from and after the said first Monday in July, Anno Domini one thousand eight hundred and fifty-nine, be repealed, and thereafter be of no force or effect, so far as the same shall conflict with the provisions of this act; and so much of said act as authorizes the qualified electors of each of the wards of the city of Philadelphia, annually on the first Tuesday in May, to elect one citizen to serve as a member of the said Board of Health, be and the same is hereby repealed.

SEC. 177. On the first Monday in July next, Anno Domini one thousand eight hundred and fifty-nine, and for ever thereafter, until otherwise provided by law, the powers, duties, rights, liberties, authorities and immunities of the Board of Health of the city and port of Philadelphia, as constituted and organized under the provisions of the Acts of Assembly mentioned in the fourth section of this Act, and any and all other laws in relation to said Board of Health, shall be transferred and assigned to, and be assumed and exercised by, nine reputable citizens and electors of said city of Philadelphia, who shall be selected in the following manner, to wit: On the first Monday in June, Anno Domini one thousand eight hundred and fifty-nine, the Judges of the District Court for the city and county of Philadelphia shall appoint three reputable citizens, and electors of said city, to be members of the Board of Health, as constituted under the provisions of this Act, one to serve one year, one to serve two years, and one to serve three years; and annually thereafter the said Court shall appoint one person to be a member of said Board; the Court of Common Pleas shall, in like manner, and at the same time, appoint the same number of members of said Board; and annually thereafter the said Court shall appoint one person to be a member of said Board; the Judges of the Supreme Court of the State shall, in like manner, and at the same time, appoint the same number of members of said Board; and annually thereafter the said Court shall appoint one person to be a member of said Board; the Select and Common Councils of the city of Philadelphia, in joint conven-

Organization of Board of Health.

177. Act of April 7, 1859, Sec. 5, P. L. 400.

tion, at any stated meeting in June next, shall elect the same number of members of said Board, one to serve one year, one to serve two years, and one to serve three years; and annually thereafter, at any stated meeting in June, said Councils, in joint convention, shall elect one member of said Board to serve for three years.

Powers of Board.

SEC. 178. The members of said Board of Health, thus appointed and elected, shall meet on the first Monday in July next, Anno Domini one thousand eight hundred and fifty-nine, at ten o'clock in the morning, and shall then assume and exercise all the powers, duties, rights, liberties, authorities and immunities of the present Board of Health.

Duties.

SEC. 179. Said Board shall elect a President and such other officers as may be necessary for the proper transaction of the business of the said Board. * * * All the estate, whatsoever, real, personal or mixed, that shall then be by law or otherwise vested in, or in possession of the Board of Health, shall be forthwith vested in the city of Philadelphia, subject to all the trusts, conditions and liabilities now legally applicable thereto, and all laws of this Commonwealth, creating, governing and regulating the Board of Health, not inconsistent herewith, shall continue in force and operation, and shall govern and regulate the Board of Health of the city of Philadelphia, except as to farmers manuring land and keeping stock in the strictly agricultural districts, as the same may hereafter be altered by law or ordinance; and all sums of money due, payable to, or received by the Board of Health, shall be paid into the city treasury; and all sums expended by or for the purposes of the Board of Health, shall be paid by the City Treasurer upon orders drawn under the appropriations regularly made by Councils.

Licenses required to clean cesspools.

SEC. 180. That from and after the passage of this Act, no person shall remove, or cause, or allow to be removed the contents of any privy-well or sink within the limits of the jurisdiction of the Board of Health, without first being licensed by the Board of Health to do so, and every person offending against the provisions of this section shall for every such offence forfeit and pay to the Board of Health the sum of fifty dollars, to be recovered as debts of that amount are by law recoverable, and also to be liable to indictment at common law for creating or maintaining a nuisance: *Provided*, That the City Councils shall, from time to time, except from the operation of this, or any other statute law, conferring on the Board of Health jurisdiction on the subject of nuisances, such portion of the territory under their jurisdiction, being a rural district or

---

178. Act of April 7, 1859, Sec. 6, P. L. 400.
179. Act of Feb. 2, 1860, Sec. 16, P. L. 31.
180. Act of March 16, 1855, Sec. 1, P. L. 89.

sparse in their population, as in their opinion they can do with safety to the health and comfort of the inhabitants thereof, which exemption shall at all times be revocable by the like authority.

SEC. 181. That every person desirous of being licensed to empty or remove the contents of privy-wells and sinks within the limits of the jurisdiction, shall make application in writing to the Board of Health, who, on being satisfied with the character of the applicant and the security and tightness of his carts, and that he is the owner of such horses and carts as represented in his application, and that he is not in collusion or combination with other persons to deceive and defraud the Board, may, under such rules and regulations as they shall make in regard thereto, both as to their own protection from fraud and imposition by such person, and as to their supervision and control of such person in his said vocation—grant him a license for one year, and renew the same from year to year, as they may deem proper, and for each license so granted and for every renewal thereof, he shall pay therefor to the Board of Health the sum of fifty dollars; and whenever any such person shall desire under his license to empty or cleanse any privy-well or sink, he shall first take from the Board of Health a permit to do so, at which time he shall furnish to the clerk, the name of the owner, agent or occupant of such property as shall have so employed him, and the name of such owner, agent or occupant shall be mentioned in said permit and recorded in the office, which permit shall particularly specify the privy-well or sink to be emptied or cleansed, and the days or hours within which it shall be done; and if any such person shall by himself, his agents or servants, remove, cause or allow or assist in removing the contents of any privy-well or sink within portions of said city not excluded from the operations of this act, without first having obtained such permit, or shall do so on any other day or days, or at any other hour or hours, than those specified in such permit, he shall for every such offence forfeit and pay to the Board of Health the sum of twenty-five dollars: *Provided*, That nothing herein, or in any other act contained shall prevent farmers and others living in rural sections from cleansing their privies without any license and without any penalty therefor. Licenses and permits, how obtained.

SEC. 182. That the price of the permit shall be paid to the Board of Health when issued, and shall in all cases be repaid by the person or persons whose privy-well or sink shall be emptied and cleansed, and when such work shall be done by order of the Board of Health, to any premises declared a nuisance, the price of the permit, shall also be re- Price of permit, when paid.

181. Act of March 16, 1855, Sec. 2, P. L. 89.
182. Ibid. Sec. 3, P. L. 90.

covered by the Board of Health, as part of the expenses of the removal of such nuisance.

Price of permit.

SEC. 183. That the price of each permit issued in the months of June, July, August and September shall be five dollars, the price of each permit issued at other times shall be fifty cents, except in cases declared by the Board of Health to be a nuisance, when the price of the permit in those eight months shall be one dollar: *Provided*, That in all cases of permits for the removing the contents of privies and sinks which are in the way of building or improvements, as also for removing the contents of all privies and sinks that have accidently become a nuisance, the charge for the permit shall be at all times fifty cents.

Penalties for depositing privy filth on highways.

SEC. 184. That if any person or persons shall deposit the contents or any part thereof, of a sink or privy-well, any where within the limits of the jurisdiction of the Board of Health, so as thereby to create and maintain a nuisance, or shall deposit or spill the same on any street, lane, alley, court, road, bridge, or other highway of the city and county of Philadelphia, such person or persons so offending shall for every such offence forfeit and pay to the Board of Health the sum of ten dollars to be recovered as debts of like amount are recoverable, and shall also be liable to indictment at common law for creating and maintaining a nuisance.

Licensed persons to give bond.

SEC. 185. That every licensed person shall give bond to the city of Philadelphia for the use of the Board of Health with surety in the penalty of two hundred and fifty dollars to be approved by the Board, conditioned for the faithful performance of all duties enjoined by this law, and the regulations of the Board of Health, and for the payment to them of all sums by this act directed to be paid to them; and the Board of Health shall in addition have power, by a vote of the majority of the whole number of members of the Board, to revoke or suspend any license for good cause shown.

Penalty for employing unlicensed persons.

SEC. 186. That any person in the city or county of Philadelphia, whether owner, agent or occupant of property, who shall employ or contract with any unlicensed person to cleanse his or her privy-well or sink, or who shall receive from any unlicensed person any portion of the contents of a privy-well or sink, emptied and cleansed within the limits of the jurisdiction of the Board of Health, shall for every such offence forfeit and pay to the Board of Health the sum of twenty-five dollars, to be recovered as debts of like amount are recoverable.

Repeal of laws appointing

SEC. 187. That the first four sections of the Act of April 1st, 1826, entitled "An Act to empower the Board of Health

183. Act of March 16, 1855, Sec. 4, P. L. 90.
184. Ibid. Sec. 5, P. L. 90.
185. Ibid. Sec. 6, P. L. 90.
186. Ibid. Sec. 7, P. L. 91.
187. Ibid. Sec. 8, P. L. 91.

to purchase and hold certain real estate, and for other purposes," the 1st, 2nd, 3rd and 4th of a series of resolutions, passed May 29, 1840, entitled "Resolution relative to James Lyon and for other purposes," the 3rd, 4th, 5th and 6th sections of an Act of February 3rd, 1848, entitled "A further supplement to the Act entitled 'An Act for establishing a Health Office and to secure the city and port of Philadelphia from the introduction of pestilential and contagious diseases and for other purposes," passed January 29th, 1818, and the several supplements thereto: the 1st and 2nd sections of the Act of March 20th, 1852, entitled "An Act relating to the Board of Health of the city and county of Philadelphia, relative to shop taxes and tavern licenses in the burnt district of Philadelphia: authorizing J. Engle Negus and Edwin L. Poulk, trustees, to sell certain real estate: authorizing the trustees of the Bustleton Academy to lease or transfer said Academy to the Controllers of public schools: to the Waterford and Erie Plank Road, and to vacate Jasper street in the county of Philadelphia," and all other laws establishing or in any way or manner relating to depositories for the contents of privies in the city and county of Philadelphia, or regulating the measurements, contracts, or charges for emptying or cleansing the same, be and the same are hereby repealed.

Places of deposit and measurers of privy filth.

SEC. 188. That all contracts made by or with the Board of Health, and all recoveries of penalties, and suits for other causes of action, under this and other acts to which this is a supplement, shall be in the name of the city of Philadelphia, for the use of the Board of Health: and nothing herein contained shall in any wise impair the authority of the City Corporation over said Board of Health, as one of the departments of said city.

Board of Health recognized as a department of the City of Philadelphia.

BIRTHS, MARRIAGES, AND DEATHS.

SEC. 189. That from and after the first day of July next, the City Commissioners of the city of Philadelphia shall supply the Health Officer with separate books, in which he shall register, in the manner hereinafter directed, the returns made to him of the marriages which may be contracted, and of the births and deaths which may occur within the said city; he shall also cause an abstract of the same to be made in the month of February next ensuing, and annually thereafter in said month, to the City Councils, through the Board of Health, which abstract shall contain a statement of the marriages solemnized, and of the number of births and of deaths, with the reported causes thereof, which have occurred in the said city during the year next preceding the first day of January, with such other infor-

Books for registration to be furnished to health officer.

Abstracts to be made to City Councils, &c.

188. Act of March 16, 1855, Sec. 9, P. L. 91.
189. Act of March 8, 1860, Sec. 1, P. L. 130.

mation and suggestions in relation thereto as he may deem of practical utility for the promotion of public health, and of general interest to the city.

Duty of clergymen.

SEC. 190. That it shall be the duty of clergymen of all denominations, of clerks or keepers of the records of all churches and religious societies, as also of every magistrate, and of other persons by or before whom any marriage may hereafter be solemnized or contracted, and of every practising physician, and of every practitioner of midwifery, and of every undertaker and superintendent or sexton of any cemetery or burying ground in the said city of Philadelphia, on or before the first day of July next ensuing, (the day in which the law goes into effect,) to report his, her, or their names and places of residence to the Health Officer, at the office of the Board of Health; and it shall be the duty of the Health Officer to have the same properly registered in index form, in suitable books to be furnished to the City Commissioners at the order of the Board of Health. In the event of any of the persons above specified removing to any other place of residence, it shall be their duty to notify the Health Officer of the fact within thirty days after such removal except where the persons removing shall cease to act in such official capacity as makes them subject to the provisions of this act.

Of physicians. Of sextons. Of health officer.

Certificates of persons dying to be furnished.

SEC. 191. That whenever any person shall die in the City of Philadelphia, it shall be the duty of the physician who attended during his or her last sickness, or of the Coroner, when the case comes under his notice, to furnish, within forty-eight hours after the death, to the undertaker or other person superintending the burial, a certificate, setting forth, as far as the same can be ascertained, the full name, sex, color, age, and condition (whether married or single) of the person deceased, and the cause and date of death.

Persons having charge of burying ground or cemetery, duty of.

SEC. 192. That no person having the charge, as sexton or otherwise, of any vault, burying-ground, or cemetery within the said city, shall inter, or allow to be interred, or place, or allow to be placed, in any vault, burying-ground, or cemetery, the dead body of any person; nor shall any undertaker or other person remove the dead body of any person who has died in the said city, and has not been buried, to any place beyond the limits of the said city, without first procuring the certificate of the attending physician or of the Coroner. To said certificate the undertaker or other person having charge of the body shall, as far as can be ascertained, add the occupation of the deceased, the place of birth, the ward, street, and number of the house in which the death occurred, the place and date of interment, and where the deceased is a minor, the full names of the

Physicians or coroner's certificate, relative to.

---

190. Act of March 8, 1860, Sec. 2, P. L. 130.
191. Ibid. Sec. 3, P. L. 130.
192. Ibid. Sec. 4, P. L. 131.

parents. In case any person shall die without the attendance of a physician, or if the physician who did attend at the time of the death refuses or neglects to furnish a certificate as aforesaid, it shall be the duty of the undertaker, or of any other person acquainted with the facts, to report the same to the Health Officer, who shall be authorized to give a certificate of death as aforesaid, provided it be not a case requiring the attendance of the Coroner. Every sexton or other person having charge of any vault, burying-ground, or cemetery within the said city, and every undertaker or other person who shall remove any dead body from or out of the said city, shall return the said certificates to the Health Officer before twelve o'clock M. on the Saturday of every week, accompanied by a schedule of the same; which returns shall be published weekly by the Health Officer, in such manner as may be designated by the Board of Health.

Persons dying without the attendance of a physician, relative to.

Removing dead bodies, relative to.

SEC. 193. That in case any physician, or the Coroner, shall refuse or neglect to furnish such certificate as aforesaid, he shall forfeit and pay the sum of five dollars for each offence; and every undertaker, sexton, or other person removing the dead body of any person, or having charge of any vault, burying-ground, or cemetery, who refuses or neglects to perform any of the duties required by this Act, shall forfeit and pay for every such offence the sum of twenty-five dollars, which sums shall in every case be recoverable in the manner and for the uses prescribed in an Act entitled "An Act for establishing a Health Office, to secure the city and port of Philadelphia from the introduction of pestilential and contagious diseases, and for other purposes."

Physician or coroner refusing to furnish certificate, penalty for.

SEC. 194. Every person practising midwifery in the city aforesaid, under whose charge or superintendence a birth shall hereafter take place, shall keep a true and exact register of such birth, and shall enter the same on a blank schedule, to be furnished by the Health Officer. The schedule shall contain a list of the births which have occurred under his or her care during the month, and shall set forth, as far as the same can be ascertained, the full name of each child, (if any name shall have been conferred,) its sex, color, the full name and occupation of its parent or parents, the day and place of its birth; and the said schedule shall be delivered, duly signed by the practitioner in the form of a certificate, on the first day of each and every month, to the Health Officer, or to any other authorized person calling for the same. In case the birth of any child shall have occurred without the attendance of a physician, or of a practitioner of midwifery, or should no other person be in attendance upon the mother immediately

Duty of persons practising midwifery.

---

193. Act of March 8, 1860, Sec. 5, P. L. 131.
194. Ibid. Sec. 6, P. L. 131.

thereafter, it shall then become the duty of the parent or parents of such child to report its birth to the Health Officer in the manner and form and within the period above required.

Dvty of clergymen.

SEC. 195. It shall be the duty of every Clergyman, and every Magistrate, and of the Clerk or Keeper of the Records of all religious and other societies, and of every other person, by or before whom any marriage may hereafter be solemnized or contracted, to make a faithful return of the same at the expiration of every three months, to the Health Officer, in the form of a certificate, which shall set forth, as far as the same can be ascertained, the full name of the husband, his occupation, the place of his birth, his residence and age, the date of marriage, the full name of the wife previous to the said marriage, and her age, the color of the parties, and the place where, and the name of the Clergyman or other person by whom the marriage ceremony was performed.

Penalty.

SEC. 196. Every Clergyman, and every Magistrate, and every Clerk or Keeper of the Records of all religious societies, and every practising Physician, and every person practising midwifery in the city aforesaid, and every Undertaker and Superintendent or Sexton of any cemetery or burying-ground in the city of Philadelphia, who shall neglect or refuse to leave his or her name and place of residence at the health office as herein provided, and who shall refuse or neglect to perform any other of the duties required as aforesaid, shall forfeit and pay for each offence the sum of ten dollars to be recovered in the manner and for the uses prescribed in an act entitled "An Act for establishing a health office, and to secure the city and port of Philadelphia from the introduction of pestilential and contagious diseases and for other purposes."

SEC. 197. The books or registers kept by the Health Officer, or a certificate duly certified by him, and authenticated by the seal of the Health Office, as containing a copy of the record of any marriage, birth or death, shall hereafter be admitted in any Court of the State as *prima facie* evidence of said marriage, birth or death.

SEC. 198. The registry of marriages, births, and deaths, shall be kept in separate books; and there shall be general indexes to the record of all marriages, births and deaths, which indexes shall also be kept in separate books.

Fees

SEC. 199. The Health Officer shall receive fifty cents for granting a certificate or certified copy of the record of any marriage, birth or death, and ten cents for making a search for either a marriage, birth or death, which sums shall be

---

195. Act of March 8, 1860, Sec. 7, P. L. 131.
196. Ibid. Sec. 8, P. L. 131.
197. Ibid. Sec. 9, P. L. 131.
198. Ibid. Sec. 10, P. L. 131.
199. Ibid. Sec. 11, P. L. 131.

paid by the party applying for the certificate or search; but the said registers shall at all times be accessible to physicians, clergymen, and lawyers, without charge.

SEC. 200. That in order to secure uniformity and dispatch in the registration herein provided for, the books shall contain, upon the margin of each page, printed title, with corresponding blanks, for suitable entries for marriages, births and deaths, in the order, to wit: To secure uniformity of registration, &c.

MARRIAGES.

Full name of husband.
Occupation.
Residence.
Birth-place.
Age when married.
Full name of wife previous to marriage.
Residence.
Birth-place.
Age when married.
Time of marriage.
Color of the parties.
Ceremony employed.
Name of person pronouncing the marriage.
Residence of the last named person.
Date of certificate.
Date of registration.

BIRTHS.

Full name of the child.
Sex.
Color.
Full name of the father.
His occupation.
Full name of the mother.

BIRTHS, *continued.*

Day, month and year of the birth.
Street and number of house where born.
Name of the physician or other person signing the certificate.
His residence.
Date of certificate.
Date of registration.

DEATHS.

Full name of the deceased.
Color.
Sex.
Age.
Married or single.
Occupation.
Birth-place.
Date of death.
Cause of death.
When a minor, the name of the father and mother.
Ward, Street, and number, of house.
Date of burial.
Date of certificate.
Date of registration.

SEC. 201. The Health Officer shall keep on hand at all times, a supply of blanks for gratuitous distribution to all persons whose duty it shall be to make returns under this Act. The said blanks shall be prepared in the form of books, and the margins shall correspond with the printed titles in the books of the Health Officer, as required by the twelfth section of this Act: *Provided*, That all books, blanks, and stationery necessary to be used in carrying out the intent and meaning of this Act shall be furnished upon an order from the Board of Health by the City Commissioners, and shall be paid for by Councils; and that the Health Officer, in consideration of such additional services, shall receive the sum of two hundred dollars, besides his present salary, to be paid to him in the manner now directed by law.

---

200. Act of March 8, 1860, Sec. 12, P. L. 131.
201. Ibid. Sec. 13, P. L. 133.

BOARD OF GUARDIANS OF THE POOR.

Abolition of elective board.

SEC. 202. That the present Board of Guardians of the Poor of the city of Philadelphia, as constituted and organized by and under an act entitled "A further supplement to the act entitled 'An Act to incorporate the city of Philadelphia,' passed February second, Anno Domini one thousand eight hundred and fifty-four," shall be abolished, and shall cease and determine from and after the first Monday in July next, Anno Domini one thousand eight hundred and fifty-nine; and that all laws and parts of laws providing for the organization of said Board, as now established, and under and by virtue of which said Board of Guardians of the Poor is now constituted, by the election of its members by the qualified electors of the several wards of the city of Philadelphia, mentioned in the eighteenth section of the act to which this is a further supplement, shall, from and after the said Monday in July, Anno Domini one thousand eight hundred and fifty-nine, be repealed, and thereafter be of no force or effect, so far as the same shall conflict with the provisions of this Act; and that so much of said Act as authorizes the qualified electors of said wards of the city of Philadelphia, annually, on the first Tuesday in May, to elect one citizen to serve as a member of said Board, be and the same is hereby repealed: *Provided,* That so much of this Act as relates to the Guardians of the Poor, shall not apply to the Twenty-second Ward, nor to such parts of the Twenty-first and Twenty-third Wards as are now under a separate organization for the support and employment of the poor.

Creation of board.

SEC. 203. That on the first Monday in July next, Anno Domini one thousand eight hundred and fifty-nine, and for ever thereafter, until otherwise provided by law, the powers, duties, rights, liberties, authorities and immunities of the Board of Guardians of the Poor of the city of Philadelphia, as constituted and organized under the provisions of the act mentioned in the first section of this Act, shall be transferred and assigned to and be assumed and exercised by nine reputable citizens and electors of the said city of Philadelphia, to be selected in the following manner, to wit: on the first Monday in June, Anno Domini one thousand eight hundred and fifty-nine, the Judges of the District Court for the city and county of Philadelphia shall appoint three reputable citizens and electors of said city to be members of the Board of Guardians of the Poor, as constituted under the provisions of this Act, one to serve one year, one to serve two years, and one to serve three years; and annually thereafter the said Court shall appoint one

---

202. Act of April 7, 1859, Sec. 1, P. L. 400.
203. Ibid. Sec. 2, P. L. 400.

person to be a member of said Board; the Court of Common Pleas shall in like manner, and at the same time, appoint the same number of members of said Board ; and annually thereafter the said Court shall appoint one person to be a member of said Board ; the Judges of the Supreme Court of this State, in like manner, and at the same time, appoint the same number of members of said Board, and annually thereafter the said Court shall appoint one person to be a member of said Board; the Select and Common Councils of the city of Philadelphia, in joint convention, at any stated meeting in June next, shall elect the same number of members of said Board, one to serve one year, one to serve two years, and one to serve three years; and annually thereafter, at any stated meeting in June, said Councils, in joint convention, shall elect one member of said Board to serve for three years.

SEC. 204. They shall enter upon the duties of their office on the first Monday of July of each year, and shall take an oath or affirmation to be administered by any alderman of the said city, that he will discharge the duties of the office of Guardian of the Poor truly and impartially to the best of his ability. *Organization of board.*

SEC. 205. They shall elect a president and such other officers as may be necessary for the proper transaction of the business of such board; and upon such organization, all the estate whatsoever, real and personal, that shall then be by law or otherwise vested in or be in possession of the Guardians for the Relief and Employment of the Poor of the City of Philadelphia, the district of Southwark, and the townships of Northern Liberties and Penn, shall forthwith vest in the city of Philadelphia, subject to all the trusts, conditions and liabilities now legally applicable thereto, and the present guardians and officers of said body shall cease their functions, and the said elective guardians shall be vested with all the powers, faculties, rights, privileges and immunities of the present Guardians of the Poor, and subject to the performance of the duties thereof, except as hereby otherwise provided; and all laws of this Commonwealth, creating, governing and regulating the said corporation, shall continue in force and operation, and shall govern and regulate the Guardians of the Poor of the City of Philadelphia, except as the same may hereafter be altered by law or ordinance; and all sums of money due, payable to, or received by the Board of Guardians of the Poor, shall be paid into the City Treasury, and all sums expended by or for the purposes of the Board of Guardians of the Poor, shall be paid by the City Treasurer upon orders drawn under appropriation regularly made by Councils. *General duties and powers*

---

204. Act of Feb. 2, 1854, Sec. 18, P. L. 33.
205. Ibid. Sec. 19, P. L. 33.

Restriction of powers.

SEC. 206. That the provisions of the twentieth and twenty-first sections of the Act of April twenty-one, one thousand eight hundred and fifty-five, entitled "A Supplement to the Act consolidating the City of Philadelphia," are hereby extended to the Board of Health and the Board of Guardians of the Poor. No contract made by either of the said boards shall be binding upon the city unless a warrant therefor shall be issued, and countersigned in such manner and by such officers as Councils may by ordinance prescribe, and such officer shall give bond to the City of Philadelphia in such amount and with surety as shall be approved by Councils, conditioned for the faithful performance of the duties imposed upon said officer by law or ordinance, and that he will not countersign any warrant upon the City Treasurer, except such as may be authorized by law or ordinance, and within the appropriations made by Councils.

Vacancies.

SEC. 207. That in case a vacancy occur in the said Board of Guardians of the Poor, or the said Board of Health, from death, resignation, or otherwise, it shall be supplied and filled, for the unexpired term of such member, by the Court which appointed, or the Councils which elected the member thus dying, resigning, or otherwise vacating his seat in the Board of which he was a member.

Criminal proceedings against members.

SEC. 208. That upon conviction in any Court of criminal jurisdiction, of any member or members of said Board of Guardians of the Poor, or the said Board of Health, of any wilful misapplication of the funds or property of the said Boards, or funds or property of the said City of Philadelphia, or of any fraudulent and corrupt official act, he or they so offending, and convicted, shall be sentenced to pay a fine of not less than one hundred, nor more than one thousand dollars, and undergo an imprisonment in the county prison for a term not exceeding one year, at the discretion of the Court.

INSPECTORS OF COUNTY PRISON.

How appointed.

SEC. 209. That the Inspectors of the County Prison shall be appointed, five by the Supreme Court of Pennsylvania, three by the District Court of the County of Philadelphia, and three by the Court of Common Pleas of said county, who shall enter upon duty on the first Monday of July next, to serve for one year, and annually thereafter the vacancies in said board shall be filled as aforesaid; they shall neither be members of the bar, nor officers or clerks of, or under any of said courts.

---

206. Act of April 21, 1858, Sec. 3, P. L. 386.
207. Act of April 7, 1859, Sec. 7, P. L. 400.
208. Ibid. Sec. 8, P. L. 400.
209. Act of May 13, 1856, Sec. 2, P. L. 567.

SEC. 210. The Board of Inspectors is authorized to adopt and enforce, from time to time, such rules and regulations as they shall deem proper for visiting prisoners in the untried department of said prison, subject to the revisal and approval of said courts.

Powers to enforce rules.

SEC. 211. That the Inspectors of the Philadelphia County Prison shall have full power to treat prisoners sentenced to be hanged, and who are not executed after an imprisonment of six months, as other convicts are who are sentenced to confinement and labor.

SEC. 212. That from and after the passage of this Act, it shall be the duty of the wardens or superintendents of the general penitentiaries and prisons of this Commonwealth in which criminals are confined, who have been convicted and sentenced by any court of justice of this State, to undergo an imprisonment of more than six months, to keep a book, in which shall be entered the name of each person so confined, and a record of every infraction or violation by him or her, of the printed and published rules of such penitentiary or prison, with the punishment (if any) inflicted on account thereof, which said book shall be laid before the Inspectors at their regular stated meetings, for examination and approval

Wardens and superintendents to have recorded the violation of rules by prisoners.

SEC. 213. That every prisoner or convict, sentenced as aforesaid, who shall have no such infraction or violation of the said rules recorded against him or her during any month of the first year of his or her imprisonment, shall be entitled to a deduction from the term of his or her sentence of one day for the first month, of two additional days for the second month, and three additional days for the third and each of the remaining months of the said first year of imprisonment, and shall also be entitled for continued good conduct during the second year, to a similar deduction of four days for each month, during which he or she shall not have violated the rules aforesaid, and to a deduction of one additional day per month for each succeeding year, until the expiration of the tenth year, and to an additional deduction of two days per month, during each year of the remainder thereof: *Provided*, That it shall be lawful for the Inspectors of said penitentiaries or prison, if any such convicts or persons shall wilfully infringe or violate any of said rules or regulations, or offend in any other way, to strike off the whole or any part of the deduction which may have been obtained previous to the date of such offence.

Deductions in favor of prisoners for obedience.

SEC. 214. That the said inspectors shall have full power and authority to discharge the said criminals, whenever they

---

210. Act of Jan. 4, 1856, Sec. 4, P. L. 711.
211. Act of May 1, 1861, Sec. 1, P. L. 462.
212. Ibid. Sec. 1, P. L. 462.
213. Ibid. Sec. 2, P. L. 462.
214. Ibid. Sec. 3, P. L. 462.

Power to discharge.

shall have served out the term of their sentence, less the number of days to which they are entitled under the provisions of this Act.

Certificate of good conduct to be given.

SEC. 215. That the said Inspectors shall direct the Warden or Superintendent to give to each prisoner who may, in consequence of good conduct be discharged at an earlier period than he would otherwise have been entitled to, a certificate thereof, stating therein the number of days that have been deducted from his original sentence for good conduct.

ELECTION DIVISIONS.

Power to create election divisions.

SEC. 216. That on or before the first Monday in May, one thousand eight hundred and fifty-four, the Commissioners of the County of Philadelphia (and thereafter the City Councils) shall lay out and establish a sufficient number, not less than six, election divisions in each of the wards established by the second section of this act, which divisions shall be, whenever practicable, bounded on all sides by streets, lanes, roads, alleys, avenues, streams of water, or by one of the boundary lines of said city, and shall be as nearly equal in number of taxable inhabitants as such boundaries will admit of, and shall be numbered respectively one, two, three, four, and so on. The said Commissioners and the said Councils, when they establish the same, shall make an accurate description thereof, and cause it to be published in one or more of the daily papers of the city of Philadelphia, and shall file a copy of such description in the office of the Clerk of the Court of Quarter Sessions in the county of Philadelphia, to be and remain on record in said office; and if, at any election thereafter, there shall be more than four hundred votes polled in any of the said divisions, then at some period, at least forty days previous to the next succeeding election, the City Councils shall rearrange the divisions of the wards wherein such vote has been polled, and increase the number thereof if necessary.

Councils to designate places of holding elections: notify the sheriff thereof. Power to remove or change the place of holding elections.

SEC. 217. That it shall be the duty of the Select and Common Councils of said city, to designate the place of holding the elections in the several election divisions of the wards in said city, and to notify the sheriff thereof, at least thirty days prior to the second Tuesday of October next, and shall have full power and authority to remove or change the place of holding the elections in any of the said election divisions, whenever by reason of inability to hold said election at the place so designated, a change shall become necessary.

SEC. 218. That the place for holding all elections in the

---

215. Act of May 1, 1861, Sec. 4, P. L. 462.
216. Act of Feb. 2, 1854, Sec. 3, P. L. 24.
217. Act of April 21, 1855, Sec. 2, P. L. 264.
218. Act of May 13, 1856, Sec. 32, P. L. 568.

city of Philadelphia, may be changed in accordance with the provisions of the fifty-sixth section of the act entitled "An Act relating to the Elections of this Commonwealth," passed the second day of July, one thousand eight hundred and thirty nine.(*v*) Places of holding elections may be changed.

ELECTIONS AND ELECTION OFFICERS.

SEC. 219. Until otherwise provided by law, in all elections for members of Congress the qualified voters of the said city shall continue to vote in their respective congressional districts, as now by law established, as if this Act had not been passed; and if any election division shall happen to comprise portions of two congressional districts, an additional and separate box shall be provided for the election of officers of such division. Until otherwise provided by law, in accordance with the provisions of the Constitution, the existing districts in the city and county of Philadelphia shall continue without change for the election of Senators and Representatives to the Legislature of Pennsylvania, and thereafter the said Representatives may be chosen in separate election districts, as they shall be established by law. Where to vote.

SEC. 220. It shall be the duty of the Sheriff of Philadelphia City and County to give notice of all elections held Duty of Sheriff.

---

219. Act of Feb. 2, 1854, Sec. 25, P. L. 27.
220. Ibid. Sec. 29, P. L. 28.

(*v*) The 56th section of the act of July 2, 1839, (P. L. Sessions 38–39, 530) ir in the following words: "It shall be lawful for the electors of any township, ward or district, to change the place for holding the election for inspectors, and other officers of such township, ward or district, in the manner following, to wit:

I. On the requisition in writing of at least thirty of the electors of the township, ward or district, in case there are one hundred or more taxables in said township, ward or district, or of ten electors in case there are less than one hundred taxables in said township, ward or district, the constables shall give notice by at least ten printed or written hand-bills, set up in the most public places within such township, ward or district, at least fifteen days before the time appointed for the purpose, that a meeting of the electors of the township, ward or district as the case may be, will be held at the usual place of holding elections therein, at a certain day and hour to be appointed in such notice, for the purpose of determining upon the expediency of changing the place of holding such elections.

II. If at least fifty electors of said ward, district or township, provided there be one hundred or more electors in said township, ward or district, or twenty electors of said township, ward or district, provided there be less than one hundred electors in said township, ward or district, be present at the time appointed, the constable shall organize the meeting, and if at such meeting a majority of the electors present shall determine by ballot that it is expedient to change the place of holding such election, two certificates thereof, and of the names of the qualified citizens voting at such meeting, shall be made out and signed by the officers of the meeting, and attested by the constable, one of which shall be delivered by the constable to the town clerk, if there be one, and the other to the Prothonotary of the Court of Common Pleas of the county, to be filed in his office.

under the provisions of this Act, designating the officers to be elected, and the time and place of such election; such notice shall be by proclamation and advertisement in at least two daily newspapers, published in the city of Philadelphia, at least twenty and not more than thirty days prior to every election, and the expenses of such advertising shall be paid out of the treasury of the city of Philadelphia. The County Commissioners of the county of Philadelphia shall immediately prior to the first election in the city of Philadelphia, and the City Commissioners thereafter shall have the respective places appointed for holding such elections put in convenient and proper order for holding and conducting the same; shall furnish to the election officers of each division the necessary blanks, stationery, &c., and a list of the taxable inhabitants of such division, and shall generally do and perform such duties appertaining to elections as they would be required by law or usage to perform had the elections or the election districts of the said City not been changed or altered: *Provided*, That the Sheriff and the other officers shall do and perform all the duties in relation to the elections under this law which are enjoined upon them by the general election laws now in force, unless otherwise provided by the Act.

Duty of City Commissioners.

Mode of voting.

SEC. 221. That the general, special, municipal, and all other, except military, elections by the qualified voters of the city of Philadelphia, shall be held in the respective election divisions of the wards of said city; the said elections shall open at or before eight o'clock in the morning, and close at eight o'clock in the evening, and the tickets to be voted at the municipal elections in the city of Philadelphia shall be on separate pieces of paper, on which shall be written or printed the name of the office to be filled, and immediately under the name of the office the name or names of the person or persons voted for to fill such office; in all general and special elections within the city of Philadelphia, each ward of the said city shall be an election district, and have a return Judge, and the return Judges of the city of Philadelphia shall meet at the State House in said city,

Power of Common Pleas to settle disputes.

SEC. 222. The Court of Common Pleas of Philadelphia county is hereby vested with power to settle summarily any question that may arise concerning the officers to conduct said elections and also to direct, according to the true intent and spirit of this act, which set of election officers shall act as aforesaid in any case or exigency which may arise or exist, not provided for by this act; and any vacancy that shall exist and continue for half an hour after the earliest time fixed by law for opening the polls, shall be filled in the manner now provided by law; *on the second Tuesday*

---

221. Act of Feb. 2, 1854, Sec. 30, P. L. 27.
222. Ibid. Sec. 31, P. L. 27.

of October, 1861, and in each year thereafter, the qualified voters of each of said election divisions shall elect, in the manner prescribed by law, one person to serve as Judge, and two persons to serve as Inspectors of elections for one year, each voter, however, to vote for one Inspector. Election of Judges, &c.

SEC. 223. That it shall be the duty of the Judge of election in every election division of said city, at every general, municipal and special election, to make out and subscribe on the night of such election, a certificate of all the votes given at such election division, for every office voted thereat; and it shall be the duty of the Judge to deliver the same to the Prothonotary of the Court of Common Pleas on the day succeeding such election, before noon of that day, which certificates shall be open to the inspection of any citizen; and any Judge who shall fail to deliver such certificates as aforesaid, to the said Prothonotary, shall forfeit fifty dollars. And the said Prothonotary shall, on the second day after such election, make out and deliver to the Sheriff of the said county a certified list of the Judges of each and every division from which such certificate shall not have been received as aforesaid, with a precept to the said Sheriff to levy and collect the said penalty from the said Judges, as is now practiced and allowed in cases of fines imposed upon defaulting jurors, provided that the said Court may, upon good cause shown, remit such fines. And in case any such certificate shall not have been placed in the office aforesaid, by noon of the day aforesaid, the Court may, on application of any citizen, issue an attachment against the Judge or Judges in default, to compel the production and filling of such certificate. Duty of election officers.

SEC. 224. That the municipal elections of the city of Philadelphia shall be conducted in the manner required by the Act of Assembly of July 2d, Anno Domini 1839, entitled "An Act relating to the elections of this Commonwealth, and its Supplements." As soon as the votes given at each division are counted, duplicate returns thereof shall be made out by the officers of such division; one copy shall be deposited in one of the ballot-boxes, as required by section 74 of the act aforesaid, the other copy shall be used for the purpose of making up full returns of the ward; and the said last copy together with a full and complete return of the votes given in such ward, signed by the Judges thereof shall be filed by one of the Judges in the office of the Prothonotary of the Court of Common Pleas of Philadelphia county as hereinafter provided. Municipal elections, how conducted. Election returns.

SEC. 225. That the returns of all municipal elections in the city of Philadelphia, and the certificates to be given to

---

223. Act of Feb. 2, 1854, Sec. 32, P. L. 28.
224. Ibid. Sec. 33, P. L. 28.
225. Ibid. Sec. 34, P. L. 28.

Manner of making out returns.

persons elected, shall be made out in the following manner, to wit: two complete copies of a return of all the votes given in each Division, and a certificate of election to each of the persons elected to office in such Divison, shall be made out and signed by the Judge, Inspectors and Clerks of such Division; and on the day succeeding the election, at nine o'clock, A. M. the Judges and Inspectors of all the Divisions of the ward shall meet and make out a return of all the votes given in such ward, and a certificate of election for each of the persons elected to office in such ward, which returns and certificates shall be signed by the Judges of such Ward, or a majority of them; the Judges shall then designate one of their number to be a Return Judge, and shall give him an accurate copy of the returns of the votes given in such wards for each municipal officer voted for, and the Return Judges of the several wards shall meet at the State House, at ten o'clock in the morning of the Thursday succeeding the day of election, and shall then and there, in the manner provided in the seventy-eighth section of the Act of Assembly of July second, Anno Domini one thousand eight hundred and thirty-nine, aforesaid, proceed to add together the number of votes given in the several wards for the several officers voted for, and shall make out full and complete returns of said votes, and a certificate of election to the persons elected, which returns shall, immediately upon the adjournment of the Return Judges, be, by the President thereof, filed in the office of the Prothonotary of the Court of Common Pleas; the certificates of election for the Ward and Division Officers, shall be delivered to the persons elected, by the Constables of the ward, within three days after the election, and the certificates for the other officers voted for shall be delivered to them by the Sheriff or his deputy, within two days after the meeting of the Return Judges. The places for the meetings of the said Judges and Inspectors in said wards, for the purposes aforesaid, shall be determined by a majority of those who are required to meet.

Return Judges to meet.

Their duties.

Places of meeting.

Proceedings for contesting elections.

SEC. 226. That the returns of all municipal elections in the city of Philadelphia, except of members of the Select and Common Councils, shall be subject to the inquiry and determination of the Court of Common Pleas of the County of Philadelphia, upon complaint of fifteen or more of the qualified voters of the proper ward or division, or in the case of Mayor, Treasurer, City Controller, Receiver of Taxes, City Solicitor or City Commissioner, by at least fifty of the qualified voters of the said city, which complaint shall be filed in the said Court within twenty days after such election; and at least two of the complainants shall take and subscribe an oath or affirmation, that the facts set forth in such

226. Act of Feb. 2, 1854, Sec. 35, P. L. 28.

complaint are true; and the said Court, in judging of such elections, shall proceed upon the merits thereof, and determine finally concerning the same, according to the laws of this Commonwealth, and shall have power, if they believe such complaint to have been made without sufficient cause, to decree that the complainants, or any one or more of them, shall pay all legal costs incurred by such investigation. The Select and Common Councils, respectively, shall in like manner as each branch of the Legislature of this Commonwealth, judge and determine upon the qualifications of their members. The trial of a contested election shall be held and conducted, and be proceeded with in the manner set forth in the several sections of the Act of Assembly passed July second, Anno Domini one thousand eight hundred and thirty-nine, providing for the trial of contested elections of the Senate and House of Representatives, excepting that the committee shall be seven in Select and eleven in Common Council. No complaint of an undue election or false return shall be acted upon, unless presented within ten days after the organization of Councils, nor unless signed by at least fifteen qualified voters of the proper ward, at least three of whom shall take and subscribe an oath or affirmation that the facts set forth in said petition or complaint are true.

Councils to judge and determine upon the qualifications of their members.

Trial of contested elections, how conducted.

SEC. 227. That whenever a new election division or divisions has been or shall be created in any of the wards of the city of Philadelphia by the Councils of said city, the officers to conduct the election next thereafter occurring shall be chosen as follows:—If such division shall be formed entirely out of an old division, the officers elected to conduct the elections in said division shall appoint the officers for the new division, the Judge appointing the Judge, and each of the Inspectors appointing one Inspector, and if the division shall be formed from several, all the Judges elected in said ward shall together appoint the Judge, the Inspectors elected in said ward, who received the highest number of votes in their respective divisions, shall together appoint one of the Inspectors, and the Inspectors elected in said ward, who received the lowest number of votes in their respective divisions, shall together appoint the other Inspector, and the officers thus chosen shall conduct all elections held in such new election division or divisions, until their successors are elected, in accordance with existing laws.

How election officers shall be appointed when a new election division made.

SEC. 228. That at all municipal elections hereafter to be held in the City of Philadelphia, all officers to be voted for by the qualified voters of the said city, shall be voted on one ticket, and be headed "City Officers," and that all officers to be voted for by the qualified voters of each ward

Tickets

227. Act of April 28, 1857, Sec. 1, P. L. 329.
228. Act of May 13, 1856, Sec. 3, P. L. 568.

6

shall be voted on one ticket, and be headed "Ward Officers" and that all officers to be voted for by the qualified voters of each election division of said ward, shall be voted on one ticket, and be headed "Division Officers."

List of taxables.

SEC. 229. That hereafter the list of taxable persons required by existing laws to be furnished to the officers of all general and municipal elections, and the list of taxable persons required to be furnished to the various Aldermen by the Receiver of Taxes, shall be that of the last assessment filed in the City Commissioners' office previous to such general or municipal election by the Assessors of the several Wards.

Return Inspectors to be elected.

SEC. 230. That the qualified citizens of the several wards of the City of Philadelphia shall meet in their respective election districts in each and every year, at the same time and places, and under the same rules and regulations as are now prescribed for holding the elections of the Judges and Inspectors of elections, and shall elect two additional Inspectors, to be styled and voted for as "Return Inspectors."

Each citizen shall vote for one.

SEC. 231. That each qualified citizen shall vote for but one person as Return Inspector of elections, and the two persons having the greatest number of votes for Return Inspectors shall be declared the Return Inspectors of elections for the ensuing year.

Duty of Inspectors.

SEC. 232. That it shall be the duty of the said Return Inspectors, once in each and every hour during the election, to count the tickets, and shall thereupon deposit the same in the ballot-boxes provided for the said purpose. That they shall make publicly known the state of the vote at each and every hour, and in like manner, immediately after the closing of the polls, make publicly known the result of said election or elections. That if any discrepancy shall occur between the tickets and the tally list kept by the clerks of the elections, it shall be the duty of the Return Inspectors to make a record of the same at the time it shall be discovered, and for this purpose the Return Inspectors and Return Clerks shall have free access to the tally list kept under the existing laws by the Inspectors and Clerks of elections. The Return Inspectors in each election district shall set their hands and seals to the certificates of elections in like manner as the Inspectors and Judges of elections are now required to do by law.

SEC. 233. That the Judges of the elections in their respective election districts are hereby required to decide between the Return Inspectors whenever they shall disagree in the performance of their duties, and the Return Inspectors shall forthwith act under such decision.

---

229. Act of April 16, 1857, Sec. 1, P. L. 221.
230. Act of May 1, 1861, Sec. 1, P. L. 575.
231. Ibid. Sec. 2, P. L. 575.
232. Ibid. Sec. 3, P. L. 575.
233. Ibid. Sec. 4, P. L. 576.

SEC. 234. That the said Return Inspectors shall meet at their respective places for holding the election before nine o'clock in the forenoon, of the day of the election in each and every year, at which said Inspectors may be elected to act, and each of said Return Inspectors shall appoint one Return Clerk, who shall be a qualified voter of such election district, and who shall continue to act as Return Clerk during the ensuing year.

SEC. 235. That in case the person who shall have received the highest number of votes for Return Inspector shall not attend on the day of any election, then the Judge of such election division shall appoint a Return Inspector in his place; and in case the person who shall have received the second highest number of votes for Return Inspector shall not attend, then the person who shall have received the second highest number of votes for Judge of the elections, at the last preceding election, shall appoint a Return Inspector in his place; and in case any Return Clerk, appointed as aforesaid, shall neglect to attend at any election during the said year, it shall be the duty of the Return Inspector who appointed such Return Clerk, or the person filling the place of such Return Inspector, to forthwith appoint a suitable person as Return Clerk, qualified as aforesaid, who shall perform the duties for the year.

SEC. 236. That the Return Inspectors and Return Clerks aforesaid, shall, before entering upon the duties of their offices, severally take and subscribe the oath or affirmation herein directed, which shall be administered by any Judge, Alderman or Justice of the Peace, and that the following shall be the form of oath or affirmation to be taken by each Return Inspector, viz.: Oath of return Inspectors, and return clerks.

I, (A. B.) do that I will duly attend to the ensuing election during the continuance thereof as a Return Inspector; that I will count the tickets as provided by law, and publicly make known the state of the votes in each and every hour, and that I will in all things truly, impartially and faithfully perform my duty to the best of my judgment and abilities, and that I am not directly or indirectly interested in any bet or wager on the result of this election.

That the following shall be the form of oath or affirmation to be taken by each Return Clerk, viz.:

I, (A. B.) do that I will impartially, carefully and truly write down the number of votes that shall be given for each candidate at the election as often as his name shall be read to me by the Return Inspectors thereof, and in all things truly and faithfully perform my duties respecting the same, to the best of my judg-

234. Act of May 1, 1861, Sec. 5, P. L. 576.
235. Ibid. Sec. 1, P. L. 576.
236. Ibid. Sec. 7, P. L. 576.

ment and ability, and that I am not directly or indirectly interested in any bet or wager on the result of this election.

Duty of return clerk.

SEC. 237. That it shall be the duty of the said Return Clerk forthwith to make out two copies of the forms of each of the said oaths or affirmations which shall be severally subscribed by each of the Return Inspectors and the Return Clerks, and the said oaths or affirmations shall be certified under the hands of the Judge, Alderman, or Justice of the Peace, by whom they shall be administered, and one of the said certificates of oath or affirmation taken or subscribed by the Return Inspectors and Return Clerks shall be deposited with the other papers in the ballot-box as now provided by law.

SEC. 238. That all the existing laws of this Commonwealth relative to elections in the City of Philadelphia, which now direct and govern the Inspectors and Clerks of elections, are hereby extended to the Return Inspectors and Return Clerks aforesaid; that the said Return Inspectors and Return Clerks shall receive the same compensation as now received by the Inspectors and Clerks of the elections under existing laws.

SEC. 239. That immediately after the polls shall have been closed and the return made out, each ballot-box shall be carefully bound by tape and sealed up, and the Judge and Return Inspectors shall severally affix their signatures with their appropriate seals to the said ballot-box before it shall be delivered up as hereinafter provided.

Duty of City Commissioners.

SEC. 240. That the Commissioners for the city of Philadelphia shall provide a fire-proof room or vault in the public buildings in the said city or some other suitable place at which the Judge of the elections after the closing of the polls and the requirements of the law have been complied with, shall forthwith there deliver to the Mayor and Recorder of the city of Philadelphia(*w*) the said ballot-boxes; that the said room or vault shall not be accessible to any other person than the Mayor and Recorder aforesaid, who shall be present and receive at the said room or vault the ballot-boxes from the Return Inspectors as aforesaid; that the Mayor and Recorder aforesaid shall not take or open, nor permit to be taken or opened, any ballot-box deposited aforesaid for the space of one year after the same

237. Act of May 1, 1861, Sec. 8, P. L. 575.
238. Ibid. Sec. 9, P. L. 576.
239. Ibid. Sec. 10, P. L. 576.
240. Ibid. Sec. 11, P. L. 576.

(*w*) By the 74th Section of the Act of July, 2, 1839, (P. L. 535,) it is provided that the ballot-boxes "shall within one day after the election be delivered by one of the Inspectors to the nearest Justice of the Peace, who shall keep the same to answer the call of any persons or tribunal, authorized to try the merits of such election." Under this section the officers have delivered the ballot-boxes to the Aldermen of the Ward; *Hereafter*, They must deliver them to the Mayor and Recorder at the place provided by the City Commissioners.

has been therein deposited, except when they shall be called upon by some court or other tribunal authorized to try the merits of such election; and after such trial or investigation it shall be the duty of the Mayor and Recorder aforesaid, to have said box or boxes returned and deposited as aforesaid.

SEC. 241. That if any officer under this Act shall neglect or fail to perform the duties herein imposed upon them, then they or either of them, shall upon conviction be sentenced to pay a fine of five hundred dollars and undergo an imprisonment by separate or solitary confinement not exceeding three years respectively for every such offence.

PORT WARDENS.

SEC. 242. The Select and Common Councils shall elect in joint meeting, by *viva voce* vote, at the last stated meeting in the month of September next, sixteen citizens having proper knowledge of the duties for Port Wardens, eight of them to serve for one year, and eight of them for two years, from the first day of June, Anno Domini eighteen hundred and fifty-five; and thereafter on or before the last stated meeting of Councils in May, in each year, elect eight such citizens to serve for two years as Port Wardens from the first day of June then suceeding, who together with the Master Warden, shall do and perform the duties which do now, or may by law or ordinance hereafter belong to the Port Wardens. It shall be the duty of the said Councils, after the requisite surveys and soundings shall have been made, to fix the lines beyond which no wharf or pier shall be constructed,(*x*) and to keep the navigable water within the said city for ever open and free from obstruction. The City Councils shall authorize the construction of wharves upon a plan and scale to meet the demands of commerce, keep the same and the avenues leading thereto open and free from obstruction; and shall, moreover, provide from time to time for the more convenient selection, appointment, regulation and compensation of pilots navigating to and from said city, and for the greater security and better disposition of vessels within the port of the same, and they may enact ordinances for the purposes in this section mentioned.

Port Wardens to be elected by Councils.

Councils to fix wharf lines.

Authority of Councils relative to the port.

SEC. 243. That the Burgess and Council of the borough of Bristol shall appoint one Assistant Warden of the port of

Borough of Bristol to

241. Act of May 1, 1861, Sec. 12, P. L. 576.
242. Act of Feb. 2, 1854, Sec. 28, P. L. 27.
243. Act of April 21, 1855, Sec. 1, P. L. 264.

(*x*) The Councils, by ordinance approved December 4, 1856, fixed the wharf line according to the power conferred upon them, and the Legislature, by an Act of Assembly, approved April 15, 1858, (P. L. 275,) recognized the line as established.

appoint a port warden. Philadelphia, to serve as a Port Warden for the time and with the authority of those appointed by the City Councils.

Preamble. SEC. 244. *Whereas*, Frequent obstructions to the safe navigation of the river Delaware and river Schuylkill, within the tide waters thereof, do frequently occur by the sinking of canal boats, barges, and other vessels trading on the said rivers, and there being no adequate remedy to compel the owner, master, or other agents having charge thereof, to raise and remove the same; therefore,

Duty of master warden. *Be it enacted*, That from and after the passage of this act, it shall be the duty of the Master Warden of the port of Philadelphia, immediately upon information of the sinking of any canal boat, barge, or other vessel, in the channel way of the tide waters of the river Delaware or river Schuylkill, within the limits of the port of Philadelphia, to give notice to the owner, master, or other agent having charge thereof, to raise and remove such obstruction within ten days after Penalty the date of said notice, under a penalty of one hundred dollars, to be sued for and recovered before any alderman, or justice of the peace within the limits aforesaid, as by law such sums are recoverable from the owner, master, or other agent having control of the same, to and for the use of the Board of Wardens of the Port of Philadelphia, subject, nevertheless, to an appeal to the Court of Common Pleas of the proper city or county, which said sum or sums so recovered shall be appropriated towards the payment of salaries and contingent expenses of the Warden's office; and in cases of the refusal or neglect of the parties interested as aforesaid to raise and remove any such obstruction within the time specified in said notice, it shall be the further duty of said Master Warden to have raised and removed at the expense of the owner, master, or agent; and the said canal boat, barge, or other vessel, together with the cargo thereof, shall be subject to a lien in the hands of the said Master Warden, until the expenses of raising and removing shall be fully paid to him; and the said Master Warden is hereby authorized to sell at public auction to the highest bidder, for cash, all such property, or so much thereof as is necessary to pay all the expenses of raising and removing, together with the penalty aforesaid, and shall return the surplus, if any, of such sale, to such person or persons as shall be legally entitled to receive the same: *Provided*, That the Master Warden before proceeding to sell any such property as aforesaid, shall give five days notice by at least twenty handbills (printed) to be posted in conspicuous places along Delaware avenue, setting forth a full description of all such property to be sold, together with time and place of selling the same.

SEC. 245. That all laws heretofore passed inconsistent with the provisions of this act are hereby repealed.

---

244. Act of April 14, 1859, Sec. 1, P. L. 643.
245. Ibid. Sec. 2, P. L. 643.

SEC. 246. That every person exercising the profession of a pilot in the bay or river Delaware, under a license duly granted, or may be hereafter granted by said Board of Wardens of the port of Philadelphia, shall, immediately after the passage of this act, take and subscribe an oath or affirmation, before the Master Warden of said port, who is hereby authorized and empowered to administer the same, that he will support the Constitution of the United States, and the Constitution and laws of Pennsylvania, and well and faithfully perform his duty as a pilot. Oath of pilots.

SEC. 247. In case any pilot, licensed under the provisions of the act to which this a supplement, and the supplement thereto, shall neglect or refuse to take and subscribe the oath or affirmation herein provided, after notice having been given by the Master Warden, it shall be the duty of the Master Warden to withdraw and cancel the license of such pilot; and it shall not be lawful for any pilot so refusing or neglecting to take and subscribe the oath or affirmation aforesaid, to perform the duties of a pilot in the bay or river Delaware. Effect of refusing to take oath.

SEC. 248. It shall be the duty of the Master Warden to give each pilot who has taken and subscribed the oath as aforesaid, a certificate of the same, which certificate shall be attached to the license and a record of the same kept in the Warden's office.

SEC. 249. That any pilot, captain, or other officer or person who shall knowingly serve in any capacity on board of any steamship, steamboat, sailing vessel, canal boat or other conveyance by water, having on board any goods, provisions or merchandise whatever, contraband of war, designed for conveyance to, or delivery at any port or place within any seceded state, or with which the United States is at war, with knowledge of such unlawful traffic, and with intent to give aid or comfort to the enemy, shall be deemed and held to be guilty of a high misdemeanor, and on conviction thereof in any competent court of criminal jurisdiction of this commonwealth, shall be punished by fine not exceeding $5000, and imprisonment at labor not exceeding ten years, or either. Treason in a pilot.

DELAWARE AVENUE.

SEC. 250. That the Councils of the city of Philadelphia are hereby authorized to widen the whole or any part of Delaware avenue, along the Delaware front of said city, to a width not exceeding fifty feet, by extending the eastern Widening of Delaware avenue authorized.

---

246. Act of May 14, 1861, Sec. 1, P. L. 745.
247. Ibid. Sec. 2, P. L. 745.
248. Ibid. Sec. 3, P. L. 746.
249. Ibid. Sec. 4, P. L. 746.
250. Act of April 15, 1858, Sec. 1, P. L. 275.

line of said avenue eastwardly as far as may be necessary; and for that purpose said Councils shall have the power from time to time, to appropriate such portions of wharf and dock properties on said avenue as may be requisite for said widening; and all damages therefor shall be sued for, ascertained and paid in the same manner as now provided by law for the opening of streets in said city, and in assessing such damages the jury shall take into consideration the advantages and disadvantages accruing to the owners of property so taken: *Provided, nevertheless*, That nothing herein contained shall be construed to authorize any reduction in the width of any part of said avenue, or Wharf street, wherever it may exceed fifty feet in width, as provided by ordinance of the Councils approved December 4th, 1856, and a supplement thereto: *And provided, also*, That the damages to property on said avenue, between Vine and South streets, shall be paid out of the fund appropriated in the will of Stephen Girard to the improvements of Delaware avenue.

Damages therefos.

Plan to be proposed.

SEC. 251. That no part of said avenue shall be deemed to be widened as aforesaid, until a plan of the same, prepared by the Board of Surveys of said city, under the direction of and approved by said Councils, shall have been first filed in the office of the said Board of Surveys for the period of thirty days, and due notice thereof given for said period by the Chief Engineer and Surveyor, once a week, in at least two of the daily papers published in said city.

Future extension of wharves.

SEC. 252. That no owner of dock or wharf property on the said avenue shall hereafter extend the same into the channel of the river beyond the present limits thereof, or to the wharf line now established by ordinance, unless a full and sufficient release of damages to the city, caused or to be caused by the widening of said avenue as aforesaid, shall have been first filed in the office of and approved by the City Solicitor: *Provided*, That in case such damages shall have been already assessed and paid to such owner prior to such extension, then the damages so paid, with interest, shall be first refunded to the city.

INCOMPATIBLE OFFICES.

SEC. 253. That no person shall, at the same time, be a member of more than one of the following bodies, to wit: The City Councils, the Guardians of the Poor, the Board of Health, the Controllers of the Public Schools, the Directors of the Public Schools, and the Inspectors of the County Prison; nor shall any person be a member of any of these bodies, who is at the same time a salaried officer under the

251. Act of April 15, 1858, Sec. 2, P. L. 275.
252. Ibid. Sec. 2, P. L. 275.
253. Act of Feb. 2, 1854, Sec. 48, P. L. 45.

same or under any of them: *Provided*, That this shall not be construed so as to prevent a Controller of the Public Schools from being at the same time a School Director.

SEC. 254. That nothing contained in the act to which this is a supplement shall prevent School Directors from holding any other office or appointment.

ADVERTISING.

SEC. 255. That all the public advertising for said city, except for municipal claims, whether for elections, taxes or otherwise, shall be inserted in no more than three daily newspapers, nor more than three times in each, nor shall there be paid for the same any greater rates than those advertised in such papers to be paid by the citizens, and the Controller shall pass no bill for advertising otherwise done; the charge for advertising delinquent tax payers shall not exceed thirty-seven cents for all advertising of each name in any one ward, which shall be payable by the person liable for the tax, but if any names of persons shall be advertised as delinquent in the payment of taxes that had been paid, the Receiver shall pay the expense thereof. Charges of advertising delinquent tax payers.

BREACHES OF ORDINANCES.

SEC. 256. That for all breaches of the ordinances of the city of Philadelphia, on and after the first day of July next, the original process shall be as now prescribed in cases of security for the peace: *Provided*, That the remedy by suit of certiorari shall be as heretofore.

SEC. 257. That for all breaches of the ordinances of the city of Philadelphia, where the penalty demanded is fifty dollars and upwards, actions of debt shall be brought in the corporate name of the city of Philadelphia; and the provisions of the act of May seventh, Anno Domini eighteen hundred and fifty seven, so far as inconsistent herewith, are hereby repealed.

PUBLIC SQUARES AND PARKS.

SEC. 258. That it shall be the duty of the City Councils to obtain by dedication or purchase, within the limits of the said city, an adequate number of squares or other areas of ground, convenient of access to all its inhabitants, and lay out and maintain such squares and areas of ground as open public places, for the health and enjoyment of the people forever. Councils to provide public squares.

---

254. Act of May 7, 1855, Sec. 28, P. L. 264.
255. Act of April 21, 1855, Sec. 13, P. L. 264.
256. Act of May 7, 1857, Sec. 2, P. L. 426.
257. Act of March 15, 1858, Sec. 1, P. L. 114.
258. Act of Feb. 2, 1854, Sec. 39, P. L. 42.

election of squares or parks regulated.

SEC. 259. That the Councils of said city, whenever they shall select any square or other area of ground, to be laid out and maintained forever as an open public place or park for the health and enjoyment of the people, shall have the power, if they cannot agree with the owner or owners thereof as to the price, to cause a petition to be filed in the Court of Quarter Sessions of the city and county of Philadelphia, on behalf of said city, setting forth by proper metes and bounds the grounds so selected, and that by ordinance the said Councils have appropriated the same for said purpose; whereupon the said Court shall appoint a jury to assess the damages in the manner now provided by law, and the proceedings thereupon shall be the same, and with the like effect, as upon the assessment of damages for the opening of streets in said city.

Viewers to appraise damages.

Whereas, The strip of ground on the west bank of the river, as hereinafter fully described, should be owned by the city of Philadelphia, to prevent the erection of breweries and factories thereon, whose refuse fluid will flow into the stream and so pass into the forebay at Fairmount;

And whereas, The natural advantages of the ground (abounding as it does in diversified scenery) fits it eminently for a park, thus securing, in the ownership thereof, a place for the health and recreation of the people and preserving forever the purity of the water they drink;

And whereas, The rapid expansion of the city on the west of the river Schuylkill urges immediate action therein; now, therefore,

Boundaries of ground to be used for a public park.

SEC. 260. *Be it enacted, &c.*, That the title to and ownership of the area of ground which, according to an accurate survey thereof, is bounded as follows: Beginning at a point on the river Schuylkill, at the intersection of the north line of Bridge street and low water mark in said river; thence along said north side of Bridge street six hundred and twenty-two feet (622) to the easterly side of the Pennsylvania railroad, thirty-seven and one-half ($37\frac{1}{2}$) feet easterly of the centre line thereof; thence along the easterly side of said railroad its several courses four thousand and eighty-two feet to the easterly side of Thirty-seventh street; thence along the easterly side of said Thirty-seventh street three thousand (3000) feet, to the water line in the dam to supply Fairmount, on the river Schuylkill; thence southerly along the said westerly water line of the river Schuylkill, its several courses and distance, to the place of beginning, excepting therefrom and thereout that part of which the Schuylkill Navigation Company is seized in fee, shall be vested in the city of Philadelphia, to be laid out and maintained forever as an open public place for the health and enjoyment of the people; and the Councils of the city of Philadelphia are

259. Act of May 13, 1857, Sec. 4, P. L. 489.
260. Act of March 31, 1860, Sec. 1, P. L. 476.

hereby empowered, within ninety days from the passage hereof, to enter upon said ground and take immediate possession thereof for the purpose aforesaid.

SEC. 261. That the owner or owners of said ground, by the first section hereof appropriated for the public purposes, shall be paid for the same according to the value, which shall be ascertained by a jury of twelve men, appointed (either upon the petition of the city of Philadelphia or of the owners) by the District Court of the county of Philadelphia, and their report upon the same shall be final and conclusive; and a mandamus may issue, within six months after the confirmation of said report, to collect the sums awarded, if not paid meanwhile. Valuation and how paid for

SEC. 262. That the Chief Engineer and Surveyor of the city of Philadelphia shall advertise, once a week for four weeks, in five daily newspapers published in the city of Philadelphia, for plans for the improvement of said grounds in the first section hereof described; and the same, when received, shall be considered by himself, in conjunction with the Mayor, Commissioner of City Property, and the Presidents of the Select and Common Councils, who shall approve one of them; and the designer thereof shall receive the sum of one thousand dollars. Plans for the improvement, relative to. Amount to be paid for approved plan.

SEC. 263. That upon the approval of the plan as provided for in the foregoing section, the Commissioners of City Property shall advertise for proposals for the improvement of said ground according to said plan, and shall award the contract to the lowest bidder, who shall perform the work under the supervision of the designer of the plan. Proposals to be received for the improvement of grounds, &c.

SEC. 264. That this Act shall not take effect until the Councils of Philadelphia shall, by ordinance, declare their approval thereof.

PUBLIC DEBT. SINKING FUND.

SEC. 265. That the net debt of the county of Philadelphia, after deducting and canceling the portion held by the sinking fund, and the several net debts of the Guardians for the Relief and Employment of the Poor of the city of Philadelphia, the district of Southwark, and the townships of the Northern Liberties and Penn, of the Mayor, Aldermen and Citizens of Philadelphia, of the Commissioners and inhabitants of the district of Moyamensing, of the Commissioners and inhabitants of the Kensington district, of the Commissioners and inhabitants of the incorporated district of the Northern Liberties, of the Commissioners and inhabitants of the district of Spring Garden, of the Commissioners and Debt of the various corporations consolidated.

---

261. Act of May 31, 1860, Sec. 2, P. L. 476.
262. Ibid. Sec. 3, P. L. 476.
263. Ibid. Sec. 4, P. L. 477.
264. Ibid. Sec. 5, P. L. 477.
265. Act of Feb. 2, 1854, Sec. 38, P. L. 244.

inhabitants of Richmond, in the county of Philadelphia, the districts of West Philadelphia and Belmont, of the boroughs of Whitehall, Manayunk, Germantown, Aramingo and Frankford, and of the Commissioners and inhabitants of the district of Penn, and the Board of Health and Controllers of the Public Schools, after deducting and canceling the portions held by the respective sinking funds of the said several corporations, is hereby consolidated and formed into one debt, to be called the debt of the city of Philadelphia, and payable at the same times that the principals of said debts are now made payable, certificates of which said debts are to be issued in sums of not less than one hundred dollars, in lieu of the present separate debts so consolidated, to the respective owners in lieu of their present certificates of the same, at the option of such owners, bearing the same rate of interest that the debts so to be exchanged now bear, and payable on the first days of January and July, at the office of the Treasurer of the city of Philadelphia. There shall be annually raised by tax, in addition to the income of the corporation property, a sufficient sum to discharge the annual interest on the said consolidated city debt, and no debt shall be incurred or loans made by the said city, without a contemporaneous appropriation of a sufficient annual income or tax, exclusive of loans, to pay the interest and sink the principal of such debt in thirty years.

Sinking Fund.

Fiscal year to commence 1st January.

SEC. 266. That the fiscal year of the city of Philadelphia, the Board of Guardians of the Poor of the city of Philadelphia, the Board of Health, and of the Controllers of Public Schools of the city of Philadelphia, and Inspectors of Prison, shall commence on the first of January in each and every year. It shall be the duty of the Board of Guardians of the Poor to furnish the Councils of the city of Philadelphia, on or before the first day of March in every year, an estimate of the amount that in their judgment will be required during the current fiscal year for the maintenance and support of the alms-house establisment of the said Board; and the Controllers of Public Schools, and the Board of Health, the Port Wardens, and Inspectors of the Prisons, severally, shall, in like manner, on or before the same day in each year, furnish to the said Councils the amount that in their judgment will be necesssary for the support of public schools and the necessary expenses of the Board of Health, the Port Wardens, and Inspectors of the Prison, respectively, for the current fiscal year and the said City Councils shall fix the rate and levy all the taxes now authorized by law within the limits of said city and county, except the State tax, and direct the amount to be applied and paid by the City Treasurer to health, school, poor, city, and other purposes, according

Estimates of appropriations to be presented by 1st of March.

Councils to levy tax.

266. Act of Feb. 2, 1854, Sec. 39, P. L. 40.

to law. The said taxes shall be voted so as to show how much is raised for said objects respectively; they shall be collected and accounted for to the Treasurer as one city and county tax. The said tax, and all State taxes accruing within said city limits, shall be paid to the Receiver of Taxes, and all allowance made by law for the collection and prompt payment of the State tax shall accrue to the City Treasury for the use of the city: *Provided*, That the said City Councils shall so discriminate in laying said city taxes as not to impose upon the rural portions those expenses which belong exclusively to the built portions of said city; for which purpose the Assessors shall distinguish in their returns what properties are within agricultural or rural sections, not having the benefit of lighting, watching, and other expenditures for purposes exclusively belonging to built portions of said city; and all lands within said agricultural or rural districts, used for the purpose of cultivation or farming, shall be assessed as farm land: *And provided*, That no money shall be hereafter borrowed on the faith and credit of said city unless the ordinance or other authority authorizing the same shall have been introduced at one stated meeting of the Common Council, and the draft thereof published in at least two of the newspapers of the city, daily, for four weeks before the final consideration and passage thereof by the said Common Council. And at any stated meeting of the Select Council, held at least one week after the final consideration of any such ordinance by the Common Councils, the Select Council may consider and act upon any such ordinance; but the Select Councils shall not originate any ordinance or other authority for borrowing money, and no loans shall be authorized without a vote of two-thirds of the whole number of the members of each Council.

All taxes to be paid to the Receiver of Taxes.

Allowance for State Tax to accrue to the city.

City Councils to discriminate as regards the rural districts in laying tax.

In what mode money shall be borrowed on the faith of the city.

SEC. 267. That it shall be lawful for Councils to authorize, by ordinance, temporary loans of moneys, whenever they shall deem it necessary: *Provided*, That each temporary loans shall at no time exceed in the aggregate the sum of five hundred thousand dollars, and no such loan shall be for a longer period than four months. And such ordinance shall be introduced at a stated meeting of the Common Council, and shall require on its final passage a vote of *two-thirds* of the whole number present of the members of Common Council; it shall then be transmitted to Select Council for their consideration, and at the next stated meeting thereafter, the Select Council may consider the same, and it shall in like manner require a vote of two-thirds of the whole number of the members of the Select Council.

Councils may authorize temporary loans by ordinances.

Such ordinances to be introduced at a stated meeting and required to be passed by a vote of two-thirds of the whole number present.

SEC. 268. That the investments which now or hereafter

267. Act of April 21, 1855, Sec. 19, P. L. 264.
268. Act of May 13, 1857, Sec. 3, P. L. 489.

Sinking fund of city.

may form a part of the sinking fund of the said city, shall not be sold except for money, nor changed except for the loan of the said city, and in case of such sale or exchange, the proceeds thereof shall be applied exclusively to the sinking fund of said city, or to the extinguishment of its funded debt. (*y*)

GENERAL PROVISIONS.

Officers to give bond. Make returns to City Controller under oath. Controller to administer oath. Perjury.

SEC. 269. That every officer or agent receiving moneys for the city, and payable to the City Treasurer, shall give bond for the faithful performance of his duty, and shall be required to make returns to the City Controller once in every week, or oftener, if Councils shall direct, under oath or affirmation of each item of the moneys received by him, and immediately upon making such return, to pay the amount in his hands to the City Treasurer. The said City Controller is hereby authorized to administer such oath or affirmation, and any person falsely making such oath or affirmation, or guilty of falsehood in any other oath or affirmation required by the provisions of this act, or by any ordinance of Councils made in pursuance thereof, shall be guilty of perjury.

No officer, agent or clerk, to be interested in any contract.

SEC. 270. That if any Councilman, Guardian of the Poor, Member of the Board of Health, Controller or Director of the Public Schools, or Warden, Inspector of the Prison, or any other member, officer or agent of the said City Corporation or of any corporation or department by this act recognized, or clerk therein, shall at any time be directly or indirectly interested in any sale to, or contract, for supplies to be furnished to said city, or to any corporation or department by this act recognized or placed under the supervision of Councils, of which he shall be a member, or officer, clerk, or agent, or shall receive any gratuity, money or property whatsoever, by reason of such sale or contract, or shall take any fee beyond that prescribed by law, he, if a Councilmen, or elective officer, or officer appointed by Court, shall be impeached in manner hereinbefore provided, and if found guilty shall forfeit and vacate his seat; and if any officer or clerk appointed by Councils, shall be removed from his ap-

---

269. Act of Feb. 2, 1854, Sec. 49, P. L. 43.
270. Ibid. Sec. 51, P. L. 43.

(*y*) At the passage of this Act, the Conncils by Ordinance of January 19, 1855, had obtained in Section 1, That the real estate belonging to the City of Philadelphia, which the said corporation are authorized, or may be authorized to sell, without being required to appropriate the proceeds specifically by the power allowing such sale; all stock in railroad, canal, plank road or other corporations, and all mortages owned by the same; and all moneys which belonged or were owing to the sinking funds of any of the corporations, which, by the Act of Assembly, approved February 2, 1854, were consolidated into the corporation of the City of Philadelphia, be and they are hereby pledged for the payment o the funded debt of the said corporation.

pointment or office; and any vendor or contractor participating in such act, shall be incapable of recovering any demand thus infected by fraud, and all such offenders shall be deemed guilty of a misdemeanor, and upon conviction of such offence in the Court of Quarter Sessions for said city and county, shall be fined and imprisoned at the discretion of said court. Penalties.

SEC. 271. That the meetings of the said City Councils, and all corporations and boards authorized or recognized as existing under this Act, except the Board of Health and Board of Inspectors of County Prison, shall be at all times open and accessible to all citizens deporting themselves with order and decorum. Councils and other bodies to sit with open doors.

SEC. 272. That nothing in this Act contained shall be so construed as to relieve the said city of Philadelphia, as hereby extended, from any engagement or contract heretofore made by the authority of City Councils to subscribe to the capital stock of any railroad company under any law of this Commonwealth; and all ordinances heretofore passed by the said city, or by any of the municipalities or districts hereby consolidated, and in force at the time of the passage of this Act, and whereby subscriptions are authorized to be made to the stock of any such railroad company, shall be binding upon and carried out by said city, municipalities and Districts, respectively, until this Act shall go into effect; and thereafter, upon, and by said City, hereby extended and consolidated, upon the performance of the conditions, if any required, by such ordinance or ordinances: and nothing in this Act shall be so construed as to interfere, in any manner, with any laws authorizing subscriptions to be made by the City of Philadelphia to any railroad company, passed prior to this Act. Railroad subscriptions to be binding. Laws authorizing subscriptions, not interfered with

SEC. 273 That the Governor is hereby authorized to appoint two Sealers and Regulators of Weights and Measures, in and for the City of Philadelphia, one of whom shall have his office north of Vine street, and the other south of said street; and they shall each perform, in their respective districts, the duties prescribed by law for the fees heretofore allowed, the sealing of each to be good and uniform throughout the said city. Governor to appoint two sealers and regulators of weights and measures.

SEC. 274. That the city of Philadelphia shall provide rooms for the accommodation of the juries of all the Courts, and thereafter no empanneled jury shall be permitted to meet at any tavern or hotel; the said City shall also provide adequate Court Rooms for the Supreme Court of Pennsylvania, when sitting in said city, and pay the tipstaves and crier thereof at such rate per day during their actual services as said Court may fix. City to provide rooms for the accommodation of juries. No jury to meet at a tavern or hotel. City to provide rooms for Supreme Court, and pay tipstaves and crier thereof.

271. Act of Feb. 2, 1854, Sec. 52, P. L. 43.
272. Ibid. Sec. 53, P. L. 43.
273. Act of April 21, 1855, Sec. 5, P. L. 264.
274. Ibid. Sec. 12, P. L. 264.

No contract for the building of school houses, bridges, culverts, new paving, or redemption of the tolls of any turnpike or plank road, to be made without an ordinance therefor. No contract shall be made by the head of any department, unless for objects authorized by Councils.

SEC. 275. That no contract for the construction of any new building, school house, bridge, culvert, new paving of streets, redemption of the tolls of any turnpike or plank road, to be paid for by the City, shall become binding thereon, without an ordinance therefor duly enacted. No contract shall be made by the head of any department for work or materials for the city, unless for objects authorized by Councils, and if for new work, the contract and sureties be approved by the City Solicitor and Councils, and the supervision of Councils shall extend to adjudge the character of all work and materials done and furnished for the city, and to the scrutiny of the accounts and vouchers therefor; but such supervision and scrutiny shall in nowise relieve the Controller from the performance of the like duty in respect to such accounts and vouchers.

Fifth street northward from York street, to be widened.

SEC. 276. That Fifth street, northward from York street, shall be widened upon the plan of streets, to one hundred feet, taking an equal quantity of ground from each side.(z)

No appropriation of moneys to be made without an ordinance therefor. The Mayor to keep a register of the amount and objects of the appropriations. Misdemeanor in office for the Controller to pass or the Treasurer to pay any bill not authorized by law.

SEC. 277. That no appropriation shall be made of the moneys of the city without an ordinance therefor, expressing the objects thereof, and the amount appropriated for each object. It shall be the duty of the Mayor to keep a register of the amount and objects of all appropriations, and to withhold his signature for all new constructions and redemption of tolls as aforesaid, until all the interest accruing on the loans of the city, and the principal of those becoming due, and the ordinary and necessary expenses of the city and the administration of justice in the county shall be adequately provided for; and without his signature any Ordinance therefor shall not go into effect. It shall be a misdemeanor in office for the Controller of the city to pass, or the Treasurer of the city to pay, any bill or order for any object not authorized by law.

The City of Philadelphia to sell the public halls, lots and real estate of the city, as rapidly as possible.

SEC. 278. That it shall be lawful for the city of Philadelphia, as rapidly as purchasers can be procured, without a sacrifice of price, to make public sale and conveyance of the public halls, lots and real estate vested in the said city, not held upon any trust and not required for authorized public purposes, and to apply the proceeds in discharge of the city debts; and if ground rents be reserved, to sell and convey the same for said purposes.

Right of redemption to owners of

SEC. 279. That all sales for registered taxes, municipal claims, assessments for removing nuisances, or other charge by the city assessed on real estate, shall be subject to re-

---

275. Act of April 21, 1855, Sec. 20, P. L. 264.
276. Ibid. Sec. 30, P. L. 264.
277. Ibid. Sec. 21, P. L. 264.
278. Ibid. Sec. 22, P. L. 264.
279. Act of May 13, 1856, Sec. 11, P. L. 568.

(z) Repealed by Act of April 26, 1862, P. L. 542. (See Section.)

demption by the owner at any time within two years from the date of the acknowledgment of the Sheriff's deed therefor, upon payment of aii costs and charges, and twenty per cent. upon the amount for which the property had sold; and any person entitled so to redeem, may present a petition to the Court from which the process to make sale had issued, setting forth the facts and his readiness to pay the redemption money as aforesaid; whereupon the Court shall grant a rule to show cause why the purchaser shall not re-convey to him the premises sold, to be served as a summons in actions of partition; and if the petitioner shall prove the facts to give him a right to redeem, the Court shall make such rule absolute, and enforce it by attachment.

property sold

SEC. 280. That it shall be the duty of the Prothonotaries of the several courts of the said city, on the expiration of each term of their respective courts, to furnish to the Controller a statement, under oath or affirmation, of the fines and penalties imposed, recognizances recovered, judgment and jury fees received, arbitrators' and witness' fees unclaimed by the parties entitled to the same, with the name of the case in which the same were imposed, recovered, or received; and it shall be the duty of the Sheriff of the county of Philadelphia to submit his account with the city to the Controller, for settlement, on the first day of January, and quarterly thereafter, and upon such settlement the Sheriff shall be charged with all sums received and recovered as aforesaid, and he shall forthwith pay over the balance, if any, to the City Treasurer; and any officer neglecting or refusing to comply with the provisions of this section, shall be deemed guilty of a misdemeanor in office, and be proceeded against in like manner as for other misdemeanors.

Duty of prothonotaries in regard to fines, &c.

Duty of sheriff.

Penalty for neglect.

SEC. 281. That so much of City avenue, between the city of Philadelphia and Montgomery county, as was surveyed by the Commissioners, without covering the old road between the east branch of Indian creek, and property of Thomas Bealer, be of the same validity as if authorized by the act under which the same was surveyed, and said avenue is hereby widened to eighty feet, taking an equal quantity of ground on each side of said road as so surveyed, for future footways: *Provided*, That such widening shall not take place by an actual taking of the ground therefor before fifteen years from the date hereof, without the consent of the owners.

City avenue widened.

SEC. 282. That the head of every department shall by the first of November of each year, report to the Controller the estimate of the appropriations that will be required for his department for the ensuing year, and of said Controller to

Reports by heads of departments, of estimated expenses.

280. Act of May 13, 1856, Sec. 17, P. L. 568.
281. Ibid. Sec. 20, P. L. 568.
282. Ibid. Sec. 23, P. L. 568.

communicate at all times to the Mayor and the Committees of Councils such information upon the condition of the finances and the accounts of all officers expending or receiving the moneys of the city, as his department can afford.

Penalty for neglect in rendering accounts, &c.

SEC. 283. That every head of the department, officer or agent of the city, who shall have made default in the rendering of any account or report, or the payment over of any money or bills collected for the city, shall be guilty of a misdemeanor, and be by Councils dismissed from his office, and the vacancy shall be filled as provided by law.

Expenditures for eating, drinking, &c., prohibited.

SEC. 284. That it shall not be lawful for any department or committee of said city, or the officers thereof, or for the Prison Inspectors, to draw any moneys out of the city treasury, or to use any savings or the proceeds of the sales of any work or materials for or in any office, department or prison, or any revenues whatsoever thereof for the entertainment, eating, drinking or smoking, furnished to any members or officers of said city, corporation, departments or officers thereof, or of said prison, but shall pay the whole of said moneys into the city treasury; and every warrant drawn for the expenses of every department of the public service and prison, shall contain the declaration that no part thereof has been used for said purposes; and it shall be lawful for the City Controller, and his duty, whenever required by any citizen, to administer an oath or affirmation to any person presenting a bill against the city, as to its accuracy, the prices actually paid or contracted to be paid therefor, whether others and who are interested therein, and as to whatsoever matter he may deem needful to protect the interest of said city.

Warrants to set forth what they were issued for.

Sale of certain lot authorized.

SEC. 285. That the corporation of the city of Philadelphia is authorized to sell and convey in fee simple, discharged of all trust, the lot, containing about two acres, used for the interment of deceased strangers, on the northwest side of George street, now intersected by Poplar and Twentieth streets, conveyed to the city by John Brown Francis.

Goods, merchandise, &c., for use of city to be supplied by contract, given to the lowest bidder.

SEC. 286. That hereafter all goods, merchandise, and other articles of any kind, and labor and service required for the city of Philadelphia, in any department thereof, shall be purchased or contracted for, only in such manner as shall be prescribed by ordinance; and for that purpose the Councils of said city are hereby required to direct by ordinance the manner and time of making the yearly estimates by the several departments of said city, and of receiving sealed proposals for such supplies as aforesaid, which proposals shall be preceded by advertisement, and no contract shall

---

283. Act of May 13, 1856, Sec. 24, P. L. 568.
284. Ibid. Sec. 25, P. L. 568.
285. Ibid. Sec. 26, P. L. 568.
286. Ibid. Sec. 27, P. L. 568.

be awarded to any but the lowest bidder, who shall give the requisite security therefor.(*aa*)

SEC. 287. That it shall be the duty of City Councils, in all cases, when making appropriations, to state the items of expenditure under separate and distinct heads for which such appropriations are intended.

Appropriations to be made and disbursed separately.

SEC. 288. That it shall be lawful for the city of Philadelphia to sell and convey, or to release and extinguish, either at public and private sale, at not less than the par value thereof, two certain small yearly ground rents, now vested in the said city, in trust, to wit: One of them being a yearly ground rent of one pound ten shillings, payable out of a lot of ground situate on the north side of Arch street and east side of Fifteenth street, in the said city, containing about one hundred and ninety-eight feet on Arch street, and extending on east side of Fifteenth street to Cherry street; and the other of them being a yearly ground rent of two pounds fifteen shillings, payable out of a lot of ground on the north side of Carter's alley, in the rear of Nos. 72 and 74 south Second street, in said city, containing in front about thirty feet, and in depth about forty feet more or less: *Provided,* That the proceeds of sale or extinguishment shall be invested and applied to the same uses, intents and purposes for which the said ground rents are how held; the purchasers of the said rents, however, not to be liable for the application or misapplication of said funds.

To release and extinguish certain ground rents.

SEC. 289. That no debt or contract hereafter incurred or made shall be binding upon the city of Philadelphia, unless authorized by law or ordinance, and an appropriation sufficient to pay the same be previously made by Councils: *Provided,* That persons claiming unauthorized debts or contracts may recover against the person or persons illegally making the same.

Debts and contracts, when binding.

Proviso.

SEC. 290. That all laws requiring municipal corporations to enter bail. or to file affidavits of defence, and all laws inconsistent herewith, are hereby repealed.

City not required to enter bail, &c.

SEC. 291. That municipal claims for taxes, liens, public assessments or charges, may be amended at any time before or at the trial, on notice given defendant under rule of Court: *Provided,* That if made on the trial, a continuance may be granted by the Court on the application of the defendant.

Amendment of municipa claims.

(*aa*) This section applies only to the *annual* supplies required in any *department* of the city. Any *extraordinary* work required by any department, or any constructions which are authorized directly by the city, are unaffected by this act. In such case the discretion is vested in Councils, and they may or may not advertise for proposals; and they may award the contract to the *best* bidder, though such may not be lowest.

287. Act of May 13, 1856, Sec. 31, P. L. 568.
288. Act of Feb. 6, 1857, Sec. 1, P. L. —.
289. Act of April 21, 1858, Sec. 5, P. L. 387.
290. Ibid. Sec. 8, P. L. 387.
291. Act of April 1, 1859, Sec. 39, P. L. 87.

Pay and mileage of jurors.

SEC. 292. That every person who shall serve or attend as a juror in any Court of the city or county of Philadelphia, and who shall reside at a distancce of more than three miles from the State House in said city, shall be entitled to receive for said service the sum of one dollar and fifty cents for each day's attendance; and shall further be entitled to receive mileage at the rate of six and one-quarter cents per mile circular for each mile traveled in going to and returning from said court house, for eac hand every week, or parts of weeks, that they may serve as jurors; the aforesaid fees to be paid by the Treasurer of said city upon a warrant by the City Commissioners, as now authorized by law.

Municipal election to be held on the 2d Tuesday of October in each year.

SEC. 293. That the election of members of Councils and of all the municipal officers of the city of Philadelphia, authorized to be elected by an act approved Februry 2d, 1854, entitled, "A further supplement to an Act to incorporate the City of Philadelphia," and by any of the supplements thereto, shall be held on the second Tuesday of October in each year, instead of the first Tuesday of May as now provided by law.

Extension of official terms.

SEC. 294. That to prevent confusion in the terms of the officers heretofore elected by the qualified voters of said city, and that no vacancy may occur, all officers, inclusive of constables, and surveyors and regulators, whose terms of office would otherwise have expired at any day succeeding said election day heretofore appointed to be held on the first Tuesday of May in each and every year, shall be continued until the last day in December following the day at which their said term would otherwise have ended, excepting the Receiver of Taxes, who shall continue until the Saturday next preceding the second Monday succeeding the fifteenth day of January following: *Provided*, That each and every officer whose term shall be so extended shall, thirty days before he shall enter upon such extended term, have given new security in the manner now required by law for the period of such extended term.

Officers to take seats on the 1st of the year, except receiver.

SEC. 295. That all officers elected by the qualified voters of the City of Philadelphia shall enter upon the performance of their duties on the first day of January next succeeding their election, excepting the Receiver of Taxes, who shall enter upon the performance of his duties on the second Monday succeeding the fifteenth of January next following his election.

Terms of office.

SEC. 296. That the terms of office of the officers hereafter to be elected shall be: of the Mayor, three years; of the

---

292. Act of April 1, 1859, Sec. 1, P. L. 598.
293. Act of March, 21, 1861, Sec. 1, P. L. 165.
294. Ibid. Sec. 2, P. L. 165.
295. Ibid. Sec. 2, P. L. 165.
296. Ibid. Sec. 4, P. L. 165.

City Controller, three years, and of the City Solicitor three years, from the day of their commencement of their term in January as aforesaid.

SEC. 297. That the city of Philadelphia is hereby empowered to make private or public sale, and convey in fee simple, or reserving ground rents, the present almshouse grounds, or any part thereof, situate in the Twenty-fourth Ward of said city, containing one hundred and eighty-seven acres, more or less, and the buildings thereon erected, subject to the following conditions: Sale of alms house grounds.

I. That the city of Philadelphia shall reserve a part of said ground, not exceeding forty acres, to be laid out and maintained as an open public place forever for the health and recreation of the people.

II. That the said city shall also reserve at Pine and South streets, on the river Schuylkill, pieces of ground sufficient in the opinion of the Chief Engineer and Surveyor of said city for abutments and approaches thereto for a bridge or bridges which may be lawfully authorized to be erected at either of said streets.

SEC. 298. That the city of Philadelphia is hereby empowered to purchase land, and erect thereon an alms or poor house, (with or without a house of correction and employment, as may be deemed expedient,) and in payment therefor to create a loan, which shall be exempt from State tax.

SEC. 299. That the proceeds arising from the sale of the grounds and buildings specified in the first section of this Act shall be specifically applied to and pledged for the payment of the loan authorized by the second section of this Act, and if ground rents shall be reserved or mortgages taken in payment, the same, when sold or paid off, shall be applied to and for the same purpose.

SEC. 300. That all that part of Ruan street, as laid down in the plan of the late Borough of Frankford, now in the Twenty-third Ward of the city of Philadelphia, running from Frankford or Main street to Paul, be and the same is hereby vacated; and in lieu thereof that the proper department of the said city of Philadelphia cause to be laid out and opened for public use two streets on the vacant ground belonging to the said city, on each side of the present police station house and market house, allowing an eight feet footway or pavement on each side of the street. Ruan street vacated.

SEC. 301. That Filbert street in the Twenty-fourth Ward of the city of Philadelphia, extending from the Schuylkill river to Lancaster Avenue, be and the same is hereby vaca- Filbert street, from the Schuylkill river to

297. Act of May 1, 1861, Sec. 1, P. L. 432.
298. Ibid. Sec. 2, P. L. 433.
299. Ibid. Sec. 2, P. L. 433.
300. Act of Feb. 28, 1861, Sec. 1, P. L. 75.
301. Act of April 12, 1861, Sec. 1, P. L. 298.

Lancaster avenue vacated.

ted, and the title to the soil over which the same is laid is hereby vested in the owners of property fronting on each side of said vacated street, to the middle thereof.

Vacation of a part of Thompson street, between Ann and Somerset.

SEC. 302. Whereas the owners of property between Ann and Somerset streets on both sides of Thompson street (formerly Duke street) in the Nineteenth Ward of the city of Philadelphia, by reason of the sixth section of an Act of the Assembly of Pennsylvania, entitled "An Act in relation to the districts of Richmond, Kensington and Penn, in the County of Philadelphia," approved the 29th day of January, 1850, have heretofore dedicated to the public use so much of their lands, on both sides of said Thompson street as under said Act was required to widen said Thompson street from 50 feet to the width of 100 feet, in order to give space for the erection of a market house in the centre of said street: *And whereas*, the market house authorized by said Act to be built on said street, has been since elsewhere erected, and the object of said Act and the dedication thereunder has failed: *Therefore*, be it enacted. * * That the 6th section of the aforesaid Act of Assembly be and the same is hereby repealed, and that so much and such parts of the land between Ann and Somerset streets, as has been dedicated or intended by said act to be given or dedicated for public use, is hereby vacated, so that the said Thompson street be reduced to its original width of 50 feet; and that the said vacated land is hereby vested in fee in the adjoining owners, according to their respective fronts on both sides of said Thompson street.

An Act to secure to Farmers certain rights in the Markets of the City of Philadelphia.

SEC. 303. *Whereas*, The authorities of the city of Philadelphia having the renting of the stalls and stands in the public market houses of said city, have recently assumed to restrict farmers from selling upon said stalls any meat except that of animals fed or fattened on their farms, and to exercise the right of denying to farmers who have been previously the occupants of particular stalls any preference over other applicants in reletting the same, thereby depriving them of the custom they have established at their respective stands: *therefore*, Be it enacted. * * * That any farmer or person whose principal occupation is that of a farmer being the lessee or occupant of a stall in any of the public market houses of the city of Philadelphia, or the occupant of a stand in any of the public streets of said city, which may now or hereafter be made stands for market wagons, may lawfully sell at such stall or stand, in any

302. Act of May 1, 1861, Sec. 1, P. L. 641.
303. Act of April 17, 1861, Sec. 1, P. L. 325.

quantity, any meat of a marketable quality slaughtered on his farm, without regard to whether the same be produced or fattened on his farm or elsewhere; and any such farmer who may now be, or hereafter become the lessee of any stall or stand, in any of the public market houses of the said city, shall be entitled to become the lessee of such stall or stand from year to year, and to continue to occupy the same in preference to any other person, so long as he may pay within the proper time the legal rent therefor, and comply with all proper rules and regulations for the government of said market houses: any Act of Assembly, ordinance of the City Councils, or requirement of the Market Department of the said City to the contrary notwithstanding.

ELECTION LAWS.

SEC. 308. That the Judges of the various election divisions of the several wards of the said city shall meet on the day following all general elections, in their respective wards, at the usual and proper time and place, and after casting up the returns of their respective divisions, select or appoint one of their number Return Judge to convey the said returns to the office of the Prothonotary of the Court of Common Pleas of said city and county, within the time prescribed by law, and the Return Judges of the several wards shall meet at the State House in said city, at the time prescribed by existing law, and shall cast up the several division and ward returns, and execute under their hands and seals one general and true return for each Senatorial and Representative District herein specified, and make, execute and deliver certificates of election in the manner prescribed by law. *Return Judges.* *Returns.*

SEC. 309. That in case a special election shall be ordered to fill a vacancy in a Senatorial district, the Judges from the wards comprising such district shall meet in their respective wards, in accordance with existing laws and the provisions of this Act, and elect Return Judges to deliver returns to be filed in the office of the Prothonotary of the Court of Common Pleas, and at the proper time meet at the State House, in said city, to cast up the returns and give certificates of election in the manner prescribed by law. *Special elections to fill vacancies.*

SEC. 310. That in case a special election shall be ordered to fill a vacancy in a Representative district, the Judges of the several election divisions composing said district shall meet at twelve o'clock, M., on the day following said elec- *Special elections.*

---

308. Act of April 22, 1858, Sec. 5, P. L. 466.
309. Ibid. Sec. 6, P. L. 466.
310. Ibid. Sec. 6, P. L. 466.

tion, at a place in said district designated by the Sheriff in his proclamation, there to cast up the returns of the divisions aforesaid, and under their hands and seals execute a certificate of election, and appoint one of their number to convey the same to the Prothonotary's office, in said city, to be recorded according to law, within two days of the time on which such election shall be held.

An Act to authorize the Controllers of the First School District of Pennsylvania to sell certain Real Estate.

Sale of Munroe School House authorized.

SEC. 311. That the Controllers of the Public Schools of the first school district of the State of Pennsylvania are hereby authorized to sell either at public or private sale, for a sum not less than fifteen thousand dollars, the lot of ground upon which the Monroe School with its appurtenances stands, situate on the south side of Buttonwood street and east of Eleventh street, in the Fourteenth Ward, in the city of Philadelphia, containing in front on said Buttonwood street eighty feet, and extending in length or depth to Pleasant street, at right angles with Buttonwood street, one hundred and fifty-nine feet eleven and five-eighths of an inch; and the said Controllers of said first district are hereby directed, with the proceeds of said sale to build within said Fourteenth Ward, in the same manner and for like purposes, as is now used and employed in said Monroe School House.

Sinkingfund not to receive the proceeds.

SEC. 312. That the proceeds of sale of said lot of ground now occupied by the said Monroe School House shall be appropriated as heretofore directed, and the same shall not merge or become invested in the sinking fund of the said city of Philadelphia, as is now by law directed, when the sale of any real estate of said city as proposed by the Act of the 2d of February, 1854, entitled "An Act to consolidate the city of Philadelphia," and several supplements hereto.

SESSION OF 1862.

An Act relating to advertising claims in the City of Philadelphia.

Four sales in each year for municipal charges.

SEC. 313. That so much of the fifth section of the Act of the ninth day of April, A. D 1861, as provides that in all cases of registered taxes, municipal claims, assessments for removing nuisances, or other charge by the city assessed on real estate, the advertising required before suit brought shall be in two newspapers, once a week for six weeks, with

311. Act of May 1, 1861, Sec. 1, P. L. 631.
312. Ibid. Sec. 2, P. L. 632.
313. Act of Jan. 31, 1862, Sec. 1, P. L. 9.

such brevity of description that the charge therefor shall not exceed one dollar and fifty cents for each property, and no sales shall take place for any such claims, taxes or assessments, except on the second Mondays of May and November be, and the same is hereby repealed; and that from and after the passage of this Act no sales shall take place for any such claims, taxes or assessments, except on the first Mondays in April, July, October and January.

SEC. 314. That all public advertisements for the city of Philadelphia, whether relating to the city departments or county officers, shall be inserted in not more than three public newspapers, nor excepting notice of municipal claims, more than three times in each, nor shall there be paid for such advertising any greater rates than those advertised in such papers to be paid by citizens, and all laws or parts of laws conflicting herewith be and the same are hereby repealed.(*bb*) **Public advertising.**

An Act to reduce the rate of Payment for Advertising Delinquent Tax-Payers and the Collection of Taxes in the City of Philadelphia.

SEC. 315. *That from and after January 1st, one thousand eight hundred and sixty-three, the charge for advertising delinquent tax-payers of the city of Philadelphia shall not exceed fifteen cents for all advertising of each name in any one Ward, which shall be payable by the person or persons liable for the tax; nor shall the same be inserted in more than two newspapers; and if the name of any person shall be so advertised, after having paid their tax, the Receiver shall pay the expenses thereof. **Reduction of the charge for advertising delinquent tax payers.**

SEC. 316. It shall be the duty of the mercantile appraisers of the city of Philadelphia, in making their returns of mercantile assessments to the Receiver of Taxes of said city, to make the said returns on or before the first day of April, one thousand eight hundred and sixty-two, and each and every year thereafter, and the said Receiver be and he is hereby directed and authorized in and for the collection of this and State taxes, to make under oath weekly returns thereof to the State Treasurer any and all delinquents of mercantile taxes, to be proceeded against by said Receiver in the same manner and within the time prescribed by existing laws, under a penalty of fifty dollars for any neglect by said Receiver, and the said Receiver shall be allowed and shall receive for the collection of said taxes the compensation now allowed by law, any act or acts hereby altered or supplied, or that are inconsistent herewith, be and the same are hereby repealed.(*cc*)

---

314. Act of Jan. 31, 1862, Sec. 2, P L. 9.
315. Act of March 22, 1862, Sec. 1, P. L. 152.
316. Act of March 22, 1862, Sec. 2, P. L. 152.

(*bb*) This section seems to enact nothing new. It has the same legal effect as the 13th section of the Act of April 21, 1855. (Ante 255.)

(*cc*) This section was repealed by act approved April 11, 1862. (P. Laws 482.)

CONGRESSIONAL DISTRICTS.

SEC. 317. That for the purpose of electing Representatives of the people of Pennsylvania, to serve in the House of Representatives, in the Congress of the United States, this State shall be divided into twenty-four districts, as follows:

I. Second, Third, Fourth, Fifth, Sixth, and Eleventh wards in the city of Philadelphia.

II. First, Seventh, Eighth, Ninth, and Tenth wards in the city of Philadelphia.

III. Twelfth, Thirteenth, Sixteenth, Eighteenth, and Nineteenth wards in the city of Philadelphia.

IV. Fourteenth, Fifteenth, Twentieth, Twenty-first, and Twenty-fourth wards in the city of Philadelphia.

V. Twenty-second, Twenty-third, and Twenty-fifth wards in the city of Philadelpha, and the county of Bucks.

An Act to grant certain rights to the Market Companies of the City of Philadelphia.

SEC. 318. That the several market companies in the city of Philadelphia shall have the same privileges upon the pavements in front of their market buildings, for exhibiting and disposing of produce, as is allowed by the city authorities to owners and tenants of other property for similar purposes.

An Act explanatory of certain Acts relative to the Inspectors of Buildings in the City of Philadelphia.

SEC. 319. That it is the true intent and meaning of section sixth of an Act passed the seventh day of May, Anno Domini one thousand eight hundred and fifty-five, entitled "An Act to provide for the regulation and inspection of Buildings," and of section first of a supplement thereto passed the eleventh day of April, one thousand eight hundred and fifty-six, entitled "An Act to provide for the better regulation of buildings in the city of Philadelphia," and of the first section of a further supplement thereto passed the twentieth day of May, one thousand eight hundred and fifty-seven, entitled "An Act in relation to party walls," that whenever the said Inspectors in settlement of their accounts pursuant to said last Act herein above mentioned, may or shall have filed a full statement of their receipts and expenditures for any year, and such account, after having been duly audited and found correct, shows that the amount of all their receipts as such Building

---

317. Act of April 10, 1862, Sec. 1, P. L. 405.
318. Act of Feb. 26, 1862, Sec. 1, P. L. 54.
319. Act of April 5, 1862, Sec. 1, P. L. 271.

Inspectors is less than the amount of their salaries, together with the clerk hire and all other necessary expenditures during said year, it shall be the duty of the city of Philadelphia to pay to said Building Inspectors the amount of such deficit so appearing by said accounts.

An Act in regard to Municipal Claims in the City of Philadelphia.

SEC. 320. That whenever a claim shall be filed in the name of the city of Philadelphia, for any charge or assessment for curbing, paving, grading, laying of water-pipes, or any other municipal debt or demand whatever, it shall be lawful for the person against whom or whose land said claim is filed, or who is entitled to take defence thereto, to give notice, in writing, to the counsel of record or person, if any, for whose use the same is filed, or if there be no such counsel or person, to the Solicitor for said city, requiring him to issue a writ of *scire facias* thereon to the next monthly return day, which shall be at least fifteen days from the date of said notice; and if no such writ be issued, the Court, in which said claim is filed, may and shall, on motion and due proof of such notice, strike said claim from the record. Writ of *scire facias* to issue in cases of certain municipal claims.

SEC. 321. That any person entitled to take defence to said claim may, at any time after the same is filed, pay into Court the amount thereof, with a sum sufficient to cover interest and costs, to abide the event of any proceedings thereon; and thereupon said claim shall cease to be a lien upon any land, and shall be stricken from the judgment index. Claims may be paid into court to abide result of proceedings.

An Act to confirm the Revised Grades and Survey Regulations as per Plan number 44, in the Eleventh Survey District in the City of Philadelphia.

SEC. 322. That the Plan number forty-four, now on file in the office of the Department of Surveys of the City of Philadelphia, being a plan of revision of survey and grades at Margaret and Filbert streets, and streets adjacent thereto, in the Twenty-fourth Ward of the said city, as ordered by Councils of the city of Philadelphia, and approved by the Board of Surveyors of the said city, March twenty-fifth, one thousand eight hundred and sixty-one, be and the same is hereby confirmed, and all the streets, street lines, heights and grades marked thereon established. Plan of a certain survey confirmed.

SEC. 323. That any law, or part of any law heretofore passed, that is inconsistent with the foregoing section, be and the same is hereby repealed. Repeal.

---

320. Act of Feb. 21, 1862, Sec. 1, P. L. 44.
321. Ibid. Sec. 2, P L. 45.
322. Act of March 4, 1862, Sec. 1, P. L. 79.
323. Ibid. Sec. 2, P. L. 80.

TAX RATE.

SEC. 324. That if the Councils of the city of Philadelphia, before or on the second stated meeting in December in each and every year, shall fail to levy and fix the rate of taxes for the ensuing year, the tax rate of the preceding year shall be continued as the rate for the ensuing year; and it shall be the duty of the City Commissioners to proceed at once to make out the tax duplicate for the ensuing year at said rates, so that the Receiver of Taxes shall be able to collect the taxes on the first Monday of February of the said year.

An Act relating to certain Records of the City of Philadelphia.

Certain records transferred to the department of surveys.

SEC. 325. That the books now in the office of the Recorder of Deeds for the county of Philadelphia, containing surveyors' returns, and descriptions of lots and tracts of land in the city and county of Philadelphia, be transferred to the office of the Department of Surveys of said city; and that it shall be lawful for the Chief Engineer and Surveyer of the city of Philadelphia to designate and cause to be copied, by an officer of his department, in a book or books, such original warrants, return of surveys, and descriptions of lots and tracts of land, in and for the city and county of Philadelphia, which may be in the Surveyor-General's office at Harrisburg, as may, in his opinion, be necessary and useful for the correct transaction of the business of the Department of Surveys of the said city; and when the latter shall have been certified by the Surveyor-General to be correct, such copies shall be of the same authority as evidence, as other records of said Department of Surveys.

Copies to be made and certified by the surveyor general.

Records of plans of streets, roads, &c., to be copied.

SEC. 326. That it shall be also lawful for the said Chief Engineer and Surveyor to procure from the office of the Clerk of Quarter Sessions of the county of Philadelphia, all detached plans of streets, roads and plots of any part of said city, and cause to be copied such other as may be parts of the records of said office, as he may designate to be necessary and useful in the said Department of Surveys; and the said Chief Engineer and Surveyor shall also cause to be copied the records which may show when the streets and roads of said city were opened, and the courses and widths thereof.

SEC. 327. That it shall be lawful for the Councils of the

324. Act of March 4, 1862, Sec. 1, P. L. 90.
325. Act of March 8, 1862, Sec. 1, P. L. 97.
326. Ibid. Sec. 2, P. L. 97.
327. Ibid. Sec. 3, P. L. 97.

city of Philadelphia, by ordinance, to cause to be made, under the direction of the Chief Engineer and Surveyor of said city, plots of ground owned by all persons in the several wards of said city, in sections, from time to time, and to make provisions for having the future changes in the ownership note thereon, and placing copies thereof in the office of the City Commissioners, to aid them in the assessment of the taxes.

Councils authorized to have certain plots made, &c.

A Supplement to An Act relating to certain Records.

SEC. 328. That the copying of the records in the Land Office provided by the ninth resolution of the joint resolution relative to the State Library and other purposes approved April sixteenth, one thousand eight hundred and thirty-eight, which have not already been so copied, shall be performed by the officer contemplated by the first section of the act to which this is a supplement, the Chief Engineer and Surveyor of the city of Philadelphia shall within thirty days after the passage of this act appoint by and with the advice and consent of the Select Council, a competent person who shall perform the service provided by the act, entitled "An Act relating to certain records of the city of Philadelphia, approved March eighth one thousand eight hundred and sixty-two," and the Councils of said city shall by ordinance determine the salary and prescribe the duties of said office.

An Act to provide for the appointment of Fence Viewers of the City of Philadelphia.

Preamble.

WHEREAS, The act of Consolidation of the city of Philadelphia, passed February two, one thousand eight hundred and fifty-four, had made no provisions for fence viewers, which prior to said act was vested in township and borough auditors:

And whereas, The office of township and borough auditors became extinct by the said act of consolidation, leaving parties without redress in case of insufficiency of partition fences; therefore

SEC. 329. That from and after the passage of this act the Board of Surveyors and Regulators of the city of Philadelphia shall, in addition to the duties now imposed upon them, perform the duties hereinafter prescribed as fence viewers; that in addition to the oath now prescribed to be taken by the said Surveyors and Regulators, they shall be sworn or affirmed to discharge their duties as such viewers, faithfully and impartially.

The board of surveyors and regulators to discharge the duties of fence viewers.

SEC. 330. That on application made to the said Board of

---

328. Act of March 27, 1862, Sec. 1, P. L. 188.
329. Act of March 11, 1862, Sec. 1, P. L. 109.
330. Ibid. Sec. 2, P. L. 109.

Their duties. Surveyor and Regulators, the president shall, at the first meeting of said Board thereafter, appoint three members thereof, who shall within five days thereafter proceed to view and examine any line or partition fence, and shall make out a certificate in writing, setting forth whether, in their opinion, the fence, if one has been already built, is lawful or otherwise; and if not lawful, or if no fence is built upon said line, then stating what proportion of costs, repairing the old or building a new fence, should be borne by each party; and in each case they shall set forth the sum each party ought to pay to the other, in case he should build or repair the other party's portion of said fence, a copy of which certificate shall be delivered to each of the parties; and they shall also present to the said board, at the next stated meeting thereafter, a report of their proceedings, which report, if approved by said board, after hearing of the parties interested, shall be final and conclusive.

Report to be final when approved.

Proceedings in cases of delinquents.

SEC. 331. That if the party who shall be delinquent in making or repairing any fence, shall not within ten days after the report shall have been approved by the said board, proceed to repair or build the said fence, and complete the same in a reasonable time, it shall be lawful for the parties aggrieved, to repair or build said fence, and he may bring suit before any alderman against the delinquent party, and recover as in other actions for work and labor done, and service performed and materials found, and either party may appeal from the decision of the alderman as in other cases.

Appeal from alderman's decisions.

Material and height of partition fence regulated.

SEC. 332. That all partition fences dividing enclosed lands within the rural districts of the said city of Philadelphia, shall be substantially made, at least four feet six inches high, and of sufficient rails or logs, the bottom rail or log to be not more than eight inches above the ground; and in built up portions of said city, a tight board or pallisade the fence, substantially built, at least six feet high; and in either case, the said viewers and Board of Surveyors and Regulators shall have power to designate the kind of fence to be built: *Provided*, The cost in the rural districts shall not exceed twelve cents per lineal foot, and in the built up portions of said city, not exceeding twenty-five cents per lineal foot.

Cost.

Cases where buildings are part of partition fences relative to.

SEC. 333. That in all cases where a building shall be a part of such party fence, the owner of the ground on which such building is erected, shall be allowed for so much of said building as forms part of the partition, as part of his share of the whole fence, in proportion to the cost of the whole; and in case the parties shall agree to divide any partition fence between them, such agreement, setting forth the kind

Agreement between par-

331. Act of March 11, 1862, Sec. 3, P. L. 109.
332. Ibid. Sec. 4, P. L. 110.
333. Ibid. Sec. 5, P. L. 110.

of fence, and what portion of the same each party shall make and keep in repair, shall be filed in the office of the Board of Surveyors and Regulators, to be there kept as a public record. ties to be filed.

SEC. 334. That all laws applying to fence viewers or partition fences in the city of Philadelphia, as are hereby altered, amended or supplied, are hereby repealed. Repealed.

SEC. 335. The Board of Surveyors and Regulators of the city of Philadelphia shall receive no compensation for the services required to be performed by them by the provisions of this act. No compensation allowed.

An Act to extend Fifteenth and Green streets in the City of Philadelphia.

SEC. 336. That it shall be the duty of the Court of Common Pleas of the city of Philadelphia within one month from the passage of this Act, to appoint Commissioners whose duty it shall be to proceed to view and lay out Fifteenth street from Carpenter street south to Reed street. said extension to be made, and damages to be assessed, and paid as it is provided by existing laws.

SEC. 337. That it shall be the duty of the Court of Common Pleas of the City of Philadelphia within one month from the passage of this act to appoint three Commissioners whose duty it shall be to proceed to view and lay out Green street in the Twenty-second Ward, from Carpenter street to Wissahickon avenue or Park street in said ward, said extension to be made, and damages to be assessed and paid as is provided by existing laws, and said Green street from Johnson to Wissahickon avenue or Park street to be put in good travelling order by the Highway Department immediately upon the confirmation of the report of said Commissioners.

An Act creating two additional Assessors for the First and Twenty-second Wards in the City of Philadelphia.

SEC. 338. That Philip H. Khlose and Patrick Fox, be and they are hereby appointed additional assessors for all that part of the First Ward, west of Passyunk road, and north of Mifflin street, including the west side of Passyunk and north side of said Mifflin street, to serve until the next annual election; and that Gideon Keyser and William Stallman, be and they are hereby appointed additional assessors for all that part of the Twenty-second Ward, Additional assessors appointed.

---

334. Act of March 11, 1862, Sec. 6, P. L. 110.
335. Ibid. Sec. 7, P. L. 110.
336. Act of April 11, 1862, Sec. 1, P. L. 498.
337. Ibid Sec. 2, P. L. 499.
338. Act of March 13, 1862, Sec. 1, P. L. 113.

lying within the boundaries of the first, second, third and fourth precincts of said ward, to serve until the next annual election.

Election of assessors for the First ward.

SEC. 339. That at the next annual election the qualified voters of said city shall elect four assessors, in lieu of the two now provided for by law, two of whom shall be for the eastern district, which shall be composed of that portion of said ward lying east of Passyunk road and south of said Mifflin street; and two of whom shall be for that portion of said ward as designated in the first section of this act; and said assessors shall be elected by general ticket, as other ward officers are now elected in said ward.

Election of assessors for the Twenty-second ward.

SEC. 340. That at the next annual election the qualified voters of the said Twenty-second Ward shall elect four assessors, in lieu of the two now provided for by law, two of whom shall be for the fifth, sixth, seventh and eighth precincts, and two of whom shall be for that portion of said ward as designated in the first section of this act; and said assessors shall be elected by general ticket, as other ward officers are now elected in said First and Twenty-second Wards.

An Act to authorize the arrest of Professional Thieves, Burglars, etc., in the City of Philadelphia.

The mayor or police magistrate authorized to commit professional thieves, &c.

SEC, 341. That from and after the passage of this act, if any person shall be charged on oath or affirmation before the Mayor or Police Magistrate of the central station of the city of Philadelphia, with being a professional thief, burglar or pickpocket, and who shall have been arrested by the police authorities at any steamboat landing, railroad depot, church, banking institution, broker's office, place of public amusement, auction room, store or crowded thoroughfare in the city of Philadelphia, and if it shall be proven to the satisfaction of the said Mayor or Police Magistrate, appointed by the Mayor for the central station, by sufficient testimony, that he or she was frequenting or attending such place or places for an unlawful purpose, he or she shall be committed by the said Mayor or said Police Magistrate to the jail of the county of Philadelphia, for a term not exceeding ninety days, there to be kept at hard labor, or in the discretion of the said Mayor or Police Magistrate of said central station, he or she shall be required to enter security for his or her good behavior for a period not exceeding one year.

Imprisonment.

Security.

Parties may apply to court for writ of *habeas corpus*.

SEC. 342 That any person who may or shall feel aggrieved at any such act, judgment or determination of the said Mayor or Police Magistrate of said central station, in and concerning the execution of this act, may apply to any

339. Act of March 13, 1862, Sec. 2, P. L. 113.
340. Ibid. Sec. 3, P. L. 113.
341. Ibid. Sec. 4, P. L. 115.

Judge of the Court of Quarter Sessions for a writ of *habeas corpus*, and upon return thereof, there shall be a re-hearing of the evidence, and the Judge may either discharge, modify or confirm the commitment.

An Act to change the width of York street, in the City of Philadelphia.

SEC. 343. That so much of York street as lies between Richmond street and the Aramingo canal, in the Nineteenth Ward, be changed to the width of fifty feet, and to conform to the width of the bridge over said canal; and all acts of Assembly contrary to this act, be and the same are hereby repealed.

An Act for the opening of Evangelist street, in the Third Ward of the City of Philadelphia.

SEC. 344. That Evangelist street, as now laid out and built upon, thirty-eight feet ten inches in width, at the distance of one hundred and thirty feet north from the north side of Catharine street, in the Third Ward of the city of Philadelphia, be continued and opened from the point where the same is now built upon and improved with permanent brick messuages, a further distance of about ninety feet, to the east line of Eighth street; and that the Court of Quarter Sessions of the city of Philadelphia, shall, upon application being made to them, appoint a jury of view to assess the damages occasioned by said opening, which jury shall, immediately after the appointment, assess said damages, and certify the same to the Court of Quarter Sessions aforesaid.

An Act to promote the efficiency of the Militia of the City of Philadelphia.

Military tax in the city of Philadelphia not to be paid into state treasury.

SEC. 345. That so much of the twenty-eighth section of an act to create a loan, and to provide for arming the State, approved the fifteenth day of May, Anno Domini one thousand eight hundred and sixty-one, as provides that the military tax imposed by the laws of this Commonwealth, should be collected and paid into the treasury of the Common wealth, be and the same is hereby repealed, so far as the city of Philadelphia is concerned; that the military tax, or commutation, payable by every person in said city, not exempt by law, shall be fifty cents, to be assessed, collected, drawn for and disbursed, as provided by an act for the regulation of the militia of this Commonwealth, approved the

How to be assessed, collected, disbursed, &c.

---

342. Act of March 13, 1862, Sec. 2, P. L. 116.
343. Act of March 22, 1863, Sec. 1, P. L. 163.
344. Act of April 10, 1862, Sec. 1, P. L. 373.
345. Act of April 11, 1862, Sec. 1, P. L. 433.

Military fund for benefit of the city.

twenty-first day of April, Anno Domini one thousand eight hundred and fifty-eight, and shall be paid into the said city treasury, as a military fund, for the benefit of the uniformed militia of said city, whether organized under general or special laws.

Appropriations by councils.

SEC. 346. The Councils of said city of Philadelphia shall have the authority, from time to time, as the necessities and efficiency of said militia, within said city, shall require, and in anticipation of the said tax, so to be assessed and collected, to appropriate out of the funds of said city, such sums as may be requisite for that purpose; and when any appropriation, as aforesaid, shall be made, it shall be drawn from the city treasury, upon the order of the proper board of officers of said militia: *Provided*, That no company shall receive a larger proportion of said fund than it would be entitled to according to the number of its uniformed members.

How to be drawn.

Proviso.

Contributing members of organized companies exempt from tax.

SEC. 347. That whenever any person in said city, who shall be subject to said military tax, shall prefer to become a contributing member of any regularly organized company, as aforesaid, he shall be exempt from said tax, upon the payment of the sum of two dollars to said company, for military purposes; and the receipt therefor, of the captain of said company, shall be a sufficient discharge to said contributing member, from the payment of said tax, for the corresponding year: *Provided however*, That each company, as aforesaid, shall yearly, or oftener, if required, make a written return to the city treasurer, and to the board of officers of the regiment to which such company is attached, of the amount of contributions so received, and the names of contributing members, which amount, so received, shall be deducted from the appropriation such company would be entitled to receive from the military fund: *And provided further*, That if the income from contributing members of any company, shall exceed the sum of five hundred dollars, in any one year, the excess shall be paid into the general fund of the regiment to which such company is attached.

Companies to make yearly returns to city treasurer.

Proviso.

An Act for the opening of Clearfield street from Amber, late Waterloo, street, to Frankford street, in the Twenty-Fifth Ward of the City of Philadelphia.

SEC. 348. That the Commissioners of Highways of the city of Philadelphia shall, within thirty days after the passage of this act, proceed and open, or cause to be opened, Clearfield street from Amber, late Waterloo, street, to Frankford road, in the Twenty-fifth Ward of the city of Philadelphia, on parallel lines with the said Clearfield street, as it is now opened east of the said Amber street.

---

346. Act of April 11, 1862, Sec. 2, P. L. 433.
347. Ibid. Sec. 3, P. L. 433.
348. Ibid. Sec. 1, P. L. 447.

An Act to vacate Culvert street, in the Twenty-third Ward of the city of Philadelphia.

SEC. 349. That Culvert street, in the Twenty-third ward of the city of Philadelphia, as laid down on the plan of said city, and not opened, be and the same is hereby vacated.

Supplement to an Act creating two additional Assessors for the First and Twenty-second Wards of the City of Philadelphia.

SEC. 350. That at the first and every other annual election, held in pursuance of an act entitled "A supplement to an act creating two additional assessors for the First and Twenty-second wards in the city of Philadelphia," each of the qualified voters of the said First ward shall be entitled to vote for two persons for the office of assessor, and the four persons receiving the highest number of votes, shall be severally declared elected to fill said office; and that so much of said supplement as is inconsistent herewith, be and the same is hereby repealed, so far as relates to said First ward.

An Act relating to certain Children's Homes.

SEC. 351. That it shall and may be lawful for any judge, mayor, alderman or justice of the peace of the city of Philadelphia, to indenture, bind or commit, to the St. John's Orphan Asylum, or the St. Vincent's Home, located in the city of Philadelphia, orphan, destitute, abandoned, or vagrant children.

An Act confirming the revised Grade and Survey Regulations of the first and second sections of the survey of West Philadelphia.

SEC. 352. That plans numbers forty-two and forty-three, being the revised grade regulations of the first and second sections of the survey of West Philadelphia, approved by the board of survey of the city of Philadelphia, on the seventeenth day of February, Anno Domini eighteen hundred and sixty-two, and now on file in the office of the department of surveys of said city, be and the same are hereby confirmed; and all the heights, grades, and distances, and street and curb lines, marked on said plans, are hereby fixed and established.

---

349. Act of April 11, 1862, Sec. 1, P. L. 485.
350. Ibid. Sec. 1, P. L. 495.
351. Act of April 16, 1862, Sec. 1, P. L. 538.
352. Act of April 17, 1862, Sec. 1, P. L. 539.

An Act to repeal so much of the 30th section of an Act entitled "A Supplement to the Act Consolidating the City of Philadelphia," passed April 21st, 1855, as relates to the widening of Fifth street, northward of York street, in said city.

SEC. 353. That so much of section thirty of an act entitled "A supplement to the act consolidating the city of Philadelphia," passed the twenty-first day of April, Anno Domini one thousand eight hundred and fifty-five, as relates to the widening of Fifth street, northward of York street, be and the same is hereby repealed; and that Fifth street, northward from York street, be shall opened of the same width as laid out in the original plan of the city of Philadelphia.

SESSION OF 1863.

A Supplement to an Act entitled "An Act to extend Fifteenth and Green streets, in the city of Philadelphia," approved the 11th day of April, A. D., 1862.

SEC. 354. That the Commissioners appointed under the second section of the act, to which this is a supplement, shall receive for their services the sum of five dollars each; and said Commissioners shall have power to employ a competent surveyor to examine and survey the said Green street so laid out, and to make such drawings and plans as shall be necessary: *Provided*, The expenses shall not exceed one hundred dollars, and the City Commissioners shall draw an order for the amount upon the City Treasurer, when certified to by a majority of the said Commissioners.

An Act to exempt from taxation the Philadelphia City Institute.

SEC. 355. That the real estate and library of the Philadelphia City Institute, situate at the northeast corner of Chestnut and Eighteenth streets, in the City of Philadelphia, be and the same is hereby exempted from taxation, except State tax.

---

353. Act of April 26, 1862, Sec. 1, P. L. 542.
354. Act of Feb. 14, 1863, Sec. 1, P. L. 65.
355. Act of March 4, 1863, Sec. 1, P. L. 101.

An Act relative to the American Mechanics' Hall Association of the City of Philadelphia.

SEC. 356. That the property situated at the northeast corner of Fourth and George streets, in the City of Philadelphia, belonging to the order of the United American Mechanics, known and organized as the American Mechanics' Hall Association of the City of Philadelphia, be and is hereby exempted from taxation: *Provided*, That nothing herein contained shall exempt said property from taxation for State purposes.

A further Supplement to the Act incorporating the City of Philadelphia, relative to certain offices.

SEC. 357. That it shall not be lawful for any member of either branch of the Legislature to hold or exercise the office of councilman in the said city, after the first of January next.

SEC 358. No member of council of said city shall be eligible to any office, employment or agency, directly, or indirectly, chosen by councils, or either branch of them, during the term for which he shall have been elected to councils.

SEC. 359. Whenever, by the requirements of any law, a particular residence is a necessary qualification for the election or appointment of any officer, a removal from such residence shall operate as a forfeiture of the office.

An Act providing for a free Bridge over the river Schuylkill, at Penrose Ferry.

SEC. 360. That the City of Philadelphia be and hereby is authorized and empowered to purchase all the bridge property, and the contiguous land appurtenant thereto, now owned and held by the Penrose Ferry Bridge Company, and erected by them in pursuance of the provisions of an act to authorize the Governor to incorporate a company to construct a bridge over the river Schuylkill, at Penrose Ferry, approved April ninth, one thousand eight hundred and fifty-four, together with the franchises of said company, and the said company is authorized and empowered to make a conveyance of all its said property, and franchises, to the said city, and upon the said conveyance being duly made

356. Act of March 10, 1863, Sec. 1, P. L. 119.
357. Act of March 18, 1863, Sec. 1, P. L. 143.
358. Ibid. Sec. 2, P. L. 143.
359. Ibid. Sec. 3, P. L. 143.
360. Ibid. Sec. 1, P. L. 153.

and completed, the said bridge shall be thenceforth free to the use of all travel, without charge or toll therefor, and the directors of said company, or others having the authority of a majority of the stockholders, are hereby authorized to make said conveyance for a sum approved by the said stockholders, and the claims of said stockholders shall be upon the consideration money paid by the city of Philadelphia, and not otherwise: and upon execution and delivery of a deed for said premises and franchises, the title thereto shall vest in the said city of Philadelphia, her successors and assigns, as fully, completely and absolutely, as the same were held or owned by the said Penrose Ferry Bridge Company.

An Act vacating Cherry street, in the Twenty-fourth Ward of the City of Philadelphia.

SEC. 361. That Cherry street, in the Twenty-fourth Ward of the city of Philadelphia, extending from the Schuylkill river to Lehman or Twenty-first street, be and the same is hereby vacated, and the title to the soil, over which the same is laid, is hereby vested in the owners of the property fronting on each side of said vacated street, to the middle thereof.

An Act to exempt from taxation the Moyamensing Institute.

SEC. 362. That the real estate and library of the Moyamensing Institute, of the city of Philadelphia, situate at the southeast corner of Eleventh and Catherine streets, of the said city, be and the same is hereby exempted from taxation, except for State purposes.

An Act relative to the school house and property of the Sisters of the Holy Cross, in the City of Philadelphia.

SEC. 363. That the school-house and property of the Sisters of the Holy Cross, in the city of Philadelphia, being number two hundred and forty-four, north Fourth street, be and the same is hereby exempted from all taxation, except taxes for State purposes.

An Act relative to the Woman's Hospital of Philadelphia.

SEC. 364. That the property, now owned and occupied by the Woman's Hospital, of Philadelphia, be and the same is hereby released and freed from the payment of municipal taxes, whilst owned and occupied by said corporation as a hospital for the treatment of diseases of women and children.

---

361. Act of March 19, 1863, Sec. 1, P. L. 169.
362. Act of April 1, 1863, Sec. 1, P. L. 193.
363. Ibid. Sec. 1, P. L. 199.
364. Ibid. Sec. 1, P. L. 201.

An Act relative to the Roxborough Lyceum.

SEC. 365. That the property of the Roxborough Lyceum, situate in the Twenty-first ward of the city of Philadelphia, be and the same is hereby exempted from the payment of all municipal taxes.

An Act to exempt from taxation the Spring Garden and Moyamensing Literary Institutes.

SEC. 366. That the real estate and library of the Spring Garden Institute, situate on the northeast corner of Broad and Spring Garden streets, and the Moyamensing Literary Institute, in the city of Philadelphia, be and the same are hereby exempted from taxation, except State tax.

An Act to authorize the Commissioners of the City and County of Philadelphia to draw their warrant for certain services in the Register of Will's office.

SEC. 367. That the Commissioners of the city and county of Philadelphia be and they are hereby authorized and required to draw their warrant upon the treasurer of said city and county, for thirteen hundred and thirteen dollars and seventy-five cents, in favor of J. A. Irwin and Edward Carrigan, for compiling, copying and perfecting the indices of wills and administrations in the Register of Wills' office, upon an order of the Court of Common Pleas, in pursuance of an Act of Assembly.

An Act relative to the house and grounds of the Sisters of Saint Joseph at Chestnut Hill, in the Twenty-second Ward of the City of Philadelphia.

SEC. 368. That the house and grounds of the Sisters of Saint Joseph, situated at Chestnut Hill, in the Twenty-second ward in the city of Philadelphia, be and the same are hereby exempted from all taxation, except taxes for state purposes.

An Act to vacate a portion of Church street in the Twenty-fourth Ward of the City of Philadelphia.

SEC. 369. That Church street, between Forty-first and Forty-second street, in the Twenty-fourth ward of the city of Philadelphia, as laid down on the plan of said city, and not opened, be and the same is hereby vacated.

---

365. Act of April 1, 1863, Sec. 1, P. L. 202.
366. Ibid. Sec. 1, P. L. 224.
367. Ibid. Sec. 1, P. L. 242.
368. Act of April 3, 1863, Sec. 1, P. L. 269.
369. Act of April 4, 1863, Sec. 1, P. L. 294.

An Act to vacate a part of Sixty-second street in the Twenty-fourth Ward of the City of Philadelphia.

SEC. 370. That that part of Sixty-second street, in the Twenty-fourth ward of the City of Philadelphia, which runs westwardly from the Darby Plank Road to the Delaware county line, be and the same is hereby vacated.

An Act relative to the property of the Orphans' Home and Asylum for the aged and infirm of the Evangelical Lutheran Church.

SEC. 371. That the property belonging to the Orphans' Home and Asylum for the aged and infirm of the Evangelical Lutheran Church, situate in the Twenty-second ward, Philadelphia, shall be exempt henceforth and hereafter, from all taxes, except state tax.

An Act relative to the American Protestant Hall and Library Association of the City and County of Philad'a.

SEC. 372. That the real estate used, occupied and owned by the American Protestant Hall and Library Association of the city and county of Philadelphia, situate on the north side of Locust street, east of Fifteenth street in the city of Philadelphia, be and the same is hereby exempt from the payment of all taxes, except state taxes, so long as the same shall be owned and used by the said association.

An Act to exempt the property of the Franklin Institute from taxation.

SEC. 373. That the hall of the Franklin Institute, of the State of Pennsylvania, for the promotion of the mechanic arts, and the lot of ground on which the same is erected, situate in the city of Philadelphia, be and the same are hereby exempted from taxation, for any purpose whatever, except for state tax.

A further Supplement to an Act, entitled "An Act to extend the width of Chatham street, and open a part of Tioga street, in the City of Philadelphia," approved the 26th day of April, Anno Domini 1855.

SEC. 374. That the width of Berks street, lately called Chatham street, between Sixth and Broad street, in the city of Philadelphia, be and the same is hereby fixed at fifty

370. Act of April 4, 1863, Sec. 1, P. L. 297.
371. Ibid. Sec. 1, P. L. 299.
372. Act of April 11, 1863, Sec. 1, P. L. 350.
373. Act of April 14, 1863, Sec. 1, P. L. 449.
374. Act of April 15, 1863, Sec. 1, P. L. 458.

feet; and that so much of an act, approved the third day of April, Anno Domini one thousand eight hundred and sixty, entitled "A supplement to an act to extend the width of Chatham street, and open part of Tioga street, in the city of Philadelphia, approved the twenty-sixth day of April, Anno Domini one thousand eight hundred and fifty-five," as fixes the width of the said Berks street at seventy feet, so far as the same conflicts herewith, be and the same is hereby repealed.

An Act vacating a part of Jones street, in the Ninth Ward of the City of Philadelphia.

SEC. 375. That Jones street, in the Ninth ward of the city of Philadelphia, extending from Fifteenth street, westward two hundred and fourteen feet, be and the same is hereby vacated, and the title to the soil, over which the same is laid, is hereby vested in the owners of the property fronting on each side of said vacated street, to the middle thereof: *Provided*, That this act shall not go into effect, until the consent of all property holders, on so much of said street as is to be vacated by this act, is first had and obtained.

An Act to appoint commissioners to lay out a State Road, in the County of Delaware and City of Philadelphia.

SEC. 376. That Spencer McIlvain, John O. Deshong, John H. Baker, Joseph E. Hinkson, Joseph Taylor, surveyor of Delaware county, and Samuel Gibsons, Robert E. Jones, John Dick, Paschall Lloyd, and Paschall J. Hoopes, of the City of Philadelphia, are hereby appointed commissioners, to view and lay out a state road from a point on a public road, called Hook Road, in the township of Darby, and county of Delaware, at or near land of Jonathan Heacock, deceased, John P. Heacock, and William D. H. Serrill; thence to and over Darby creek, to the most suitable point on the Island road, in the Twenty-fourth Ward of the city of Philadelphia.

Commissioners.

Route.

SEC. 377. That it shall be the duty of said Commissioners, or a majority of them, after taking oath or affirmation before a Justice of the Peace, to perform the duties enjoined upon them by this Act with fidelity and impartiality, to carefully view the ground on which the said road may pass, and lay out and mark the same upon the ground, on the route agreed upon them for the road aforesaid, in such a manner as to enable the supervisors readily to find the same; and for the purpose of fulfilling the duties enjoined in this Act, the

Duties of Commissioners.

---

375. Act of April 15, 1863, Sec. 1, P. L. 481.
376. Ibid. Sec. 1, P. L. 481.
377. Ibid. Sec. 2, P. L. 481.

Compensation of Surveyor, &c.

said Commissioners, or a majority of them, are hereby enjoined to employ a surveyor, at a per diem allowance of not more than three dollars, and two chain carriers, at a per diem allowance not exceeding one dollar and fifty cents each, and one axeman, at a per diem allowance not exceeding one dollar and fifty cents; and the said Commissioners shall receive a per diem allowance, not exceeding two dollars, for each day necessarily employed in the discharge of their duties, enjoined by this Act, which shall be paid, one-half by the treasurer of the county of Delaware, and the other half by the city of Philadelphia.

Drafts.

SEC. 378. That it shall be the duty of the Commissioners, as aforesaid, to make out two separate and accurate drafts of the location of said road, respectively noting the courses and distances as they occur, with such other matters as may serve for explanation; one copy to be deposited in the office of the clerk of the Court of Quarter Sessions, in the respective counties through which the road may pass, and from thenceforth the said road shall be a public highway.

Bridge to be erected over Darby Creek.

Cost of.

Proviso.

SEC. 379. That when the said road shall have been laid out and located, as aforesaid, it shall be the duty of the Commissioners of the County of Delaware and the City Commissioners of the City of Philadelphia to cause to be erected upon the line of said road, a bridge, over Darby creek, with a draw of sufficient capacity to permit the passage of vessels navigating said creek; one-half the cost thereof shall be defrayed by each county; and upon the refusal or neglect of either of said Board of Commissioners of said county and city to perform the duties hereby enjoined, it shall be lawful for either of the Boards of Commissioners aforesaid to cause the said bridge to be erected, and to recover one-half the cost of the same from the city or county neglecting or refusing to perform the duties hereby enjoined: *Provided*, That nothing contained in this Act shall require the Commissioners of the aforesaid counties to commence the building of said draw-bridge before the thirty-first day of December next.

An Act to vacate a portion of Kingsessing avenue, in the Twenty-fourth Ward of the City of Philadelphia.

SEC. 380. That Kingsessing avenue, between Forty-fourth street and a street formerly called Beckett street, in the Twenty-fourth Ward of the city of Philadelphia, as laid down on the plan of said city and not opened, be and the same is hereby vacated; and that Beckett street aforesaid shall be continued westward from Forty-second street to

378. Act of April 15, 1863, Sec. 3, P. L. 481.
379. Ibid. Sec. 4, P. L. 481.
380. Act of April 17, 1863, Sec. 1, P. L. 510.

Forty-fourth street, at right angles to said Forty-second street, as laid out on a certain plan and dedication to public use of said Beckett street, dated the twenty-fifth day of March, Anno Domini one thousand eight hundred and fifty-one, and recorded at Philadelphia, in Deed Book G. W. C., number ninety-one, page two hundred and fifty, &c.

An Act creating two additional Assessors for the Twentieth Ward of the City of Philadelphia.

Sec. 381. That the City Commissioners of the city of Philadelphia are hereby authorized and directed to appoint two additional assessors, for all that portion of the Twentieth Ward of said city lying west of Broad street, to serve until the next election of assessors.

Commissioners authorized to appoint two additional Assessors.

Sec. 382. That at the next election of assessors, the qualified voters of the said Twentieth Ward, shall elect four assessors, in lieu of the two now provided by law, two of whom shall be for that portion of the ward lying east of Broad street, and two of whom shall be for that portion of said ward lying west of said Broad street; that each of the qualified voters of the said Twentieth Ward shall be entitled to vote for two persons for the said office of assessor, and the four persons receiving the highest number of votes shall be severally declared elected to fill said office.

Four to be elected at next election.

An Act vacating a part of Mud lane, or Old Montgomery street in the Nineteenth Ward of the City of Philadelphia.

Sec. 383. That so much of Mud lane, or Old Montgomery street, in the Nineteenth Ward of the city of Philadelphia, as lies east of Hancock street, and is not included in, or does not form a part of Columbia avenue, as at present laid out, on the approved plan of that part of the city of Philadelphia, be and the same is hereby vacated; and the title to that part of the soil of the said Mud lane, or Old Montgomery street, hereby vacated, is hereby vested in the owners of the property fronting on each side of said vacated lane, or street, to the middle thereof.

An Act to authorize Woodland street, in the Twenty-fourth Ward of the City of Philadelphia, to be graded, curbed and paved.

Sec. 384. That the city of Philadelphia may, at any time hereafter, grade, curb and pave, or cause to be graded,

381. Act of April 22, 1863, Sec. 1, P. L. 552.
382. Ibid. Sec. 2, P. L. 552.
383. Ibid. Sec. 1, P. L. 553.
384. Act of May 27, 1863, Sec. 1, P. L. 586.

curbed and paved, Woodland street, from the intersection of the same with Market street, in the Twenty-fourth Ward, of the proper width, as laid down on the plan of said city; and it shall be the duty of the Chief Commissioner of Highways of the said city, immediately, to give thirty days' notice of the intention so to grade, curb and pave said street, or any portion thereof, to any plank road, turnpike, or passenger railway company, occupying or using the same portion of said street; and upon the expiration of said notices, shall enter into a contract, with a competent paver or pavers, to do said work, which shall be paid for by warrants drawn by the Chief Commissioner of Highways, duly countersigned by the Controller, on the Treasurer of said city; and the said city shall collect the cost of said curbing and paving, from the owners of property fronting on said street, as provided by law; the said city, before commencing to curb and pave, as aforesaid, shall pay unto the Delaware County Turnpike Road Company the sum of thirty-three hundred and twenty-five dollars, in full consideration for their chartered privilege to collect tolls on said portion of said street; and said company shall not be entitled to demand, or receive, any toll for the use of said street thereafter, or exercise any chartered privilege over the same; and so much of the capital stock of the Delaware County Turnpike Road Company, as was specifically subscribed for making that part of their road, as above mentioned, shall become extinguished upon repayment to the holders thereof, by the company, the par value of such stock; the Philadelphia and Darby Passenger Railway Company shall be required to keep in repair only so much of said street as may be within their tracks; that the city of Philadelphia, before taking possession of that portion of the Darby Turnpike or Plank Road Company, between Thirty-ninth and Forty-first streets, the said city of Philadelphia shall pay, or cause to be paid, to the Treasurer of the said the Darby Turnpike or Plank Road Company, the cost of that portion of said road; the same to be computed at the average of the original cost of the whole of said road.

An Act in relation to the plans of survey of certain streets in the Twenty-fourth Ward, of the City of Philadelphia.

Whereas, A certain tract, or piece of land, commonly known as the Maryland Dam property, lying and being between the Darby road and the Baltimore turnpike, and between Forty-second and Forty-sixth streets, in the Twenty-fourth Ward, of the City of Philadelphia, with certain adjoining smaller strips, in all containing about twenty-five acres, have been recently acquired, with the intention of laying out the same as a park, at the private expense of the owners and of the contributors thereto: *And whereas,* The irregularities of surface and other causes render the said tract of land unsuitable for building purposes, and prevent the streets of the said city from being extended across and through the same, according to the established plan of survey thereof, without great expense to the city: *Therefore, be it enacted,*

SECT. 385. That it shall be lawful for the owners of said tracts of land, not exceeding twenty-five acres in extent, or the majority of them, or any one duly authorized to act in their behalf, within six months after the passage hereof, to file, in the Department of Surveys of said city, a plan of said tract of land, by courses and distances, with a declaration of the period of time it may be intended to keep and maintain the same as a park; and upon the receipt of said plan and declaration, the president of said Board of Survey shall cause said plan to be marked upon the established plan of survey of the proper district, in such manner as shall indicate the outlines and exact situation of the same; whereupon, so much of the said plan of survey of said city, as may be included within the limits of the said tract of land, shall thenceforth be suspended; and no street shall be opened, or continued across, or within the limits of said tract of land, during the period it shall be held and used as a park; as aforesaid, without the consent of the owners thereof; which time may be extended as often as it may expire, by and with the consent of the said owners, or their trustee, and of the Board of Survey, upon a like declaration being so filed: *Provided, however,* That nothing herein contained shall suspend, effect, or alter, the established plan of the Darby road, or Baltimore avenue, or the grades thereof, adjoining said premises, nor shall prevent the City of Philadelphia, at any time, from using any portion of said tract of land, that may be required for the drainage, or sewerage of said ward, according to the established plan of surveys thereof.—July 18, 1863.—P. L. 1113.

A further Supplement to an Act to incorporate the City of Philadelphia.

SEC. 386. That whenever, hereafter, the report of any jury, assessing damages for opening, or widening, of any road, or street, in the City of Philadelphia, shall be finally confirmed by the Court of Quarter Sessions of the said city and county, the sums assessed as damages, against the owners of the properties found to be benefitted by the opening, or widening, of such street, or road, shall be and remain liens on the said properties, against which they are severally assessed, for the space of six months, from the said confirmation of such report; and that it shall be lawful to file, in the office of the Court of Common Pleas, of the City and County of Philadelphia, a claim against the owners of the said several properties, for the amount so assessed, as damages against such property, in the name of the City of Philadelphia, for the use of the persons, in favor of whom said damages shall have been awarded; which claims, so filed, shall continue and have the same effect and lien as municipal claims, when filed, now have, and be recovered by *scire facias,* in the same way and manner as municipal claims are now recoverable, in the said City of Philadelphia.—January 6, 1864.—P. L. 1131.

A further Supplement to an Act to establish a Board of Wardens, for the port of Philadelphia, and for other purposes, approved March twenty-ninth, one thousand eight hundred and three.

SEC. 387. That from and after the passage of this act, no license shall be granted to any person to act as pilot, unless he has served a regular apprenticeship of six years on board a pilot boat.—January 7, 1864.—P. L. 1141.

SESSION OF 1864.

A Further Supplement to an Act passed the thirteenth day of March, one thousand eight hundred and sixty-two, to authorize the arrest of Professional Thieves, Burglars, et cetera, in the City of Philadelphia.

SEC. 388. That the provisions of the first section of an act to authorize the arrest of professional thieves, burglars, et cetera, in the City of Philadelphia, approved March thirteenth, one thousand eight hundred and sixty-two, be and the same are hereby extended to authorize the arrest of professional thieves, burglars, or pickpockets, at any hotel, restaurant, auction sale, in private residence, passenger car, or at any other gathering of people, whether few or many, in the Cities of Philadelphia, Allegheny, Lancaster, Harrisburg and Pittsburg.—March 16, 1864.—P. L. 16.

An Act to vacate Stump lane, in the City of Philadelphia.

SEC. 389. That a certain lane, commonly called Stump lane, from Columbia avenue, west of Fifteenth street, to Turner's lane, in the City of Philadelphia, be and the same is hereby vacated; and the title to the land, over which the same passes, is hereby vested, in fee simple, in the several owners of grounds adjoining, and fronting, on the said lane, respectively; each owner to have, and to take, one-half part to the middle thereof, so far as his respective lot adjoins, and fronts, on the said lane. March 17, 1864.—P. L. 22.

An Act to authorize a change of investment in the City of Philadelphia.

SEC. 390. That the City of Philadelphia shall have power, by deed, to extinguish any of the ground rents devised by James Dutton to the Guardians of the Poor, and to invest the consideration thereof in certificates of the debt of the City of Philadelphia, in trust for the uses and purposes created by said will. March 17, 1864.—P. L. 24.

An Act to change the width of York street in the City of Philadelphia.

SEC. 391. That so much of York street as lies between Edgemont street and the Aramingo canal, in the Nineteenth ward, be changed to the width of fifty feet, and to conform to the width of the bridge over said canal; and all Acts of Assembly contrary to this be and the same are hereby repealed.—March 17, 1864.—P. L. 31.

An Act to vacate a certain fifty feet wide street, in the late village of Holmesburg, now Twenty-third Ward, in the City of Philadelphia.

SEC. 392. That all that certain fifty feet wide street, running from Baker street north-eastward, between land of the estate of Joseph Brown, deceased, and land of George Clark, formerly Paul Crispin's estate, to the Welsh road; thence crossing the said Welsh road, and continuing the same course, through land of John Solly, to Pennypack creek, be and the same is hereby vacated. —March 17, 1864.—P. L. 33.

An Act to repeal certain portions of the Ninth Section of an Act to provide for the Regulation and Inspection of Buildings in the City of Philadelphia, approved May seventh, one thousand eight hundred and fifty-five.

SEC. 393. That so much of the ninth section of the said act as requires the party or division wall to extend above the line of the roof, and the division or separation of wooden cornices, be and the same is hereby repealed, so far as it relates to blocks of not more than two houses, having a side yard to each house: *Provided*, The same be covered with slate, metal, tin, or other incombustible material.—March 17, 1864.—P. L. 37.

A Supplement to an Act incorporating the City of Philadelphia.

Repeal of provision relative to constables.

SEC. 394. That so much of the Act of Consolidation, and the supplements thereto, relative to the term of time for which Constables are elected in the City of Philadelphia, be and the same is hereby repealed.

Official term of, changed.

SEC. 395. And that in lieu of the term of years for which Constables of the various wards, boroughs and townships of the said city are now elected, t hereafter be elected for the term of five years, from and after the expiration of the various terms, to which they have been elected.—March 18, 1864.—P. L. 60.

An Act relating to the occupancy of certain Squares and Highways, in the City of Philadelphia, for the Great Central Fair, in aid of the Sanitary Commission.

SEC. 396. That the Executive Committee of the Great Central Fair, in aid of the Sanitary Commission, to be held in the City of Philadelphia, be and they are hereby authorized to occupy, by temporary frame, or other building, or buildings, so much of any of the public highways, and squares, in the said City of Philadelphia, as may be necessary for the use of the said Fair, the said occupancy to be for as short a period as may be reasonably possible, and every such building to be removed on or before, the fifteenth day of July, one thousand eight hundred and sixty-four, and the said highways, and squares, restored to their former condition, by that day: *Provided*, That the same shall be done under the direction of the Commissioner of City Property of said city.—March 25, 1864.—P. L. 72.

A further Supplement to an Act to incorporate the City of Philadelphia.

SEC. 397. That all that certain part of what is now known as the First ward of the City of Philadelphia, included and contained within the following boundaries, shall hereafter constitute and form the First ward of said city, to wit: beginning at a point on the Passyunk road, where it intersects Wharton street; thence along the south side of the said Wharton street to the river Delaware; thence along the river Delaware, to League island; thence along the southern boundary of said island, so as to include the whole of the same; thence along the back channel to Broad street; thence along the east side of said Broad street to Passyunk road; thence along said Passyunk road to place of beginning.

Boundaries of the First Ward changed.

SEC. 398. All the remaining portions of what is now known as the First ward, and not embraced in the above described boundaries, shall hereafter constitute, and form, a new ward, and shall be known as the Twenty-sixth ward of the City of Philadelphia.

New Ward formed, to be called the Twenty-sixth.

SEC. 399. Each of the above wards shall be entitled to one member of the Select Council, and also to two mem-

Representation of each, in Select and Common Councils, relative to.

bers of the Common Council of said city; at the next annual election, the qualified voters of the said First ward, shall elect one member of Select Council, to serve for three years, from the first day of January, one thousand eight hundred and sixty-five, and the term of the present Select Councilman, of the First ward, shall expire on the first day of January, one thousand eight hundred and sixty-five, and one member of Common Council, who shall serve for two years, from the first of January, next ensuing his election, and shall thereafter elect members of Councils, as is now, or may hereafter be, provided by law. The qualified voters of the Twenty-sixth ward, shall, at the next annual election, elect one member of Select Council, who shall serve for three years, and, also, one member of Common Council, who shall serve for two years, from the first day of January, next ensuing his election, and shall thereafter elect members of Councils, as is now, or may hereafter be, provided by law.

Common Councilmen elected to continue until expiration of terms.

SEC. 400. The members of Common Council, now residing within the boundaries of the above created First ward, and the members of the Common Council, now residing within the boundaries of the above created Twenty-sixth ward, shall continue to represent their respective wards, in said Councils, until the time, for which they were elected, shall have expired.

Aldermen and Constables.

SEC. 401. Each of the above wards shall be entitled to two Aldermen, and, also, to two Constables, and at the next annual election, the qualified voters of each of said wards, shall elect one person to serve as Alderman, and one person to serve as Constable of their respective wards, and the Alderman, and Constable, at present acting, in said wards, shall continue to act as such until the time, for which they were elected, shall have expired; all vacancies in the office of Alderman, and Constable, shall be supplied as is now, or may hereafter be, provided by law.

Vacancies in School Boards.

SEC. 402. The qualified voters of the said wards, shall, at the next election, elect School Directors, to fill any vacancies in the several Boards of School Directors, of said wards, caused by the passage of this act: *Provided*, That the persons elected as School Directors of the old First ward shall continue to act as School Directors, of the new ward until their term of office shall have expired.

Proviso.

Assessors.

SEC. 403. The Assessors, residing within the bounds of the above wards, shall continue to act as Assessors, for the wards, in which they may respectively reside, until the term, for which they were elected, shall have expired;

after which, the Assessors, for said wards, shall be elected, as is now, or may hereafter be, provided by law.

SEC. 404. Immediately upon the passage of this act, it shall be the duty of the City Commissioners, and they are hereby required, to divide each of the above wards into not less than eight precincts, and fix the places of holding the elections therein.

City Commissioners to divide both Wards into Precincts.

SEC. 405. The officers now elected to conduct the elections, in the now First ward, shall appoint election officers to conduct the elections in the precincts, to be founded in the First and Twenty-sixth wards, until the next election, when election officers shall be elected as is now provided for by law.—March 29, 1864.—P. L. 111.

Election office.

A further Supplement to an Act to extend Fifteenth and Green streets, in the City of Philadelphia, approved the eleventh day of April, one thousand eight hundred and sixty-two.

SEC. 406. That the Commissioners appointed by the Court of Common Pleas, May fifth, one thousand eight hundred and sixty-two, to lay out Green street, from Carpenter to Park street, in the Twenty-second ward, are hereby authorized to proceed to view and lay out Green street, in the Twenty-second ward, from Park street to Cottage street, in said ward; said extension to be made, and damages to be assessed, and paid, as is provided by existing laws; and said Green street, from Park street to Cottage avenue, to be put in good travelling order, by the Highway Department, immediately upon the confirmation of the report of said Commissioners; and said Commissioners are hereby authorized to employ a competent Surveyor, at an expense, not exceeding fifty dollars; and said Commissioners shall each receive, for their services, five dollars per day, warrants for same to be drawn by City Commissioners, on the City Treasurer.—March 30, 1864.—P. L. 135.

An Act to regulate places of Public Amusement in the City of Philadelphia.

SEC. 407. That it shall not be lawful to exhibit, to the public, in any building, garden, grounds, concert-room, saloon, or other place, or room, within the City of Philadelphia, any interlude, tragedy, comedy, opera, ballet, play, farce, negro minstrelsy, or other dancing, or any other entertainment of the stage, or any part thereof, or

Proprietors, or managers of places of Amusement required to take out a license.

any representation, in which a drop curtain, and scenery, or theatrical costumes are used, or any equestrian, circus, or dramatic performance, or any performance of jugglers, rope dancing, or acrobats, or any entertainment of vocal or instrumental music, or any menagerie, until a license for such exhibition, performance, or entertainment, shall have been first had, and obtained, from the Mayor of the City of Philadelphia; which license shall be granted by him, for each and every place, or building, in which such exhibitions, performances, or entertainments, are held, upon the payment, by the owner, or manager, of the sum of ten dollars, to the City Treasurer, for the whole, or for any portion, of each calendar year; and every manager, proprietor, or director, of any such exhibition, performance, or entertainment, who shall neglect to take out such license, or who shall allow, or cause, any such exhibition, performance or entertainment, without such license, and every owner, or lessee, of any building, room, garden, grounds, concert-room, or other place, who shall lease, or let, the same, for the purpose of any such exhibition, performance, or entertainment, or shall assent to the use thereof, for any such purpose, except as permitted by such license, and without such license having been previously obtained, and then, in force, shall be guilty of a misdemeanor, and upon conviction thereof, shall be sentenced to pay a fine, not exceeding one hundred dollars, or undergo an imprisonment, not exceeding three months, or both, or either, at the discretion of the Court.

How to be granted.

Penalty for Exhibitions, Performances, &c., without such license.

Attendance of females, as waiters, prohibited.

SEC. 408. It shall not be lawful for any female to attend among, or wait upon, the audience, or spectator, at any of the exhibitions, performances, or entertainments, mentioned hereinbefore, or at any other place of public amusement, in the City of Philadelphia, to procure, offer, furnish, or distribute, any description of commodities, or refreshments, whatsoever; nor shall it be lawful for any manager, or proprietor, of any such exhibition, performance, entertainment, or place of public amusement, to employ or permit the employment of any female, to attend among, or wait upon, the audience, or spectators, thereat, to procure, offer, furnish, or distribute, any description of commodities, or refreshments, whatsoever; and any person, violating any of the provisions of this section, shall be guilty of a misdemeanor, and, upon conviction thereof, shall be sentenced to pay a fine, not exceeding five hundred dollars, or undergo an imprison-

Penalty for violating this provision.

ment, not exceeding one year, or both, or either, at the discretion of the court.

SEC. 409. That it shall be lawful for the Mayor of the City of Philadelphia, upon satisfactory proof, under oath, or affirmation, of the violation of any of the provisions of this act, to vacate, annul, and render void, and of no effect, any license, which shall have been obtained, as aforesaid, by any manager, proprietor, owner, or lessee, for the holding such exhibition, performance, or entertainment, or allowing, or letting, any part of a building, or other premises, for the purposes thereof; and it shall also be lawful, for the said Mayor, to prevent any such exhibition, performance, or entertainment, from being held, exhibited, or performed, until the license, hereinbefore provided for, shall be paid, or, if the same shall have been annulled, or vacated, for violation of any of the provisions of this act, and, to that end, to direct the police to close the building, room, or other place, in which, the said exhibition, performance, or entertainment, is intended to be held, and to prevent the entrance of auditors, or spectators.

Mayor may annul license, upon proof of violation of this Act.

Authorized to prevent Performances, and close buildings, in certain cases.

SEC. 410. That all sums of money, received by the City Treasurer, in payment for licenses, under this act, shall be paid into the treasury of the said city, for municipal uses; and it is hereby enacted, that nothing, in this act contained, shall, in any wise, be taken, or deemed to revoke, modify, or interfere with, the provisions of the several acts of the General Assembly, requiring license from the State, for theatrical, or other exhibitions.—March 30, 1864.—P. L. 141.

License fees, under this Act, to be paid into City Treasury.

An Act to exempt the Citizens' Volunteer Hospital of Philadelphia from taxation.

SEC. 411. That the real estate, now occupied as the Citizens' Volunteer Hospital, situate at the corner of Broad and Washington streets, in the City of Philadelphia, be and the same is hereby exempt from taxation, so long as the same shall be occupied for that purpose.—March 31, 1864.—P. L. 170.

An Act to provide for the more accurate indexing of liens against Real Estate, in the City of Philadelphia.

SEC. 412. That it shall be the duty of the Prothonotaries of the Court of Common Pleas, and of the District Court of the City and County of Philadelphia, to keep a locality index, in which, shall be registered the street front of real estate, against which, claims are, or shall be, filèd, to enforce liens for taxes, municipal work, or of mechanics, and material men; said index to state the amount of feet front, of said real estate, with the determining distances as they may be stated in said claims; said Prothonotaries shall receive, in addition to the fees allowed by existing laws, the sum of twenty-five cents for each claim filed, to defray the expense in keeping said index, which said sum shall be included in the costs, and collected as such; it shall be the duty of said Prothonotaries to give certificates of search of all claims filed, as they shall be required by any written order therefor, in which, the property shall be described; for which certificate, for each property, they shall receive the sum of forty cents; inclusive of the stamp required by any act of Congress, and no more.—March 31, 1864.—P. L. 171.

An Act to authorize the macadamizing of the streets, in certain portions of the City of Philadelphia.

SEC. 413. That the Councils of the City of Philadelphia are hereby authorized, upon the petition of a majority of the owners of the ground, on any of the streets, in the First, Second, Twentieth, Twenty-first, Twenty-second, Twenty-fourth, and Twenty-fifth wards of the said city, for a continuous distance of not less than one thousand feet, and not already paved, to direct, and provide, that said street or streets shall be macadamized in a suitable manner, instead of being paved; and that all laws, and ordinances, in reference to curbing, and paving, in said city, and repairing the same, and for the assessment, and collection, of the cost thereof, be and the same are hereby extended to the curbing, and macadamizing, of any of the streets in the wards aforesaid: *Provided*, That the said councils shall prescribe the width of gutter, on said streets, to be paved with flagging, or cobble stones, and that no more than the cost of said work shall be assessed to, and collected from, the owners of the respective fronts upon said streets; which cost shall be established and declared by said Councils, as near the actual expense of the same as may be: *And provided further*, That nothing herein contained shall interfere with the curbing, and paving, of any streets already directed to be done by any law or ordinance.—April 1, 1864.—P. L. 187.

An Act relating to the opening of streets, and payment of damages therefor, in the City of Philadelphia.

SEC. 414. That when any street, in the City of Philadelphia, is ordered to be opened, in accordance with law, the jury appointed to assess the damages for said opening after having determined the amount of said damages, and to whom they shall be paid, shall also make inquiry as to the advantages of opening said street, to property in the immediate vicinity of the same; and said jury shall determine what amount of the damages, if any, shall be paid by the City of Philadelphia, and what amount, if any, shall be paid by the property owners benefitted.

Juries authorized to inquire as to advantages accruing to property owners by opening of streets.

SEC. 415. If the jury determine that the property owners shall pay said damages, or any part thereof, it shall specify the properties benefitted, and state the amount each is benefitted; and due notice having been given, by advertisement, or otherwise, as the court may direct, of the award of the jury in the case; when said award is confirmed by the court, the street shall forthwith be opened by the proper authorities of the City of Philadelphia; and said city shall pay, to the respective owners of the property damaged, or their legal representatives, the damages so assessed for said opening.

Properties benefitted to be specified.

Notice of award to be given.

Payment of damages.

SEC. 416. When the court has confirmed the award of the jury as aforesaid, the Solicitor of the City of Philadelphia shall notify the property owners benefitted, of the amount assessed against the property of each, and have delivered to them bills for the sum so assessed; and if said assessments are not paid, within thirty days after the delivery of the bill, said Solicitor shall, without delay, file a claim in the proper court, for the amount thereof, against said property, which claim shall be a lien against the premises assessed, and shall be collected in the same manner as municipal claims are now by law collected.—April 1, 1864.—P. L. 207.

City Solicitor to notify property owners benefitted, of the amount assessed against them.

LEGISLATIVE APPORTIONMENT.

An Act to fix the number of Senators, and Representatives, and to form the State into Districts, in pursuance of the provisions of the Constitution.

Senatorial districts.

SEC. 417. That until the next septennial enumeration of the taxable inhabitants, and an apportionment thereon, the Senate shall consist of the thirty-three members, and be apportioned as follows, to wit:

I. The First, Second, Third, Fourth, Seventh Eighth, and Twenty-sixth, wards, of the City of Philadelphia, shall compose the First District, and elect one Senator.

II. The Ninth, Tenth, Thirteenth; Fourteenth, and Fifteenth, wards, of the City of Philadelphia, shall compose the Second District and elect one Senator.

III. The Fifth, Sixth, Eleventh, Twelfth, Sixteenth, Seventeenth, and Eighteenth, wards, of the city of Philadelphia, shall compose the Third District, and elect one Senator.

IV. The Nineteenth, Twentieth, Twenty-first, Twenty-second, Twenty-third, Twenty-fourth, and Twenty-fifth, wards, of the City of Philadelphia, shall compose the Fourth District, and elect one Senator.

XIX. The Senators shall be chosen in the several districts, at the following times, to wit:

In the First District, one Senator shall be chosen at the general election, in the year of our Lord, one thousand eight hundred and sixty-six.

In the Second District, one Senator shall be chosen at the general election, in the year of our Lord one thousand eight hundred and sixty-five.

In the Third District, one Senator shall be chosen at the general election, in the year of our Lord one thousand eight hundred and sixty-four.

In the Fourth District, one Senator shall be chosen at the general election, in the year of our Lord one thousand eight hundred and sixty-five.

Representative districts.

SEC. 418. That until the next septennial enumeration of taxables, and apportionment thereon made, the House of Representatives shall consist of one hundred members, and be apportioned as follows: The City of Philadelphia shall be divided into eighteen districts, viz:

I. The First ward, and the Twenty-sixth ward, except

the seventh, and eighth, election divisions, shall compose the First District, and elect one member.

II. The Second ward, except the tenth, and eleventh, divisions, and the first, second, and third divisions of the Third ward, shall compose the Second District, and elect one member.

III. The tenth, and eleventh divisions of the Second ward; the fourth, fifth, sixth, seventh, and eighth divisions of the Third ward; the Fourth ward; and the first, and third divisions of the Fifth ward, shall compose the Third District, and elect one member.

IV. The seventh, and eighth divisions of the Twenty-sixth ward, and the Seventh ward, shall compose the Fourth District, and elect one member.

V. The second, fourth, fifth, sixth, seventh and eighth divisions of the Fifth ward, and the Eighth ward, shall compose the Fifth District, and elect one member.

VI. The first, fourth, fifth, sixth, seventh, and eighth divisions of the Sixth ward; and the first, second, third, fourth, fifth, sixth, and seventh, divisions of the Ninth ward, shall compose the Sixth District, and elect one member.

VII. The Thirteenth ward, and the third, fifth, and sixth divisions of the Fourteenth ward, shall compose one District, and elect one member.

VIII. The Tenth ward; the eighth division of the Ninth ward, and the first, second, and fourth divisions of the Fourteenth ward, shall compose the Eighth District, and elect one member.

IX. The second and third divisions of the Sixth ward; the Eleventh ward, and the first, second, fifth, and sixth divisions of the Twelfth ward, shall compose the Ninth District, and elect one member.

X. The Fifteenth ward, except the eighth division, shall compose the Tenth District, and elect one member.

XI. The first, second, third, fourth, fifth, sixth and eighth divisions of the Sixteenth ward; the third, fourth and seventh divisions of the Twelfth ward, and the first, and second divisions of the Twentieth ward, shall compose the Eleventh District, and elect one member.

XII. The Eighteenth ward; the first division of the Seventeenth ward; the third and sixth divisions of the Nineteenth ward and the fourth division of the Twenty-fifth ward, shall compose the Twelfth District, and elect one member.

XIII. The Seventeenth ward, except the first division; the seventh division of the Sixteenth, and the second, and seventh divisions of the Nineteenth ward, shall compose the Thirteenth District, and elect one member.

XIV. The seventh and eighth divisions of the Fourteenth ward; the fourth, fifth, sixth, seventh, eighth, ninth and tenth divisions of the Twentieth ward; and the eighth division of the Fifteenth ward, shall compose the Fourteenth District, and elect one member.

XV. The first, third,* fourth, fifth, ninth, and tenth divisions of the Nineteenth ward; the third and eleventh divisions of the Twentieth ward; the first division of the Twenty-first ward; and the fifth and sixth divisions of the Twenty-fifth ward, shall compose the Fifteenth District, and elect one member.

XVI. The Twenty-second ward, and the third, fourth, fifth, sixth and seventh divisions of the Twenty-first ward, shall compose the Sixteenth District, and elect one member.

XVII. The Twenty-third ward; the first, second, and third divisions of the Twenty-fifth ward, and the eighth division of the Nineteenth ward, shall compose the Seventeenth District, and elect one member.

XVIII. The Twenty-fourth ward, and the second, and eighth divisions of the Twenty-first ward, shall compose the Eighteenth District, and elect one member.

---

* *A Supplement to an Act to fix the number of Senators and Representatives, and to form the State into districts, in pursuance of the provisions of the Constitution, approved May fifth, one thousand eight hundred and sixty-four.*

**Whereas*, By a clerical error in the act, to which this is a supplement, the third election division of the Nineteenth ward, of the City of Philadelphia, was included in the twelfth, and also in the Fifteenth Representative District, of the said city:

And whereas, It was intended that the said election division should form a part of the first named Representative District; therefore:

Be it enacted, &c., That the third election division of the Nineteenth ward, of the City of Philadelphia, shall be included in and form a part of the Twelfth Representative District, of the said City; and so much of said act, as constitutes the said Division a portion of the Fifteenth Representative District, of the said City, be and the same is hereby repealed.—August 24, 1864.—P. L. 1014.

A Supplement to a Further Supplement to an Act to incorporate the City of Philadelphia, passed February second, one thousand eight hundred and fifty-four.

SEC. 419. That the burgess, and council, of the borough of Chester, in the county of Delaware, shall appoint one assistant warden, of the port of Philadelphia, to serve as a port warden, for the term of four years, from the first day of June next, with the same power, and authority, as those appointed by the Councils of Philadelphia, under and by virtue of the act to which this is a supplement.

Burgess and Council of Chester to appoint an assistant Port Warden.

SEC. 420. That it shall be the duty of the surveyor, of the county of Delaware, to prepare, within twelve months from the passage of this act, a plan of the Delaware river front, of said county, showing the present line of low water, with the depths of water for seven hundred feet, out from said line of low water, at distances of fifty feet from said line, and at distances not more than five hundred feet apart; and, upon the receipt of said plan, by the wardens for the port of Philadelphia, they shall define a wharf-line for Delaware county, beyond which, it shall not be lawful for them to authorize the construction of any wharf, or pier; and if any person shall trespass on the tide-way of the river, beyond the line of low water, as defined by the survey now authorized, without a license from the port wardens, he, or they, so offending, shall be liable to the penalties, as provided in existing acts for like offences.

Surveyor of Delaware county to prepare a plan of river front, &c.

Wharf line for Delaware county to be defined by Wardens.

SEC. 421. That the map, or plan, directed to be prepared by the second section of this act, shall be placed on file, in the office of the wardens, for the port of Philadelphia; and the necessary expense, incurred in preparing said map, or plan, shall be paid by the commissioners of Delaware county.—March 31, 1864.—P. L. 304.

Plan to be filed.

An Act to repeal a portion of the twenty-first section of an Act entitled, "A Supplement to the Act Consolidating the City of Philadelphia."

SEC. 422. That so much of the twenty-first section of the act entitled "A Supplement to an Act Consolidating the City of Philadelphia," approved the twenty-first day of April, in the year of our Lord one thousand eight hundred and fifty-five, as provides that the ordinance, therein mentioned, shall not go into effect without the signature of the Mayor of the City of Philadelphia, be and the same is hereby repealed; and it shall be competent for the Select and Common Councils, of the said City, by a two-thirds vote, of each Council, in the usual way, to pass any bill whatever its nature, which may have been returned by the Mayor, without his signature.—March 31, 1864.—P. L. 305.

A further Supplement to the Act consolidating the City of Philadelphia.

SEC. 423. That from, and after, the passage of this act, it shall not be lawful for any person to act as a member of the Board of Control, of the First School District of Pennsylvania, unless such person shall be a member of the Board of School Directors, of the section by which he was elected, nor after his term, as a member of said Board of School Directors, shall have expired.

A further Supplement to the Act to incorporate the City of Philadelphia.

SEC. 424. That the City of Philadelphia shall have power to construct sewers in the streets of the said City, and to charge, therefor, the sum of seventy-five cents for each lineal foot, against each front, the same to be recovered, as liens, for the laying of water pipe, are now recovered in said City, and with the same allowance for corner lots: *Provided, however,* That for branch sewers, the consent, or request in writing, of the majority of the owners of property, fronting on the street, or streets, intended to be culverted, be first obtained, and filed, in the office of the Department of Sewers: *Provided, also,* That the request, in writing, of a majority of the property owners, only, on the line of any street, lane, or alley, shall be requisite, to authorize the improvement of the same; and that all acts, which conflict herewith, be and the same are hereby repealed.—April 8, 1864.—P. L. 324.

An Act to authorize the sale of certain real estate in the City of Philadelphia.

Preamble. SEC. 425. *Whereas,* On the twentieth day of August, one thousand eight hundred and sixty-three, there was conveyed to the Master and Assistant Wardens of the Port of Philadelphia, a piece of ground, forty feet in width, or front, upon the road leading to Gloucester Point, and in length, or depth, extending from said road into the Delaware, at low water mark; the southern boundary of said piece of land being distant eight hundred feet, or thereabouts, from the north side of the wharf of Greenwich Point: *And whereas,* Said land was conveyed, to said Wardens, in trust for, and to the use of, the Commonwealth of Pennsylvania, for the purpose of erecting a pier, at which, vessels might unload, and load, gunpowder, to be stored in a magazine, then conveniently thereto: *And whereas,* The location of said. magazine, having been changed, no gunpowder has been unloaded, or loaded, upon said pier, for a great number of years, and said pier having become so dilapidated, as to be useless, it is to the interest of all parties, that the same be sold, and the money received, therefrom, be appropriated to the general purposes of the Commonwealth of Pennsylvania.

SEC. 426. That the Board of Wardens, of the port of Philadelphia, shall be, and they are hereby authorized, and required, to sell, within three months, said powder pier, at public sale, after public notice, in at least two daily newspapers, published in said City, three times a week, for two weeks, and to convey the same, in fee simple, to the purchasers, by a deed, executed under their seal, signed by the Master Warden, and attested by the Clerk, which deed shall vest an absolute title in the purchaser, free, clear, discharged, from all, and every trust, use, and limitation.

Sale of powder pier authorized.

Notice.

SEC. 427. That no sale of said property shall be confirmed by said Board of Wardens, except at a stated meeting regularly convened, at which a majority of the members of the Board shall be present; and the purchase money arising from said sale, shall be paid into the State treasury.—April 9, 1864.—P. L. 372.

Confirmation of sale.

Purchase money to be paid to State.

A Supplement to an Act to provide for the taxation of non-resident venders of merchandize, in the City of Philadelphia, and for other purposes, approved the twelfth day of April, one thousand eight hundred and fifty-one.

SEC. 428. That if any person, not residing within this State, and paying, under the laws thereof, a license, now required by law, shall, within the City and County of Philadelphia, sell, or exhibit for sale, by sample, specimen, card, or otherwise, any goods, wares, or merchandize, for, or on account of, any merchant, manufacturer, or other person, not having his principal place of business within the said State, and not having a license under the laws of this Commonwealth, for the sale of such goods, wares, or merchandize, such person, so offending, shall be guilty of a misdemeanor, and, on conviction, shall be sentenced to an imprisonment, not exceeding thirty days, and to pay a fine, not exceeding three hundred dollars, or both, or either, in the discretion of the Court.—April 9, 1864.—P. L. 375.

An Act to open parts of Columbia avenue, and Bedford street, in the City of Philadelphia.

SEC. 429. That within one month, after the approval of this act, the Court of Common Pleas shall appoint three commissioners, whose duty it shall be to lay out, and open, Columbia avenue, and straighten it from Fifth to Sixth streets, and from Hancock to Mascher street, also, Bedford street, from Fifteenth to Broad streets, in the City of Philadelphia, and all damages shall be assessed, as is now provided for by existing laws; and within one month, after the confirmation of the report of the said commissioners, the Chief Commissioner of Highways shall put the said street in good traveling order. — April 14, 1864.—P. L. 423.

An Act to change the width of Wildey (formerly Bedford) street, in the City of Philadelphia.

SEC. 430. That so much of Wildey street as lies, between Shackamaxon and Hanover (now called Columbia avenue) streets, in the Eighteenth Ward, of the City of Philadelphia, be changed to the width of thirty feet, as formerly laid out, and located, agreeably to legislative enactment, dated March sixth, one thousand eight hundred and twenty.—April 18, 1864.—P. L. 438.

An Act to open Ninth and Twenty-ninth streets, in the City of Philadelphia.

SEC. 431. That within one month after the approval of this act, the Court of Common Pleas shall appoint three commissioners, whose duty shall be to lay out, and open

Ninth street, from Master street to Germantown, road and also Twenty-ninth street, from Pennsylvania avenue to the Township Line road, in the City of Philadelphia; and all damages shall be assessed, as is now provided for by existing laws; and within one month after the confirmation of the report of the said commissioners, the Chief Commissioner of Highways shall put the said streets in good traveling order.—April 18, 1864.—P. L. 445.

An Act to open Eighth street, in the City of Philadelphia.

SEC. 432. That within one month after the approval of this act, the Court of Common Pleas shall appoint three commissioners, whose duty shall be to lay out and open Eighth street, from Montgomery street to Germantown road, in the City of Philadelphia; and all damages shall be assessed, as is now provided for by existing laws; and within one month after the confirmation of the report, of the said commissioners, the Chief Commissioner of Highways shall put the said street in good traveling order.—April 18, 1864.—P. L. 447.

A Further Supplement to an Act to incorporate the City of Philadelphia, passed February second, one thousand eight hundred and fifty-four, relative to the election of School Directors.

SEC. 433. That the twentieth section of the above act is hereby amended, to entitle the qualified voters, in the Twenty-first Ward, of said City, to elect eighteen citizens, qualified to serve as members of the Senate of this commonwealth; six of whom shall be elected to serve for one year; six, for two years, and six for three years, as Directors of the Public Schools; said directors to be elected at the next election, held for city officers; and annually, thereafter, the qualified voters of the said Twenty-first Ward shall elect six citizens, of like qualifications, to serve as Directors of the Public Schools, for three years.—April 18, 1864.—P. L. 468.

A Further Supplement to an Act to incorporate the City of Philadelphia.

SEC. 429. *Whereas*, The owner of the fire alarm telegraph, is also the superintendent of the police and fire alarm telegraph, connected with the Police Department of the City of Philadelphia, and is the only person from whom the privileges and supplies, necessary for the management of such telegraph, can legally be obtained:

And whereas, The provisions of the act, to which this is a supplement, forbid any officer, of the said City corporation, to be directly, or indirectly, interested in any sale to, or contract for supplies, to the said City, or to any department thereof:

SEC. 434. That no provision in the act, to which this is a supplement, shall prohibit, or prevent, the employment of the owner of the fire alarm telegraph patents, as an officer of the City of Philadelphia, or prohibit any payment to him, of any sum of money, by the said City, for extension of the said telegraph, or for supplies furnished by him, for its management.—April 19, 1864.—P. L. 491.

An Act relating to the office of Fire Marshal of the Police Department of the City of Philadelphia.

Fire Marshal authorized to enter buildings for the purpose of examinations as to causes of fires.

SEC. 435. That the Fire Marshal, appointed by the Mayor of the City of Philadelphia, under the ordinance of the Select and Common Councils of said City, approved March twenty-fifth, Anno Donini one thousand eight hundred and sixty-four, shall, under the instructions and orders of the Mayor, be authorized to enter any building or premises, wherein a fire has at any time occurred, for the purpose of making such examination as may be deemed necessary to ascertain the cause of the burning; and any person preventing or obstructing, or attempting to prevent, or obstruct, said Fire Marshal, while in the discharge of the duty aforesaid, shall be guilty of a misdemeanor; and, on conviction thereof, shall be fined in a sum not exceeding fifty dollars, or undergo an imprisonment, not exceeding three calendar months, or both, at the discretion of the Court.

Penalty for attempting to obstruct him while in discharge of duty.

Mayor may issue *Subpœna* for witnesses.

SEC. 436. And that the Mayor of the City of Philadelphia shall be and he is hereby authorized, whenever, in his judgment, the occasion demands it, to issue *subpœna,* in the name of the State of Pennsylvania, to any person, or persons, requiring them to attend before him, or the Fire Marshal, at such time and place, as may be named in said *subpœna,* then and there to testify, under oath or affirmation, which the Fire Marshal, in the absence of the Mayor, is hereby empowered to administer, as to the origin of any fire occurring within the bounds of the consolidated City of Philadelphia; and also as to any facts or circumstances that may be deemed important to secure

Marshal may administer oaths in absence of mayor.

the detection and conviction, of any party, or parties guilty of the offences of arson, or attempted arson.

SEC. 437. That such *subpœna* may be directed to any police officer, of the City of Philadelphia, who is hereby empowered to serve the same. *Subpœna may be directed to any policeman.*

SEC. 438. That this act shall go into effect from, and after, the date of its passage, and approval by the Governor of the Commonwealth.—April 20, 1864.—P. L. 515. *To go into effect immediately.*

A Supplement to an Act entitled "An Act for the registration of Births, Marriages and Deaths, in the City of Philadelphia," passed the eighth day of March, one thousand eight hundred and sixty.

SEC. 439, That the health officer, in lieu of the compensation provided by the thirteenth section of said act, shall be paid in the manner therein provided, the sum of nine hundred dollars per annum.—April 23, 1864.—P. L. 549.

An Act relative to Railroads using steam in the City of Philadelphia.

SEC. 440. *Whereas,* The public safety, and convenience, require that the railroads using steam should, whenever it is reasonably convenient, pass over, or under, the public highways:

That the tenth section of the act, approved the twenty-first day of April, Anno Domini one thousand eight hundred and fifty-five, entitled "A supplement to the Act Consolidating the City of Philadelphia," shall not apply to any railroad chartered, or which may hereafter be chartered, authorized, by law, to use steam as a motive power and shall only apply to passenger railways using public streets, laid out according to law.—April, 23, 1864.—P. L. 550.

An Act vacating Wharf street, in the Second and Third Wards, of the City of Philadelphia.

SEC. 441. That that part of Wharf street, in the Second and Third Wards of the City of Philadelphia, extending from Queen to Washington streets, be, and the same is, vacated; and that the title of the owners of property, fronting on each side of the said vacated street, shall extend to, and include, the portions of the soil of the said street, intervening between the front lines of their respective lots, and the middle of the said street. April 27, 1864.—P. L 614

An Act relating to certain streets in the Twenty-fourth Ward, of the City of Philadelphia.

Certain streets and parts of streets to be vacated.

SEC. 442. That such streets, and part of streets, as lay within the boundaries of the Powelton estates, of the Pennsylvania Railroad Company, in the Twenty-fourth Ward of the City of Philadelphia, as may be designated, upon a plan to be filed, by said company, in the office of the Chief Engineer, and Surveyor, of said City, as requisite to be vacated, within the limits of the property of said company, for the more convenient construction of depots, shops, and other buildings, for the use of said company, and for the more convenient arrangement of tracks, and sidings, be and the same are hereby declared to be vacated, from the time of the filing of said plan, as aforesaid.

Plan to be filed.

Parties injured may apply for juries to assess damages.

SEC. 443. That it shall, and may, be lawful for any party, injured thereby, if such there be, to apply for a jury, in the manner prescribed by existing laws, in force in the City of Philadelphia, in relation to the vacating of streets, and the award of such jury, when finally confirmed, shall be paid by said railroad company: *Provided,* That public notice, by advertisement, be given of the filing of said plan: *And provided also,* That such application, for a jury, be made, within three months after such notice is first published.—April 27, 1864.—P. L. 615.

Award of Jury.

Proviso.

Proviso.

A Supplement to an Act to Change the width of York street, in the City of Philadelphia, approved the seventeenth day of March, one thousand eight hundred and sixty-four.

SEC. 444. That so much of York street, as lies between Moyer (formerly Brown) street, and the Aramingo canal, in the Nineteenth Ward, be changed to the width of fifty feet, and to conform to the width of the bridge, over said canal; and all Acts of Assembly, contrary to this, be and the same are hereby repealed. April 27, 1864.—P. L. 617.

An Act to open Franklin street, in the City of Philadelphia.

SEC. 445. That within one month after the approval of this act, the Court of Common Pleas shall appoint three commissioners, whose duty shall be to lay out and open Franklin street, from Montgomery to Dauphin streets in the City of Philadelphia, and all damages shall be assessed as is now provided for by existing laws; and within one month after the confirmation of the report of the said commissioners, the Chief Commissioner of Highways shall put the said street in good traveling order.—April 27, 1864.—P. L. 637.

A Further Supplement to the Act to incorporate the City of Philadelphia, relative to filling vacancies in Councils.

SEC. 446. That in case of a vacancy occurring, hereafter, in either branch of the Councils of Philadelphia, the qualified voters of the Ward, at the next election, shall elect a person for the unexpired term. *Relative to Vacancies in Councils.*

SEC. 447. That from and after the passage of this act, it shall be lawful for any member of the Select and Common Councils of the City of Philadelphia, to tender his resignation, to take effect, at a given time stated; and it shall be the duty of the president of the chamber, wherein such resignation shall be tendered, to direct the clerk to notify the sheriff of the county of Philadelphia, of such resignation, within one week after the same. *Resignations* *Sheriff to be notified of same.*

SEC. 448. The sheriff of the City and County of Philadelphia, shall give notice, in the usual manner, of all elections, to be held, under the provisions of the foregoing sections, in case such vacancy shall occur twenty days previous to the election.—April 27, 1864.—P. L. 638. *Notice of elections to be given by Sheriff.*

An Act to open Lehigh avenue and a part of Fourth street, in the City of Philadelphia.

SEC. 449. That, within two months after the approval of this act, the Court of Common Pleas shall appoint three commissioners, whose duty it shall be to open Lehigh avenue, according to surveys now on record in the Survey Department of Philadelphia, between the intersection of Frankford road and Sixth street, in the City of Philadelphia; and, also, Fourth street, from Oxford street, to Montgomery street, in the said City; and all damages shall be assessed as now provided by existing laws; and within one month after the report of the said Commissioners, the Chief Commissioner of Highways, shall put the said streets in good traveling order. —April 27, 1864.—P. L. 640.

A Further Supplement to an Act to incorporate the City of Philadelphia.

SEC. 450. That hereafter the return judges of the several Wards of the City of Philadelphia, shall meet at the State House in said City, at ten o'clock in the morning of the Friday succeeding the day of election; and such part or parts of any law as requires them to meet on Thursday, is hereby repealed.–April 27, 1864.–P. L. 643.

A Supplement to an Act entitled "A Supplement to the Act consolidating the City of Philadelphia," relative to Taxes in the Twenty-third Ward of said City, approved May third, one thousand eight hundred and sixty.

SEC. 451. That the compensation allowed to the Receiver of Taxes, in the said Twenty-third Ward, for his services, shall hereafter be two and one-half per centum of all moneys received by him during the current year, for which the said taxes shall have been levied; said compensation to be computed for this year from the first day of January Anno Domini one thousand eight hundred and sixty-four.—April 30, 1864.—P. L. 677.

An Act for macadamizing a portion of Broad street, in the City of Philadelphia.

SEC. 452. That the Councils of the City of Philadelphia shall cause to be commenced, at a period not later than will allow of the completion thereof before the first day of January, one thousand eight hundred and sixty-five, the macadamizing of the centre of Broad street, of the width of thirty-two feet, from Prime street or Washington avenue, to Moyamensing or Jefferson avenue, the same to be done in a substantial manner and of the most approved character of material and construction.—May 3, 1864.—P. L. 696.

An Act relating to the Election Divisions of the Twenty-first Ward in the City of Philadelphia.

SEC. 453. That all that part of the eighth division of the Twenty-first Ward, in the City of Philadelphia, lying between the sixth and seventh divisions of said Ward, and the river Schuylkill, and the north line of said sixth division, extending westwardly to Domino lane, in said ward, shall be attached to, and constitute a part of, the seventh division of said ward.—May 3rd, 1864.—P. L. 721.

An Act to provide for the payment of Salaries of the Secretaries of the Sectional Board of School Directors, in the City of Philadelphia.

SEC. 454. That it shall be the duty of the City Councils of Philadelphia to provide, by ordinance, for the payment of the secretaries of the several wards of directors, in the First School District. Councils to provide for payment of Secretaries.

SEC. 455. That from and after the first day of January; one thousand eight hundred and sixty-four, the salary of each of said officers shall be one hundred dollars per annum; and warrants for the payment thereof, shall be drawn in same manner as are the warrants for the payment of teachers in the said District. Salary fixed.

SEC. 456. All laws in conflict with the provisions hereof, or supplied by this act, are hereby repealed.—May 4th, 1864.—P. L. 806 Repeal.

A Further Supplement to an Act to establish a Health Office, and to secure the City and Port of Philadelphia from the introduction of Pestilential and Contagious Diseases, approved January twenty-ninth, Anno Domini one thousand eight hundred and eighteen.

SEC. 457. That the Port Physician shall, from and after the passage of this act, receive annually, a salary of twelve hundred dollars, to be paid quarterly by an order drawn by the Board of Health on their treasurer, any law to the contrary notwithstanding.—May 5th, 1864.—P. L. 820.

An Act to vacate Hamilton, late Pleasant street, between Ninth and Canton, (late Charles street,) in the City of Philadelphia.

SEC. 458. That so much of Hamilton street, lately called Pleasant street, as is laid out on the plan of streets in the Thirteenth Ward of the City of Philadelphia, late the district of Spring Garden, and extending from Ninth to Canton, late Charles street, be and the same is hereby vacated—May 6th, 1864.—P. L. 861.

A Supplement to an Act, passed March twenty-ninth, Anno Domini one thousand eight hundred and three, to establish a Board of Wardens for the Port of Philadelphia, and for other purposes.

Repeal of certain provisions relative to the rates of pilotage.

SEC. 459. That so much of the act, passed February ninth, one thousand eight hundred and thirty-seven, as provides, that when any vessel is towed by a steamboat, from the City of Philadelphia to the buoy of the brown or the breakwater, or from the buoy of the brown, or the breakwater, to the City of Philadelphia, the rates of pilotage shall continue to be as established by the act to which this is a supplement; and so much of the act passed March twenty-fourth, one thousand eight hundred and fifty-one, as provides, that when vessels taking steam down as far as Reedy island, between the twentieth day of November and the tenth day of March, inclusive, in any year, there shall be a deduction of five dollars, or to the buoy of the brown, there shall be a deduction of the whole charge of winter pilotage, be and is hereby repealed.

Rates fixed.

SEC. 460. That from and after the passage of this act in lieu of the compensation now allowed to pilots, for conducting ships or vessels from the City of Philadelphia, to the capes of the Delaware, or from the capes of the Delaware to the City of Philadelphia, the rates of pilotage shall be, for every half foot of water, which any inward bound vessel shall draw under and up to twelve feet, the sum of one dollar and eighty-seven cents; and for every inward bound vessel drawing over twelve feet, the sum of two dollars and eight cents for every half foot of water; and for every half foot which any outward bound vessel shall draw under and up to twelve feet, the sum of one dollar and fifteen cents; and for any outward bound vessel drawing over twelve feet, the sum of one dollar and fifty cents for every half foot of water; and shall also receive over and above the said sums, for conducting ships or vessels to or from the City of Philadelphia, forever, between the first day of November and the first day of April, inclusive, in any year the additional sum of ten dollars: *Provided.* They are not towed by a steamboat to and from the buoy of the brown; and shall also re-, ceive three dollars per day, whenever detained by any master, owner, or consignee, or by the ice: *Provided always,* That whenever it shall appear to the Wardens that, in case of an inward bound vessel, should a pilot not

Proviso.

Proviso.

offer before such vessel reached a line, drawn from Fenwick's island to the light boat, or five-fathom bank, the rates of inward pilotage shall continue to be established by the act of ninth February, one thousand eight hundred and thirty-seven.—May 6th, 1864.—P. L. 877.

An Act relating to certain Public Improvements, in the City of Philadelphia.

SEC. 461. That it shall be the duty of the Commissioners of Highways, of the City of Philadelphia, forthwith to cause Broad street to be graded for public use, from the Germantown road, northward, to Fisher's lane, and the culverts to be enlarged under the Philadelphia and Reading railroad, near Thompson street, and under Thompson street near Thirty-first street, in connection with said railroad company; all said work to be approved by the Chief Engineer of the said City.—May 6th, 1864.—P. L. 878.

An Act to authorize the appointment of an Inspector of stationary Steam Engines and Steam Boilers, in and for the City of Philadelphia.

SEC. 462. That the Mayor of the City of Philadelphia may nominate, in the month of June, annually, and by and with the advice of the Select Council of the said city, appoint a person skillful and competent, for the discharge of the duties hereinafter directed to be performed by him, to be the inspector of stationary engines, in and for the City of Philadelphia; he shall, before entering upon the duties of his office, give bond in the sum of ten thousand dollars with security, to be approved by the Mayor; he shall enter upon the performance of his duties on the first Monday of July in every year hereafter, and shall hold until his successor be duly qualified; any vacancy shall be filled in like manner and the Mayor may at any time suspend the said inspector from the further performance of the duties, until the Councils of the City of Philadelphia shall otherwise direct.

An inspector of stationary engines, boilers, &c., to be appointed, annually, by the mayor, with the advice of Select Council.

To give bond.

Official term, when to commence.

Mayor may suspend.

SEC. 463. It shall be the duty of the Inspector carefully to examine and inspect all stationary steam engines and steam boilers, erected or in use at the time this goes into effect; and thereafter no stationary steam engine or steam boilers shall be erected and put into use and operation in the City of Philadelphia, without being first inspected and certified to be competent and safe, under

Duties and powers of inspector.

the hand and seal of the officer created by this act; and he shall furnish to the owner, proprietor or other person using such engine or steam boiler, a certificate, under his hand and the seal of his office that it has been so inspected and found to be competent and safe; he shall, from time to time, and as often as he may deem expedient, examine all or any such engines or steam boilers in use or operation and for such purpose, he, together with his assistants, may enter upon any premises and require the removal of any part of the building, fixtures, or machinery and he shall note in a book, to be kept for that purpose, the result of every such examination; and he shall at least once in every year make such examination and give certificate of the result thereof, whenever required.

Certificates to be given.

Councils to make regulations, establish an office, fix compensation, &c.

SEC. 464. The Councils of the City of Philadelphia shall have power to make all needful rules and regulations for the purpose of carrying the foregoing provisions into effect and shall provide for the establishment of an office for the said Inspector; also, for so many and such assistants and other officers as they may deem necessary, shall fix adequate rates of compensation for the said Inspector and all other officers, shall establish the fees for services under this act, which shall be paid into the treasury of the City of Philadelphia and shall provide such other regulations as may be necessary to carry into effect the provisions of this act; and they may provide for the performance of the duties hereinbefore enjoined by the deputies or other assistants of the said inspector, as they may deem necessary.

Assistants.

Fees to be paid into City Treasury.

Deputies, relative to.

Penalty for using engines, or boilers without the certificate of the Inspector.

SEC. 465. If any person shall on or after the first Monday of July next maintain, or keep in use or operation, or shall thereafter put in use or operation, any stationary steam engine orsteam boiler, within the said City of Philadelphia, without having first received a certificate that the same has been found to be safe and competent, as is hereinbefore provided for, or shall put or keep in use or operation, any such stationary steam engine or steam boilers, within the said City after notice from the said Inspector, that the same is not competent and safe, he or she so offending, shall be deemed guilty of a misdemeanor and upon conviction in the Court of Quarter Sessions for the said County, shall be sentenced to pay a fine not exceeding five thousand dollars and to undergo imprisonment in the jail of said County, either with or without labor, as the Court may direct, for a term not exceeding two years; and each and every such person shall be liable for all damages that may accrue directly or indirectly, to any person or persons whatever. Liable for damages.

SEC. 466. So much of any law or laws, as shall be inconsistent herewith, shall be and the same are hereby repealed.—May 7, 1864.—P. L. 861. Repeal.

An Act regarding the Port of Philadelphia.

SEC. 467. That the first section of the act entitled "An Act relative to the duties of the Port Warden of Philadelphia," approved April fourteenth, eighteen hundred and fifty-nine, shall be so construed as to authorize said Master Warden to recover from the owner, master, or other agent having control of said vessel, all the expenses of raising, removing and selling said vessel, together with the penalty aforesaid and costs of suit in one suit, in like manner as is provided for the recovery of all fines, forfeitures, penalties, sum and sums of money, by the act entitled "An Act to establish a Board of Wardens for the Port of Philadelphia," approved March twenty-ninth, eighteen hundred and three. Construction of certain section in relation to recovery, by master Warden, of expenses of raising, removing and selling vessels, with penalty, &c.

SEC. 468. That the powers vested in the Councils of Philadelphia, by an act approved April twenty-second, eighteen hundred and fifty-eight, entitled "A Further Supplement to the act incorporating the City of Philadelphia," and by the twelfth section of an act approved May thirteenth, eighteen hundred and fifty-six, entitled "A Further Supplement to the act consolidating the City of Philadelphia," be and the same are hereby vested in the Port Wardens: *Provided*, That all liens filed to collect the expenses of said work, shall be filed by the City Solicitor and the lien for said work shall have the same force and effect as liens for municipal work in the City of Philadelphia, under existing laws and the claims filed for the same shall be governed by the same rules of evidence, as those filed in the City of Philadelphia, for the removal of nuisances by the Board of Health. Certain powers relative to cleansing docks vested in Port Wardens. Liens for work to be filed by City Solicitor. Effect of. Rules of evidence, relative to.

SEC. 469. That hereafter the Master Warden shall be appointed and commissioned by the Governor for three years, and until his successor is appointed and qualified, and in default of such appointment by the Governor for ninety days, a Master Warden may be chosen by the Board of Wardens, at a regular stated meeting, at which a majority of the members shall be present; and the obligation and duties of the said Master Warden, as heretofore defined by law, shall be and remain as heretofore. Master Warden to be appointed by governor. In default of such appointment, to be chosen by board. Obligations and duties, relative.

in addition to the obligations and duties now imposed by this act.

Duties of captains, as to entry and clearance of vessels.

SEC. 470. That the captains of all vessels arriving in the Port of Philadelphia, shall enter such vessels at the Warden's office, in a book kept for the entry and clearance of vessels, within twenty-four hours next after their arrival; and when such vessel shall be outward bound, it shall also be his duty to clear such vessel at said office under the same rules, regulations, fees and penalties, as are now provided by law.

Masters of vessels required to give to pilots an account of draught. Penalty for false return thereof.

SEC. 471. That masters of vessels shall give an account to the pilot when boarding, of the draught of such vessel and in case he shall misrepresent said draught and give it as less than the actual draught, he shall forfeit and pay the sum of twenty-five dollars, to be sued before and recovered before any alderman of the City of Philadelphia, by the Master Warden who shall pay the same over when collected, to the society for the relief of decayed pilots, their widows and orphans, he first having deducted the expenses incurred recovering the same.

Chief Engineer and Surveyor to prepare map of the entire Delaware front.

SEC. 472. That by direction of the Board of Wardens the Chief Engineer and Surveyor of the City of Philadelphia, shall be required to prepare a map or plan from actual survey, to be made within twelve months from the passage of this act, of the entire Delaware front of the City of Philadelphia, specifying the depths of water from the fast land to the wharf line as already established; and it shall be the duty of the Port Wardens, upon receipt of said map or plan, to fix and determine an arbitrary line of low water, beyond which no encroachments or improvements of any kind, shall be made without license had and obtained from the Board of Port Wardens, agreeably to the Acts of Assembly of this Commonwealth; and in case any person shall trespass upon the tide-way of the river Delaware, beyond the line of low water so defined, they shall be subject to a penalty of not less than five hundred dollars, nor exceeding four thousand dollars, with costs of suit and shall, if the Board of Wardens so direct, remove any or all obstructions at their own proper cost and expense; the penalty so incurred may be collected, as other penalties, under the original act and the supplements thereto, establishing a Board of Port Wardens, are collectable and shall be appropriated to the use of said Board of Wardens.

Port Wardens to fix a low water line.

Penalty for trespassing upon tide-way, beyond line defined

Removal of obstructions, relative to. How penalties to be collected and appropriated.

SEC. 473. That hereafter a quorum of the Board of

Wardens for the Port of Philadelphia, shall consist of a majority of the members of the said Board. Quorum of Board.

SEC. 474. That it shall be lawful for the Burgess and Council of the borough of Bristol, in Bucks County, by a majority of their whole number in the month of May one thousand eight hundred and sixty-four and every second year thereafter, to elect a suitable person, he being a citizen of said borough, as a member of the Board of Wardens of the City of Philadelphia, to serve for two years from the first Monday of June, following: *Provided*, That no member of the Bristol borough Council, shall be eligible to the office of warden, during his term as a member of said Council. Burgess and Council of Bristol authorized to elect a member of the Board. Proviso.

SEC. 475. That this act shall go into effect from and after the first day of June next; and so much of any act or acts as are hereby altered or supplied, or are inconsistent with this act, be and the same are hereby repealed.—May 20, 1864.—P. L. 908. When this act to go into effect. Repeal.

An Act to open and straighten Highland and Union avenue, and Thirtieth street, in the Twenty-second Ward, and Church and Adams streets, in the City of Philadelphia.

SEC. 476. That it shall be the duty of the Court of Common Pleas of the City of Philadelphia, within one month from the passage of this act, to appoint three commissioners, whose duty it shall be to proceed to view and lay out, widen and straighten Highland avenue to a sixty feet street, from Thirtieth street to the Montgomery County line; also to lay out, widen and straighten Union avenue, a fifty feet street, from Thirtieth to the Montgomery County line; also, to lay out, widen and straighten Thirtieth street, from Highland avenue to Park street; to lay out Adams street between Tulpehocken street and Johnson street and Church street, from Musgrove street, as laid out on City plan, to Main street, on the north-west side of said street and on south-east side, from Musgrove to Nash street, as laid out on City plan, Twenty-second ward, making the said Church street, between Musgrove and Nash street, to be forty feet in width and run in a straight line with that part, as conformed by the Court of Common Pleas, between Musgrove and Chew streets; and the said Church street, from Nash street to Main street, to be twenty feet wide. Said extension to be made and damages to be assessed and paid, as is provided by existing laws, and said streets to be put in good traveling order by the Highway Department, immediateiy upon the confirmation of the report of said Commissioners.—May 20, 1864.—P. L. 908.

An Act to vacate two intended streets, in the Twenty-fourth Ward of the City of Philadelphia.

SEC. 477. WHEREAS, Two streets, each thirty feet in width, one thereof situate one hundred and twenty feet west of Fortieth street and intended to lead south from Baltimore avenue to Woodland street, and the other thereof situate the like distance east of Forty-first street, and intended to lead south from said Baltimore avenue to Kingsessing avenue, a distance of about four hundred feet, in the Twenty-fourth ward of the City of Philadelphia, were laid out on the plan of the revised grade and survey regulations of the fourth section of the survey of West Philadelphia, but said streets were never dedicated to public use and are not intended to be opened, the same not being required for public use; now, therefore, *Be it enacted, &c.,* * * * * * *

SEC. 478. That the said two streets are hereby vacated and the soil therein vested in fee in the adjoining owners, to the middle thereof, respectively.—May 20, 1864.—P. L. 910.

An Act for the opening of Evergreen street, from Twenty-first street to Twenty-second street, in the Twenty-sixth Ward, and Venango street, in the Twenty-first Ward, of the City of Philadelphia.

SEC. 479. That the Chief Commissioner of Highways of the City of Philadelphia shall, within thirty days after the passage of this act, proceed and open, or cause to be opened for public use, Evergreen street, from Twenty-first street to Twenty-second street, in the Twenty-sixth ward of the City of Philadelphia, and Venango street, from Twentieth street to Twenty-first street, in the Twenty-first ward of said City; said Evergreen street to commence on the west side of said Twenty-first street, at the distance of one hundred and fifteen feet northward from the north side of Catharine street and to extend westwardly of the width of thirty feet, between lines parallel with said Catharine street, to the east side of Twenty-second street and Oxford street, Eighth to

Tenth, Diamond street, from Seventh street to Broad street, Twentieth ward.—May 20th, 1864.—P. L. 911.

A Further Supplement to the Act to incorporate the City of Philadelphia.

Repeal of provision relative to publishing, in newspapers, certain accounts, &c.

SEC. 480. That so much of the twelfth section of an act entitled, "A Further Supplement to the act to incorporate the City of Philadelphia," approved February second, one thousand eight hundred and fifty-four, as requires the City Controller to publish in two or more newspapers annually, verified by his oath or affirmation, the public accounts of the said City and of the trusts in their care, exhibiting all the receipts and expenditures of the City, the sources from which the revenues and funds are derived and in what manner the same have been disbursed, each account to be accompanied by a statement in detail in separate columns, of the several appropriations made by the City Councils, the amount drawn on each appropriation and the balance standing to the debit or credit of each such appropriation, be and the same is hereby repealed.

Validity of ordinances not recorded relative to.

SEC. 481. That no law shall be construed to impair the validity of an ordinance of the City of Philadelphia, if the same is not recorded; and all ordinances heretofore passed, or which may hereafter be enacted, shall be valid and effectual, although the same may not have been, or may not be recorded in the office of the Recorder of Deeds.

Vacancies in Councils.

SEC. 482. That in case of a vacancy occurring in either branch of the Councils of Philadelphia, the same shall be filled at the next general election, for the unexpired term.

Salaries of officers.

SEC. 483. That the Councils shall have power to fix the salaries of all municipal officers elected by the people.—May 20, 1864.—P. L. 911.

An Act to extend and open Pulaski street, in the City of Philadelphia.

SEC. 484. That the Chief Commissioner of Highways of the City of Philadelphia shall, within three months after the passage of this act, proceed and open or cause to be opened for the public use, Pulaski street, from Seventeenth street to Broad street, in the City of Philadelphia, which said Pulaski street is hereby extended from the west side of said Seventeenth street sixty feet, the same course it runs and is opened west thereof, to the east side of Broad street, and Seventeenth street to Master street to Dauphin street: *Provided,* That no expense shall be incurred or paid by the City of Philadelphia for grading said street.—May 20, 1864.—P. L. 912.

An Act for the opening of Jackson street, in the Second Ward of the City of Philadelphia.

SEC. 485. That Jackson street as now laid out and opened, northward from Ellsworth street, twenty-five feet in width, at the distance of one hundred and nineteen feet, and from the west side of Tenth street and parallel thereto, in the Second Ward of the City of Philadelphia, be continued and opened in a direct line from the point where the same is now built upon and improved with permanent brick messuages, a further distance of about ninety feet to the south line of Washington avenue; and that the Court of Quarter Sessions of the City of Philadephia shall, upon application being made to them, appoint a jury of view to assess the damages occasioned by said opening, which jury shall, immediately after the appointment, assess said damages and certify the same to the Court of Quarter Sessions aforesaid.—May 20, 1864. —P. L. 913.

An Act relating to Hamilton and Thirty-first streets, in the Twenty-fourth Ward, of the City of Philadelphia.

Parts of Hamilton and Thirty-first streets vacated.

SEC. 486. That so much of Hamilton street as lies between Mansion street and Bridgewater or Thirtieth street, and so much of Thirty-first street as lies between the Powelton estate of the Pennsylvania Railroad Company and Hamilton street, in the Twenty-fourth ward of said City of Philadelphia, be and the same are hereby vacated.

Damages to be paid by Pennsylvania Railroad Company.

SEC. 487. That it shall and may be lawful for any party injured thereby, if such there be, to apply for a jury in the manner prescribed by existing laws in force in the City of Philadelphia, in relation to the vacating of streets; and the award of such jury when finally confirmed, shall be paid by said Pennsylvania Railroad Company: *Provided,* That public notice of the closing of the parts of said streets hereby vacated, be given by advertisement in three newspapers, published in said City: *And provided also,* That such application for a jury be made within three months after such notice is first published.—July 7, 1864.—P. L. 951.

Notice of closing of streets to be given.

Application for jury, when to be made.

An Act to authorize the sale of certain Real Estate, in the City of Philadelphia.

SEC. 488. WHEREAS, On the twentieth day of August, one thousand eight hundred and six, there was conveyed to the Master and Assistant Wardens of the Port of Philadelphia, a piece of ground forty feet in width or front, upon the road leading to Gloucester Point, and in length or depth, extending from said road into the Delaware at low water mark, the southern boundary of said piece of land being distant eight hundred feet or thereabouts, from the north side of the wharf of Greenwich Point:

And whereas, Said land was conveyed to said Wardens in trust for and to the use of the Commonwealth of Pennsvlvania, for the purpose of erecting a pier at which vessels might unload and load gunpowder, to be stored in a magazine then conveniently thereto:

And whereas, The location of said magazine having been changed, no gunpowder has been unloaded or loaded upon said pier for a great number of years, and said pier having become so dilapidated as to be useless, it is to the interest of all parties that the same be sold and the money received therefrom be appropriated to the general purposes of the Commonwealth of Pennsylvania:

SEC. 489 That the Board of Wardens of the Port of Philadelphia, shall be and they are hereby authorized and required to sell, within three months, said powder pier at public sale after public notice, in at least two daily newspapers, published in said City, three times a week for two weeks and to convey the same, in fee simple to the purchasers by a deed executed under their seal, signed by the Master Warden and attested by the Clerk, which deed shall vest an absolute title in the purchaser, free, clear and discharged, from all and every trust, use and limitation; and the whole of the purchase money arising from said sale, shall be paid into the State Treasury; and all acts inconsistent herewith, are hereby repealed.—July 22, 1864.—P. L. 953.

To exempt the Penn Asylum of Philadelphia, for Indigent Widows and Single Women, from taxation.

SEC. 490. That the building and grounds thereto attached of the Penn Asylum of Philadelphia, for Indigent Widows and Single Women, situate in Belgrade street above Otis, in said City, be and the same are hereby exempted from taxation for City and County purposes; and all such taxes assessed thereon for the present year, are hereby exempted.—August 18, 1864.—P. L. 964.

A Further Supplement to an Act to incorporate the City of Philadelphia.

SEC. 491. That the Select and Common Councils of the City of Philadelphia, shall have the power to levy a tax for municipal purposes, on all subjects of taxation specified by the thirty-second section of the act of April twenty-ninth, one thousand eight hundred and forty-four, and to provide, by ordinance, a system for the assessment thereof, and for the collection of taxes thereon.

SESSION OF 1865.

A Further Supplement to an Act to incorporate the City of Philadelphia, relative to the election of School Directors in the Twenty-fifth Ward.

Time and manner of electing school directors.

SEC. 492. That at the next general election, the qualified voters of each election division of the Twenty-fifth Ward, of the City of Philadelphia, shall vote for three citizens of the said division, to serve as School Directors, and the three persons having the highest number of votes, in such division, shall be elected, one of whom shall serve for one year, one for two years, and one for three years; and at each annual election thereafter, the qualified voters, of each election division, shall vote for one citizen of said division to serve for three years, and the whole number of directors, elected from the several divisions, shall constitute the Board of Directors for said Twenty-fifth Ward; the term of each director to be determined by lot, at the first meeting of the board after their election.

Repeal.

SEC. 493. That all laws, or parts of laws, conflicting with the provisions of this act, be and the same are hereby repealed. —February 2, 1865.—P. L. 77.

An Act supplementary to an Act entitled "An Act in relation to Inspection," approved April fifteenth, one thousand eight hundred and thirty-five, relating to the compensation of the Bark Inspector of the Port of Philadelphia.

SEC. 494. That from and after the passage of this act, the Bark Inspector of the port of Philadelphia shall receive, in lieu of the compensation allowed him by the act to which this is a supplement, the sum of one dollar and sixty cents, for inspecting every ton weight of bark, and a proportionate sum for tierces and barrels; and that so much of the act to which this is a supplement, as is inconsistent herewith, be and the same is hereby repealed.—February 2, 1865.—P. L. 86.

A further Supplement to an Act to incorporate the City of Philadelphia, passed February second, Anno Domini one thousand eight hundred and fifty-four, relative to the election of School Directors in the Twenty-first Ward.

SEC. 495. That the true intent and meaning of the act, entitled "An Act to elect School Directors in the Twenty-first Ward," shall be but eighteen, and that the eighteen School Directors elected by the qualified citizens of the Twenty-first Ward, on the second Tuesday of October, Anno Domini one thousand eight hundred and sixty-four, shall constitute the School Board of said ward; and that the term of the School Directors, heretofore elected by the citizens of Manayunk, Roxborough and Penn District, in the Twenty-first Ward, shall expire and terminate on the thirty-first of December, Anno Domini one thousand eight hundred and sixty four, and the said act of April eighteenth, eighteen hundred and sixty-four, shall be construed as if the provision of this declaratory act had been therein inserted.—February 2, 1865.—P. L. 87.

An Act to amend the Fee Bill as to Aldermen, in and for the City of Philadelphia.

SEC. 496. That from and after the passage of this act, the fees to be received by Aldermen in the City of Philadelphia, shall be as follows: For information or complaint, on behalf of the commonwealth, thirty cents; docket entry of action, on behalf of the commonwealth, twenty five cents; warrant, *mittimus* or *capias*, on behalf of the commonwealth, fifty cents; writing an examination or confession of defendant, fifty cents; hearing in criminal cases, fifty cents; administering oath or affidavit in criminal or civil cases, ten cents; taking recognizance in criminal case, thirty cents; transcript in criminal case, including certificate, fifty cents; entering judgment on conviction for fine, fifty cents; recording conviction, twenty-five cents; warrants to levy fine or forfeiture, thirty cents; bail piece and return supersedeas, thirty cents; discharge to jailor, thirty-five cents; entering discontinuance in case of an assault and battery, fifty cents; entering complaint of master, mistress or an apprentice, thirty cents; notice to master, mistress or apprentice, twenty-five cents; hearing parties, fifty cents; holding inquisition, under landlord and tenant act, or in case of forcible entry, each day, each justice two dollars; process, et cetera, to sheriff, each justice, seventy-five cents; recording proceedings, each justice, one dollar and fifty cents; writ of restitution, each justice, seventy-five cents; warrant to appraise damages, thirty cents; warrant to sell strays, thirty cents; warrant to appraise swine, thirty-five cents; receiving and entering return of appraisement of swine, twenty-five cents; publishing proceedings of appraisers of swine, seventy-five cents; entering action in civil case, twenty-five cents; summons or *subpœna*, twenty five cents; *capias* in civil case, fifty cents; every additional name after the first, all witnesses' names to be in one *subpœna*, unless separate subpœnas be requested by the parties, ten cents; *subpœna duces tecum*, twenty-five cents; entering return of summons, twenty-five cents; entering *capias* and bail bond, twenty-five cents; every continuance of suit, twenty cents; trial and judgment in case, fifty cents; taking bail or plea of freehold, twenty-five cents; entering satisfaction, fifteen cents; entering discontinuance of suit, fifteen cents; entering amicable suit, fifty cents; entering rule to take deposition of witnesses, fifteen cents; rule to take depositions, twenty-five cents; interrogatories annexed to rule to take depositions, twenty-five cents; entering return of rule in any case, fifteen cents; entering rule to refer, fifteen cents; rule of reference, twenty-five cents; notice to each referee, twenty-five cents, entering report of referees and judgment thereon, thirty cents; written notice in any case, twenty-five cents; execution, thirty cents; entering return of execution, fifteen cents; *scire facias*, in any case, thirty-five cents; opening judgment for a re-hearing, twenty-five cents; transcript of judgment and certificate, fifty cents; return of proceedings on *certiorari*, or appeal, including recognizance, one dollar; receiving the amount of a judgment and paying the same over, if not exceeding ten dollars, twenty five cents; if exceeding ten and not exceeding thirty dollars, thirty-five cents; if exceeding thirty dollars, sixty-five cents; every search service, to which no fees are attached, twenty cents; affidavit in case of attachment, thirty cents; entering action in case of attachment, twenty-five cents; attachment in any case, thirty-five cents; recognizance, fifty cents; interrogatories, thirty-five cents; rule on garnishee, twenty-five cents; return of rule on garnishee, twenty-five cents; bond in case of attachment fifty cents; entering return, and appointing freeholders, twenty-five cents; advertisement, each, twenty-five cents; order to sell goods, thirty-five cents; order for the relief of a pauper, thirty cents; entering transcript of judgment from another justice or alderman, fifty cents; order for the removal of a pauper each justice or alderman, one dollar; order to seize good for the maintenance of wife and children, fifty cents; order for premium for wolf, fox or other scalps, to be paid by the county, twenty-five cents; every acknowledgment, or probate of deed or other instrument of writing, for the first name, fifty cents; each additional name, after the first, twenty-five cents; taking and signing acknowledgment of indenture of an apprentice, fifty cents; assignment and making record of indenture, fifty cents; cancelling indenture, fifty cents; comparing and signing tax duplicates, each alderman, seventy-five cents; marrying each couple, making record thereof, and certificates to the parties, five dollars; certificate of approbation of two justices, to the binding as apprentice of a person, by the directors of the poor, each justice. thirty-five cents; certificate to obtain land warrant, seventy-five cents; swearing or affirming county commissioner, assessor, director of the poor, or other township officer, or county officer, and certificate, fifty cents; administering oaths or affirmations, in any case not herein provided for, twenty-five cents; justifying parties on bonds for tavern licenses, one dollar; entering complaint, in landlord and tenant proceedings, act one thousand eight hundred and thirty, twenty-five cents; issuing process, in landlord and tenant proceedings, act one thousand eight hundred and thirty, twenty-five cents; hearing and determining case, in landlord and tenant proceedings, act one thousand eight hundred and thirty, fifty cents; record of proceedings, in landlord and tenant proceedings, act one thousand eight hundred and thirty, fifty cents; writ of possession, (and return,) in landlord and tenant proceedings, act one thousand eight hundred and thirty, fifty cents; when more than one magistrate is required, in landlord and tenant proceedings, the above fees shall be charged by each magistrate; entering complaint, in landlord and tenant proceedings, act one thousand eight hundred and sixty-three, seventy-five cents; issuing process, in landlord and tenant proceedings, act one thousand eight hundred and sixty-three, seventy-five cents; hearing and determining case, act one thousand eight hundred and sixty-three, one dollar; record of proceedings, act one thousand eight hundred and sixty-three, one dollar and fifty cents; issuing writ of restitution, (and return,) act one thousand eight hundred and sixty-three, one dollar.

SEC. 497. (To remain as heretofore, to wit:) The fees for services, under the laws of the United States shall be as follows: For certificate of protection, fifty cents; for certificate of lost protection, twenty-five cents; warrant, twenty-five cents; commitment, twenty-five cents; summons for seamen, in admiralty case, twenty-five cents; hearing thereon, with docket entry, fifty cents; for certificate to clerk of the district court, to issue admiralty process, twenty-five cents.—February 3, 1865.—P. L. 92.

A Supplement to an Act to open and straighten Highland and Union avenue, and Thirtieth street, in the Twenty-second ward, and Church and Adams street, in the City of Philadelphia, approved the Twentieth of May, Anno Domini one thousand eight hundred and sixty-four.

Construction of certain provisions.

SEC. 498. That so much of the above act that reads, from Nash street to Main street, to be twenty feet wide, shall so be construed by the Commissioners in making their report to the Court, so as to read, and the said Church street, from Nash street to Main street, to be twenty feet wide, leaving the house of the late Nathan Birchalls, on the north west corner of Main and Church street, remain as it is, on the line of said street, and no curbing or foot pavement shall be required to be laid along the grave yard wall, on the south-easterly side of said Church street, between Nash street and Germantown avenue.

Duty of chief commissioners of highways. SEC. 499. That thirty days after the confirmation of the report of the commissioners, appointed by the Court of Common Pleas, it shall be the duty of the Chief Commissioners of Highways to notify the property holders, on said Church street, to set in their fences on the line of the aforesaid confirmed street: *Provided*, The property owners, to whom damages have been awarded by the commissioners, shall have been duly paid the said award.—February 4, 1865.—P. L. 97.

Proviso.

An Act regulating the Fees of the Clerk of the Quarter Sessions of the Peace, and so forth, for the City and County of Philadelphia.

SEC. 500. That during the term of the present Clerk of the Quarter Sessions of the Peace, the Court of Oyer and Terminer, and General Jail Delivery, of the City and County of Philadelphia, all fees, which are now, by law, chargeable and receivable by him, shall be increased fifty per centum, and that the amount of tax, to be by him paid to the commonwealth, shall be fifty per centum on the excess received over fifteen hundred dollars per annum.—February 8, 1865.—P. L. 109.

An Act relative to the Pay of Assessors, in the City of Philadelphia.

SEC. 501. WHEREAS, It is important to the state, that competent persons be chosen as assessors, the justness and equalization of taxes depending upon the valuation by them:

And whereas, By reason of the many changes and transfers of real estate, in the City of Philadelphia, the Assessors of said city are compelled to make a full and complete assessment, yearly, as well as attend appeals, extra assessments, enroll militia soldiers, et cetera, which said duties require their personal attention the greater part of the year, and as it is but just that they should be remunerated for their services; therefore

SEC. 502. That from and after the passage of this act, the pay of each of the Assessors, of the City of Philadelphia, shall be five hundred and fifty dollars per annum; which said sum shall be a full compensation for all services imposed by law, or be hereafter imposed by the State or municipal authorities; and so much of any act, heretofore passed, as may be inconsistent herewith, be and the same is hereby repealed.—February 10, 1865.—P. L. 136.

A further Supplement to an Act to Incorporate the City of Philadelphia, providing for the Time of Meeting of Sectional School Board, and Filling Vacancies therein.

SEC. 503. That the Board of Directors of each school section, in the City of Philadelphia, shall hereafter meet and organize their respective boards, by the election of a president and secretary, on the first Monday of January next succeeding the annual election for directors.

When school boards to meet and organize.

SEC. 504. If any person, duly elected a School Director, shall refuse to attend a regular meeting of the board, after having personally received written notice from the secretary, to appear and enter upon the duties of his office, or if any person, having taking upon him the duties of his office, as director, shall neglect to attend any three regular meetings of the board, in succession, unless detained by sickness, or prevented by absence from the district, or shall refuse to act in his official capacity, when in attendance, for three regular meetings, the directors present shall have power to declare his seat, in the board vacant, and appoint another in his stead to serve until the next municipal election.—February 16, 1865.—P. L. 151.

The seats of directors neglecting to attend meetings may be declared vacant.

An Act for the Better Security of Life and Limb in the City of Philadelphia.

SEC. 505. That in any store, or building, in the City of Philadelphia, in which there shall exist, or be placed, any hoistway, hatchway, elevator, or well hole, or in which there shall be made any opening through the floor, the same shall be properly protected, or covered, by a good and sufficient trap-door, or such other appliances as may be necessary to secure the same from being or becoming dangerous to life, or limb, and on the completion of the business of each, the said trap-door, or other appliances, shall be safely closed by the occupant having the use and control of the same; any violation of the provision of this act shall subject the offender, or offenders, to a fine of fifty dollars, for each offence, to be recovered, with cost of suit, in an action of debt, in any court having cognizance thereof, by, to and for the use of the Philadelphia Association for the Relief of Disabled Firemen.—February 16, 1865.—P. L. 152.

An Act to amend an Act, entitled "An Act to Incorporate the City of Philadelphia," approved February second, one thousand eight hundred and fifty-four, so far as Relates to the Board of School Controllers.

SEC. 506. That the controllers of the public schools, of the First school district of Pennsylvania, shall establish a system for the examination of the qualifications

Controllers to establish a system of examination of teachers.

of all persons, who may desire to become teachers, in the public schools of said district, the said examinations to be held at such times and places, and under such system, rules and regulations, as the said Controllers shall, from time to time, adopt.

Teachers, hereafter elected, required to have a certificate of qualification.

SEC. 507. No person shall, from and after the passage of this act, be elected to the position of teacher, in any of the public schools of said district, by any of the sectional Boards of School Directors, within the same, unless such person shall have been found duly qualified for the position to which he, or she, shall have been elected, nor unless he, or she, shall have received a certificate of qualification, duly issued by the authority of said controllers, after his or her examination, provided for in the first section of this act: *Provided*, The exclusive right of the several sectional boards of school directors, within said district, to elect the teachers of their respective sections, shall be and remain unimpaired, except in so far as the same is qualified by this act.

Proviso.

Directors to certify, to controllers, names and grade of teachers, heretofore elected, and by them to be certified to City Controller.

SEC. 508. It shall be the duty of the several sectional Boards of School Directors, within said district, to certify to the said Controllers, within thirty days from the passage of this act, a complete list of the names and grade of all teachers, in the respective sections, who had been duly elected as such, prior to the passage of this act; which said list shall be, within sixty days from the passage of this act, duly certified by said Controllers, under their common and corporate seal, to the Controller of the City of Philadelphia.

Directors to certify names and grade of teachers, hereafter elected, &c.

SEC. 509. It shall be the duty of the Directors of the Public Schools, of the several sections, in like manner, from time to time, to certify to the Controllers of the public schools of said district, the names and grade of all persons qualified as aforesaid, who shall hereafter be elected to the position of teacher in the said district; which said names and grade shall also be certified, by said Controllers, to the said City Controller.—February 17, 1865.—P. L. 176.

A further Supplement to An Act to Incorporate the City of Philadelphia, relating to Fire Alarm and Police Telegraph.

SEC. 510, WHEREAS, The signal boxes of the fire alarm telegraph, within the corporate limits of the City of Philadelphia, are frequently broken open, and false alarms of fire given, and the wires and poles of the police and fire alarm telegraph disturbed and broken, by malicious persons:

And whereas, There is now no law, under which the said person, or persons, thus offending, can be punished; therefore,

SEC. 511. That if any person or persons shall wilfully give, or cause to be given, any false alarm of fire, from a fire alarm telegraph box or boxes, or shall break, or cause to be broken, any fire alarm box, or any pole, post, or wire, connected with the police and fire alarm telegraph, within the City of Philadelphia, or shall injure, or in any manner intefere with, or interrupt, the working of the same, he, she or they, shall be deemed guilty of a misdemeanor, and on conviction thereof, shall be punished by a fine, not exceeding five hundred dollars, for each offence, or by imprisonment, for a term not exceeding two years, or by both.—February 28, 1864.—P. L. 238.

An Act for the better security of the City of Philadelphia from dangers incident to the refining or improper and negligent storage of Petroleum, Benzine, Benzole or Naptha.

SEC. 512. That after ninety days from the passage of this Act, no petroleum, benzine, benzole or naptha shall be refined or manufactured within the City of Philadelphia, on the eastern side of the river Schuylkill, between Allegheny avenue and Mifflin street, excepting thereout the area southward of Washington street, and between the river Schuylkill and Thirtieth street, or on the western side of the river Schuylkill, south of Girard avenue and east of Forty-third street; nor shall the same be kept or stored in any building or other premises within such limits, in any greater quantity, at any one time, than twenty-five barrels of refined petroleum, and one barrel of crude petroleum, and one barrel of benzine, benzole or naptha respectively; the said barrels to be kept or stored in buildings with cellars of sufficient depth, or in premises properly excavated or embanked to prevent any overflow of the fluids therefrom, under forfeiture, as hereinafter directed, of the entire quantity of each and all of the said articles of merchandize, that shall be so refined, kept or stored, contrary to the restrictions of this Act: *Provided*, That it shall not be lawful to keep or store the said quantities of refined petroleum, crude petroleum, benzine, benzole, or naptha, within the designated limits without license therefor, first had from the Mayor of the City of Philadelphia, upon due certificate, to be given by the Fire Marshal of the said city, that the cellar, excavation or premises, in which storage, as aforesaid, shall be authorized, will afford reasonable security from special danger, in case of accidents or fire, for which license the sum of ten dollars shall be paid to the City Treasury; and such license to be renewed for each calendar year, upon annual payment as aforesaid: *Provided*, That those persons engaged in the business of refining petroleum within the above limits, who have erected iron tanks and other suitable and safe protection against the escape and dispersion of the same, which fact shall be certified by the Fire Marshal to

The refining or manufacturing of petroleum within certain limits, prohibited.

Restrictions as to storage of the same.

License therefor to be obtained from the Mayor, upon certificate of Fire Marshal.

Persons, who have erected iron tanks &c., not liable to provisions, until one year after passage of act.

the Mayor, shall not be subject to the provisions of this Act, until the expiration of one year from the passage hereof: *And provided further*, That nothing herein contained shall prevent the refining, storing or depositing of crude or refined petroleum, or coal oil, on the west side of the Schuylkill, east of Thirtieth street, between Bridge street and Arch street, and between Chestnut street and South street, on premises, with sufficient excavations or embankments to prevent the overflow or escape of the oil so refined, stored or deposited, in case of fire or accident: *And provided further*, That no refining of petroleum, benzine, benzole, or naptha shall be carried on within five hundred feet of the east or west side of the river Schuylkill, within the said city, north of the line of Girard avenue.

Proviso.

Proviso.

Petroleum, &c., may be manufactured, refined and stored within certain limits.

SEC. 513. That it shall be lawful to refine, manufacture, store and keep petroleum, benzine, benzole and naptha in such quantities as may be desired, in those portions of the City of Philadelphia, east and west of the river Schuylkill, not included within the limits designated in the first section of this Act, for prohibition therefrom: *Provided*, That the same be at least one hundred feet distant from any dwelling, without the written consent of the owner thereof: *And provided further*, That a license be first had from the Mayor of the City of Philadelphia, for which ten dollars shall be paid into the City Treasury, and likewise, for the annual renewal thereof, after certificate, to be given by the Fire Marshal of the said city, upon actual survey and inspection of the building or premises in which said commodities shall be refined, kept or stored, or are designed so to be, that the said buildings or premises have suitable tanks, cellars, excavations or embankments, to prevent the overflow or escape of petroleum and like commodities in the event of accident or fire; which certificate of survey and inspection shall be returned to the Mayor; whereupon, if the same be approved by him, he shall issue his license in accordance with the provisions of this Act.

Proviso.

License therefor.

Certificate to be given by Fire Marshal.

Mayor may issue warrant for search and seizure, upon information made of any violation of the provisions of this Act.

SEC. 514. Whenever any inhabitant of the said city shall make oath or affirmation, before the Mayor of the City of Philadelphia, which shall afford probable cause to believe that any petroleum, benzine, benzole or naptha, is improperly stored, kept or refined, contrary to the provisions of this Act, it shall be lawful for the said Mayor to issue his warrant or warrants, to any police officer of the said city, or other fit persons commanding him or them to search for such petroleum, benzine, benzole or naptha, wherever the same may be, in violation of any of the provisions of this Act, and if found, to seize and take possession of the same, and cause the same to be removed to such safe place as the Mayor shall thereupon designate, in writing

SEC. 515. All actions or suits, for the recovery of any petroleum, benzine, benzole or naptha, which may have been seized and detained, by virtue of the provisions of this Act, or for the value thereof, or for damages sustained by the seizure or detention thereof, shall be brought against the Philadelphia Association for the Relief of Disabled Firemen, and shall be commenced within one calendar month after such seizure shall have been actually made; and in case no action or suit shall have been commenced within such period, such petroleum, benzine, benzole or naptha shall be deemed absolutely forfeited to said Philadelphia Association for the Relief of Disabled Firemen, and may be immediately delivered up to the proper officers thereof, for its use.—March 2, 1865.—P. L. 264.

Actions for recovery of petroleum, &c. seized how to be brought.

An act to promote the more certain and equal Assessment of Taxes in Philadelphia.

SEC. 516. That the Court of Common Pleas of Philadelphia county, shall, once in every three years, before the time of the revision of the taxes for the succeeding year, and as often as vacancies shall occur, appoint two persons, deemed the most competent, who, with the Senior City Commissioner, for the time being, shall compose the Board of Revision of Taxes, of the county; a majority of whom shall be a quorum; who shall have the power to revise and equalize the assessments, by raising or lowering the valuations, either in individual cases, or by wards, to rectify all errors, to make valuations where they have been omitted, and to require the attendance of the assessors or other citizens before them, for examination on oath or affirmation, either singly or together, with power to forfeit the pay of assessors, rateably to their annual compensation, for each day's absence, when their attendance is required; and the said Board of Revision shall hear all the appeals and applications of the tax-payers, subject to an appeal from their decision to the Court of Common Pleas of the county, whose decision shall be final, and if the appeal to the court shall be groundless, the appellant shall pay their costs of court; the City Commissioners shall have no power to correct or revise the taxes, but shall receive, in writing, the request of tax-payers to have their taxes reduced, and lay them before the Board of Revision, at the next meeting; the Board of Revision shall hear the tax-payers of their respective wards, in succession, of which notice shall be given as now required by law, by the commissioners and assessors; and the said Board of

Court of Common Pleas to appoint, triennially, two persons to act with the senior commissioner, as a board of revision.

Their powers and duties.

Revision shall alone, by a majority of them, exercise all the powers heretofore vested in the County Board of Revision, but shall not in any instance lower the aggregate valuation of the county; they shall meet as often, but not oftener than is necessary to despatch the business which their duties require of them, and shall hold stated meetings on the first Saturday of each month, and receive the same compensation as the City Commissioners; but the Senior Commissioner shall receive no additional pay for his services in the Board of Revision.

Meetings, when to be held.

Compensation.

Chief Engineer and Surveyor to have books of plans of the city made out.

SEC. 517. The Chief Engineer and Surveyor of the City of Philadelphia, under an ordinance and appropriation by the Councils thereof, shall cause to be made books of plans of the said city, divided into sections, so far as the streets of the said city are or shall be laid out, which shall show the situation and dimensions of each property therein, with the city numbers thereof, and who are the owners, with such succession of blank columns as will permit the names of future owners to be entered therein, with the dates of transfer, and with index for recording such names alphabetically; and the person or persons who shall be employed to perform such duty, shall have access to all plans of survey in the offices of any surveyor of the said city, to all books in the Recorder of Deeds' office, and all records of the courts, and in the Register's office, and may take copies or extracts thereof without any charge therefor.

The originals to be kept in the Department of Surveys, and duplicates thereof, in office of Commissioners.

SEC. 518. The original books, when made, shall be kept in the fireproof of the Department of Surveys of the said city, and a duplicate set thereof shall be placed by the Chief Engineer and Surveyor in the office of the City Commissioners, and be there safely preserved in the fireproof; and the said Chief Engineer and Surveyor shall keep up the books in his office, so as to show at all times who are the owners of the lots on the plans, and before the annual meeting of the Board of Revision, for revising the valuations for taxation, shall cause the books in the Commissioners' office, to be brought up to that time; and such books shall be kept in such manner as not to destroy the evidence of the ownerships, at any previous time, but by additions which will show the subdivisions of property, and the owners thereof, as transmissions of title may take place; and the said Chief Engineer and Surveyor may furnish copies of the said books, or parts thereof, for such price as may be fixed by councils, for the use of the city; and his certificate shall be received in evidence, as and for such proof as the assessment books would be, and lithographed copies

Duties of the Chief Engineer and Surveyor in relation thereto.

He may furnish copies thereof.

of the said books may be multiplied and sold for the profit of the said city.

SEC. 519. To enable the Chief Engineer and Surveyor of the city to keep up the said books of plans, it shall be the duty of every seller and buyer of ground upon the planned plot of the City of Philadelphia, to make report to him of every conveyance made, with the precise dimensions and locality of the premises, and so doing the same shall be received without charge, and noted on the deed of conveyance, by the assistant of the said Chief Engineer and Surveyor; but if said seller and buyer shall both omit said duty, the Recorder of Deeds of the said county of Philadelphia, shall not admit the deed of conveyance to record in his office, without charging fifteen cents for each lot described therein; and it shall then be his duty to furnish the proper description of such lot or lots, with the date of conveyance, and names of grantor or grantee, within one month, into the office of the Department of Surveys, under the penalty of one dollar for each omission, to be recovered as penalties for taking unlawful fees are recovered, for the use of the said city; and it shall be the duty of every purchaser of houses and lands at judicial sales, and of every one to whom an allotment in partition shall have been made, and of every devisee by will, to make return to the Chief Engineer and Surveyor of the purchase he has made, or allotment he has received, and of all devises made to him by will, with descriptions as aforesaid, which the said Chief Engineer and Surveyor shall receive without charge; but if he shall not have done so simultaneously with the completion of his purchase, or on partition effected, or if on probate of any will, the devisee shall not have done so, as to any houses or lands in the said city, purchased, allotted, or devised, it shall be the duty of the clerk or prothonotary of the proper court, under whose authority such judgment or partition shall have been made, and for the Register of Wills, to furnish such descriptions as are above required of the Recorder of Deeds, so far as the wills to be proved in his office shall enable him to do so, for the like charge, and under the same penalty; and the clerk or prothonotary, and, Register, may make such charge against such purchaser, or party taking in partition, or devisee, on delivery of the deed, certifying proceedings in partition, or granting probate of the will, and that whether the same be in trust, or for any estate for life only, or otherwise, unless the party interested shall produce to him or

Sellers and buyers of property to make report to Engineer of all conveyances made.

To be noted on deed.

In case of neglect to do so, the Recorder of Deeds shall, upon payment of charges, return the description to the Department of Surveys.

Penalty for omission.

Purchasers at judicial sales, devisees by will, &c., to make similar returns.

Duties of clerks of courts and Registers of Wills in cases of omission by parties above mentioned.

them, the certificate of the Chief Engineer and Surveyor that such duty has been performed.

Liability for taxes.

SEC. 520. If neither the seller or buyer, devisee or heir, or other party, who has acquired title to houses and lands, in the said city, shall have furnished the description of the property sold as aforesaid, both he who may have parted with and he who acquired title, shall be liable for the taxes thereafter assessed thereon, without right of reclamation, or contribution therefor, either against the other, and if the lands or houses sold be afterwards sold for taxes, thereafter accruing, as a lien by record, before said duty shall have been performed, the purchaser shall acquire title as now he may by law, within the county of Philadelphia; but if the said duty of making the return, as required by this act, shall have been discharged by the party who shall have acquired title, in whatsoever manner, before the tax accrued, as a lien of record, for which the same shall have been sold, the purchaser at the tax sale shall not acquire the title of such person, who shall have performed said duty, or of his heirs or assigns, unless the sale shall have been made in the name of such owner, after service of process upon him, as in case of suit by summons.

Tax sales, relative to

Engineer may make searches for conveyances devises, &c., not reported.

SEC. 521. And should the Chief Engineer and Surveyor apprehend that conveyances, or devises, or descents, of houses or lands, shall have taken place, without being reported to him, he shall cause search to be made therefor, and perfect his books of plans; and every person found delinquent for six months after acquiring title, as aforesaid, in making report as aforesaid, shall be liable to a fine of five dollars, to be recovered by the said Chief Engineer and Surveyor, in the name of the city, as debts of that amount are by law recoverable.

Penalty for failure to make report.

Reports of descriptions to be arranged, &c.

SEC. 522. The Chief Engineer and Surveyor shall preserve on file, arranged alphabetically and according to date, all reports made to him of descriptions of houses and lands, and for twenty-five cents shall give his certificate, at the foot of a duplicate of the description or descriptions, that report has been made into his office of the description of the designated property or properties, when a duplicate of descriptions shall be produced to him, with the certificate written out for his signature, and his certificate shall be evidence for the receiver of it, and any clerk, prothonotary and Register, and all others, that this law has been complied with.

Certificates to be given by Engineer, and to be evidence.

Assessment books and duplicates to be made by Commissioners.

SEC. 523. It shall be the duty of the City Commissioners to cause to be made assessment books, and duplicates, in the form that shall be prescribed by the

Councils of the city, and no other, and to have the same bound and permanently preserved in their office, the duplicates whereof shall be kept in the office of the Receiver of Taxes, and they shall be made in conformity with the books of plans, to be furnished by the Chief Engineer and Surveyor, whenever and as furnished by the successive wards, omitting no property thereon, nor the name of any owner; and it shall be the duty of every assessor, whenever he shall find any property to be owned differently from the name in the proper assessment book, to report such change to the Chief Engineer and Surveyor without delay, and the Chief Engineer and Surveyor, if finding such report correct, shall make the book of plans conform, by the proper entry, but without erasure of any name; and the failure of the assessor to perform this duty shall subject him to a charge or penalty of five dollars for each such omission, to be recovered as debts of the amount thereof are recoverable by law.

Duplicates to be kept in office of the Receiver of Taxes.

Duty of assessors, in reference to errors in book.

Penalty for neglect to report.

SEC. 524. It shall be the duty of all owners of houses and lots to furnish, forthwith, descriptions of their property to the Chief Engineer and Surveyor, to aid him in making up the books of plans; and whensoever such descriptions shall have been so furnished, and the certificate of the Chief Engineer and Surveyor shall be received, no property so returned shall be subject to sale for taxes, thereafter to accrue, as a lien of record thereon, except in the name of the owner, as returned, and after recovery by suit, and service of the writ on him, made as in case of a summons, and all such returns shall be arranged and filed alphabetically.—March 14, 1865.—P. L. 324.

Duty of owners of property.

An Act to amend the Fee Bill, as to Constables, in the City of Philadelphia.

SEC. 525. That from and after the passage of this act, the fees to be received by constables, in the City of Philadelphia, shall be as follows: for executing warrants, on behalf of the commonwealth, sixty cents; for taking body into custody, or conveying to jail, on *mittimus*, or warrant, fifty cents; for arresting a vagrant, disorderly person, or other offenders against the law, (without process) and bringing before a justice, fifty cents; for levying a fine, or forfeiture, on a warrant, thirty-five cents; for serving *subpœna*, twenty-five cents; for serving summons, notice on referee, suiter, master, or mistress, or apprentice, personally, each, twenty-five cents; for serving, by leaving a copy, twenty-five cents; for executing attachment, thirty-five cents; for arresting, on *capias*, fifty cents; for taking bail bond, on *capias* or for delivery of goods, twenty-five cents; for notifying plaintiff, where defendant has been arrested, on *capias*, to be paid by plaintiff, twenty-five cents; for serving summons, landlord and tenant proceedings, fifty cents; for executing writ of possession, landlord and tenant proceedings, one dollar; for executing landlord's warrant, fifty cents; for serving execution, thirty-five cents; for taking inventory of goods, on landlord's warrant, (each item,) two cents; for levying or distraining goods, and selling the same, for each dollar, not exceeding one hundred dollars, six cents; and for each dollar, above one hundred dollars, four cents; (and one-half of said commission shall be allowed, where the money is paid after the levy without sale, but no commission shall, in any case, be taken on more than the real debt, and then only for the money actually received by the constable, and paid over to the creditor;) for advertising the same, fifty cents; for copy of a vendue paper, when demanded, each item, two cents; for putting up notice of distress, at mansion house, or at any other public place, on the premises, twenty-five cents; for serving *scire facias*, personally, twenty-five cents; for serving, by leaving a copy, twenty-five cents; for executing bail piece, fifty cents; for travelling expenses, on an execution returned *nulla bona*, and *non est inventus*, where the constable has been at the defendant's last residence, each mile circular, five cents; for executing order for removal of a pauper, seventy-five cents; for traveling expenses, in said removal, each mile circular, fifteen cents; for traveling expenses, in all other cases, each mile circular, five cents.—March 14, 1865.—P. L. 344.

An Act to authorize the Chief Engineer and Surveyor of the City of Philadelphia to revise the Grades of certain portions of Bridgewater street, in the Twenty-fourth Ward of the City of Philadelphia.

SEC. 526. That the Chief Engineer and Surveyor of the City of Philadelphia be and he is hereby authorized and directed to revise the grade of Bridgewater street, between Market and Bridge streets, in the Twenty-fourth Ward of the City of Philadelphia, in such way and manner as will permit the free use for railroad purposes, of the front, on the river Schuylkill, between said Market and Bridge streets, and of the wharf or wharves, that may be erected on the same; and when said revision shall have been made, the said Chief Engineer and Surveyor is hereby further directed to make and file a report thereof, in the office of the Court of Common Pleas of the City and County of Philadelphia: *Provided*, That the City of Philadelphia shall be at no expense for said revision.—March 17, 1865.—P. L. 419.

An Act to vacate Ellwood lane, between Fourth and Sixth streets, in the Twenty-fifth Ward of the City of Philadelphia.

SEC. 527. That so much of Ellwood lane, as lies between the east side of Fourth street and the west side of Sixth street, in the Twenty-fifth Ward of the City of Philadelphia, be and the same is hereby vacated.—March 21, 1865.—P. L. 446.

An Act to vacate so much of Carpenter street, as lies west of Twenty-sixth street, in the City of Philadelphia.

SEC. 528. That so much of Carpenter street as lies west of Twenty-sixth street, and east of the Schuylkill river, in the Twenty-sixth Ward of the City of Philadelphia, be and the same is hereby vacated.—March 21, 1865.—P. L. 452.

A Supplement to an Act, entitled "An Act to provide for the appointment of Fence Viewers in the City of Philadelphia," approved March 11, 1862.

Building and repairing fences, relative to.

SEC. 529. That if the party, who shall be delinquent in making or repairing any fence, in accordance with the provisions of the Act, of which this is a supplement, shall not, within ten days after the report shall have been approved by the Board of Surveyors, proceed to repair or build said fence, and complete the same in a reasonable time, it shall be lawful for the parties aggrieved, to repair or build said fence; and if the costs for the work done and materials furnished, are not paid by the delinquent party, within three months after the completion of the same, a lien may be filed against the premises, for said costs and expenses, which shall be of the same effect, and may be sued out and collected in the same manner, as municipal claims are now, by law, collected.

Repeal of certain section.

SEC. 530. That the third section of the Act, of which this is a supplement, is hereby repealed.—March 22, 1865.—P. L. 538.

An Act authorizing the paving of a part of Ridge avenue, in the City of Philadelphia.

SEC. 531. That the Chief Commissioner of Highways shall enter into a contract to curb and pave a footway six feet in width, along the northwest side Ridge avenue, from Columbia street to Wissahickon avenue; the contractor to accept, as cash, the claims against the land, fronting thereon, who shall have the power to use the name of the City of Philadelphia in filing said claims for collection.—March 22, 1865.—P. L. 554.

Supplement to an Act for the registration of Births, Marriages and Deaths in the City of Philadelphia, passed March 8, 1860, providing for the registration of Marriages, which occurred prior to the passage of said Act.

SEC. 532. That the Health Officer of the City of Philadelphia shall register, in a book for that purpose, to be furnished by the City Commissioners of said city, upon presentation to him, of certificates properly authenticated by either the affidavit of the clergyman, who performed the marriage service, or in case of his death, the affidavit of two persons that they were acquainted with his handwriting, and knew his signature, and that the signature, attached to such certificate of marriage, is the genuine signature of such clergyman, such marriages as have occurred prior to the passage of the Act to which this is a supplement; and upon demand made of him, by any persons interested, he shall give a certificate of such registration of marriage, duly certified by him, which shall be of like force and effect as evidence, or otherwise, as the certificates provided for in the Act to which this is a supplement; and for such certificate, he shall be entitled to receive the same fees as are allowed in the said Act. —March 22, 1865.—P. L. 560.

An Act to authorize the paving of Foot-ways in the Twenty-second and Twenty-fourth Wards of the City of Philadelphia.

Upon the petition of a majority of property owners, Councils may direct footways to be paved.

SEC. 533. That when a majority of the property owners, or the owners of a majority of the feet frontage, for a continuous distance of five hundred feet or more, on any one, or both sides of any street, road or lane used as a public highway, in the Twenty-second and Twenty-fourth Wards, shall petition Councils of said city for a paved footway along the same, they shall state, in their petition, the kind of pavement wanted by them; and Councils shall, when such petition is received, direct the Highway Department of said city, to notify the owners of property on said street, or such parts thereof as may have been included in the petition, to have such footway paved in front of their respective premises, in the manner indicated in the petition, within thirty days after receiving said notice.

Refusal or neglect to make pavement, relative to.

SEC. 534. That should any of the property owners refuse or neglect to make said pavement, for thirty days after notice has been given, the High Department shall proceed, without delay, to have it made, and charge the cost thereof to the property in front of which it is made; and if said cost is not paid within thirty days after a bill for the same has been presented, a claim shall be filed in the proper court for the amount thereof; which claim shall be a lien against the property, and shall be collected in the same manner as other municipal claims are now, by law, collected.

In case of neglect of owners to repair pavements, the Highway Department shall have the same done.

SEC. 535. That when said pavement requires repairing, and the owner or owners of property in front of which the repairs are needed, neglect or refuse, after ten days' notice, to make such repairs, it shall be the duty of the Highway Department to have them made without delay; and the costs thereof shall be collected in the same manner as the cost is ordered to be collected by the second section of this Act.

Councils may direct curbstones to be set, &c., whenever streets are opened.

SEC. 536. That nothing in this Act shall prevent Councils of the City of Philadelphia, from directing the curb stones to be set, and brick pavements laid, on the footways of any of the streets, in said Ward, whenever said streets are opened and graded according to confirmed surveys and the advance of improvements may demand the same.

Councils may order paving on any street in which public lamps have been erected, upon petition of two citizens.

SEC. 537. That should a majority of owners of property upon any of the said streets, upon which public lamps have been erected, refuse to petition Councils for a pavement, it will be competent for any two citizens living upon the said street, to petition the Councils for the said pavement, setting forth the condition of the sidewalk, sworn to before a magistrate; and Councils shall order the Commissioners of Highways, as is provided in section first of this Act, to notify said owners to put down a pavement, in conformity with this Act.—March 22, 1865.—P. L. 562.

An Act supplementary to the Health Laws of the City of Philadelphia.

SECT. 538. That no bone-boiling establishment, or compost manufactory, or depository of dead animals, shall be erected within the bounds of the First Ward, and of the Twenty-sixth Ward, of the City of Philadelphia; and all such establishments and depositories, within the limits aforesaid, are hereby declared a public nuisance; and the Board of Health of the City of Philadelphia are hereby empowered to enter the premises wherein such nuisances exist, and destroy the sheds or enclosures used for such purposes, and to seize and sell the implements and utensils used in the bone-boiling establishment or compost manufactory so entered; the net proceeds whereof to be paid over to the said Board, for the use of the City of Philadelphia: *Provided*, That this Act shall not take effect until first of June next.—March 22, 1865.—P. L. 564.

An Act to divide the Twenty-fourth Ward of the City of Philadelphia, into two School Sections.

Twenty-fourth Ward divided into two school sections.

SEC. 539. That from and after the third Tuesday in June next, all that part of the Twenty-fourth Ward of the City of Philadelphia, lying north of the centre of Market street, shall constitute one school section, and the remaining part of said Ward shall constitute another school section; and that each of the said sections shall possess and be vested with all the rights, powers and privileges, enjoyed by any other section of said city.

Number and terms of directors.

SEC. 540. That the number of members of the School Board for the section, north of Market street, shall be eighteen, and for the section, south of that street, shall be fifteen, and the terms of office shall be as is now prescribed by law; the qualified electors of each of the said sections shall vote for the School Directors, by general ticket, on the ticket designated "Ward Officers;" and certificates of election shall be issued to those who may be elected by the judges of the ward, as to other ward officers.

Mode of electing.

Organization of boards.

SEC. 541. That on the third Tuesday in June next, the directors in each of the sections hereby erected, shall assemble in some convenient place and organize; they shall elect a president and secretary to serve until the first Monday of January next, and they shall also elect a controller, for such term as is or may be prescribed by law for controllers.—March 22, 1865.—P. L. 567.

A further Supplement to an Act to Incorporate the City of Philadelphia.

Time of holding election of controllers of public schools.

SEC. 542. That the election of members of the Board of Controllers of the public schools, of the First School District of Pennsylvania, authorized by an Act, approved February second, one thousand eight hundred and fifty-four, entitled "A further Supplement to an Act to Incorporate the City of Philadelphia," and by any of the supplements thereto, shall be held on the third Tuesday in June, as now provided by law, and shall serve until December thirty-first, one thousand eight hundred and sixty-five; and thereafter, the said Controllers shall be elected on the third Tuesday in December, in each year, and shall serve for one year.

Directors, when to meet and organize.

SEC. 543. That the Directors of the several sections of the First School District of Pennsylvania shall meet, at their respective places of meeting, on the third Tuesday of December, as aforesaid, and elect one of their number, to serve as Controller of Public Schools, for one year, from the first Monday in January, next ensuing his election; and the said directors shall meet and organize, by the election of a president and secretary, on the first Monday in January, in each and every year, thereafter.

SEC. 544. That from and after the fourth day of July, the Controllers of Public Schools, of the First School District of Pennsylvania, shall meet and organize, at ten o'clock, A. M., on the first Monday in January, in each and every year thereafter, instead of the first Monday in July, as now required by law. Organization of board of control.

SEC. 545. That all acts, or parts of acts, inconsistent with the foregoing, be and the same are hereby repealed.—March 22, 1865.—P. L. 578. Repeal.

An Act to prevent Imposition in the Renting of Stalls and Stands, in the Market Houses belonging to the City of Philadelphia.

SEC. 546. That from and after the passage of this act, the Commissioners of Markets, of the City of Philadelphia, be and he is hereby empowered to administer an oath, or affirmation, to such person, or persons, renting stalls, or stands, in any of the market houses, belonging to said city; for which service, he shall be entitled to charge and receive the same fees, as are authorized to be charged for similar services, by aldermen of said city.—March 23, 1865.—P. M. 592.

A further Supplement to an Act to Incorporate the City of Philadelphia, approved February fourth, Anno Domini one thousand eight hundred and sixty-four, equalizing the Territories and Taxable Inhabitants of the Eighteenth and Nineteenth Wards of the City of Philadelphia.

SEC. 547. That from and after the passage of this act, that all that portion of the Nineteenth Ward of the City of Philadelphia, lying within the following limits and boundaries, viz.: commencing at a point on Norris street and Gunner's Run canal; thence northwardly by the said Gunner's Run canal to Lehigh avenue; thence eastwardly by Lehigh avenue to the river Delaware; thence by the river Delaware to Norris street; thence westwardly by Norris street to Gunner's Run canal, the place of beginning, is hereby attached to the Eighteenth Ward, of the City of Philadelphia, and shall form the Eleventh Election Division of the said Eighteenth Ward.—March 23, 1864.—P. L. 603.

An Act to vacate a part of Ash street, in the Eighteenth Ward of the City of Philadelphia.

SEC. 548. That Ash street, north-westwardly, from Thompson street to Almond street, in the Eighteenth Ward of the City of Philadelphia, be and the same is hereby vacated.—March 23, 1865.—P. L. 616.

An Act to authorize a Change in the Grade of Bridge street, in the Twenty-fourth Ward, Philadelphia, at the crossing of the Pennsylvania Railroad.

Change of grade authorized. SEC. 549. That the Chief Engineer and Surveyor, of the City of Philadelphia, be and he is hereby authorized and directed to prepare a plan, and proceed to change the grade line of Bridge street, in the Twenty-fourth Ward, of the City of Philadelphia, at the crossing of the Pennsylvania Railroad, so that said street may pass either under, or above, the railroad: *Provided*, That the plan be submitted to, and be approved by, the Board of Surveyors of the City of Philadelphia; and that all the expenses, incurred in making such change, and putting said street in as good condition as it now is, shall be paid by the Pennsylvania Railroad Company.

When work to be commenced. SEC. 550. Said work shall commence as soon as the Chief Engineer receives official notification from said Railroad Company, that it is ready to comply with the provisions of the first section of this act.—March 23, 1865.—P. L. 643.

An Act in reference to the Manufacturing of Fire Works, in the City of Philadelphia.

SEC. 551. That it shall not be lawful for any person, or association, or incorporaiion, to manufacture any species of pyrotechnic, or fire works, cartridges, nor any kind of fixed ammunition, in the built up portions of the City of Philadelphia.—March 23, 1863.—P. L. 744.

A Supplement to an Act for the better security of the City of Philadelphia, from dangers incident to Refining, or Improper and Negligent Storage, of Petroleum, Benzine, Benzole, or Naptha, approved March second, one thousand eight hundred and sixty-five.

Persons refining, manufacturing, or storing petroleum, within certain limits, required to obtain license. SEC. 552. That all persons refining, or manufacturing, depositing, or storing, petroleum, or coal oil, benzine, benzole, or naptha, on the west side of the river Schuylkill, east of Thirtieth street, between Arch street and Bridge street, and between Chestnut street and South street, as authorized by the Act to which this is a Supplement, shall, besides having on their premises suitable tanks, excavations, or embankments, to prevent the overflow, or escape, of the oil so refined, stored, or deposited, be required to obtain a license from the Mayor of the City of Philadelphia, for which, the sum of ten dollars shall be paid into the City Treasury, and likewise, for the annual renewal thereof, upon due certificate, to be given by the Fire Marshal, and approved by the Mayor, of said City, that such premises are so constructed and arranged as to afford reasonable security from danger, in case of accident, or fire.

SEC. 553. That so much of the first section of the Act, to which this is supplementary, as prohibits the refining of petroleum, benzine, benzole, or naptha, within five hundred feet of the east, or west, side of the river Schuylkill, shall not be construed to apply to the Belmont Petroleum Works, located on the river road, above the Columbia bridge, in the Twenty-fourth Ward of the City of Philadelphia. Certain provisions not to apply to the Belmont Petroleum Works.

SEC. 554. That it shall be lawful to refine, manufacture, store and keep petroleum, benzine, benzole, and naptha, in such quantities as may be desired, in that portion of the said City of Philadelphia, lying south of Dickinson street, and east of Otsego street, subject to all the provisions and restrictions of the second section of the Act to which this a supplement. Petroleum, &c., may be refined, stored, &c., within certain limits.

SEC. 555. That the Fire Marshal shall be entitled to charge, demand and receive, for his own use, from each applicant, for examination of the premises, and license, under this Act, and the Act to which this is a supplement, before such examination is made, the following fees, to wit: for every examination of a storage depot, where the quantity, allowed by law, shall exceed twenty-five barrels, and for every refinery, or manufactory, the sum of ten dollars; for all other examinations, required by law, the sum of five dollars. Fees of Fire Marshal, for examinations.

SEC. 556. That any part of the Act, to which this is supplemental, which is inconsistent herewith, is hereby repealed. —March 24, 1865.—P. L. 749. Repeal.

An Act to vacate so much of Amber street, Tulip street and Lemon street, now Memphis street, in the Twenty-fifth Ward of the City of Philadelphia, as lies between the north side of Lehigh avenue and the south side of the Philadelphia and Reading Railroad.

SEC. 557. That so much of Amber street, Tulip street, and Lemon, now Memphis street, as lies between the north side of Lehigh avenue and the south side of the Philadelphia and Reading Railroad, in the Twenty-fifth Ward of the City of Philadelphia, be and the same are hereby vacated.—March 24, 1865.—P. L. 777.

A Supplement to an Act to promote the more certain and equal assessment of Taxes in Philadelphia, approved the fourteenth day of March, Anno Domini, one thousand eight hundred and sixty-five.

SEC. 558. That the Court of Common Pleas of the County of Philadelphia shall, immediately after the passage of this act, appoint the two persons who, with the Senior City Commissioner, as provided for in the act to which this is a supplement, shall be the Board of Revision of Taxes; and the said two persons, so to be immediately appointed, shall remain in office until the period of time fixed in the said act, to which this is a supplement, for the appointment of such officers, when the time of the officers hereby authorized to be appointed shall expire, and their successors shall be appointed, as is provided in the act to which this is a supplement, and the duties of said officers, together with the Senior City Commissioner, shall be such as are prescribed by law for the Board of Revision, for all matters to be done for other years than that of the year of the triennial assessment.—March 27, 1865.—P. L. 786.

A further Supplement to the Act to incorporate the City of Philadelphia, authorizing the construction of sewers or drains.

SEC. 559. That the City of Philadelphia shall have power to construct sewers or drains in the streets of said city, and to charge the sum of seventy-five cents per lineal foot against each front; the same to be recovered as liens for the laying of water pipe are now recovered in said city, and with the same allowance for corner lots; and from the passage of this act it shall be lawful for any tenant of any property, wherever the owner or owners of property so assessed for the construction of any sewer or drain as aforesaid, neglect or refuse to pay the said assessment, the tenant of such property owner may pay the assessment against such property to the contractor, and hand the receipt thereof to the property owner, as so much cash, paid for rent, as tenants are now required to pay taxes for delinquent property owners.—March 27, 1865.—P. L. 791.

A further Supplement to the Act passed April twentieth, Anno Domini one thousand eight hundred and fifty-eight, entitled "An Act establishing a mode of selecting and drawing jurors, in and for the City of Philadelphia."

SEC. 560. That the period for which a citizen, whose name has been duly drawn, and who has served as a juryman for one full term, is exempted, by the eighth section of the act approved April twentieth, Anno Domini one thousand eight hundred and fifty-eight, from again serving as a juror, shall be limited to one year instead of three years.—March 27, 1865.—P. L. 799.

An Act vacating a part of Nicetown lane, and reducing the width of Juniata avenue, in the Twenty-fifth Ward of the City of Philadelphia.

Part of Nicetown lane vacated.

SEC. 561. That Nicetown lane, as the same is now laid out and opened and used, from the west line of the old York road to the south line of Juniata avenue, in the Twenty-fifth Ward of the City of Philadelphia, be and the same is hereby vacated; and that the title to the soil over which the same passes, be and the same is hereby vested in fee simple in the several owners of the ground adjoining and fronting upon the same respectively, each owner to have and to take one-half part thereof, so far as his respective lot adjoins and fronts upon the same lane: *Provided, nevertheless,* That the said line shall not be closed until Roxborough street, from westerly line of said Old York road, to the easterly line of the Germantown road, shall have been laid out and opened by the owners of the ground through which the said street passes, free from cost to the City of Philadelphia.

Proviso.

SEC. 562. That Juniata avenue, as the same is laid down on the plan of the City of Philadelphia, extending from the Old York road to Germantown avenue, in Twenty-fifth Ward of the said city, be reduced from the width of one hundred and twenty feet to the width of sixty feet; and that thirty feet of the space of sixty feet so taken from said avenue, as now laid out, be vested in fee in the owner or owners of the real estate fronting on the northern line of said avenue, as now laid out; and that thirty feet of the said space of sixty feet so taken from said avenue, as now laid out, be vested in fee in the owner or owners of the real estate fronting on the southern line of said avenue, as now laid out.—April 4, 1865.—P. L. 818.

Width of Juniata avenue reduced.

An Act vacating certain streets, roads and lanes, in the First Ward of the City of Philadelphia.

SEC. 563. That Greenwich Point road and Jones's lane, wherever the same extend through or into the property owned, or which may be acquired within six months from the passage of this act, by the Pennsylvania Railroad Company, in the First Ward of the City of Philadelphia, be and the same are hereby vacated; and no street shall hereafter be opened into or through the said property, acquired or to be acquired, as aforesaid, by the said company, at or near the present Delaware terminus of their said road, without the consent in writing of said company: *Provided,* That Greenwich Point road and Jones's lane shall not be closed, until a street parallel with the river Delaware, and westwardly of the limits of the said property, acquired or to be acquired, and connecting the said Jones's lane with the Greenwich point road, shall have been opened and put in fit condition for public use, without expense to the City of Philadelphia.—April 4, 1865.—P. L. 819.

An Act to vacate a part of Buist lane, in the Twenty-fourth Ward of the City of Philadelphia.

SEC. 564. That Buist lane, from the Darby plank road to Wickersham avenue, in the Twenty-fourth Ward of the City of Philadelphia, be and the same is hereby vacated.—April 4, 1865. —P. L. 820.

An Act to enable the Councils of the City of Philadelphia to comply with an Act of Assembly, approved April thirteenth, one thousand eight hundred and forty-four.

SEC. 565. That the Select and Common Councils of the City of Philadelphia be and they are hereby authorized to create a loan, for the purpose of complying with section eleven of an act of Assembly, approved April thirteenth, one thousand eight hundred and forty-four, as per Pamphlet Laws, one thousand eight hundred and forty-four, pages two hundred and sixty-four, two hundred and sixty-seven: *Provided,* The amount thereof shall not exceed the sum of four hundred and fifty thousand dollars, and that the same shall become a law when it shall have been passed by a majority of each branch of said Councils; any law to the contrary notwithstanding.—April 4, 1865.—P. L. 823.

An Act to vacate the easternmost nineteen feet in width of a certain road or street in the Twenty-fourth Ward, Philadelphia.

SEC. 566. *Whereas,* Wyoming street has been laid out and opened from Haverford road to the Lancaster Turnpike, in the Twenty-fourth Ward, Philadelphia, in accordance with the general survey of the city of Philadelphia, at the distance of about thirty-eight feet eastward from a certain old road or lane, laid out also from said Haverford road northward to said Lancaster turnpike:

And whereas, The opening of said Wyoming street has rendered said road, of its full width, entirely unnecessary; therefore,

SEC. 567. That the easternmost nineteen feet in width of said road or lane, extending from said Haverford road to said Lancaster turnpike, be and the same is hereby vacated, and the title to the strip of land thus vacated, vested in the owners of the property bounding on the eastern side of said road.—April 4, 1865.—P. L. 825.

An Act vacating a portion of the Ford road, in the City of Philadelphia, and Montgomery county.

SEC. 568. That so much of the Ford road as lies between the Belmont avenue, in the Twenty-fourth Ward of the City of Philadelphia, and the Righter's Ferry road, or Ott's road, in the County of Montgomery, be and the same is hereby declared to be vacated and closed to the public use.—April 4, 1865.—P. L. 826.

An Act to widen Cadwalader street in the Seventeenth Ward of the City of Philadelphia.

SEC. 569. That the Commissioners of Highways, of the City of Philadelphia, are hereby required, from and after the passage of this act, to open and widen Cadwalader street, in the Seventeenth Ward in said City of Philadelphia, from Master street to Thompson street, of the full width, according to the survey originally made.—April 4, 1865.—P. L. 828.

APPENDIX.

CONTAINING THE CHARTERS OF THE

VARIOUS PASSENGER RAILWAYS,

WHICH ARE SUBJECT TO THE CONTROL OF THE

COUNCILS OF PHILADELPHIA,

AND OF THE

LAWS AND ORDINANCES THERETO.

PREPARED UNDER THE SUPERVISION OF THE

Law Department of the City of Philadelphia.

CITY PASSENGER RAILWAYS.

Frankford and Southwark Philadelphia City Passenger Railroad Company.

SECTION 1. *Be it enacted by the Senate and House of Representatives of the Commonwealth of Pennsylvania, in General Assembly met, and it is hereby enacted by the authority of the same,* That John Robbins, Jr., William H. Witte, John P. Verree, Peter Rambo, John Clouds, Hugh Clark, Michael Day, John H. Bringhurst, J. D. Anderson, William Overington, Joseph Jeans, Harvey Rowland, Isaac Shallcross, James P. Verree, Jr., John Rupert, Amos A. Gregg, Sam'l. H. Crawford, Isaiah J. Williamson, Samuel Branson, James C. Hand, Joseph McDowell, Samuel Megarge, Alexander Derbyshire, Edward D. Potts, Joseph Barnet, Franklin A. Comly, John Farnum, Marmaduke Watson, of Philadelphia county, John Walton, John Shelmire, Hugh Warner, John Smith, John Hallowell, Jr., Charles Blaker, James Fenton, George Kenderdine, Joseph B. Yerkes, Jonathan Iredell, Charles H. Hill, Henry Stout, Jonathan Jarrett, Oliver Fretz, Hiram Reading, George J. Mitchell, Asa Comly, David Jeans, Charles Jarrett, Jacob L. Walton, John Iredell, Jervis S. Smith, Daniel Carr, Charles Palmer, Lukens Paid, Jacob Kirk, Thomas Iredell, of Montgomery county, John Davis, Louis S. Coryell, Joseph Morrison, Hugh Murns, Robert Banes, Griffith Miles, Erasmus N. Hilles, William Stavely, Simon Geer, Charles Waters, John E. Kenderdine, Lukens Thomas, Howard H. Sager, Captain Evan Groom, Colonel David Marple, Charles A. Dubois, John Banes, James M. Boillian, Robert Darrah, Amos Snyder, Joseph Barnesly, John Blackford, Luther Calvin, John Betz, George Jamison, Thomas Dungan, Joshua Fell, Jonathan Walton, Elias Ott and William Fenton, of Bucks county, or any three of them, be and they are hereby appointed Commissioners to open books

1. Act of April 4, 1854, P. L. 759.

receive subscriptions, and organize a company, by the name, style and title of the "Philadelphia and Delaware River Railroad Company," (1,) with power and authority to construct a railroad, beginning at a point north of Cherry street, Kensington, in the county of Philadelphia, and thence through the eastern part of Montgomery county, by way of the Pennepeck creek to or near the village of Hatborough, and thence by way of New Hope, or Riegersville, or any point between said New Hope or Riegersville, to the borough of Easton, in Northampton county, subject to all the provisions and restrictions of an Act regulating railroad companies, approved the nineteenth day of February, Anno Domini one thousand eight hundred and forty-nine, so far as the same is not altered or repealed by this Act. And the said Philadelphia and Delaware River Railroad Company shall have the right to connect with the North Pennsylvania Railroad, at any point north of Cherry street, and within the present bounds of the District of Kensington, county of Philadelphia, on such terms as may be mutually agreed upon, and with the concurrent action of the State of New Jersey, and subject to the provisions and restrictions of the Act aforesaid, to construct a bridge across the river Delaware, and to connect, by one or more lateral or branch roads, with any railroad or other public improvements in the State of New Jersey: *Provided,* That if said company shall construct a bridge across the river Delaware, the said bridge shall be so constructed as not to interefere with the free navigation of said river.

SEC. 2. That the capital stock of the said company shall consist of twenty thousand shares, of fifty dollars each: *Provided,* That the said company may, from time to time, by a vote of the stockholders, at a meeting called for that purpose, increase the capital stock, if it should be deemed necessary, to an amount sufficient to carry out the true intent and meaning of this Act. For the purpose of completing and equipping the railroad, the said company shall have the power of borrowing any sum, at a rate of interest not exceeding seven per centum per annum, and to secure the payment of the same by the issue of a bond and mortgage of the said railroad, together with the corporate rights and franchises granted by this act, and to annex to the said bond and mortgage the privilege of converting the same into capital stock of the said company, at par, at the

(1.) The title changed by Act of April 9, 1858, Section 14.
2. Act of April 4, 1854, P. L. 759.

option of the holders, if they shall signify their election one year before their maturity: *Provided also,* That the said company shall issue no certificate of loan of a less denomination than one hundred dollars: *Provided,* That any railroad now incorporated, or hereafter to be incorporated, connecting with the New York and Erie Railroad, shall have the right of connection with said road.

SEC. 3. That said company shall have power to connect with any railroad belonging to any other company, using part of the said route in any and every case where it may be deemed inexpedient, for a time, to build the whole of the road authorized by this act, and the said company shall have as full power and control over the part or parts built by the said company in every respect, as if the said company had built the whole of the road authorized by this Act.

SEC. 4. That the president and directors of the said company shall have the power, if it shall be deemed expedient to exercise the same, to contract to pay to the stockholders of the said company, at such times as the president and directors, or a majority of them shall designate, interest at the rate of six per centum per annum on all shares or instalments paid on the shares of the said stock until the said railroad shall be completed, and the profits and earnings of the said railroad within the same time shall be credited to the cost of the same: *Provided,* That interest shall not be paid on any share of stock upon which any instalment which has been duly called for remains unpaid: *Provided further,* That the stock of the said company shall not be subject to any tax in consequence of the payment of the interest hereby authorized, nor until the net earnings shall realize at least six per centum per annum upon the capital invested.

SEC. 5. That if the said company shall not commence the construction of said railroad within five years, and complete it in ten years from the passage of this act, the same shall be null and void, except so far as the same may be necessary to settle the affairs and pay the debts of said company.

SEC. 6. That the capital stock of the Philadelphia and Delaware River Railroad Company be and the same is

3. Act of April 4, 1854, P. L. 760.
4. Act of April 4, 1854, P. L. 760.
5. Act of April 4, 1854, P. L. 760.
6. Act of March 12, 1856, Section 1, P. L. 115.

hereby reduced to ten thousand shares, subjec to all the provisions of the Act to which this is a supplement, and that John F. Lamb, John Foulkrod, Peter Castor, Charles E. Kreamer, Harvey Quicksall, William W. Stratton, Jos. Deal, Richard Garsed, Charles B. Gilbert, N. Field Campion, A. K. Colhoun, James Burnes, Albert G. Rowland, and Edward G. Lee, are hereby appointed additional commissioners to open books, sell stock, and organize said company. (2.)

SEC. 7. That the Philadelphia and Delaware River Railroad Company shall have authority to extend their road southerly, from its present terminus at Sixth and Cherry streets, Kensington, along the former street to Morris street, in Southwark, with a single track; thence easterly along the same to Fifth street; thence northerly along the latter street to the aforesaid Cherry street, with the privilege of occupying Germantown Road, from its intersection with Fifth street, until the said Fifth street shall be duly declared open: *Provided,* That the said road shall be used exclusively for a City Passenger Railway by horse locomotion: *Provided further,* That the gauge of said road shall be five feet two inches, and that before the said company shall use and occupy the said streets, the consent of the councils of the City of Philadelphia shall be first given, and said consent shall be taken and deemed to be given if the said councils shall not, within thirty days after the passage of this Act, by ordinance duly passed, signify their disapproval thereof, (3,) and said councils may, from time to time, by ordinance, establish such regulations in regard to said railway as may be required for the paving, repaving, grading, culverting, and laying of water and gas pipes in and along said streets, and to prevent obstructions thereon.

SEC. 8. That it is hereby provided that the Philadelphia and Delaware River Railroad Company shall, in constructing their tracks along the highways referred to, conform to the grades established, or which may be hereafter established by the Board of Survey of the City of Philadelphia, and be subject to any ordinances passed by the

(2.) The letters patent were issued to this company by Governor Pollock, March 22, 1856.

(3.) This consent was given by the Ordinance of July 7, 1857. Sec. 9, page

7. Act of June 9, 1857, Section 1, P. L. 802.

8. Act of June 9, 1857, Section 2, P. L. 803

councils of the said city relating thereto: *Provided,* That the streets thus occupied by the aforesaid railway shall be kept in repair by the said railway company, and no burden trains be carried over said road.

SEC. 9. That the said railroad company shall not connect with any railroad other than for passenger purposes, and of the same gauge, and no freight or freight cars shall be permitted to pass over said railway under the penalty of a forfeiture of their charter; and the said company shall annually pay into the treasury of the City of Philadelphia, for the use of said city, whenever the dividends shall exceed six per centum per annum on the capital stock, the sum of six per centum on the sub-dividends thus declared; and the said company, before commencing to run their cars upon the said streets, shall purchase, at the option of the owners, the stock of horses, omnibuses, sleighs, and harness, owned and used upon the said streets at the time of the completion of the said road, at a price to be assessed in the following manner, to wit: The said owners shall choose one disinterested person, and the said company shall chose a second person, and the two thus chosen shall choose a third, who, together, shall appraise the stock, and the value thus arrived at shall be binding and final: *Provided,* That whenever any damages may be sustained by reason of this company taking possession of lands or other property, other than above described, except so far as the use of the before-named streets are necessary to the full and perfect enjoyment of the purposes by this act designed, the said damages shall be assessed and paid in the manner and according to the provisions of the eleventh section of the Act of nineteenth of February, Anno Domini one thousand eight hundred and forty-nine, entitled "An Act Regulating Railroad Companies:" *Provided further,* That so much of the act, to which this is a supplement, as authorizes the construction of a railroad, or the use of any railroad out of the limits of the City of Philadelphia, be and the same is hereby repealed, and any road built or to be built by the said company shall be confined to the limits of the said City, but the authority vested in the said Company to borrow money on the terms mentioned in the said Act, shall be extended to the road herein authorized in the same manner as if the railroad herein authorized had been authorized to have been built by the said act.

9. Act of June 9, 1857, Section 3, P. L. 803.

SEC. 10. That the right to use and occupy said streets for the purposes aforesaid shall continue for twenty years from the passage of this act, and no longer, unless renewed or extended by the Legislature.

SEC. 11. That the rail to be used on said road shall be that now adopted by the company, (part of which is now upon said road,) and no change shall be made in the shape thereof, unless by consent of councils.

SEC. 12. That the Philadelphia and Delaware River Railroad Company shall have power to cross with their tracks the Philadelphia and Reading Railroad at Frankford avenue, in the City of Philadelphia, at the present grade of said avenue, and on a level with the said Reading Railroad: *Provided*, That when the City of Philadelphia shall require the grading of Frankford avenue at the present confirmed grade, that then the said Philadelphia and Delaware River Railroad Company shall conform their tracks to the same.

SEC. 13. It shall be the duty of said company, at its own expense, to erect upon their said road, on either side of the said crossing, one gate, to be kept securely closed, under the care and supervision of some sober and competent person, to be appointed by the said company, which person shall be permanently stationed at the said crossing, whose duty it shall be to open the said gate for the passage of the cars of the said company only when the same can be done without danger of collision with any of the trains passing over the road of the said Reading Railroad: *Provided*, Every violation of the provisions of this section, information and proof thereof having been made before any Alderman of the City of Philadelphia, the said Delaware River Railroad Company shall pay a fine of one hundred dollars, one-half to go to the city treasury, and the other half to the informer, and the informer shall be a competent witness in the case.

SEC. 14. That the occupancy by the Philadelphia and Delaware River Railroad Company of portions of Frankford avenue and Frankford street, in the City of Philadelphia, for the purpose of the passenger railway track, be and is hereby confirmed and approved, and that the said company shall have power to extend their tracks from the company's

10. Act of June 9, 1857, Section 4, P. L. 804.
11. Act of June 9, 1857, Section 5, P. L. 804.
12. Act of April 8, 1858, Section 1, P. L. 225.
13. Act of April 8, 1858, Section 2, P. L. 225
14. Act of April 9, 1858, Section 1, P. L. 237.

present southern terminus at Morris street, southerly to Greenwich Point, with a single track on Fifth and Sixth streets; and that from and after the passage of this act, the title of the said Philadelphia Delaware River Railroad Company, shall be changed and known by the title of the "Frankford and Southwark Philadelphia City Passenger Railroad Company."

SEC. 15. That the Frankford and Southwark Philadelphia City Passenger Railroad Company, (formerly known by the corporate name of the Philadelphia and Delaware River Railroad Company,) be and they are hereby authorized and empowered to sell and convey such portion of the real estate now owned by them as the board of directors may deem it unnecessary for the said company to hold for the uses and purposes of the said rail road; such sales to be made either at public or private sale, and for such prices and upon such terms as the said board of directors may think fit.

SEC. 16. The said railroad company are hereby authorized to construct and lay a railway track in Washington street, in the Second Ward, in the City of Philadelphia, and connect the same with their railroad in Fifth street and Sixth street, in the said city; or the said company may connect their roads in Fifth and Sixth streets with any railroad now laid in said Washington street, or use, for the purpose of making such connection, any part of such existing railroad: *Provided*, The owners of such railroad consent thereto: *And provided*, That nothing herein shall be construed to authorize the Frankford and Southwark Philadelphia City Passenger Railroad Company to use, as aforesaid, any part of said Washington street, except that between Fifth and Sixth street; nor to authorize the said company to use the said road for the transportation of freight, but may, in the same, for baggage: *And provided further*, That the said company shall not use any railroad hereby authorized to be built, or used in such way as to diminish the present traveling facilities upon that portion of their road which is south of said Washington street.

SEC. 17. The said company are hereby authorized to lay a single track of railroad in Powell street, in the

15. Act of May 16, 1861, Section 1, P. L. 698.
16. Act of May 16, 1861, Section 2, P. L. 698.
17. Act of May 16, 1861, Section 3, P. L. 699.

Fifth Ward, and connect the same with their road in the said Fifth and Sixth streets.

SEC. 18. That so much of the fourth section of an act, approved June ninth, Anno Domini one thousand eight hundred and fifty-seven, entitled "A Supplement to an Act to incorporate the Philadelphia and Delaware River Railroad Company, passed April fourth, one thousand eight hundred and fifty-four," as allows the said company to occupy the streets in the said act mentioned, for no longer a period than twenty years, be and the same is hereby repealed; and the right of the corporation therein named, and the right of the Frankford and Southwark Philadelphia City Passenger Railroad Company to occupy the streets therein mentioned, for the purposes in the said act mentioned, shall be held to have been granted as if the restriction in the said fourth section had never formed part thereof.

SEC. 19. The said corporation is hereby authorized to invest its sinking fund, contingent fund or repair fund, in the loans or capital stock of any railroad or plank road company incorporated by the Commonwealth of Pennsylvania, and located in the City of Philadelphia: *Provided*, The amount shall not exceed twenty thousand dollars in any one corporation.

SEC. 20. That no provision in the act incorporating said company, or in any of the Acts of Assembly forbidding the said company from carrying freight, shall be construed to prohibit or forbid the said company from carrying the baggage of passengers using their cars.

SEC. 21. That the Frankford and Southwark Philadelphia City Passenger Railroad Company be and they are hereby authorized to use steam power to propel cars upon so much of their road as lies north of their depot on Berks street; and the said company is hereby authorized to use that part of their said road, heretofore mentioned, for the transportation of merchandize.

18. Act of May 16, 1861, Section 4, P. L. 699.
19. Act of May 16, 1861, Section 5, P. L. 689.
20. Act of May 16, 1861, Section 6, P. L. 699.
21. Act of March 4, 1863, P. L. 107.

Resolutions and Ordinances specially applicable to the Frankford and Southwark Passenger Railway Company.

1. *Resolved,* That the City Solicitor be requested to take legal measures to compel the Frankford and Southwark Passenger Railway Company to file their statement in detail of the cost of the road, in compliance with the eighth section of an ordinance, entitled "An Ordinance to regulate Passenger Railways."

2. *Resolved,* That the Chief Commissioner of Highways be, and he is hereby required to take measures forthwith to stop the laying down of the curves and intersections now in progress at Fifth and Sixth streets and Washington avenue, until it has been determined whether the same is legal and proper, and if the privilege for doing said work has been given by the said commissioner, that he is hereby required to report to councils by what authority such permission has been given.

3. *Resolved,* That the Chief Commissioner of Highways be, and he is hereby instructed to take immediate measures to cause the railroad crossing Front street at Chatham street, and connecting the Frankford and Southwark Passenger Railway Company with the depot of the Trenton Railroad Company; also, the connection of said Frankford and Southwark Passenger Railway Company, with the railroad of the Philadelphia, Wilmington and Baltimore Railroad Company, at Sixth and Washington streets, and Fifth and Washington streets, to be removed.

4. *Resolved,* That permission is hereby granted by the City of Philadelphia to the Frankford and Southwark Philadelphia City Passenger Railway Company to connect their road with the Kensington Depot of the Trenton Railroad Company, by continuing the same across the curb and sidewalk of Front street, opposite to Chatham street, to and across ground now belonging to said passenger railway

1. Resolution of October 16, 1858, Ordinances 1858, p. 381.
2. Resolution of December 27, 1858, Ordinances, 1858, p. 503.
3. Resolution of January 1, 1859, Ordinances, 1859, p. 1.
4. Resolution of May 16, 1859, Ordinances, 1859, p. 247.

company, and thence to the depot premises of said railroad company—the same to be done under the supervision of the Department of Surveys.

5. SECTION 1. That the Frankford and Southwark Railway Company be authorized to make a connection with the railway laid in Washington street, at the intersection of Fifth and Sixth streets: *Provided*, That this license may be revoked at any time, and the connection removed: *And provided further*, That before the said railroad company shall make the said connections, they shall enter into an obligation satisfactory in law to the City Solicitor, that, in case the said connections shall at any time be removed by the city, the said railroad company will bind itself to pay to the city all expenses that may be incurred by such removal: *Provided, however*, That said company shall not use said connection in such a way as to diminish the present traveling facilities upon that portion of the route south of said Washington avenue.

5. Ordinance of December 22, 1860, Ordinances, 1860, p. 446.

The Philadelphia and Gray's Ferry Railroad Company.

SECTION 1. That Edward Brady, W. Young, C. J. Eastwick, J. S. Struthers, John J. Hoopes, J. Gibson, J. M. Williams, D. M. Jones, J. Dick, W. A. Woods, J. Leech, Jr. George McHenry, Thomas B. Florence, William M. Reilly John H. Bryant, Jacob J. Walters, Charles Lafferty, E. R. Helmbold, Charles Dingee, C. Haisley, P. Lafferty, R. F Christy, James McCahan, F. A. Servor, Thomas Allison, Luke Keegan, Michael McGinnis, Charles Whitson, John Murphy, William E. Skillman, William Struthers, George Whitson, John Melligan, John H. Whiston, Alexander Henry, James D. Campbell, John McIntire, A. J. Riley, George Kirkpatrick, David McClain, Andrew Morrow, George W. Middleton, Theodore G. Gauss, B. H. Bartol, S. Benton, Charles L. Jordan, James Baird, John Alexander, L. C. Wells, James W. Flinn, Henry Y. Smith, William H. Cooper, William B. Hood, Jesse Johnson, Alfred Day, R. K. Neff, S. F. Betts, T. H. Speakman, William Young, Jr., T. J. Muirhead, John S. Thackara, John Campbell, N. Weannemacher, W. J. Jackson, John Reid are hereby appointed commissioners to open books, receive subscriptions and organize a company under the name and title of the Philadelphia and Gray's Ferry Passenger Railroad Company, to continue for a period of twenty years from the passage of this act.

SEC. 2. That said company are hereby authorized and empowered to construct a railway, to be worked by horse power, and to convey passengers over the same, and for such toll as may from time to time be established, from a point at or near the Schuylkill river, at Gray's Ferry Bridge, as they think fit, by a double track along the Gray's Ferry road eastwardly and northeastwardly, to the intersection of South street, thence by a single track along said South street, eastwardly, to Twenty-first street, thence along said Twenty-first street northwardly to Pine street, thence along said Pine street eastwardly to Second street, thence along said Second street northwardly to Dock

1. Act of April 9, 1858, Section 1, P. L. 237.
2. Act of April 9, 1858, Section 2, P. L. 238.

street, thence along said Dock street westwardly and north-westwardly to Walnut street, thence along said Walnut street westwardly to Third street, thence along said Third street southwardly to Spruce street, thence along said Spruce street westwardly to Twenty-third street, thence along said Twenty-third street southwardly to the intersection of Gray's Ferry road, aforesaid: *Provided*, That the said company, before commencing to run their cars upon the said streets, shall purchase the stocks of omnibuses, sleighs, horses and harness owned and used upon the Spruce street and Pine street lines of omnibuses, at the time of the completion of the said railway, at a price to be assessed in the following manner, to wit: the owners shall choose one disinterested person and the said company shall choose a second person, and the two persons thus chosen shall choose a third person, whom together shall appraise such said stocks, and the value thus arrived at shall be binding and final; and the said company shall have the right to purchase real estate and to erect thereon such buildings and improvements as may be deemed expedient for the purposes of the said company, and also to purchase the necessary equipments for said railroad; and no locomotive shall be allowed to pass over the same; and shall not obstruct the said streets, by permitting freight cars to pass over any portion of said railway; and said company shall have power to cross with their tracks, at grade, any other lines of railroads, and said company may connect with any other railway for passenger purposes; and said railroad shall be of the gauge of five feet two inches: *Provided*, That in running over the roads of other railroad companies, the company shall conform to the rules and requirements of the companies whose road they may occupy, as to time and direction of running their cars.

SEC. 3. That the capital stock of said company shall consist of twenty thousand shares, of twenty-five dollars each; and said company shall have power to raise on bonds any sum not exceeding one-half of their capital stock, for the purpose of carrying out the true intent of this act.

SEC. 4. That dividends of so much of the profits of said company as may appear advisable to the board of managers, shall be declared in the months of January and

3. Act of April 9, 1858, Section 3, P. L. 239.
4. Act of April 9, 1858, Section 4, P. L. 239.

July in each and every year, and shall be paid at the office of said company, after ten days from the time of declaring the same: *Provided*, said dividends shall not in any case exceed the amount of the net profits of said company, so that the capital stock shall never be impaired thereby. And the said company shall annually pay into the treasury of the City of Philadelphia, for the use of said city, whenever the dividends shall exceed six per centum per annum on the capital stock, the sum of six per centum on the said dividends thus declared: *And provided*, That the said company shall pave and keep in good repair such portions of said streets as may be occupied by said railway: *Provided*, That the road hereby authorized to be laid out and constructed shall be a trunk passenger railway; and all passenger railway companies now incorporated, or hereafter to be incorporated in the City of Philadelphia, shall be at liberty to intersect with and use the tracks of said company, upon such terms as the companies concerned may agree upon; and should the companies concerned fail to agree upon proper terms, then they shall each appoint one disinterested person, who shall be approved of by the Court of Common Pleas of the said city, and the two thus chosen shall choose a third person, also disinterested, who shall also be approved of by said court, and the three thus chosen shall determine on the terms of compensation on which the company hereby incorporated shall grant the use of its road to such other railway company, or any of them.

SEC. 5. That the said company shall make and have a common seal, and also shall ordain and establish such by-laws and regulations as may appear necessary or convenient for the government of said company, and not being contrary to the constitution and laws of the United States or of this commonwealth; and generally to do all and singular the matters and things which to them it may lawfully appertain to do, for the well-being of said company and the due ordering and management of the affairs thereof, in accordance with the provisions of the act regulating railroad companies, approved the nineteenth day of February, A. D. one thousand eight hundred and forty-nine, and the supplements thereto. And at every annual election for said president, treasurer, and eleven directors, each share of stock shall entitle the holder thereof to one vote: *Pro*

5. Act of April 9, 1858, Section 5, P. L. 239.

vided further, That before the said company shall use and occupy the said streets, the consent of the Councils of the City of Philadelphia shall be first obtained, and said consent shall be taken and deemed to have been given, if said Councils shall not within thirty days after the passage of this act, by ordinance duly passed, signify their disapproval thereof; and the said company shall also be subject to an ordinance of the City Councils, entitled "An Ordinance to regulate Passenger Railways within the City of Philadelphia," approved the seventh day of July, one thousand eight hundred and fifty-seven (1857). (*a*)

SEC. 6. That the Philadelphia and Gray's Ferry Passenger Railway Company shall have the right to lay a single or double track to and from their proposed new depot, when completed, to intersect with their tracks on Pine, Spruce and Twenty-third streets; and shall also have the right of extending their track, either on Twenty-first or Twenty-second streets, (as the board of directors may direct,) southwardly to Christian street; thence westwardly to the intersection of their track, on Gray's Ferry road, and also the right to form a connection with the Philadelphia and Darby Railroad Company, near Gray's Ferry bridge, by extending their track over the Gray's Ferry bridge to a point along said Philadelphia and Darby railroad at or near the Gray's Ferry depot, upon such terms and conditions as the City Councils, or such parties as may own and control the said bridge may agree upon.

SEC. 7. That hereafter, the annual meetings of the stockholders, and election of officers of the company, shall be held on the third Tuesday of January in each year, instead of the second Monday, as heretofore; and that on and after that time the Board of Directors shall consist of six instead of eleven members, three of whom, in connection with the President, shall constitute a quorum; or, in the absence of the President, four directors shall constitute a quorum to transact business.

SEC. 8. The said company shall have the right, at any time, to sell any real estate they may have or acquire over and above what may be necessary for the construction of

6. Act of April 16, 1864, Sec. 1, P. L. 662.
7. Act of April 16, 1864, Sec. 2, P. L. 662.
8. Act of April 16, 1864, Sec. 3, P. L. 662.

(*a*) The consent of the Councils was given by the ordinance set forth on page 15.

their depot and stables. The charter of the company shall be and is hereby made perpetual.

SEC. 9. It shall be lawful for the President and Directors of the company to reduce the number of shares actually issued, by substituting full paid shares in proportion to the instalments actually paid in, so that the certificate for each share of stock hereafter issued shall represent twenty-five dollars of the capital paid in: *Provided*, That the right to issue the whole, or any part of the whole number of shares authorized to be issued by the charter, shall not be thereby impaired: *And provided also*, That the tax on dividends to be paid to the City of Philadelphia, shall not thereby be increased; and it is hereby declared to be the true intent and meaning of the Act of Incorporation in reference thereto, and the same shall be so construed as to apply to the authorized capital of the company.

An Ordinance relating to certain Passenger Railway Companies.

WHEREAS, By the provisions of the Act of Assembly, approved April 9, 1858, entitled "An Act to incorporate the Philadelphia and Gray's Ferry Passenger Railway Company," and of a certain other Act of Assembly, approved April 10, 1858, entitled "An Act to incorporate the Second and Third street Passenger Railway Company of Philadelphia," and of a certain other Act of Assembly approved April 10, 1858, entitled "Act to incorporate the North Branch Passenger Railway Company of the city of Philadelphia," and of a certain other Act of Assembly, approved April 13, 1858, entitled "An Act to incorporate the Fairmount Passenger Railroad Company," and of a certain other Act of Assembly, approved April 9, 1858, entitled "A further supplement to an Act to incorporate the North Philadelphia Plank Road Company and for other purposes," the right is reserved to the City Councils to disapprove of the said Acts of Assembly respectively, and of the right therein respectively granted to the said companies to occupy streets and highways of the said city therein, respectively within thirty days from the passage of the said Acts of Assembly; therefore

9. Act of April 16, 1864, Sec. 4, P. L. 662.

SEC. 1. That in pursuance of the power and authority in them vested by the said Acts of Assembly, Councils do hereby declare their disapproval of each and every of the said Acts of Assembly in the above preamble mentioned, and of the rights therein respectively granted to "The Philadelphia and Gray's Ferry Passenger Railway Company," "The Second and Third Street Passenger Railway Company of Philadelphia," "The North Branch Passenger Railway Company of the City of Philadelphia," "The Fairmount Passenger Railway Company," and "The North Philadelphia Plank Road Company," to occupy the streets and highways of the City of Philadelphia.

SEC. 2. That if any company in the said preamble named shall within ninety days from the passage of this ordinance, and before such company shall occupy any of the said streets or highways, file in the office of the City Solicitor a written obligation, sufficient in law, to bind such company to observe and be subject to all ordinances of the city in relation to passenger railways then in force, and thereafter to be passed, then the provisions of the first section of this ordinance as to each and every such company as shall file such written obligation, asaforesaid, shall cease to have effect.(*a*)

1. Ordinance April 16, 1858, Section 1, 143.
2. Ordinance April 16, 1858, Section 2, 143.

(*a*) The Philadelphia and Gray's Ferry Passenger Railway, filed an obligation, June, 1858. The Fairmount, on June 5, 1858. The North Branch, July 10, 1858. The Second and Third, June 16, 1858. The Philadelphia Plank Road Company, July 7, 1858.

Second and Third Street Passenger Railway Company.

SECTION 1. That John Robbins, Junior, James Verree, Samuel Megargee, William O. Kline, Anthony Miskey, Paul J. Field, Hugh O'Donnell, M. S. Buckley, John P. Verree, James V. Watson, George Read, Curwen Stoddart, Peter Rambo, John H. Bringhurst, Henry Crilley, Henry Bumm, John K. Gamble, S. D. Anderson, John Horn, Henry Nicholas Marselis, Joseph P. Loughead, Harry Connelly, John F. Mascher, Lambert Towns, B. F. Hart. Wm. A. Mitchell, A. A. Gregg, Harry Conrad, Stephen Robbins, George Fisher, Jacob Jones, John Dorlan, Lewis Wunder, Charles D. Robbins, Alexander Cummings, Daniel M. Fox, George Earp, Edward S. Lawrance, Henry Bickley, W. P. Cooper, E. Cameron, Joseph Singerly, John McGreger, J. E. Ridgway, Samuel S. Warthmann, Thomas W. Higgins, Jno. O'Brien, Francis McManus, Charles Harlan, Ferdinand Giesler, Dendy Sharswood, Wm. H. Kichline, Henry Gerker, Jacob Bender, Andrew McBride, Robert Kelton, Robert Cabeen, Samuel B. Jones, William Read, Lewis Shinnic, John Blair, Thomas J. Potts Charles S. Peall, Charles E. Roberts, Richard M. Berry, Charles Doran, H. R. Cogshall, George H. Hart, John Anspach, junior, Joseph Glenat, Henry K. Strong, Joseph B. Myers, or a majority of them, be and they are hereby constituted and appointed commissioners to open books, receive subscriptions and organize a company by the name, style and title of the Second and Third Street Passenger Railway Company of Philadelphia, with power and authority to lay out and construct a railway, commencing at Third and Dock streets, extending northwardly along Third street to Brown street; along Brown to Beach street; along Beach to Maiden street; along Maiden street, or the opening north of the public square, to Frankford road; along Frankford road to Queen street; along Queen to Richmond street; thence along Richmond street to Allegheny avenue, and returning along Richmond to Norris street; along Norris street to Franklin Avenue; along Franklin avenue to Second street; along Second street to Mifflin street; southward, along Mifflin street, to Third street, and along

1. Act of April 10, 1858, Sec. 1, P. L. 240.

Third street to Dock street, with the right to extend the said railway from Third and Brown streets, northwardly along Third street to Germantown road; along Germantown road to Oxford street; along Oxford street eastwardly, to Third street; along Third street to Norris street; along Norris street to Second, and along Second street to Franklin avenue, also diverging at Frankford road and Franklin avenue; thence along Frankford road to the foot of Queen street, with a single track from thence along Frankford road, with a double track to Maiden street; thence along Maiden street with a single track to Penn street; thence along Penn street to Coates, and thence along Coates street to Second street, to connect at Second street with the main track, and with the further right to extend the said railway from Frankford road and Queen street northwardly along Frankford road to Amber street; southwardly along Amber street to Front street, and along Front street to Franklin avenue, or along such other streets east of Third street as the councils of the City of Philadelphia may authorize for the purpose of carrying out the object of this act, with a single track on each of said streets, except Richmond street, which may have a double track east of Norris street and Frankford road, which may have a double track north of Franklin avenue, with the privilege of extending the same north and south along Third and Second streets and Jefferson avenue, and eastwardly along Richmond street and Frankford road to any point within the city limits as public convenience may from time to time require, subject to all the provisions and restrictions of an act regulating railroad companies, approved the nineteenth day of February, one thousand eight hundred and forty-nine, and the several supplements thereto, so far as the same are not altered or supplied by this act, and, also, to an ordinance of the city councils entitled, an ordinance to regulate passenger railways within the City of Philadelphia, approved the seventh day of July, one thousand eight hundred and fifty seven: *Provided, however,* That nothing contained in this act shall be construed to authorize the construction of a double track on Second and Third street, or on Frankford road north of Franklin avenue.

Sec. 2. That the capital stock of the said company shall consist of five thousand shares of fifty dollars each: *Provided,* That the said company may from time to time, by a

2. Act of April 10, 1858, Sec. 2, P. L. 241.

vote of the stockholders, at a meeting called for that purpose, increase the capital stock, if it should be deemed necessary, to an amount not exceeding ten thousand shares, for the purpose of completing and equipping the railway; the said company shall have the power of borrowing any sum not exceeding in amount the one-half of their capital stock, at a rate of interest not exceeding seven per centum per annum, and to secure the payment of the same by the issue of a bond and mortage of the said railroad, together with the corporate rights and franchises granted by this act, and to annex to the said bond and mortgage the privilege of converting the same into the capital stock of the said company at par at the option of the holders, if they shall signify their election one year before their maturity: *Provided, also,* That the said company shall issue no certificate of loan of a less denomination than one hundred dollars.

SEC. 3. That the said railway company shall not use a locomotive for the purpose of transporting cars over their road under the penalty of a forfeiture of their charter; and whenever the said company shall declare dividends exceeding the rate of six per centum per annum in addition to any tax imposed by general laws of their capital stock, they shall pay into the treasury of the City of Philadelphia, for the use of the said city, a tax of six per centum per annun on the excess of dividend above said rate of six per centum per annum; and the said company, before commencing to use the said road upon said streets, shall purchase, at the option of the owners, the stock of horses, omnibuses, sleighs, and harness, owned and used upon the said streets at the time of commencing the said road, at a price to be assessed by three disinterested persons to be appointed in the following manner: the said owners shall choose one disinterested person, and the said company shall choose a second person, and the two thus chosen shall choose a third, who also shall be a disinterested person, and the three shall appraise such stock; and the value thus arrived at shall be binding and final upon both parties, and said appraisers shall be sworn to faithfully perform all the duties incident to said appointment, and who shall make the appraisement within thirty days from the time of their appointment.

SEC. 4. That before the said railway company shall commence to use the said streets, the consent of the councils of

3. Act of April 10, 1858, Sec. 3, P. L. 242.
4. Act of April 10, 1858, Sec. 4, P. L. 242.

the City of Philadelphia shall be first obtained, and said consent shall be taken and deemed to have been given if said councils shall not within thirty days after the passage of this act, by ordinances duly passed, signify their disapprobation thereof; and the said councils may from time to time, by ordinances, establish such regulations in regard to said railway as may be required for the purposes of paving, re-paving, grading, culverting and laying gas and water pipes in and along said streets, and to prevent obstructions thereon; and that the said company in constructing said road shall conform to the grades established by councils of the several streets and avenues traversed by said railway, and keep said streets in perpetual good repair at the proper expense of the said company.

SEC. 5. That the said railway company shall have the right to cross at grade any railroad that is now or that hereafter may be built within the limits of the City of Philadelphia, and to connect with any other passenger railway within the said city.

SEC. 6. That it shall be the duty of said company, at every point of crossing at grade any railroad upon which locomotive steam engines are employed, to have flagmen stationed, and use all the precaution and means of safety, excepting the gates that are provided in the supplement to an act to the Philadelphia and Delaware River Railroad Company, authorizing said company to cross the Philadelphia and Reading Railroad at grade at Frankford avenue, and the company hereby incorporated shall be subject to all the penalties in said supplement provided for the Philadelphia and Delaware River Railroad Company.

SEC. 7. The said railway on the route described, shall be subject to the use of any part or parts thereof by any other Passenger Railway Company, for the purpose of completing a route or making a circuit, upon such conditions as may be agreed upon by such other company and the said Second and Third Street Passenger Railway Company, and in case the companies cannot agree, then upon such terms and conditions as shall be prescribed by the Councils of the City of Philadelphia.

SEC. 8. That the capital stock of the Second and Third

5. Act of April 10, 1858, Sec. 5, P. L. 242.
6. Act of April 10, 1858, Sec. 6, P. L. 243.
7. Act of April 10, 1858, Sec. 7, P. L. 243.
8. Act of April 13, 1859, Sec. 1, P. L. 558.
(*a*) The ordinance whereby the councils gave consent is at page 15.

Street Passenger Railway Company of Philadelphia, shall be increased to ten thousand shares of fifty dollars each, to be issued in such manner as the board of directors shall deem best for the interests of the company: *Provided*, The stockholders shall accept this amendment to their charter within thirty days after the approval thereof.

SEC. 9. That the company shall be required within sixty days from the passage of this act, to extend their road from the Reading Railroad to Allegheny avenue; and shall also extend said road from Allegheny avenue, along Richmond street and Point road, to within two hundred feet of the bridge over Frankford creek in Bridge street, in Bridesburg, in the Twenty-third ward, with a single track, within nine months after the passage of the act.

SEC. 10. That so much of the provisions of the said act to which this act is a further supplement, and of any other act of assembly, as may be construed to authorize any other railroad company to use or run their cars over or upon the railroad of the said Second and Third Street Passenger Railway Company, of Philadelphia, without their consent, be and the same is hereby repealed: *Provided*, That nothing herein contained shall be so construed as to effect any rights that the Fairmount and Arch Street Passenger Railway Company, or the Fairmount Passenger Railway Company, now have to use said Second and Third Street Passenger Railway track, nor the corporate rights and privileges of the Green and Coates Street Philadelphia Passenger Railway Company.

SEC. 11. That the said railway company be and are hereby authorized to take up their railway track now laid on Third street, from Oxford street to Norris street, and to discontinue the use thereof; and that the said company be and are hereby authorized to lay out, construct, continue and extend their said railway on Second street, northward, along the said Second street, from Norris street, to Lehigh avenue, in the City of Philadelphia.

SEC. 12. That in all cases where the said railway company has redeemed, or shall hereafter redeem, any of its bonds, it shall be lawful for the directors to issue new stock, to the amount of the bonds so redeemed, to the stockholders thereof.

9. Act of April 13, 1859, Sec. 2, P. L. 558.
10. Act of April 10, 1862, Sec. 1, P. L. 409.
11. Act of April 10, 1862, Sec. 2, P. L. 409.
12. Act of April 10, 1862, Sec. 3, P. L. 410.

Resolutions and Ordinances specially applicable to the Second and Third Street Passenger Railway Company.

WHEREAS, The interest of the citizens of Philadelphia, residing upon the line of the Fairmount Railway Company, demands that a connection should be made between that road and the Second and Third Street Railroad, at the intersection of Race and Second streets, for the purpose of preventing a conflict in the travel between said railway companies, and enabling them to adopt such direction of travel as will accommodate the residents thereon. And whereas, by an Act of Assembly, incorporating the Second and Third Street Railway Company, approved April 10th, 1858, the Councils of the City of Philadelphia are empowered to grant the Second and Third Street Railway Company privilege to construct such connecting links between their lines on Second and Third streets, as may be required by them: therefore,

1. *Resolved*, That the Second and Third Street Passenger Railway Company are hereby authorized to construct a single track passenger railway on the line of Race street, from Second to Third street; provided, they conform to existing laws and ordinances.

2. That the Second and Third Street Passenger Railway Company be, and the same is hereby authorized to lay out and construct an additional track of Railway, beginning at Oxford and Third streets, and extending along Oxford street to Front Street· and also, a track beginning at Jefferson street and Frankford road, and extending along Jefferson street to Second streeet, in accordance with the grades and regulations established by the Board of Surveyors and Regulators: *Provided*, That nothing herein contained shall be construed to authorize the construction of a double track on either of the streets hereby designated: *And provided further*, That the ordinance shall not take effect until the said Second and Third Street

1. Resolution August 20, 1858, p. 239.
2. Ordinance December 17, 1858, p. 485.

Passenger Railway Company shall have filed in the office of the City Solicitor a full and complete account of the cost of their road so far as the same has been constructed.

3. That the Second and Third Streets Passenger Railway Company are hereby authorized to construct a double track of railway on Lehigh avenue from the intersection of their road at Richmond street and Lehigh avenue to their property on said Lehigh avenue: *Provided*, That a single track shall be laid each side of the market sheds on said avenue.

4. That the said Second and Third Streets Passenger Railway Company are hereby authorized to lay the necessary railway on Dock street, from the intersection of their road at Second and Dock streets, to effect a circuit into Third street for their Richmond cars; and are also authorized to use the southwestern railway track in Dock street: *Provided*, That the City of Philadelphia shall have the power, at all times, without notice to the said railway company, to order the said tracks to be removed at the expense of the said company.

3. Sec. 1, Ordinance November 5, 1861, p. 308.
4. Sec. 2, Ordinance November 5, 1861, p. 308.

North Branch Passenger Railway.

SECTION 1. That Robert Weight, Robert Buchanan, John L. Crawford, Charles Whitson, Thomas O. Plum, Samuel Hultz, Patrick Kelly, John H. Whitson, M. Davis, Daniel T. Moore, John Powers, N. R. Moseley, A. B. Ivins, G. W. Whitson, C. T Thomas, John Weaver, Daniel Dougherty, S. Morton Zulick, and Isaac M. Ashton, or any five of them, are hereby appointed commissioners to open books, receive subscriptions, and organize a company by the name, style and title of the North Branch Passenger Railway Company of the City of Philadelphia, with power to lay out and construct a railway from the intersection of Fifteenth and Chestnut streets, thence along Fifteenth street to Vine street, thence along Vine street to Sixteenth street, thence along Sixteenth street to Walnut street, and to connect with any passenger railway now constructed or hereafter to be constructed, so as to give the said company a complete route from Fairmount to the Exchange in the said City of Philadelphia,(*a*) and the said company shall have power to convey passengers over the said route to and from Fairmount to the Exchange, as aforesaid; and they shall have the right to purchase real estate and to erect thereon such buildings and improvements as may be necessary or deemed expedient for the purposes and convenience of said company, and also to purchase the necessary equipments, such as horses, cars, or other vehicles for the conveyance of passengers on the said railway, and no freight or burden trains or locomotives shall be permitted to pass over said railway: *Provided,* That before the said company shall run their cars on the track or tracks of any other passenger railway, they shall agree with such other company or companies upon the terms or compensation to be paid said company or companies for the privilege of so using said roads, and that if the said parties shall not be able to agree upon terms, the determination of the dispute shall be submitted to the councils of Philadelphia, whose adjustment shall be binding and conclusive: *Provided,* That it may be

1. Act of April 10, 1858, Sec. 1, P. L. 245.

(*a*) The nature of this grant has been adjudicated in North Branch Passenger Railway Company *vs.* City Passenger Railway Company, 2 Wright, 361.

lawful for any other railroad within the City of Philadelphia, upon which horse power is used as a motive power to connect with the said North Branch Passenger Railway, upon the same terms and in the same manner upon which the said North Branch Passenger Railway is authorized to connect with other passenger railways.

SEC. 2. That the capital stock of the said company shall consist of three thousand shares of fifty dollars each: *Provided*, That said company shall have power, by a vote of the stockholders convened for that purpose, to increase their capital stock, as much as in their opinion shall or may be necessary to complete said railway, and to carry out the full and true intent and meaning of this act.

SEC. 3. That dividends of so much of the profits of said company as shall appear advisable to the directors thereof, shall be declared in the months of January and July, in each and every year, and be paid at the office of the said company at any time after ten days from the time of declaring the same, but said dividends shall in no case exceed the amount of the net profits of said company, so that the capital stock shall never be impaired thereby; and if said directors shall make any dividends impairing the capital stock of said company, the directors consenting thereto shall be liable in their individual capacities to said company for the amount so divided, and each director present when such dividends shall be declared, shall be considered as consenting thereto, unless he or they enter their written protest upon the minutes of the Board, and give public notice of the same.

SEC. 4. That the said company shall make and have a common seal, and the same to alter and renew at pleasure, and also shall have power to ordain, establish, and put in execution such by-laws, ordinances and regulations, as shall appear necessary or convenient for the government of said corporation, and not being contrary to the constitution and laws of the United States, or of this commonwealth, and generally to do all and singular the matters and things which to them it shall lawfully appertain to do for the well being of said corporation, and the due ordering and managing of the affairs thereof.

SEC. 5. That said company shall have power to elect or

2. Act of April 10, 1858, Sec. 2, P. L. 245.
3. Act of April 10, 1858, Sec. 3, P. L. 246.
4. Act of April 10, 1858, Sec. 4, P. L. 246.
5. Act of April 10, 1858, Sec. 5, P. L. 246.

appoint a president and five directors, a majority of whom shall, with the president, be citizens of Philadelphia, and such other officers as shall be deemed necessary or expedient, and in every election for officers each share of stock shall entitle the holder to one vote.

SEC. 6. That the said company shall have power to raise on their bonds or other security, any sum of money not exceeding one-half of their capital stock, for the purpose of carrying out the true intent and meaning of this act.

SEC. 7. That the said railway company shall not connect with any railroad other than for the purpose of carrying or conveying passengers, and their railway shall be of the same uniform gauge as other city passenger railways now constructed in said City of Philadelphia, under the penalty of a forfeiture of their charter; and the said company shall annually pay the treasury of the City of Philadelphia, for the use of said city, whenever the dividends shall exceed six per centum on the capital stock the sum of six per centum on the said dividends thus declared; and the said company before commencing to use said road upon the said streets, shall purchase, at the option of the owners, the stock of horses, omnibuses, sleighs and harness, owned and used upon said streets at the time of commencing the said road, at a price to be assessed in the following manner: the said owners shall choose one disinterested person, and the said company shall choose a second person, and the two thus chosen shall choose a third, who also shall be a disinterested person, and the three shall appraise such stock, and the value thus arrived at shall be binding and final upon both parties: *Provided*, That whenever any damages shall be sustained by reason of this company taking possession of lands or other property other than above described, except so far as the usufruct of the before mentioned streets necessary to the full and perfect enjoyment of the purposes of this act designed, the said damages shall be assessed and paid in the manner and according to the provisions of the eleventh section of the act of nineteenth of February, Anno Domini one thousand eight hundred and forty-nine, entitled "An Act regulating railroad companies," and the several supplements thereto: *And provided further*, That before the said company shall use and occupy said streets, the consent of the councils of the City of Philadelphia shall

6. Act of April 10, 1858, Sec. 6, P. L. 246.
7. Act of April 10, 1858, Sec. 7, P. L. 247.

be first obtained, and said consent shall be taken and deemed to have been given, if said councils shall not within thirty days after the passage of this act by ordinance duly passed signify their disapproval thereof; and said councils may from time to time, by ordinance, establish such regulations in regard to said railway as may be required for the paving, re-paving, grading, culverting, and the laying of gas and water pipes in and along said streets, and to prevent obstruction thereon.(*a*)

SEC. 8. That the said company in constructing said railway shall conform to the grades now established or hereafter to be by law established of the several streets and avenues traversed by said railway, and keep said streets and avenues in perpetual repair at the proper expense of said company.

SEC. 9. The road therein authorized shall be commenced within one year and finished within three years from the passage of this act: *Provided*, That the privileges thereby granted shall continue for twenty years and no longer, unless extended or renewed by the Legislature.

8. Act of April 10, 1858, Sec. 8, P. L. 247.
9. Act of April 10, 1858, Sec. 9, P. L. 247.
(*b*) The ordinances whereby the Councils gave consent is at page 15.

Fairmount Passenger Railroad Company.

SECTION 1. That Robert Morris, E. F. Prentis, R. Coulton Davis, Joseph B. Hanson, George Chandler, James M. Smith, Seneca E. Malone, William H. James, Joseph C. Kern, James Stroup, Thomas Allman, William Penrose, Aaron B. Ivins, Richard Stokes, George C. Bower, Henry Grambo, Stephen N. Winslow, William K. Bray, John Derbyshire, Morris Davis, Lafayette Baker, Peter C. Ellmaker, John Ashton, M. D., Jonathan Loyd, James Steel, S. J. Ray, John White, William Anspach, Solomon Bunn, Joseph Harrison, Jr., William H. Harding, D. R. Smith, Isaac M. Krupp, Charles A. Jones, N. R. Moseley, Isaac W. Ashton, S. Martin Zulic, or any five of them, are hereby appointed commissioners to open books, receive subscriptions, and organize a company by the name, style, and title of the Fairmount Passenger Railway Company, and as such shall have power to lay out and construct a railway in the City of Philadelphia, according to the following routes: From the south side of Fairmount to Callowhill street respectively, thence east on Callowhill street to Twenty-third, thence south to Vine street, thence east to Second street, thence south to Walnut or Dock streets, thence west to Third street, thence north to Race street, thence west to Twenty-second street, thence north to Callowhill street, with a double track on Callowhill street to Fairmount, the place of begining, with the right to intersect and run their cars over any railroad already incorporated, or which may hearafter be incorporated and located on Second street, from Vine to Dock street, from Dock to Third street, and from thence to Race street in said city, upon such terms as may be agreed upon by the parties interested, or in case the parties interested cannot agree upon the terms aforesaid, then the city councils, upon petition of either of the parties interested, shall fix the terms in such a manner as shall be deemed right and equitable, and shall have power to convey passengers over the same; and the said company shall also have the right to purchase real estate, and to erect thereon such buildings and improvements as may be deemed expedient and necessary for the purposes of said company, and also to purchase the necessary

1. Act of April 13, 1858, Sec. 1, P. L. 257.

equipments for said railways; and no freight or burden trains or locomotives shall be permitted to pass over the same.

SEC. 2. That the capital stock of said company shall consist of six thousand shares, of fifty dollars each: *Provided*, That said company may from time to time by a vote of the stockholders, at a meeting convened for that purpose, increase their capital stock as much as in their opinion may be necessary to complete said railway, and to carry out the true intent and meaning of this act.

SEC. 3. That dividends of so much of the profits of said company as shall appear advisable to the directors, shall be declared in the months of January and July in each and every year, and be paid at the office of said company any time after ten days from the time of declaring the same, but said dividends shall in no case exceed the amount of the net profits of said company, so that the capital stock shall never be impaired thereby; and if said directors shall make any dividend impairing the capital stock of said company, the directors consenting thereto shall be liable in their individual capacities to said company for the amount so divided, and each director present when such dividend shall be declared shall be considered as consenting thereto, unless he or they enter protest upon the minutes of the board, and give public notice of the same.

SEC. 4. That the said company shall make and have a common seal, and the same to alter and renew at pleasure, and also to ordain, establish, and put in execution such by-laws, ordinances and regulations, as shall appear necessary or convenient for the government of said corporation, and not being contrary to the constitution and laws of the United States or of this commonwealth, and generally to do for the well-being of said corporation, and the due ordering and managing of the affairs thereof.

SEC. 5. That said company shall have power to elect or appoint a president and five directors, a majority of whom, with the president, shall be citizens of Philadelphia, and such other officers as may be deemed necessary or expedient; and in every election for officers each share of stock shall entitle the holder to one vote.

2. Act of April 13, 1858, Sec. 2, P. L. 258.
3. Act of April 13, 1858, Sec. 3, P. L. 258.
4. Act of April 13, 1858, Sec. 4, P. L. 258.
5. Act of April 13, 1858, Sec. 5, P. L. 258.

SEC. 6. That said company shall have power to raise on bonds any sum not exceeding one-half of their capital stock, for the purpose of carrying out the true intent of this act: *Provided*, That no bond shall be issued for a less sum than one hundred dollars.

SEC. 7. That the said railroad company shall not connect with any railroad other than for passenger purposes, and of the same gauge, under the penalty of a forfeiture of their charter, and the said company shall annually pay into the treasury of the City of Philadelphia for the use of said city whenever the dividends shall exceed six per centum on the said dividends thus declared, and the said company before commencing said road upon the said streets, shall purchase, at the option of the owners, all the stock of horses, omnibuses, sleighs and harness, and incidentals owned and used upon the said streets at the time of commencing the said road, at a price to be assessed in the following manner, to wit: The said company shall choose one disinterested person, and the said owners shall choose a second person and the two thus chosen shall choose a third person, who, together, shall appraise such stock, and the value thus arrived at shall be binding and final: *Provided*, That whenever any damages may be sustained by reason of this company taking possession of lands or other property other than above described, except so far as the usufruct of the before named streets, necessary to the full and perfect enjoyment of the purposes by this act designed, and the said damages shall be assessed and paid in the manner and according to the provisions of the eleventh section of the act of nineteenth of February, Anno Domini one thousand eight hundred and forty-nine, and the several supplements thereto, entitled "An Act regulating Railroad Companies:" *And provided further*, That before the said company shall use and occupy the said streets, the consent of the councils of the City of Philadelphia shall be first obtained, and said consent shall be taken and deemed to have been given, if said councils shall not within thirty days after the passage of this act, by ordinances duly passed, signify their disapproval thereof; and said councils may from time to time, by ordinances, establish such regulations in regard to said railway, as may be required for paving, repaving, grading,

6. Act of April 13, 1858, Sec. 6, P. L. 259.
7. Act of April 13, 1858, Sec. 7, P. L. 259.

culverting, and laying of gas and waterpipes in and along said streets, and to prevent obstructions thereon.(*a*)

SEC. 8. That said company in constructing said road, shall conform to the grades now established, or hereafter to be by law established, of the several streets traversed by said roads, and keep said streets in perpetual good repair at the proper expense of said company.

WHEREAS, The Fairmount Passenger Railway Company has become greatly embarrassed by numerous unsettled claims and complicated legal questions arising from improvident expenditures, and from misconduct of its former officers, which cannot be determined for many years to come:

And whereas, The bondholders, stockholders and creditors interested in said Company have, by very general consent, agreed to the terms of a proposed compromise, whereby the difficulties and embarrassments of said Company are to be adjusted and settled; and it is proper that the litigation likely to grow out of the complicated affairs of said Company should be avoided and prevented; therefore,

SEC. 9. That the number of shares of stock authorized to be issued by the said Company shall be sixteen thousand, and that the shares of stock heretofore issued by the said Company, and which have been purchased or hypothecated for valuable consideration, shall be estimated and taken as a part of the said sixteen thousand shares, and shall be as good and valid stock as though the same had been regularly and lawfully issued by the said Company.

SEC. 10. That all the notes heretofore issued by the said Company, and for which a valuable consideration has been given or paid, shall be valid and binding upon the said Company to the extent of whatever value has been given or paid for the same, with interest at the rate of six per cent. per annum therefor; and the holders thereof shall be entitled to collect and receive that amount.

SEC. 11. That the mortgage heretofore executed by the said Company, dated the fourteenth day of January Anno Domini one thousand eight hundred and sixty-one, in favor

8. Act of April 13, 1853, Sec. 8, P. L. 1863, 259.
9. Act of July 17, 1862, Sec. 1, P. L. 1863, 672.
10. Act of July 17, 1862, Sec. 2, P. L. 1863, 672.
11. Act of July 17, 1862, Sec. 3, P. L. 1863, 672.

(*a*) The ordinance whereby the Councils gave consent is at page 15.

of Pearson S. Peterson and John Roache, trustees, and recorded in , upon all the property, real and personal, of the said Company, shall be valid and binding upon the said Company to the extent and for the uses and purposes therein contained, mentioned and set forth; and the lien thereof shall be held to commence from the execution and delivery of the said mortgage.

SEC. 12. That the bonds issued by the said Company for a valuable consideration, under and in pursuance of the terms and provisions of the said mortgage, as certified to have been so issued by the said Pearson S. Peterson and John Roache, trustees, shall be valid and binding upon the said Company; and the holders thereof shall be entitled to all the rights intended to be secured to them, under and by virtue of the said mortgage, to the extent of whatever value has been given or paid for the same, with interest at the rate of six per cent. per annum therefor; and the holders thereof shall be entitled to collect and receive that amount.

SEC. 13. That it shall be the duty of the President and Directors of the said Company, within twenty days after the passage of this act, to call a meeting of the stockholders of the said Company, to be held at the office of the Company, in the City of Philadelphia, fifteen days after the date of such notice, for the purpose of taking into consideration the adoption or rejection of this Act of Assembly; and at such meeting the vote shall be taken according to the number of shares held by each stockholder, respectively; and if, upon such vote being taken, it shall appear that a majority of the votes, according to the number of shares held by the persons voting, each share being entitled to one vote, shall have been cast in favor of the adoption of this act, then this Act of Assembly shall be and become an amendment to the charter of the said Company, and be binding upon the said Company from and after the date of its said adoption.

SEC. 14. That as soon thereafter as it can conveniently be done, it shall be the duty of the President and Directors of the said Company to cause to be presented to the Supreme Court for the Eastern District of Pennsylvania, a petition setting forth the names of all the persons claiming

12. Act of July 17, 1862, Sec. 4, P. L. 1863, 672.
13. Act of July 17, 1862, Sec. 5, P. L. 1863, 672.
14. Act of July 17, 1862, Sec. 6, P. L. 1863, 672.

to be stockholders and creditors (whether as noteholders, bondholders or otherwise), of the said Company, and setting forth the difficulties and embarrassments existing in the affairs of the said Company, and praying the said Court for the appointment of some person with the powers of a Master and Examiner in Chancery, for the purpose of taking testimony, and deciding and reporting a decree, settling and adjusting the rights of all the parties, both stockholders and creditors, interested in the said Company.

SEC. 15. That it shall be the duty of the said person, so appointed by the said Court, within thirty days after his said appointment, to give notice by a public advertisement, to be published twice in the Legal Intelligencer, and to be published for two weeks in two daily newspapers in the City of Philadelphia, of his appointment; and that all persons claiming to be stockholders and creditors, whether noteholders, bondholders or otherwise, are required to appear before him, at a time and place to be appointed by him, and present their claims as stockholders and creditors of the said Company; and it shall be the duty of the said person so appointed, to examine the said claims, to take proof thereon, and to determine and decide upon the rights of the respective claimants who shall appear before him; and for those purposes to adjourn from time to time, for such period and so often as may be necessary, in order to fulfill the duties of his appointment; and, after having fully heard and determined the questions so submitted to him, it shall be his duty to report a decree to the said Court, settling and deciding who are the stockholders in said Company, what number of shares of stock each stockholder is entitled to, who are the creditors of the said Company, and whether such creditors are noteholders, bondholders, or in whatsoever other manner the said Company is indebted to such creditor; that such report or decree shall be made and filed in the office of the Prothonotary of the said Court; and, unless the same is excepted to within ten days after it is so filed, it shall become final and binding upon all parties or persons interested in the said Company, without appeal or writ of error, and shall be conclusive evidence of the fact and rights of persons as therein found reported and decreed.

15. Act of July 17, 1862, Sec. 7, P. L. 1863, 672.

SEC. 16. That it shall be the duty of the person so appointed by the said Court to give notice of the filing of his said decree, for ten days before the same shall be filed, by publication in two daily newspapers in the said city, and by one insertion in the Legal Intelligencer, also published in said city.

SEC. 17. That it shall be the duty of the said Court to examine and decide upon the said exceptions, if any such shall be filed, according to the rules of practice prevailing in courts of chancery, in similar cases coming within their jurisdiction, and to refer the case back to the said Master for further proof, with proper directions to him, or to make and enter a final decree, in such form and manner as may be in accordance with equity and the rights of the parties, and in pursuance of the provisions of this Act of Assembly; and such decree, when so made, shall be final and binding, without appeal or writ of error, upon the said Company, and upon all parties or persons, whether stockholders or creditors, interested in said Company; and shall be conclusive evidence of the fact, and the rights and equities of all persons interested in the said Company, as therein found reported and decreed.

SEC. 18. That the said Master and the said Court shall hold and declare any stockholder who has heretofore paid valuable consideration for his said stock, to be a stockholder of the said Company; and also all such persons as have advanced money upon the said stock, and are holders thereof by pledge or hypothecation, to be such holders; and shall also decree the amount due to them on account of such advance loan or hypothecation; and that all noteholders and bondholders shall have their rights respectively determined, declared and decreed, according to the amounts in money or other valuable consideration, which they have, respectively, given, advanced or loaned, for or on account of such bonds or notes as they may hold.

SEC. 19. That it shall be the duty of Joseph J. Sharpless, the receiver of the estate and effects of the said Company, to file with the said Master an account, showing the balance of money in his hands, at such time as he shall be required so to do by the said Master; and it shall be the duty of the

16. Act of July 17, 1862, Sec. 8, P. L. 1863, 672.
17. Act of July 17, 1862, Sec. 9, P. L. 1863, 672.
18. Act of July 17, 1862, Sec. 10, P. L. 1863, 672.
19. Act of July 17, 1862, Sec. 11, P. L. 1863, 672.

said Master to report a distribution of the said balance, after deducting all the expenses and costs of the proceedings taken in the said Court as herein provided, *pro rata*, among the said various creditors of the said Company, according to the amounts which may be found and decreed to be due to each, respectively.

SEC. 20. That the Board of Directors, elected heretofore on the twenty-fourth day of March, one thousand eight hundred and sixty-two, shall take the charge, control and management of all the books and papers of the said Company; and after the decree, hereinbefore provided for shall have been made, the said Board of Directors shall allow, regulate and control the issue and transfer of stock in the said Company, as so found and decreed in the manner provided by the charter and by-laws of the said Company; and do all other acts necessary and proper in the transaction of the business of said Company.

SEC. 21. That all proceedings in any and all suits now pending, by stockholders or creditors, whether as noteholders, bondholders or otherwise, against said Company, shall be suspended until the said decree shall be made; and no suit shall be brought against said Company by any stockholder or creditor until said decree shall have been made; but, so soon as such decree shall have been made, all creditors of said Company shall have the right to proceed for the collection of the amounts found to be due to them, by said decree, according to law; and the suits now pending against said Company may thereafter be proceeded with, in accordance with the rules of law and equity, applicable to the courts in which such suits are pending.

SEC. 22. That the fifth section of said act be so construed, as to permit said Fairmount Passenger Railway Company, at its annual election, to elect a president and twelve directors; and in case it shall be deemed expedient to increase the present number of the directors of said company, before the period of another annual election shall arrive, the present board of directors may order an election of additional directors by the stockholders, who shall have the same power as if duly elected at the last annual election, prior to said election.

20. Act of July 17, 1862, Sec. 12, P L. 1863, 672.
21. Act of July 17, 1862, Sec. 13, P. L. 1863, 672.
22. Act of July 18, 1863, Sec. 1, P. L. 1864, 1114.

SEC. 23. That the said railway company be and they are hereby authorized to lay a track, from the terminus of their road, Second and Vine streets; thence east, on Vine to Front street; thence south to Race street; thence west to connect the same with the present road: *Provided*, That they first liquidate the debt for constructing the square from Third and Vine, to Second and Vine streets.

SEC. 24. That the Fairmount Passenger Railroad Company are hereby authorized and empowered to increase the capital stock of said company to twenty thousand shares, of fifty dollars each.

SEC. 25. That the provisions of the act, approved the seventeenth day of April, one thousand eight hundred and sixty-three, entitled "An Act to enable the District Court of the City and County of Philadelphia, to quash the writ of sequestration now existing against the Hestonville, Mantua and Fairmount Passenger Railroad Company," shall be and the same are hereby extended to the Fairmount Passenger Railroad Company, and its creditors, in the District Court, Supreme Court, Court of Common Pleas, or any other court, in which proceedings touching the affairs of said company are now pending, subject to all the provisos contained in said act.

23. Act of July 18, 1863, Sec. 2, P. L. 1864, 1114.
24. Act of May 21, 1864, Sec. 1, P. L. 923.
25. Act of May 21, 1864, Sec. 1, P. L. 924.

North Philadelphia or Central Passenger Railway Company of Philadelphia.

SECTION 1. That William Schaffer, William M. Kennedy, JacobO. Ewing, John Fallon, William Greene, Geo. Hergesheimer, Robert Thomas, Joseph King, Jr., Samuel Culp, George W. Carpenter, Frederick Emhart, F. William Buckius, Jabez Gates, Enoch Taylor, or any five of them, be, and they are hereby appointed Commissioners to open books, receive subscriptions, and organize a company with the rights, and subject to the restrictions of the "Act regulating Turnpike and Plank Road Companies," approved January twenty-sixth, one thousand eight hundred and forty-nine, to be called "The North Philadelphia Plank Road Company," to lay out and construct a plank or hard road, commencing at the north line of South Penn District, in Schuylkill Sixth street, or with the consent of the commissioners of said district, at any point within said district, thence northward along the line of said Sixth street continued to a point not further than a quarter of a mile either to the north or south of Nicetown lane, and thence to connect with the old York turnpike road, at the nearest and best point to be determined by the managers of said company, also from said point to continue the said road northwestwardly to and along the line of either Green street or Wayne street, as laid down on the plan of the borough of Germantown, and to continue the same northwestwardly in the same direction on the line of either of said streets, continued as far through the borough of Germantown as may from time to time be deemed expedient; all of which said plank road shall be opened, laid out, and constructed of the width of not less than sixty-five feet, the capital stock of which said company shall consist of eight hundred shares of fifty dollars each: *Provided,* That the county of Philadelphia shall not be liable for any damages on account of the opening of any street or road for the use of said "Plank Road Company:" *And provided further,* That whenever hereafter any incorporated district through which this road may pass, shall deem it necessary to curb and pave the street or road occupied by said company, the commissioners of said district shall have full power

1. Act of April 29, 1852, Sec 1, P. L.

and authority to remove the planks from said road as far as it may be necessary to enable them to curb and pave said street or road, but no further: *Provided further*, That the consent of the council of the borough of Germantown shall be obtained before said company shall occupy any street or any portion of any street now open to public use in said borough.

SEC. 2. That the North Philadelphia Plank Road Company be and they are hereby authorized to borrow money to the extent of twenty thousand dollars, and to issue their bonds therefor, convertible into the stock of the company or otherwise, and in such form and for such amounts, not less than one hundred dollars each, as the managers of said company may think proper, and to mortgage their road and franchises to secure the payment of said bonds, the said bonds to bear such rate of interest, and to be sold or disposed of by the company at such rates as they shall deem best.

SEC. 3. That the said North Philadelphia Plank Road Company shall also be and they are hereby authorized to continue their road by lateral branches, so as to connect at one or more points with the Germantown Turnpike or Main street, in the borough of Germantown: *Provided*, That no public street or road be appropriated for that purpose without the consent of the councils for said borough, and the said company are hereby further authorized to continue their road so as to connect with the Germantown and Roxborough township line road, at any point north of Harvey street, and thence up the said township line without the consent of the councils of said borough, and road to the Wissahickon turnpike road, also to continue their road from the intersection thereof at Schuylkill Sixth street with the Lamb tavern road, southeastwardly along the Lamb tavern road aforesaid to Broad street.

SECTION 4. That the North Philadelphia Plank Road Company be and they are hereby authorized to construct a railroad, to be used exclusively with horse power and passenger travel, with one or two tracks of five feet two inches gauge along the line on which, by the act to which this is a supplement and the supplements thereto, they are authorized to construct their plank road, as aforesaid, and from the point of intersection of Seventeenth street and

2. Act of March 31, 1851, Sec. 2, P. L.
3. Act of March 31, 1851, Sec. 2, P. L.
4. Act of April 9, 1858, Sec. 1, P. L. of 1860, 799.

Tioga street, to continue the said railroad down the said Tioga street to Broad street and down Broad street to Lehigh avenue; thence to continue said road down Broad street to Columbia avenue, and there to connect with the Citizens' Passenger Railroad Company; and thence over their road on Columbia avenue and Lancaster street and Tenth and Eleventh streets; and shall further have the right to lay a branch of the said road with one or two tracks, as aforesaid, up Broad street from said Lehigh avenue to Fisher's lane, and shall have power to convey passengers over the same; and the said company shall also have the right to purchase real estate, and to erect thereon such buildings and improvements as may be necessary for the purposes of said company, and also to purchase the necessary equipments for said railways; and no freight or burden trains, or locomotives, shall be permitted to pass over the same.

SEC. 5. That the said North Philadelphia Plank Road Company shall have the right, subject to such general regulations as the city councils shall, from time to time, establish and ordain for the government of passenger railroads connecting and running on other roads than their own, to connect with any other passenger railway of the same gauge, which is now constructed or which may hereafter be constructed, occupying or crossing any part of the route above indicated, and to run their cars and carry passengers on such roads, with which they shall so connect, on paying to the company or companies owning such roads, a fair compensation for the use of their road or roads; and if said North Philadelphia Plank Road Company and the company or companies, owning any road with which they shall so connect, should fail to agree on a fair compensation, as aforesaid, then they shall each appoint one disinterested person, who shall be approved of by the Court of Common Pleas in said city, and the two thus chosen shall choose a third person, also disinterested, and who shall also be approved of by said court, and the three thus chosen shall determine on the terms and compensation on which said North Philadelphia Plank Road Company shall use, as aforesaid, any other road: *Provided also*, That all passenger railways now constructed, or hereafter to be constructed, having a right to occupy or cross any part of said route, shall also have the right to connect with and use the road

5. Act of April 9, 1858, Sec. 2, P. L. of 1860, 799.

of the North Philadelphia Plank Road Company, on the same terms and conditions and to the same extent as aforesaid.

SEC. 6. That said North Philadelphia Plank Road Company, in constructing said road, shall conform to the grades now established, or hereafter to be by law established, of the several streets and avenues traversed by said road, and keep said streets and avenues in perpetual good repair, at the proper expense of said company: *Provided*, That before the said company shall use and occupy the said streets, the consent of the councils of the City of Philadelphia shall be first obtained; and said consent shall be taken and deemed to have been given, if said councils shall not, within thirty days after the passage of this act, by ordinances duly passed, signify their disapproval thereof; and said councils may, from time to time, by ordinance, establish such regulations in regard to said railway, as may be required for the paving, re-paving, grading, culverting and the laying of gas and water pipes in and along said streets, and to prevent obstructions thereon.(*a*)

SEC. 7. That to enable the said company to carry out the provisions of this act, they shall be and are hereby authorized to increase their capital stock two hundred thousand dollars above their present capital; and if they find it necessary, they shall further have the right to raise money by means of a loan, and for that purpose to mortgage their road, property and franchises, for any sum not exceeding three hundred thousand dollars, and to issue bonds, secured by such mortgage, of an amount of not less than one hundred dollars each payable at such time as the stockholders shall determine, and bearing interest not exceeding six per cent.; and shall further be authorized to dispose of said bonds on any terms and for any price which the directors of said company, or their authorized agent or agents, shall deem expedient.

SEC. 8. That the said railroad company shall not connect with any railroad, other than for passenger purposes, and of the same gauge, under the penalty of a forfeiture of their charter; and the said company shall annually pay into the treasury of the City of Philadelphia, for the use of said city, whenever the dividends shall exceed six per centum per annum on the capital stock, the sum of six per

6. Act of April 9, 1858, Sec. 3, P. L. of 1860, 4.
7. Act of April 9, 1858, Sec. 4, P. L. of 1860, 800.
8. Act of April 9, 1858, Sec. 5, P. L. of 1860, 800.
(*a*) The consent of Councils was given. See Ordinance, page 15.

centum on the said dividends thus declared; and the said company, before commencing said road upon the said streets, shall purchase, at the option of the owners, the stock of horses, omnibuses, sleighs and harness owned and used upon the said streets at the time of commencing the said road, at a price to be assessed in the following manner: The said owners shall choose one disinterested person, and the said company shall choose a second person, and the two thus chosen shall choose a third, who together shall be disinterested persons, and shall appraise such stock, and the value thus arrived at shall be binding and final: *Provided,* That said company shall in all respects be subject to the provisions of the general act regulating railroad companies, of nineteenth of February, Anno Domini one thousand eight hundred and forty-nine, and the several supplements thereto: *Provided also,* That said North Philadelphia Plank Road Company shall be subject to an ordinance of the city councils, entitled "An Ordinance to regulate Passenger Railways within the City of Philadellhia," approved the seventh day of July, Anno Domini one thousand eight hundred and fifty-seven.

SEC. 9. That the North Philadelphia Passenger Railway Company be and they are hereby authorized and empowered to adopt and use, for the purpose of drawing and propelling their cars, on any road or railway which they now have built and constructed, and also on any road which they may hereafter build and construct, under any power or authority whatever, steam passenger cars: *Provided* That no cars propelled by steam upon said road shall be permitted to run south of Columbia avenue.

SEC. 10. That should said road, or any part thereof, be sold, at judicial sale, under any judgment obtained on the mortgage which is now on said road, for any sum less than the price or sum which said company have contracted to give for the building and construction of said road, then Emanuel Peters, the builder and constructor thereof, his legal representatives or assigns, shall have the right, at any time within three years from the date of such sale, to claim or redeem the road, which shall have been sold as aforesaid, from any person or persons who shall have purchased the same at said sale, by paying to such purchaser or purchasers the price or sum which he, she or

9. Act of May 16, 1861, Sec. 1, P. L. 695.
10. Act of May 16, 1861, Sec. 2, P. L. 695.

they shall have paid for the same with interest at said sale; and the purchaser or purchasers at said sale, upon being paid or tendered the price or sum for which said road shall have been sold as aforesaid, shall make, execute and deliver a good and lawful deed for said road to the said Emanuel Peters, his legal representatives or assigns; and thereupon the said Emanuel Peters, his legal representatives or assigns, shall be vested with all the rights, powers, privileges, immunities, franchises and appurtenances which shall have belonged to and been enjoyed by said company, at the time of said sale.

SEC. 11. That all and every the provisions of the act aforesaid shall be and the same are hereby extended to and shall apply to and embrace a sale to John Loutey by John Welsh and William L. Schaffer, trustees under power to sell, given to them in a certain mortgage, dated the twenty-eighth day of July, Anno Domini one thousand eight hundred and fifty-nine, and recorded at Philadelphia in Mortgage Book A. D. B., number thirty-five, page five hundred and fifty-one, et cetera, as though made under process or decree of Court; and it shall not be deemed necessary for the said purchaser to give any further notice, but he shall, within thirty days after the passage of this act, organize the new corporation under the name, style and title of the Central Passenger Railway Company of the City of Philadelphia, as fully and effectually as though a formal meeting had been called, after full public notice had been given, as mentioned in the said act to which this is a supplement; and he shall select a President and Board of Directors for the time mentioned in said act, and do and perform all and singular the matters and things in the said act specified, with like effect as though the sale or conveyance had been made to two or more persons.

SEC. 12. That the said Company shall, in all respects, not by acts under which it is organized or hereby modified, be subject to the provisions of the general act regulating railroad companies, approved the nineteenth day of February Anno Domini one thousand eight hundred and forty-nine, and the several supplements thereto, and to so much as is now in force and applicable, of an act incorporating the North Philadelphia Plank Road Company, approved the twenty-ninth day of April, Anno Domini one thousand eight hundred and fifty-two; to the second section of a

11. Act of March 14, 1863, Sec. 1, P. L. 128.
12. Act of March 14, 1863, Sec. 2, P. L. 129.

supplement thereto, approved the thirty-first day of March, Anno Domini one thousand eight hundred and fifty-four; to the first section of a further supplement, approved the ninth day of April, Anno Domini one thousand eight hundred and fifty-eight; to the first section, except the proviso thereto, of a further supplement, passed the ninth day of April, Anno Domini one thousand eight hundred and sixty-one; and to the fifth section of an act relating to said Company, approved the twentieth day of April, Anno Domini one thousand eight hundred and fifty-three; and that all other acts or parts of acts relating to said Company be and the same are hereby repealed; that the word "borough," in the first section of the act aforesaid, approved the twenty-ninth day of April, Anno Domini one thousand eight hundred and fifty-two, shall be taken and construed to mean "township;" and that nothing in said section contained shall prevent the said Company from extending their road and railway, by the best and most practicable route to the northern limits of said township, now Twenty-second Ward, and the southwestern limits of the Twenty-first Ward, which they are hereby authorized, from time to time, to do; or straightening any part or parts of their road and railway, using such streets or avenues as may be necessary for such purposes; and with the consent of the owners of any land, or subject to the provisions of the general act aforesaid, they may pass over such land, or part or parts of any artificial road, for the purposes aforesaid, as they may deem necessary: *Provided,* That any Director of said Company shall be at liberty to act in any other capacity, and receive such compensation as the by-laws may prescribe.

SEC. 13. That the said Company shall have the right, from time to time, as they deem it advantageous to the public, to extend their road or railway, by single or double track, eastwardly north of Oxford street, as well as southwardly from their present terminus to the south side of Green street, so as to cross at grade, and to connect with other passenger railways or railroads intersecting this road or railway, when so extended; and for the purpose of such extensions, and to complete their circuits, shall use such streets or avenues as may be necessary: *Provided,* That the said Company, in laying unlaid portions, and re-laying parts already laid of their road or railway, shall use the best style of rail conducive to the safety of passengers, and

13. Act of March 14, 1863, Sec. 3, P. L. 129.

shall lay the same in the best manner; and shall keep the paving within the lines of their railway on the streets and avenues over which they pass, in perpetual good repair; that the said Company shall have the right to connect their road or railway with, and run their cars on and over, any passenger railway or railroad which now crosses, or may hereafter cross or connect with their present or future road or railway, the consent of the owners thereof having been first had and obtained; and shall have and enjoy all the rights and privileges in regard to their extended road or railway which they now have on any other portion of their said road or railway; and shall have and enjoy, all and singular, the same rights and privileges which are now or may hereafter be extended to any other passenger railway company: *Provided also,* That said Central Passenger Railway Company of the City of Philadelphia shall not have the right to use any portion of any railroad, turnpike or artificial road, except for the purpose of crossing the same, without first obtaining the consent of the company or parties owning the same; nor shall the said Railroad Company have the right to use any other street than Wayne street running parallel therewith, between Manheim and Johnson streets, in the late borough of Germantown, in the Twenty-second Ward, nor construct any branch road over School lane, Rittenhouse or Tulpehocken streets, in said ward; nor shall they be permitted to locate their road upon any portion of Ninth or Twelfth streets in the City of Philadelphia: *And provided further,* That in case the said Company shall combine a turnpike, paved or plank road with their said railroad, they shall not be authorized to erect or maintain any toll-gate between Manheim and Johnson streets, in the late borough of Germantown; nor collect any toll from persons who only pass over that portion of their road located between said streets.

WHEREAS, By the several acts relating to and under which the Central Passenger Railway Company of the City organized, plank road and turnpike privileges were conferred on the Company;

SEC. 14. That should the Board of Directors of said Company, by resolution, a copy of which shall be filed in the office of the Secretary of the Commonwealth, declare it to be the intention of the Company to abandon or re-

14. Act of April 12, 1864, Sec. 1, P. L. 394.

linquish their plank road and turnpike privileges, that then and thereafter, all plank road and turnpike privileges now vested in the Company shall cease and determine; and thereupon, such parts of the plank road heretofore occupied by the Company, and not upon the route of their railroad, shall be taken, and deemed public highways, and be subject to like control as though originally laid out and opened in accordance with the general road laws of this Commonwealth: *Provided, however*, That the said Company shall be at liberty to remove any toll-houses or other structures erected thereon.

SEC. 15. That the said Company be and they are hereby authorized to extend their road, by single or double track, from any point on the line of their road, in a northwardly direction, to any point on the North Pennsylvania Railroad, southward of Edge Hill, in Montgomery County, and north of Susquehanna avenue, City of Philadelphia, and to build branches, not exceeding two miles in length, using, for such purposes, such parts of any streets, lanes or avenues as may by them be deemed expedient, and to connect their road with the North Pennsylvania Railroad, the Chestnut Hill Railroad and such other railroads as now, or hereafter may cross or intersect their present or future road; and the said Company shall have, exercise and enjoy all and every the rights, powers, liberties, privileges, franchises and immunities mentioned in the general act for regulating railroad companies, approved the nineteenth day of April, Anno Domini one thousand eight hundred and forty-nine, and conferred upon other railroad companies by said general act, by an act approved the eleventh day of February, Anno Domini one thousand eight hundred and fifty-three, and any other general act relating to railroad companies, now in force in this Commonwealth; and all acts or parts of acts conflicting herewith are hereby repealed: *Provided*, That the said Central Passenger Railway Company shall not have the right to use any portion of any railroad, turnpike or artificial road, except for the purpose of crossing the same, without first obtaining the consent of the company or parties owning the same; nor shall the said railroad company have the right to use any other street than Wayne street, running parallel therewith between Manheim and Johnson streets, in the late Borough of Germantown, in

15. Act of April 12, 1864, Sec. 2, P. L. 394

the Twenty-second Ward; nor construct any branch road over School lane, Rittenhouse street, Walnut lane or Tulpehocken street, in said ward, nor on Ninth or Twelfth streets: *Provided further,* That in constructing their road over any of the streets of the City of Philadelphia, except Wayne street, the said Central Passenger Railway Company shall conform to the grade of said streets as now or shall hereafter be established by the Board of Survey, and shall also use such form of rail on Broad street, south of Turner's lane as shall be approved by the said Board of Survey of said city: *And provided also,* That the said Central Passenger Railway Company shall not be authorized to construct any branch of said road between Manheim and Johnson streets, in the late Borough of Germantown, except on Chelton avenue, east of their road, to the Philadelphia, Germantown and Perkiomen turnpike.

WHEREAS, In transcribing an act entitled "An Act relating to the Central Passenger Railway Company," approved April twelfth, one thousand eight hundred and sixty-four, House bill number five hundred and ninety-three, the words "April" and "February," where they occur in the second section, were transposed:

SEC. 16. That the error in the second section of the said act be corrected by striking out on the twelfth line the word "April" and inserting "February," and striking out on the fourteenth line the word "February" and inserting "April."

16. Act of April 28, 1864, Sec. 1, P. L. 652.

Citizens' Passenger Railway Company.

SECTION 1. That Amos Ellis, Jacob Peters, William Bonsall, James S. Reeves, Almon B. Walters, Edward P. Dunn, Peter Ambruster, Volney I. Frazier, Bejamin Shell, Thomas H. Forsyth, Gillias Dallett, Lewis T. Mears, Andrew Benner, Edward R. Helmbold, David McClain, Benjamin H. Shedaker, John Alexander, Stephen Benton, George Kirkpatrick, David M. Uber, Hugh Clark, T. R. G. Hinckle, George Simpson, James H. Stroup, William G. Audenreid, John Kensel, Michael Cahill, John J. Meany, William M. Randall, Benjamin Barton, Dr. D. B. Whipple, Benjamin Davis, Willis J. Hocker, N. R. Moseley, M. D., Joseph Collins, John McCarthy, and William Seybert, of the city of Philadelphia, or a majority of them, be and they are hereby appointed Commissioners to open books for the purpose of receiving subscriptions to the capital stock of the company hereby directed to be incorporated by the name, style and title of the *Citizens' Passenger Railway Company of Philadelphia*, with power to lay out and construct a railway from the intersection of Tenth and Lancaster streets, thence along said Lancaster street to Broad street, thence along said Broad street to Columbia street, thence along Columbia street to Eleventh street, thence along Eleventh street to Reed street, thence along said Reed street to Tenth street, thence along said Tenth street to the place of beginning: *Provided*, That any passenger railroad that may be hereafter incorporated, connecting with or crossing the Citizens' Passenger Railroad, shall have the right, by paying one-half of the expenses of construction of that part of the road used to run their cars over said road lying between Ridge avenue and Arch street, and shall have power to convey passengers over the same; and the said company shall also have the right to purchase real estate, and erect thereon such buildings and improvements as may be deemed expedient and necessary for the purposes of said company, and also to purchase the necessary equipments for said railway, and no freight or burden trains or locomotives shall be permitted to pass over the same.

1. Act of March 25, 1858, Sec. 1, P. L. 166.

SEC. 2. That the capital stock of said company shall consist of ten thousand shares of fifty dollars each: *Provided*, That said company may, from time to time, by a vote of the stockholders, at a meeting convened for that purpose, increase their capital stock as much as may be necessary to complete said railway or railways, and to carry out the true intent and meaning of this act.

SEC. 3. That dividends of so much of the profits of said company as shall appear advisable to the directors, shall be declared in the months of January and July, in each and every year, and be paid at the office of said company any time after ten days from the time of declaring the same; but said dividend shall in no case exceed the amount of the net profits of said company, so that the capital stock shall never be impaired thereby; and if said directors shall make any dividend impairing the capital stock of said company, the directors consenting thereto shall be liable in their individual capacities to said company for the amount so divided, and each director present when such dividend shall be declared, shall be considered as consenting thereto, unless he or they enter protest upon the minutes of the Board, and give public notice of the same.

SEC. 4. That the said company shall make and have a common seal, and the same to alter and renew at pleasure, and also to ordain, establish, and put in execution such by-laws, ordinances and regulations as shall appear necessary or convenient for the government of said corporation, and not being contrary to the Constitution and laws of the United States or of this Commonwealth, and generally to to do all and singular the matters and things which to them it shall lawfully appertain to do for the well being of said corporation, and the due ordering and managing of the affairs thereof.

SEC. 5. That said company shall have power to elect or appoint a president and five directors, a (majority of whom, with the president, shall be citizens of Philadelphia,) and such other officers as may be deemed necessary or expedient, and in every election of officers each share of stock shall entitle the holder to one vote.

SEC. 6. That said company shall have power to raise on

2. Act of March 25, 1858, Sec. 2, P. L. 166.
3. Act of March 25, 1858, Sec. 3, P. L. 166.
4. Act of March 25, 1858, Sec. 4, P. L. 167.
5. Act of March 25, 1858, Sec. 5, P. L. 167.
6. Act of March 25, 1858, Sec. 6. P. L. 167.

bonds any sum not exceeding one-half of their capital stock actually paid, for the purpose of carrying out the true intent of this act.

SEC. 7. That the said railroad company shall not connect with any railroad other than for passenger purposes, and of the same gauge, under a penalty of a forfeiture of their charter; and the said company shall annually pay into the treasury of the City of Philadelphia for the use of said city, whenever the dividend shall exceed six per centum per annum on the capital stock, the *sum of six per centum* on the said dividends thus declared, and the said company, before commencing to use said road upon the said streets, shall purchase, at the option of the owners, the stock of horses, omnibuses, sleighs, and harness owned and used upon the said streets at the time of commencing the said road, at a price to be assessed in the following manner:—the said owners shall choose one disinterested person, and the said company shall choose a second person, and the two thus chosen shall choose a third, who together shall be disinterested persons, and shall appraise such stock, and the value thus arrived at shall be binding and final: *Provided*, That whenever any damage may be sustained by reason of this company taking possession of lands or other property other than above described, except so far as the usufruct of the before-named streets, necessary to the full and perfect enjoyment of the purposes by this act designed, the said damages shall be assessed and paid in the manner, and according to the provisions of the eleventh section of the Act of ninteenth of February, Anno Domini one thousand eight hundred and forty-nine, entitled an Act regulating Railroad Companies, and the several supplements thereto: *And provided further*, That before the said company shall use and occupy the said streets, the consent of the councils of the City of Philadelphia shall be first obtained, and said consent shall be taken and deemed to have been given if said councils shall not, within thirty days after the passage of this act, by ordinance duly passed, signify their disapproval thereof; and said councils may from time to time, by ordinance, establish such regulations in regard to said railway, as may be required for the paving re-paving, grading, culverting, and the laying of gas and water pipes in and along said streets, and to prevent obstructions thereon.(*a*)

7. Act of March 25, 1858, Sec. 7, P. L. 197.
(*a*) This was done by the Ordinance set forth as Secs. 12 and 13.

SEC. 8. That said company, in constructing said road, shall conform to the grades now established, or hereafter to be by law established, of the several streets and avenues traversed by said road, and to keep said streets and avenues in perpetual good repair at the proper expense of said company.

SEC. 9. The said railway on the route described shall be subject to the use of any part or parts thereof by any other passenger railroad company for the purpose of completing a route, or making a circuit, upon such terms and conditions as may be agreed upon by such other companies and the said Citizens' Passenger Railroad Company, and in case the companies cannot agree, then upon such terms and conditions as shall be prescribed by the councils of the City of Philadelphia.

SEC. 10. That the Citizens' Passenger Railway Company be and the same is hereby authorized to extend their railway by laying a single track, with sufficient turnouts or sidelings. along Poplar street, from Tenth street to Nineteenth street, and shall have the right to connect the tracks already laid, by a single track along Columbia avenue, from Tenth to Eleventh street, conforming to the established grades of said streets.

SEC. 11. That the President and Directors of the Citizens' Passenger Railway Company of the City of Philadelphia be and the same are hereby authorized to grant, bargain and sell, lease, release, convey and confirm to such person or persons, and for such consideration, price or prices as they may deem proper, all or any part of their lot of ground situated on the west side of Tenth street, in the City of Philadelphia, beginning at the distance of three hundred feet northward of the north-west corner of Tenth and Montgomery; thence extending along Tenth to Berks street, and being in depth westwardly one hundred and seventy-three feet to a forty feet wide street; and that the vendee or vendees of said property be and they are hereby vested with the fee simple title of, in and to the same, their heirs and assigns, forever.

8. Act of March 25, 1858, Sec. 8, P. L. 168.
9. Act of March 25, 1858, Sec. 9, P. L. 168.
10. Act of March 26, 1859, Sec. 1, P. L. 263.
11. Act of March 18, 1861, Sec. 1, P. L. 193.

SEC. 12. That the Citizens' Passenger Railway Company of Philadelphia be and they are hereby authorized to take up their track on Columbia avenue, from Tenth to Eleventh street, and to lay a track on Montgomery street, from Tenth to Eleventh street, with the necessary sidelings, and to connect the same with their present road, by a track on Eleventh street, from Columbia avenue to Montgomery street.

SEC. 13. That the President and Directors of the Citizens' Passenger Railway Company of the City of Philadelphia be and the same are hereby authorized to grant, bargain, sell, release, convey and confirm to such person or persons, and for such consideration, price or prices as they may deem proper, all or any part of their buildings and lot of ground situated on the east side of Tenth street, in the City of Philadelphia, beginning at the distance of sixty-five feet southward from the south side of Columbia avenue, containing in front or breadth, on said Tenth street, eighty feet, and extending in length or depth, eastward of that width, between lines parallel with said avenue, on the north line two hundred and thirty-four feet eight and a quarter inches, and on the south line thereof two hundred and forty-three feet seven-eighths of an inch; and that the vendee or vendees of said property be and they are hereby vested with the fee simple of, in and to the same, their heirs and assigns forever.

12. Act of April 11, 1863, Sec. 1, P. L. 319.
13. Act of April 11, 1863, Sec. 2, P. L. 319.

An Ordinance respecting "The Citizens' Passenger Railway Company."

WHEREAS, By the act of Assembly entitled "An Act to incorporate the Citizens' Passenger Railway Company," approved 25th day of March, A. D. one thousand eight hundred and fifty-eight, it is provided that "before the said company shall use and occupy the said streets, the consent of the councils of the City of Philadelphia shall be first obtained, and said consent shall be taken and deemed to have been given if said councils shall not, within thirty days after passage of the act, by ordinances duly passed, signify their disapproval thereof;" and whereas, the said period of thirty days will probably elapse before the said company will be so organized as to act in a corporate capacity; therefore

That the councils of the City of Philadelphia do hereby, in pursuance of the authority in them vested by the said act of assembly, declare their disapproval of the said act, and of the right therein granted to the Citizens' Passenger Railway Company to use and occupy the streets of the city therein named.

SEC. 15. That if the said company shall, within ninety days, from the passage of this ordinance, and before they shall use or occupy any of the said streets, file in the office of the City Solicitor a written obligation, sufficient in his opinion, in law, to bind the said company to observe and be subject to all ordinances of the City of Philadelphia in relation to passenger railways, then in force, or at any time thereafter to be passed, then the provisions of the first section of this ordinance shall be of no effect.

14. Ordinance, April 16, 1858, Sec. 1, p. 145.
15. Ordinance, April 16, 1858, Sec. 2, p. 145.

Fairmount and Arch Street Passenger Railway Company.

SECTION 1. That William L. Hurst, Henry M. Phillips, Benjamin Shedan, Pearce Butler, William Randall, George Kirkpatrick, H. B. Whipple, Isaac Leech, junior, E. P. Camp, George Thomas, W. Marshall, Thomas Pritchett, Job R. Tyson, William Boyd, James B. Smith, Lewis Bitting, R. J. Hemphill, Daniel Dougherty, John J. Boland, John Powers, Joseph J. Lipp, Jeremiah King, Ellis S. Archer, Jacob Dock, William H. Moore, Benjamin W. Tingley, Benjamin H. Frederick, Samuel R. Brick and Bernard Berens, be and they are hereby appointed commissioners to open books, and to sell stock, in accordance with the provisions of the general railroad law, and organize a company by the name, style and title of the Fairmount and Arch Street City Passenger Railway Company; which said company shall have power to lay out and construct a railway, commencing at Tenth and Arch streets, and continuing westwardly along the same, with a double track, to Twentieth and Twenty-first streets, respectively, with single track to Callowhill street; and thence westwardly, with double track, to wire bridge, at Fairmount, and shall have power to convey passengers over the same; and the said company shall also have the right to purchase real estate, and to erect thereon such buildings and improvements as may be deemed expedient and necessary for the purposes of said company; and also to purchase the necessary equipments for said railways: *Provided*, That no freight or burden trains, or locomotives, shall be permitted to pass over the same.

SEC. 2. That the capital stock of said company shall consist of four thousand shares of fifty dollars each: *Provided*, That said company may from time to time, by a vote of the stockholders at a meeting convened for that purpose, increase their capital stock as much as, in their opinion, may be necessary to complete said railway or railways, and to carry out the true intent and meaning of this act.

SEC. 3. That dividends of so much of the profit of said

1. Act of April 16, 1858, Sec. 1, P. L. 320.
2. Act of April 16, 1858, Sec. 2, P. L. 321.
3. Act of April 16, 1858, Sec. 3, P. L. 321.

company, as shall appear advisable to the directors, shall be declared in the months of January and July in each and every year, and be paid at the office of said company any time after ten days from the time of declaring the same; but said dividends shall in no case, exceed the amount of the net profits of said company, so that the capital stock shall never be impaired thereby; and if said directors shall make any dividend impairing the capital stock of said company, the directors consenting thereto shall be liable, in their individual capacities, to said company for the amount so divided; and each director present when such dividend shall be declared, shall be considered as consenting thereto, unless he or they enter protest upon the minutes of the board, and give public notice of the same.

SEC. 4. That the said company shall make and have a common seal, and the same to alter or renew at pleasure; and also to ordain, establish and put in execution such by-laws, ordinances and regulations as shall appear necessary or convenient for the government of said corporation, and not being contrary to the constitution and laws of the United States, or of this commonwealth; and generally do all and singular the matters and things which to them it shall lawfully appertain to do for the well being of said corporation, and the due ordering and managing of the affairs thereof.

SEC. 5. That said company shall have power to elect or appoint a president and five directors, a majority of whom, with the president, shall be citizens of Philadelphia, and such other officers as may be deemed necessary or expedient, and in every election for officers each share of stock shall entitle the holder to one vote.

SEC. 6. That said company shall have power to raise on bonds any sum not exceeding one-half of their capital stock, for the purpose of carrying out the true intent of this act: *Provided*, That said bonds shall not be issued for a less sum than one hundred dollars each.

SEC. 7. That the said railroad company shall not connect with any railroad other than for passenger purposes, and of the same gauge, under the penalty of a forfeiture of their charter; and the said company shall annually pay into the treasury of the City of Philadelphia, for the use of said city, whenever the dividends shall exceed six per centum

4. Act of April 16, 1858, Sec. 4, P. L. 321.
5. Act of April 16, 1858, Sec. 5, P. L. 322.
6. Act of April 16, 1858, Sec. 6, P. L. 322.
7. Act of April 16, 1858, Sec. 7, P. L. 322.

per annum on the capital stock, the sum of six per centum on the said dividend thus declared: *Provided*, That whenever any damages may be sustained by reason of this company taking possession of lands or other property other than above described, except so far as the usufruct of the before named streets, necessary to the full and perfect enjoyment of the purposes by this act designed, the said damages shall be assessed and paid in the manner and according to the provisions of the eleventh section of the act of nineteenth of February, Anno Domini one thousand eight hundred and forty-nine, entitled "An Act regulating Railroad Companies:" *And provided further*, That before the said company shall use and occupy the said streets, the consent of the councils of the City of Philadelphia shall be first obtained; and said consent shall be taken and deemed to have been given, if said councils shall not within thirty days after the passage of this act, by ordinances duly passed, signify their disapproval thereof; and said city councils may from time to time by ordinance establish such regulations in regard to said railway, as may be required for the paving, re-paving, grading, culverting and the laying of gas and water pipes in and along said streets, and to prevent obstruction thereon.

SEC. 8. That said company, in constructing said road, shall conform to the grades now established or hereafter to be by law established, of the several streets and avenues traversed by said road, and keep said streets and avenues in perpetual good repair, at the proper expense of said company.

SEC. 9. And the company shall purchase, at the option of the owners, the stock of horses, omnibuses, sleighs and harness owned and used upon the said Arch street at the time of making the road, (not exceeding those now in use on said avenue,) at a price to be assessed as follows: The owners to choose one disinterested person and the said company another person, and the two thus choosen shall choose a third, who shall appraise said stock, and the value thus arrived at and reported within ten days, shall be final: *Provided*, That this company shall be subject to an ordinance of the city councils, entitled, "An Ordinance to regulate passenger railways within the City of Philadelphia," approved the seventh day of July, Anno Domini one thousand eight hundred and fifty-seven.

8. Act of April 16. 1858, Sec. 8, P. L. 322.
9. Act of April 16, 1858, Sec. 9, P. L. 322.

SEC. 10. The said company shall have the power to connect and run over any railway or portion of railway, that now is or may be hereafter constructed; and shall have power to build a road or portion of a road for the purpose of connecting with, or completing a route on such streets as may be necessary, and shall have power to convey passengers over the same: *Provided*, That before the said company shall run their cars on the track or tracks of any other passenger railway, they shall agree with such other company or companies, upon the terms or compensation to be paid said company or companies, for the privilege of using said roads; and that if the said parties shall not be able to agree upon terms, then either parties shall apply to the Court of Common Pleas, who shall appoint three disinterested persons, whose adjustment shall be binding and final: *Provided*, That the West Philadelphia Passenger Railway Company shall have the right to connect with the said Fairmount and Arch Street Passenger Railway Company, by way of Twentieth and Twenty-first streets, upon such terms and conditions as may be agreed upon in the tenth section of this act: *Provided further*, That any passenger railroad that is now, or may be hereafter incorporated, connecting with or crossing the same, shall have the right to run their cars upon said road, upon terms to be agreed upon by said parties interested; and if the said parties cannot agree, then the District Court of the City of Philadelphia shall upon petition presented by either party, appoint two persons, who shall fix the amount to be paid by the parties using the same: *Provided*, That the said company shall be subject in all respects to the general provisions of the general law regulating railroads, approved the nineteenth of February, one thousand eight hundred and forty-nine, and the several supplements thereto.

An Ordinance

Relating to "an Act to Incorporate the Fairmount and Arch Street City Passenger Railway Company," approved April 16, 1858.

WHEREAS, By the provisions of an Act of Assembly, approved April 16, 1858, entitled "An Act to Incorporate the Fairmount and Arch street City Passenger Railway Company," the right is reserved to the city councils to disapprove of the said act of assembly, and of the right of the said company to occupy the streets and highways of the said city within thirty days from the passage of the said act of assembly; therefore,

SEC. 11. That in pursuance of the power and authority in them vested by the said act of assembly, councils do hereby declare their disapproval of the said act of assembly in the above preamble mentioned, and of the rights therein respectively granted to "The Fairmount and Arch street City Passenger Railway Company," to occupy the streets and highways of the City of Philadelphia.

An Ordinance

Expressing the consent of Councils to the construction, by the Fairmount and Arch Street City Passenger Railroad Company, of Railway Tracks upon Arch, Twenty-first and Twenty-second Streets.

SEC. 12. That the consent of the councils of the City of Philadelphia be, and the same is hereby given to the use and occupation by the Fairmount and Arch street City Passenger Railway Company of the following streets, viz.: —commencing at Tenth and Arch streets continuing westwardly along the same with double track to Twentieth and Twenty-first streets, respectively, with single track to

10. Act of April 16, 1858, Sec. 10, P. L. 323.
11. Ordinance of May 5, 1858, p 177.
12. Ordinance of December 16, 1858, p. 488.

Callowhill street, and thence westwardly with double track to Wire Bridge at Fairmount, as provided for in an act of the general assembly of the commonwealth, entitled "An Act to incorporate the Fairmount and Arch street City Passenger Railway Company," approved April 16th, 1858, and upon no other streets, and this consent and allowance is given upon the condition that the said company shall not exercise any power conferred upon them to build any road on any other streets than those hereinbefore designated, and should they at any time hereafter construct or commence to construct, without further express consent of councils thereto, any road upon any other street or streets than those hereinbefore designated, then the consent hereby given shall cease and terminate, and the said company shall have no longer the right to run and use the said railway on the streets aforementioned; and provided further, that within ninety days from the date of approval of this act, and before the said company shall in anywise use the said streets, the said company shall file in the office of the City Solicitor, a covenant under their common seal to observe and be subject to all ordinances of the City of Philadelphia then in force, or at any time thereafter to be passed, and especially to comply with the provisions of this ordinance and to construct no other railroad or portion of a railroad than is hereby consented to and allowed, without the express consent of councils thereto, first had and obtained, and also within ninety days from the approval of this ordinance, and before occupying any of said streets to execute and file in the office of the Department of State, an instrument in writing, surrendering to the Commonwealth of Pennsylvania all and every power, franchise and right to construct any road or portion of a road under the authority of the tenth section of their charter, and any ordinance that may be inconsistent herewith be and the same is hereby repealed.

A Supplement

To an Act to incorporate the Fairmount and Arch Street City Passenger Railway Company, approved April sixteenth, Anno Domini one thousand eight hundred and fifty-eight.

WHEREAS, Heretofore, to wit; on the sixteenth day of April Anno Domini one thousand eight hundred and fifty-eight, the general assembly of this commonwealth passed an act to incorporate the Fairmount and Arch Street Passenger Railway Company:

And whereas, It was provided amongst other things in said act, that before the said company should use and occupy the streets for the purpose of constructing a passenger railway, the consent of the councils of the City of Philadelphia should be first obtained, and that said consent should be deemed to have been given, if said councils should not within thirty days after the passage of the act signify their disapproval thereof:

And whereas, Afterward, to wit: the fifth day of May, Anno Domini one thousand eight hundred and fifty-eight, the said City Councils, by ordinance duly passed, did disapprove of the said act of assembly, which ordinance was passed for the purpose of preventing the said act from taking effect within thirty days aforesaid:

And whereas, Subsequently to the passage of the same, to wit: on the eleventh day of August, one thousand eight hundred and fifty-eight, the company was duly organized under said act of assembly, for the purposes mentioned therein, letters patent being on the said day issued by the governor of the commonwealth:

And whereas, On the sixteenth December, one thousand eight hundred and fifty-eight, the consent of the councils of the City of Philadelphia was duly given to the use and occupation of certain streets mentioned in said ordinance, the said company, for the purpose of constructing a passenger railway thereon;

And whereas, Relying on said act of assembly and the said ordinance, the said company have expended large sums of money in purchasing materials, making contracts in the actual execution of said work, a considerable portion of it having been already fully completed:

And whereas, Under certain proceedings commenced in the Supreme Court of this state, said company has been enjoined from the further prosecution of the work, for the reason that the said City Councils had no power to pass the ordinance, giving their assent to the occupancy of the streets, after having dissented therefrom within thirty days mentioned in the said act:

And whereas, Common justice requires that the corporate powers heretofore given to said company, should be maintained; therefore,

SEC. 13. That the Fairmount and Arch Street City Passenger Railway Company be and they are hereby authorized to construct a railway on the route mentioned and set forth in the first section of the act to which this is a supplement, and that they shall have power to convey passengers over the same, as if the consent of the Councils of the City of Philadelphia, to the use and occupation of the streets mentioned in said first section, had been given in due form of law, within thirty days after the passage of the act to which this is a supplement, as provided for by the seventh section of said act.

SEC. 14. That the tenth section of said act to which this is a supplement, is hereby repealed; and in lieu thereof the said company are hereby authorized to connect with and run over any passenger railroad or railoads, that is now or may hereafter be constructed, so as to give the said company a complete route from Fairmount to the Exchange, in the said City of Philadelphia: *Provided,* That before the said company shall run their cars on the track or tracks of any passenger railway or railways, they shall agree upon the terms of compensation to be paid said company or companies, for the privilege of using said road or roads; and that if the said parties shall not agree, then either parties shall apply to the court of common pleas, who shall appoint three disinterested persons, whose adjustment shall be final.

SEC. 15. That said company may, after the special consent of Councils of the City of Philadelphia shall have been first obtained, by ordinance duly passed, in lieu of two tracks on that part of Callowhill street which is between Hamilton and Twenty-second street, construct one of their tracks on Twenty-second street, from Callowhill to Hamil-

13. Act of March 24, 1859, Sec. 1, P. L. 235.
14. Act of March 24, 1859, Sec. 2, P. L. 235.
15. Act of March 24, 1859, Sec. 3, P. L. 235.

ton, and thence west on Hamilton street to Callowhill street: *And provided*, That said company shall be subject, in all respects, to the general provisions of the general law regulating railroads, approved the nineteenth day of February, Anno Domini one thousand eight hundred and forty-nine, and the several supplements thereto.

SEC. 16. That the charter of the said company shall be and remain in as full force as if said councils had assented thereto by ordinance, within thirty days from the passage thereof.

An Ordinance

Relative to the Fairmount and Arch Street City Passenger Railway Company.

WHEREAS, By an Act of Assembly, approved March 25th, 1859, entitled, "A Supplement to an Act entitled 'An Act to incorporate the Fairmount and Arch Street City Passenger Railway Company, approved April 16th, A. D. one thousand eight hundred and fifty-eight,'" the said company are authorized, after the special consent of the councils of the city shall have been first obtained, by ordinance duly passed, in lieu of two tracks in that part of Callowhill street which is between Hamilton and Twenty-second street, to construct one of their tracks on Twenty-second street, from Callowhill street to Hamilton street, and thence westward, on Hamilton street to Callowhill street; therefore,

SEC. 17. That the consent of the said councils is hereby given to the construction, by the Fairmount and Arch Street City Passenger Railway Company, of one of their tracks on Twenty-second street, from Callowhill street to Hamilton street, and thence west on Hamilton street to Callowhill street, in lieu of two tracks on that part of Callowhill street which is between Hamilton and Twenty-second street.

16. Act of March 24, 1859, Sec. 4, P. L. 236.
17. Ordinance of April 23, 1859, Sec. 5, p. 199.

Girard College Passenger Railway Company.

An Act to incorporate the Girard College Passenger Railway Company.

SECTION 1. That Robert A. Parrish, William F. Emlen, Robert Ralston, James Page, Edward D. Stokes, D. T. Pratt, Harry Conrad, Robert Morris, Theophilus, Cauffman, William Trego Coates, Walton Macgregor. J. Mitcheson, J. Austin Parrish, James F. Nicholas, Charles Thompson Jones, Jacob Esher, or any five of them, are hereby appointed commissioners to open books, receive subscriptions, and organize a company, under the provisions of the general Railroad law of eighteen hundred and forty-nine and the supplements thereto, by the name, style and title of the Girard College Passenger Railway Company, and as such, shall have power to lay out and construct a railway in the City of Philadelphia, from or near the Girard College, down Ridge avenue to Tenth and Ninth streets respectively, thence down said streets to Arch street thence down Arch to Second street, with a double track on said avenue and Arch street, and shall have power to convey passengers over the same; and the said company shall also have the right to purchase real estate, and to erect thereon such buildings and improvements as may be deemed expedient and necessary for the purposes of said company, and also to purchase the necessary equipments for said railway; and no freight or burden trains or locomotives shall be permitted to pass over the same: *Provided,* That the said company, before commencing to build said road upon said streets, shall purchase, at the option of the owners, the stock of horses, omnibuses, sleighs and harness, owned and used upon said streets at the time of commencing said road at a price to be assessed in the following manner: The said owners shall choose one disintested person, and the said company shall choose a second person, and the two thus choosen shall choose a third, who, together, shall be disinterested persons, and shall appraise such stock, and the value thus arrived at shall be reported to the parties interested within twenty days, and the decision thus arrived

1. Act of April 15, 1858, Sec. 1, P. L. 300.

at shall be binding and conclusive: *Provided further*, That any passenger railroad that is now or may be hereafter incorporated, connecting with or crossing the same, shall have the right to run their cars upon the said road, on payment of an equal part of all the cost thereof, upon terms to be agreed upon by the said parties interested; and if the said parties cannot agree, then the District Court of the City of Philadelphia shall, upon petition presented by either party, appoint two persons, who shall fix the amount to be paid by the parties using said road.

SECT. 2. That the capital stock of said company shall consist of ten thousand shares, of fifty dollars each: *Provided*, That said company may from time to time, by a vote of the stockholders, at a meeting convened for that purpose, increase their capital stock as much as in their opinion may be necessary to complete said railway or railways, and to carry out the true intent and meaning of this act.

SECT. 3. That dividends of so much of the profits of said company as shall appear advisable to the directors, shall be declared in the months of January and July in each and every year, and be paid at the office of said company, any time after ten days from the time of declaring the same; but said dividend shall in no case exceed the amount of the net profits of said company, so that the capital stock shall never be impaired thereby. And if said directors shall make any dividend impairing the capital stock of said company, the directors consenting thereto shall be liable in their individual capacities to said company for the amount so divided, and each director present when such dividend shall be declared, shall be considered as consenting thereto, unless he or they enter protest upon the minutes of the board, and give public notice of the same.

SECT. 4. That the said company shall make and have a common seal, and the same to alter and renew at pleasure; and also to ordain, establish, and put in execution such by-laws, ordinances and regulations as shall appear necessary or convenient for the government of said corporation, and not being contrary to the constitution and laws of the United States or of this Commonwealth; and generally to do all and singular the matters and things which to them it shall lawfully appertain to do for the well being of said

2. Act of April 15, 1858, Sec. 2, P. L. 301.
3. Act of April 15, 1858, Sec. 3, P. L. 301.
4. Act of April 15, 1858, Sec. 4, P. L. 302.

corporation, and the due ordering and managing of the affairs thereof.

SECT. 5. That said company shall have power to elect or appoint a president and five directors, a majority of whom, with the president, shall be citizens of Philadelphia, and such other officers as may be deemed necessary or expedient; and in every election for officers each share of stock shall entitle the holder to one vote.

SECT. 6. That said company shall have power to raise on bonds any sum not exceeding one-half of their capital stock, for the purpose of carrying out the true intent of this act: *Provided,* That no bond shall be issued for a less amount than one hundred dollars.

SECT. 7. That the said railroad company shall not connect with any railroad other than for passenger purposes, and of the same gauge, under the penalty of a forfeiture of their charter; and the said company shall annually pay into the treasury of the City of Philadelphia, for the use of said city, whenever the dividends shall exceed six per centum per anum on the capital stock, the sum of six per centum on the said dividend thus declared: *Provided,* That whenever any damages may be sustained by reason of this company taking possession of lands or other property other than above described, except so far as the usufruct of the before named streets necessary to the full and perfect enjoyment of the purposes by this act designed, the said damages shall be assessed and paid in the manner and according to the provisions of the eleventh section of the act of nineteenth of February, Anno Domini one thousand eight hundred and forty-nine, entitled an act regulating railroad companies: *And provided further,* That the City Councils may, from time to time, by ordinance, establish such regulations in regard to said railway as may be required for the paving, re-paving, grading, culverting, and the laying of gas and water pipes in and along said streets, and to prevent obstructions thereon: *And provided further,* That before the said company shall use and occupy the said streets, the consent of the City Councils shall be first obtained, and said consent shall be taken and deemed to have been given if said councils shall not, within thirty days

5. Act of April 15, 1858, Sec. 5, P. L. 303.
6. Act of April 15, 1858, Sec. 6, P. L. 303.
7. Act of April 15, 1858, Sec. 7, P. L. 303.

after the passage of this act, by ordinance duly passed, signify their disapproval thereof.

SECT. 8. That said company, in constructing said road, shall conform to the grades now established, or hereafter to be by law established, of the several streets and avenues traversed by said road, and keep said streets and avenues in perpetual good repair, at the proper expense of said company: *Provided*, That said Girard College Passenger Railway Company shall be subject to an ordinance of the City Councils, entitled "An Ordinance to regulate Passenger railways within the City of Philadelphia," approved the seventh day of July, Anno Domini one thousand eight hundred and fifty-seven.

An Ordinance

Relating to certain Passenger Railway Companies.

WHEREAS, By the provisions of an Act of Assembly, approved April 15, 1858, entitled "An Act to incorporate the Girard College Passenger Railway Company," and of a certain other Act of Assembly, entitled "An Act to incorporate the Green and Coates street Philadelphia Passenger Railway Company," approved April 21, 1858, and of a certain other Act of Assembly, entitled "An Act to incorporate the Germantown Passenger Railway Company," approved Apiil 21, 1858, the right is reserved to the City Councils to disapprove of the said Acts of Assembly, respectively, and of the right therein respectively granted to the said companies to occupy the streets and nighways of the said city, therein respectively, within thirty days from the passage of the said acts of assembly; therefore,

SEC. 9. That in pursuance of the power and authority in them vested by the said Acts of Assembly, Councils do hereby declare their disapproval of each and every of the said acts of assembly in the above preamble mentioned, and of the rights therein respectively granted to "The Girard College Passenger Railway Company," "The Green and Coates street Philadelphia Passenger

8. Act of April 15, 1858, Sec. 8, P. L. 303.
9. Sec. 1, Ordinance of May 5, 1858, p. 176.

Railway Company," and "The Germantown Passenger Railway Company," to occupy the streets and highways of the City of Philadelphia.

SEC. 10. That if any company in the said preamble, named, shall, within ninety days from the passage of this ordinance, and before such company shall occupy any of the said streets or highways, file in the office of the City Solicitor a written obligation, sufficient in law to bind such company to observe and be subject to all ordinances of the city in relation to passenger railways, then in force, or thereafter to be passed, then the provisions of the first section of this ordinance as to each and every such company as shall file such written obligations as aforesaid, shall cease to have effect.

10. Sec. 2, Ordinance of May 5, 1858, p. 176.

The Green and Coates Street Passenger Railway Company.

SECTION 1. That Harry Connelly, George Read, David Scull, George A. Binder, Henry Crilly, Hugh Clark, James F. Stillman, Willoughby Rex, Samuel B. Jones, Abel C. T. Smith, William Downie, Henry Gerker, Lewis Shinnick, Samuel Wilt, William Read, John Schaffer, James J. Arbuckle, George Fritz, Daniel Kensil, John Deemer, A. Eugene Smith, Frederick Gerker, Milton Miller, George W. Hamersly, Peter Fisher, Andrew McBride, Charles Wister, Alfred R. Lentz, Daniel T. Moor, William M. Wilson, Alexander Crawford, Wilson Kerr, Eugene Woodward, John P. Rice, John Steper, Thomas Hankinson, or a majority of them, be and they are hereby appointed Commissioners to open books, receive subscriptions and organize a company, by the name, style and title of the Green and Coates street Philadelphia Passenger Railway Company, with power and authority to construct a passenger railway, begining at Oak street, running west along Green street, to Twenty-second street; thence northwardly, along Twenty-second to Coates street; thence westwardly, along Coates street, with a double track, to river Schuylkill; thence eastwardly, along Coates street, to the place of beginning; subject to all the provisions and restrictions of an act regulating railroad companies, approved the nineteenth day of February, Anno Domini, one thousand eight hundred and forty-nine, and the several supplements thereto, so far as the same is not altered or repealed by this act. And the said Green and Coates street Philadelphia Passenger Railway Company, shall have the right to cross, at grade, and connect with, any other railroad now built, or that hereafter may be built, in the City of Philadelphia.

SEC. 2. That the capital stock of the said company shall consist of two thousand shares of fifty dollars each, and that the said company may from time to time, by a vote of the stockholders, at a meeting called for that purpose, of which meeting thirty days notice shall be given, in two or more papers in the City of Philadelphia, increase the capital stock to an amount sufficient to carry out the true

1. Act of April 21, 1858, Sec. 1, P. L. 447.
2. Act of April 21, 1858, Sec. 2, P. L. 447.

intent and meaning of this act, for the purpose of completing and equiping the said railway; the said company shall have the power of borrowing any sum of money not excluding one hundred thousand dollars, at a rate of interest not exceeding seven per centum per annum, and to secure the payment of the same by the issue of a bond and mortgage of the said railway, together with the corporate rights and franchises granted by this act, and to annex to the said bond and mortgage the privilege of converting the same into the capital stock of the said company at par, at the option of the holder, if they shall signify their election one year before the maturing of the same: *Provided*, That the said company shall issue no certificate of loan of a less denomination than one hundred dollars.

SEC. 3. That the said road shall be used exclusively as a passenger railway, by horse locomotion, and that the gauge of said road shall be five feet two inches. And before the said company shall use and occupy the said streets, the consent of the councils of the City of Philadelphia shall be given; and said consent shall be taken and deemed to be given if the said councils shall not, within thirty days after the passage of this act, by ordinance duly passed, signify their disapproval thereof.(*a*) And said councils may from time to time, by ordinance, establish such regulations in regard to said railway as may be required, for the paving, re-paving, grading, culverting, and laying of water and gas pipe in and along said streets, and to prevent obstructions thereon. And the said company, before commencing to use said streets, shall purchase, at the option of the owners, the stock of horses, omnibuses, sleighs and harness, owned and used upon said streets at the time of commencing the said road, at a price to be assessed in the following manner: the said owners shall choose one disinterested person, and the said company shall choose a second person, and the two thus chosen shall choose a third, who together shall be disinterested persons, and shall appraise such stock, and the value thus arrived at shall be binding and final.

SEC. 4. That it is provided that the said Green and Coates street Philadelphia Passenger Railway Company shall, in constructing their branch along the highways referred to,

3. Act of April 21, 1858, Sec. 3, P. L. 448.
4. Act of April 21, 1858, Sec. 4, P. L. 448.
(*a*) The Ordinance whereby the consent of Councils was given, is at page [15,] with which Ordinance this Company complied.

conform to the grades established, or which may hereafter be established by the Board of Surveyors of the City of Philadelphia, and be subject to any ordinances passed by the councils of the said city relating thereto: *Provided*, That the streets thus occupied by the aforesaid railway company shall be kept in repair by the said company: *And provided further*, That said passenger railway shall have power to cross all railroad tracks of all railroad companies now incorporated, or hereafter to be incorporated, whose grade conform to theirs.

SEC. 5. That the said railway company shall not connect with any railroad, other than for passenger purposes, and of the same gauge; and no freight or freight cars shall be permitted to pass over said railway, under the penalty of a forfeiture of its charter. And the said company shall annually pay into the treasury of the City of Philadelphia, for the use of said city, whenever the dividend shall exceed six per centum per annum on the capital stock, the sum of six per centum on the excess above six per centum thus declared: *Provided further*, That any passenger railroad that is now, or may be hereafter incorporated, connecting with or crossing the same, shall have the right to run their cars upon said road upon terms to be agreed upon by said parties interested. And if the said parties cannot agree, then the District Court of the City of Philadelphia shall, upon petition presented by either party, appoint two persons, who shall fix the amount to be paid to the parties using the same.

SEC. 6. And it is hereby provided, that the said company hereby incorporated shall have the right to run their cars upon any other passenger railway now incorporated, or that may be hereafter incorporated, in said City of Philadelphia, upon such terms as provided for in section five.(*a*)

SEC. 7. That the Green and Coates Street Philadelphia Passenger Railway Company shall have the power to extend their tracks from the present terminus, at Coates street to Landing avenue, along Landing avenue to a point opposite Kerns's mill; and that said company are also authorized to remove their track from Twenty-second street, and to

5. Act of April 21, 1858, Sec. 5, P. L. 448.
6. Act of April 21, 1858, Sec. 6, P. L. 449.
7. Act of April 3, 1860, Sec. 1, P. L. 623.
(*a*) Legislation relative to this Company is to be found in an Act, also in relation to the Germantown Passenger Railway, p. 69.

extend their track along Green street from Twenty-second street to Pennsylvania avenue; thence along said avenue to Coates street: *Provided*, That in case the City of Philadelphia shall at any time determine to extend Fairmount Park so as to include said avenue, then the said railroad company shall immediately remove their tracks from said avenue: *Provided*, That this Act shall not go into effect until councils of the City of Philadelphia shall, by ordinance, first give their assent thereto.

SEC. 8. That the proviso to the fifth section of the act of assembly, entitled "An Act to incorporate the Green and Coates Street Philadelphia Passenger Railway Company," and the first and second provisos to the act, entitled "A supplement to an Act to incorporate the Green and Coates Street Philadelphia Passenger Railway Company," be and the same are hereby repealed; and that so much of any act of assembly as may, or might, be construed to give to any other railway company the right to run their cars upon the railroad of the Green and Coates Street Philadelphia Passenger Railway Company, without their consent, be and the same is hereby repealed: *Provided*, That the sixth section of the act, entitled "An Act to incorporate the Green and Coates Street Philadelphia Passenger Railway Company," shall not be in any manner affected by this act, but shall have the same force and effect and meaning as if this act had not been passed.

Resolution

To authorize the laying of a sideling on Green street.

SEC. 9. That the Chief Commissioner of Highways be and he is hereby authorized to grant a permit to the Green and Coates streets Passenger Railroad Company to lay a sideling on the south side of Green street, between Ninth street and Linden place, subject to all ordinances of councils heretofore passed or that hereafter may be passed.

8. Act of March 21, 1862, Sec. 1, P. L. 150.
9. Resolution of December 19, 1859, p. 414.

Resolution

Relative to the removal of certain Railway Curves.

SEC. 10. That the Chief Commissioner of Highways be, and he is hereby authorized and directed to notify the Green and Coates streets Railway Company to remove the railway curves at Second and Green, and at the corner of Third and Coates streets, in the Eleventh Ward, within ten days from the date of such notice; and if not then removed, the said Chief Commissioner of Highways to remove the same, and charge the cost and expense thereof to the Green and Coates Streets Passenger Railway Company.

Resolution

To authorize the laying of turnouts on Coates street.

SEC. 11. That the Commissioner of Highways be, and he is hereby authorized to grant a permit to the Green and Coates Street Passenger Railway Company to lay turnouts on the north side of Coates street, east of Landing avenue, into their car house, formerly occupied by Messrs. Moore & Co., subject to all the ordinances of councils heretofore passed, or that hereafter may be passed.

10. Resolution of April 14, 1860, p. 191.
11. Resolution of July 11, 1860, p. 291.

The Germantown Passenger Railway Company.

SECTION 1. That Charles Megarge, William S. Perot, Samuel Maupay, Thomas A. Biddle, Ellison P. Morris, William W. Wister, Cornelius S. Smith, James Kempton, Frederick Collins, Samuel Huston, Mordecai L. Dawson, Henry J. Williams, Joseph Jones, John Morris, Sr., Charles W. Johnson, Philip R. Freas, Charles P. Perot, John R. Knoor, George W. Hammersly, William Millward, William Struthers, Jeremiah Eldridge, J. H. Wheeler, Charles Goepp, Charles W. Otto, Henry J. Smith, James P. Gibson, Edward Chase, Jabez Gates, John J. Griffith, John K. Gamble, Henry P. Brunner, Charles Weiss, David McLean, W. M. Reilly, J. S. Struthers, Vincent L. Bradford, Charles Wister, Henry E. Wallace, Robert P. King, and Thomas H. Town, be and they are hereby appointed commissioners to procure books and make therein the following entries:— We, whose names are hereunto subscribed, do promise to pay to the treasurer of the Germantown Passenger Railway Company, for the use of the said company, the sum of fifty dollars for each and every share of stock set opposite to our respective names by us hereunto subscribed, in such manner, times, and proportions, as may be determined upon by resolutions of the board of managers of the said company, and shall give notice in at least two daily papers of the City of Philadelphia for two weeks, of the times and places at which the said books shall be opened to receive subscriptions for the capital stock of the said company, at which respective times and places, at least one of the commissioners shall attend and keep the said books open for at least two hours in each day for three periodical days, if so many shall be necessary, and allow any person or persons of the age of twenty-one years, and the Germantown and Perkiomen Turnpike Road Company, to subscribe therein, in his, or their name, or in the name or names of any other person or persons by whom he shall, by a written power of attorney to be signed by the said person or persons, or by the said turnpike road company before a competent witness, and to be produced to and left with the said commissioners for such number of shares as he may take; but no person or corporation shall be permitted to

1. Act of April 21, 1858, Sec. 1, P. L. 494.

subscribe in his or their names, or in the name of any other person or persons, for more than ten shares each on the first day, nor for more than twenty shares each on the second day, and on the third, or any succeeding day, for such number as he or they may think proper; and if, at the expiration of the said third day, the full number of four thousand shares shall not have been subscribed, then the attending commissioner or commissioners may adjourn from time to time, and from place to place, as he or they shall think proper, of which adjournment public notice shall be given as aforesaid, but whenever the number of shares subscribed shall amount to four thousand, then the said books shall be closed, and if, before the said books shall have been declared to be closed, more than four thousand shares shall be subscribed, then the said commissioners shall apportion the said four thousand shares among the subscribers in proportion to the number of shares subscribed by each person, but so that each subscriber shall have at least one share: *Provided always,* That every person offering to subscribe in his own name, or in the name of other persons, shall previously thereto, pay to the attending commissioner or commissioners, the sum of five dollars for every share so to be subscribed for, out of which sum the expenses of the commissioners shall be defrayed, and the remainder shall be paid over to the treasurer of the corporation to be created by virtue hereof, as soon as the same shall be organized, and the officers chosen, as is hereinafter directed.

SEC. 2. That when four thousand shares of stock shall have been subscribed as aforesaid, or if after the books have been kept open for three days, the whole number of four thousand shares shall not have been subscribed, then when not less than two thousand shares shall have been subscribed, the said commissioners, or any three of them, shall certify, under their hands and seals, the names of the subscribers, and the number of shares subscribed by or apportioned to each subscriber, to the Governor of the Commonwealth, and it shall thereupon be his duty, by letters patent, under his hand, and the seal of the State, to create and erect the said subscribers and their assigns into one body politic and corporate in deed and in law, by the name, style and title of the "Germantown Passenger Railway Company," and by the said name the subscribers shall

2. Act of April 21, 1858, Sec. 2, P. L. 495.

have perpetual succession, with power to make a corporate seal, and the same to alter, break, and renew at pleasure, and all the rights, privileges and franchises belonging or incident to a corporation, and shall be able and capable of taking and holding their said capital stock, and the increase and profits thereof; and of adding to or enlarging the same by order of any stated meeting of the stockholders, or of any special meeting duly covened for that purpose, if such enlargement shall be found necessary to fulfil the objects and purposes of this act, and of purchasing, taking, receiving and holding all such real estate as may be necessary for station-houses, depots, shops, stables, and for such other purposes as may be or become necessary to enable them to carry on the traffic of their said road and the other purposes for which they were incorporated, with economy, facility, and dispatch, and the same to sell, let, or lease on ground rent, mortgage, lease, or dispose of at their pleasure, and of suing and being sued, and of doing all and every other matter and thing which a corporation may lawfully do: *Provided*, That the said company shall not in the aggregate, hold at any one time more than twenty acres of land.

SEC. 3. That the persons named in the letters patent, or any five of them, shall as soon as conveniently may be after the same shall have been sealed, give at least ten days' notice in two or more daily newspapers printed at Philadelphia, of a time and place to be by them appointed, at which the subscribers shall proceed to organize the said corporation, and shall choose by a majority of the said subscribers, by ballot, to be delivered in person, one president, nine managers, one treasurer, and such other officers as may be necessary to carry on the business of the company, who shall serve until others are regularly chosen, and to make such by-laws, rules and regulations as they may think proper for the well ordering of the affairs of this company, and for the government of the Board of Managers: *Provided, however,* That the same shall not be inconsistent with the Constitution and laws of this State or the United States: *Provided further,* That no person or corporation shall have more than one hundred votes at any meeting or election, and that each stockholder shall be entitled to one vote for each share held by him or them, not exceeding ten shares, and shall also have one vote for

3. Act of April 21, 1858, Sec. 3, P. L. 496.

every additional ten shares held by him or them, not, however, to exceed in all, one hundred votes.

SEC. 4. That the stockholders shall meet on the second Monday in June, Anno Domini one thousand eight hundred and fifty-nine, after their organization, and annually thereafter, at such place within the City of Philadelphia, as may be fixed upon by the by-laws of the corporation, or in default of any such by-law, by a resolution of the board of managers, for the purpose of choosing such officers as aforesaid, for the ensuing year, but no failure to hold any such election shall be a cause of forfeiture of this charter, but the officers previously elected shall continue in office until others shall be regularly chosen.

SEC. 5. That the president and managers aforesaid shall procure certificates for the shares of stock, of the said company so subscribed as aforesaid, and shall deliver the same, signed by the president, and countersigned by the treasurer, and sealed with the seal of this corporation, to each subscriber for the number of shares subscribed or then held by him, which certificate shall be transferred at his or her pleasure, in person or by attorney, upon the books of the company in presence of the president or of the treasurer, subject always to all payments due or to become due thereon, and every such assignee shall become a member of the said corporation, and be entitled to all the rights and privileges belonging to him as such: *Provided,* That the said company shall not be obliged to allow the transfer of any share of stock until all the instalments actually due or called for thereon, have been satisfied and paid: *And provided further,* That no assignment of such share shall release the holder thereof from a liability to pay the instalments which were actually due or called for before the said assignment: *And provided further,* That if any stockholder shall omit for the space of six months to pay any instalment which may be called for, the managers of the company may either declare the shares of stock on which the instalments are unpaid as aforesaid, to be forfeited, or may, at their option, bring suit to recover the said instalments with interest at the rate of twelve per cent. per annum, as debts of a like amount are recoverable against the person or persons appearing by their books to be the owner of those shares: *Provided,* That the Councils of said City

4. Act of April 21, 1858, Sec. 4, P. L. 496.
5. Act of April 21, 1858, Sec. 5, P. L. 497.

shall have power to lay a tax on the gross receipts of said company, not exceeding five per cent.

SEC. 6. That the board of managers shall meet at such days and times and at such places as may be fixed by the by-laws of the corporation, or in the absence of such by-laws, at such times and places as may be determined by themselves; five members shall form a quorum, they shall have full power to make by-laws, rules and regulations for their own government, and to carry on the business of the corporation, dispose of their funds, to employ such engineers, superintendents, assistants, or other officers as may be found necessary, to direct and determine their duties, fix their salaries or compensation, and generally to do, perform, exercise and carry out all the matters and things, powers and authorities, objects and purposes for which this Act of incorporation was granted, and which are therein contained, subject only to the direction of this Act and the control of the by-laws or resolutions of the meetings of stockholders.

SEC. 7. That the said corporation shall and may lay down, construct, and complete a passenger railway, with single or double tracks, on all or any part of the Germantown turnpike road, within the City of Philadelphia, with such branches as may be necessary to connect them with any other railway or railways within the said City, and to procure the cars, carriages, and other appliances required for the objects and purposes of this Act, and erect or procure the necessary offices, depots, station-houses, workshops, stables, and such other buildings as may be required for the economical and convenient transaction of their business, and the accommodation of their passengers: *Provided,* That the gauge of the said railway shall be five feet and two inches, and the form of the rails laid down shall be approved by the City Councils or by their officers: *Provided always,* That no work shall be commenced upon the line of the said railway until an agreement authorizing the company hereby created, to construct and lay down their said road upon the bed of the Germantown turnpike shall have been made and executed by and between the Germantown and Perkiomen and Turnpike Road Company and the said Passenger Railway Company, upon such terms and conditions, and with such restrictions as may be agreed

6. Act of April 21, 1858, Sec. 6, P. L. 497.
7. Act of April 21, 1858, Sec. 7, P. L. 497.

on by the said parties, who are hereby respectively authorized to make and enter into such agreement, nor until the Select and Common Councils of the City of Philadelphia shall have passed an Act permitting and allowing the construction of the said road; the said agreement to be acknowledged and recorded in the office for recording deeds, et cetera, in the City of Philadelphia, as deeds are, by the present laws, required to be acknowledged and recorded: *And provided further,* That the consideration to be paid to the said The Germantown and Perkiomen Turnpike Road Company for the use of their road, if any may be paid either in cash or by the issue of such a number of shares of stock as may be required, which shares, so issued by the company, shall be upon the same footing with other shares of stock, and entitle the holders thereof to all the privileges of other stockholders.

SEC. 8. That the president and managers shall keep a just and true account of all their receipts and expenditures, and shall and may, twice in each year, on such days as may be fixed by the by-laws, make a dividend of the clear net profits derived from the tolls received by them, first deducting all charges for repairs and other expenses, whether regular, incidental or contingent, and shall give public notice of the time and place at which such dividend shall be paid, and shall cause the same to be paid accordingly: *Provided, always,* That the said company shall pay to the City of Philadelphia a tax of six per cent. per annum upon so much of any dividend as shall exceed six per cent. per annum in any one year, to be paid to the said City at the end of each year: *And provided further,* That the capital stock of the said company shall not be subject to any further or other assessment for taxes by the said City.

SEC. 9. That the said Germantown Passenger Railway Company, with the consent and approbation of the said Germantown and Perkiomen Turnpike Company, and of the Councils or board of surveyors of the City of Philadelphia, shall and may have power and authority to alter and regulate the ascents and descents of their said railway, and to cut down or raise the present bed of the turnpike road, so far as may be required to enable them to use their railway with ease and convenience; but no such work shall in any case be commenced or carried on until plans and

8. Act of April 21, 1858, Sec. 8, P. L. 498.
9. Act of April 21, 1858, Sec. 9, P. L. 498.

specifications of the said proposed alterations shall have been submitted to the managers of the Germantown and Perkiomen Turnpike Road Company, and to the Councils or board of surveyors of the City of Philadelphia, nor until their consent to and approval thereof shall have been obtained and filed in the office of the said Germantown Passenger Railway Company.

SEC. 10. That when the said railway, or any part or parts thereof, shall be constructed and completed, the said company shall be authorized to charge and receive as tolls for the carriage of passengers, not more than five cents for each passenger for any distance under two miles, and for two miles and any distance beyond two miles at the rate of not more than three cents per mile, all fractional parts of a mile being considered and charged as one mile.

SEC. 11. That if any person or persons shall wilfully break, remove or destroy, with intent to injure any part of the said railway, or the cars, carriages, station-houses, or other buildings of the said company, or shall, without the consent of the said company, wilfully and maliciously obstruct or impede the passage on or over the said railway, or any part thereof, the person or persons so offending shall forfeit and pay for every such offence the sum of five dollars, to be recovered as debts of a like amount are by law recoverable, but no such suit shall be brought unless commenced within sixty days after such offence has been committed, and the persons so offending shall remain liable to actions at the suit of said corporation, if the sums so recovered shall not be sufficient to repay and satisfy the damage occasioned by their acts as aforesaid: *Provided*, That before the said railroad company shall go into operation, they shall purchase all the omnibuses running over the said route, together with the horses and harness belonging to the same, at a price to be agreed upon in the following manner, to wit:—The said company shall choose one person, and the proprietor or proprietors of any such omnibuses shall choose one other person, and the two so chosen shall choose a third, who shall value the omnibuses, horses and harness aforesaid, and whose decision shall be final: *Provided*, That said company shall be subject in all respects to the provisions of the general law regulating railroads, passed nineteenth February, Anno Domini one

10. Act of April 21, 1858, Sec. 10, P. L. 499.
11. Act of April 21, 1858, Sec. 11, P. L. 499.

thousand eight hundred and forty-nine, and the several supplements thereto.

SEC. 12. That said company may issue bonds and borrow money to an amount not exceeding fifty per cent. of their capital stock, and secure the same by mortgage on their road: *Provided,* That no bond shall be issued of a less denomination than one hundred dollars.

An Act

To authorize the Germantown Passenger Railway Company, and the Green and Coates Street Philadelphia Passenger Railway Company, jointly, to lay a single track on Fourth and Eighth streets, Philadelphia.

SEC. 13. That the Germantown Passenger Railway Company be and are hereby authorized and empowered, subject to the rights hereinafter conferred on the Green and Coates Streets Philadelphia Passenger Railway Company, to lay down and construct, and use a railway from the point where Fourth street intersects the Germantown and Perkiomen turnpike, in the city of Philadelphia, and running thence southwardly along said Fourth street, in said city, to Dickinson street; thence westwardly along said Dickinson street to its intersection with Eighth street; and thence northwardly on said Eighth street to its intersection with the said Germantown and Perkiomen turnpike, with the right and power to make and lay a track on Walnut street, between their said tracks on Fourth and Eighth streets, so as to connect the said tracks on Fourth and Eighth streets by the said track on Walnut street; and it is hereby further enacted, that all that part of the said railway track in Fourth street, from the centre of Coates street; thence southwardly along Fourth street to Dickinson street; thence up Dickinson street to Eighth street; thence northwardly along Eighth street to the centre of Coates street, and also the track on Walnut street, between Fourth and Eighth streets, connecting the track on Fourth and Eighth streets, as hereinbefore authorized to be built, shall be constructed, laid down, and used by the said Germantown Passenger

12. Act of April 21, 1858, Sec 12, P. L. 499.
13. Act of March 22, 1859, Sec. 1, P. L. 284.

Railway Company and the Green and Coates Street Philadelphia Passenger Railway Company, at their joint and equal expense, and shall be the joint property of the said two companies, each owning one-half thereof; and that part of the said track to be laid on Walnut street, as aforesaid, shall be subject to be used by any other passenger railway company that may be authorized to lay and use a track on Walnut street, on payment by said company to the said Germantown Passenger Railway Company, and the said Green and Coates Street Philadelphia Passenger Railway Company, of one-half of the cost of construction of the said railway on Walnut street, and of the repairs thereof, and of the expense of keeping that portion of said street in repair; and the Germantown Passenger Railway Company are hereby authorized and empowered, at such times and in such portions as in their discretion they shall see proper, to lay down and construct a branch railway track or tracks along Broad street, northward from its intersection with the Germantown and Perkiomen turnpike, to the intersection of said Broad street with the Old York road; thence along said Old York road to Milestown, or Branchtown, with the right to extend the same to the point where the North Pennsylvania railroad crosses said road; and the said Germantown Passenger Railway Company, and the Green and Coates Street Philadelphia Passenger Railway Company, shall also have the right and privilege of running their cars over, or connecting their said road hereby authorized, with or crossing any other passenger railway in the City of Philadelphia, on such terms as may be mutually agreed upon; and in case the said companies cannot agree as to such terms, then the District Court of the City of Philadelphia shall, upon petition presented by either party, appoint two disinterested persons, who shall fix the amount to be paid by the parties using the same, and whose decision in the premises, when confirmed by said court, shall be final and conclusive: *Provided*, That the persons so appointed shall be duly sworn or affirmed before entering upon the discharge of their duties, and shall file their report in the Prothonotary's office of said court within thirty days after their appointment as aforesaid: *Provided further*, That until said Eighth street shall have been opened and graded, the said Germantown Passenger Railway Company shall have power and authority to construct and lay a single track on and along such streets as may be necessary to connect the track as laid upon Fourth and Eighth streets, and make the same a continuous track, in order to carry out the full intent and meaning of this act: *And provided further*, That if the Germantown Passenger Railway Company shall be able to agree with the Germantown and Perkiomen Turnpike Company for the right of way for their said railway over said turnpike, within thirty days after the passage of this act, then the said Passenger Railway Company shall, within one year after such agreement, lay a railway track or tracks, and run their cars thereon, as provided in the original act incorporating said company, from the intersection of said turnpike with Eighth street, and northwardly as far as Washington lane, in said City; but if the said passenger railway company shall fail, within the said time, to agree with the said turnpike company for the right of way, then the said passenger railway company and the said turnpike company shall each, within a reasonable time thereafter, choose one person, and the two persons so chosen shall select a third person, all of whom shall be disinterested; or if the two first chosen shall fail to agree upon a third person within seven days after they are chosen, then the District Court of the City of Philadelphia shall select such third person; and the three persons so chosen, or a majority of them, shall proceed to fix and determine, by a yearly rental or otherwise, as they shall see proper, the fair value of the said right of way; and the valuation so fixed shall be filed of record in the said court, and shall be confirmed by the said court. And within ten months after the said proceedings shall be finally settled and confirmed, the said passenger railway company shall lay a railway track or tracks to said Washington lane, and run their cars thereon, as before provided in this section; but nothing in this proviso shall prevent the Germantown Passenger Railway Company from taking immediate possession of, and ascertaining and settling damages for, the right of way on that portion of the Germantown and Perkiomen turnpike which lies between Fourth and Eighth streets in said City, according to the provisions of the act regulating railroad companies, approved the nineteenth day of February, Anno Domini one thousand eight hundred and forty-nine: *And provided further*, That if any part of the Germantown and Perkiomen turnpike road comes into the possession of the City of Philadelphia, it shall be the duty of the Germantown Passenger Railway Company to keep said portion of the road in repair for such length as it may be occupied by them with their railway.

SEC. 14. That it shall be lawful for the said Germantown Passenger Railway Company to increase their capital stock to ten thousand shares, of fifty dollars each, and to borrow any sum of money by them required, not exceeding in amount one-half of their capital stock as hereby increased, at a rate of interest not exceeding seven per centum per annum, and to issue bonds therefor, in the sum of not less than one hundred dollars each, and to secure the payment thereof by a mortgage or mortgages upon the whole or any part of their railway, including their interest in the said road to be constructed upon Fourth and Eighth streets and Dickinson and Walnut streets, and the appurtenances thereof, and upon their corporate rights, franchises and privileges, or any part thereof.

SEC. 15. That all general meetings or elections by the stockholders of the Germantown Passenger Railway Company shall be conducted, and the vote shall be given, according to the provisions of the fifth section of an act entitled "An Act regulating railroad companies," approved the nineteenth day of February, Anno Domini one thousand eight hundred and forty-nine.

SECT. 16. That whenever it may be expedient to follow the bed of the said Germantown and Perkiomen turnpike, in the construction and laying of said railway, it shall be lawful for said company to diverge therefrom and use and occupy any street or land that may be necessary for the said route: *Provided however*, That the said Germantown Passenger Railway Company shall pay damages for any land so used and occupied; which damages shall be ascertained and settled in the manner directed by the above mentioned Act regulating railroad companies, approved the nineteenth day of February, Anno Domini one thousand eight hundred and forty-nine.

SEC. 17. That if the said Germantown Passenger Railway Company shall, within thirty days after the passage of this Act, file in the office of the City Solicitor, a written obligation under their common seal, covenanting to comply with all the ordinances of the Select and Common Councils of the City of Philadelphia, regulating passenger railways,

14. Act of March 22, 1859, Sec. 2, P. L. 286.
15. Act of March 22, 1859, Sec. 3, P. L. 286.
16. Act of March 22, 1859, Sec. 4, P. L. 287.
17. Act of March 22, 1859, Sec. 5, P. L. 287.

the same shall be deemed and taken to be a full compliance with the ordinance of said Councils authorizing the construction of said railway, approved one thousand eight hundred and fifty-eight; and the said company shall be thereupon entitled forthwith to commence the construction of said roads; and the said company shall be subject to such rates of taxation as are now, or may hereafter be imposed on other passenger railways in the City of Philadelphia.

SEC. 18. That it shall be lawful for the said Green and Coates Street Philadelphia Passenger Railway Company to increase their capital stock eight thousand shares, of fifty dollars each, and to borrow any additional sum of money by them required, not exceeding one hundred and fifty thousand dollars, at a rate of interest not exceeding seven per centum per annum, and to issue bonds therefor, in the sum of not less than one hundred dollars each, and to secure the payment thereof by a mortgage or mortgages upon the whole or any part of their railway upon Green and Coates streets, and the appurtenances thereof, and upon their interest in the said road so to be constructed upon Fourth and Eighth streets and Dickinson and Walnut streets, and upon their corporate rights, franchises and privileges, or any part thereof.

SEC. 19. That nothing in this Act contained shall be construed to give the Germantown Passenger Railway Company the right to run their cars upon the railways on Green and Coates streets, or to give the Green and Coates Street Philadelphia Passenger Railway Company the right to run their cars upon that part of Fourth or Eighth streets north of Coates street; nor shall any other passenger railway company have such right, unless by contract.

SEC. 20. That the said Green and Coates Street Philadelphia Passenger Railway Company may use their road to Fourth street, or to any point eastward thereof, at their discretion; and may remove their tracks eastwardly of said Fourth street, without prejudice to their right to relay the same, and to continue the said road, according to the route prescribed by their charter, at any time hereafter; and the fifth section of this Act shall apply to the said company, in respect of the said railway hereby authorized to be built by them as aforesaid; and all the rights, powers and privi-

18. Act of March 22, 1859, Sec. 6, P. L. 287.
19. Act of March 22, 1859, Sec. 7, P. L. 287.
20. Act of March 22, 1859, Sec. 8, P. L. 287.

leges granted by this Act may be exercised by the said companies respectively, at their discretion, in whole or in part, and from time to time, as they may deem advisable.

SEC. 21. That if any one or more of the stockholders of either of the said two railway companies shall or may dissent from the exercise of any of the powers by this Act granted, then it may be lawful for such dissenting stockholder to apply, by petition, to the District Court of the City of Philadelphia, to have his stock valued and appraised by three disinterested persons, to be appointed by said court; and it shall be lawful for either of the said companies to purchase such stock, and to pay therefor such sum as may be found due to such dissenting stockholder.

SEC. 22. That it shall be lawful for either of them, the said Germantown Passenger Railway Company, or the said Green and Coates Street Philadelphia Passenger Railway Company, whenever a majority of the holders of the stock of either company shall, at a meeting called for that purpose, so authorize, grant, sell and convey to the other of said companies all their right and interest to and in the said railway so hereby authorized to be jointly built, with its appurtenances, and to and in all the rights, privileges and franchises thereof; and when so granted and conveyed, the same shall be held and enjoyed by the purchasing company, as though the same had been by due authority made, constructed, and enjoyed by them alone.

SEC. 23. That all laws, or parts of laws, inconsistent herewith, be and the same are hereby repealed.

SEC. 24. That it shall and may be lawful for a majority of the stockholders of the Germantown Passenger Railway Company, and they are hereby empowered, to reduce the number of their Board of Managers of said Company from nine to three, including the President; and if, at any future period, the stockholders may desire to add to their number of managers, they may increase the same to any number, not exceeding twelve, including the President: *Provided, however,* That such diminution or increase shall be made at a meeting of the stockholders specially convened for such purpose, to be held at their usual place of business, after two weeks' notice, in one or more of the daily papers of the City of Philadelphia: *And also provided,* That such meeting

21. Act of March 22, 1859, Sec. 9, P. L. 288.
22. Act of March 22, 1859, Sec. 10, P. L. 288.
23. Act of March 22, 1859, Sec. 11 P. L. 288.
24. Act of April 3, 1863, Sec. 1, P. L. 270.

shall be held at least one month before the second Monday in June, being the annual period for electing managers for said Company.

SEC. 25. That the managers of the said Company are hereby authorized and empowered to sell and convey, either upon ground rent or in fee simple, or taking a mortgage for the whole or part of the consideration money, any portion of the real estate now owned by them, as the Board of Managers may deem it unnecessary for the said Company to hold for the use of the said railway; such sales to be made, either at public or private sale, and for such price and upon such terms as the Board of Managers may think fit.

Resolution.

To authorize the Germantown Passenger Railway Company to lay rails upon certain streets.

SEC. 26. *Resolved,* That the Germantown Passenger Railway Company be and they are hereby authorized to lay rails temporarily on Columbia avenue, between Seventh and Eighth streets, and along Seventh street, to connect with their road at Montgomery street, until the culvert now being constructed on Montgomery avenue shall be completed: *Provided,* That they shall place said streets in as good condition as they were before they used them.

25. Act of April 3, 1863 Sec. 2, P. L. 270.
26. Resolution July 18, 1860, page 332.

Hestonville, Mantua and Fairmount Passenger Railroad.

SECTION 1. That Albert S. Ashmead, Charles M'Calla, H. R. Harnish, Charles B. Truit, William Patterson, J. R. Gheen, Jacob S. Yost, Robert Glendenning, Robert Morris, Samuel Smedley, Jacob Ziegler, Samuel Hutchins, W. D. Kelley, James Hunter, Isaac Heston, Thomas A. Andrews, J. R. Vogdes, John C. Keffer, D. B. Paul, H. A. Dreer, Nehemiah Evans, Robert Selfridge, John A. Brown, G. C. Franciscus, G. H. Bardwell, B. R. Miller, H. E. Wallace, S. Morton Zulick, D. D. Jones, John Steele, Jesse T. Vodges, Stephen P. Hill, Isaac M. Ashton, William P. M'Calla, John F. Beatty, E. W. Carr, Peter Packer, and George M. Hill, or a majority of them, are hereby appointed commissioners to open books, and receive subscriptions, and organize a company, by the name style and title of the Hestonville, Mantua and Fairmount Passenger Railroad Company and as such shall have power to lay out and construct a railway in the City of Philadelphia, according to the following route: Commencing at Hestonville; then eastward along Lancaster avenue or the Merion plank road with double track to Belmont avenue; thence with double or single track, by Belmont avenue and Lancaster avenue, and such other street or streets as may be requisite, to Haverford street and Bridge street; thence along Haverford street, with single track, to Thirtieth street; thence southward to Bridge street: thence eastward, with double track, over the bridge to Fairmount; thence westward, with single track along Bridge street, from Thirtieth street to Lancaster avenue, or such other street or streets as may be requisite, with the privilege of extending south-eastward, with double track, to the middle of Market street, and by single track along Thirty-sixth street, from Haverford street southward to Walnut street; thence by single track to Thirty-fourth street; thence northward by Thirty-fourth street and Lancaster avenue and Thirty-fifth street to Haverford street to the place of beginning; with the privilege of laying a single or double track upon Garden street and Hamilton street with the right to intersect and run

1. Act of April 6, 1859, Sec. 1, P. L. 389.

their cars over any passenger railway now constructed, or which may hereafter be constructed, so as to give the said company a complete route from Hestonville to the eastern limits of the City of Philadelphia; and the said company shall have power to convey passengers over said route to and from Hestonville and the eastern limits of the City aforesaid; and they shall have the right to purchase real estate, and to erect thereon such buildings and improvements as may be necessary or deemed expedient for the purposes and convenience of said company, and also of purchase the necessary equipments, such as horses, cars and other vehicles for the conveyance of passengers over said railway; and no freight or burden trains, or locomotive, shall be permitted to pass over said railway: *Provided*, That before the said company shall run their cars on the track or tracks of any other passenger railway, they shall agree with such other company or companies upon the terms of compensation to be paid said company or companies for the previlege of so using and running cars on said road or roads; and if the parties shall not be able to agree upon the terms of compensation as aforesaid, then the determination of all such disputes shall be submitted to three competent and disinterested citizens of the City of Philadelphia, who shall be appointed by the Judges of the Court of Common Pleas of said City, on petition, in writing, presented to said judges, whether in vacation or at their chamber; and it shall be the duty of said judges, on the presentation of said petition, forthwith to appoint the said three referees, whose duty it shall be, without delay, to adjust and determine the compensation to be paid by the said Hestonville, Mantua and Fairmount Passenger Railroad Company as aforesaid; and the decision of said referees as aforesaid made, shall be in writing, and deposited within five days after their appointment with the Judges of the Court of Common Pleas as aforesaid; which decision so aforesaid made, shall be final and conclusive upon both parties.

SECT. 2. That the capital stock of said company shall consist of six thousand shares, of fifty dollars each, and that said company shall have power, by a vote of the stockholders, convened for that purpose, to increase their capital stock as much as in their opinion shall or may be necessary to complete said railway and to carry out the full and true intent and meaning of this act: *Provided*,

2. Act of April 6, 1859, Sec. 2, P. L. 390.

That said capital stock shall not exceed five hundred thousand dollars.

SECT. 3. That dividends of so much of the profits of said company as shall appear advisable to the directors, shall be declared in the months of January and July in each and every year, and be paid at the office of said company any time after ten days from the time of declaring the same; but said dividends shall in no case exceed the amount of the net profits of said company, so that the capital stock shall never be impaired thereby; and if said directors shall make any dividend impairing the capital stock of said company, the directors consenting thereto shall be liable in their individual capacities to said company, for the amount so divided; and each director present when such dividend shall be declared, shall be considered as consenting thereto, unless he or they enter protest upon the minutes of the transactions of the board, and give public notice of the same.

SECT. 4. That said company shall have a common seal and the same to alter and renew at pleasure, and also to ordain, establish and put in execution such by-laws, ordinances and regulations as shall appear necessary or convenient for the government of said corporation, and not being contrary to the laws and constitution of the United States or of this Commonwealth, and generally to do for the well-being of the said corporation and the due ordering and managing of the affairs thereof.

SECT. 5. That the said company shall have power to elect or appoint a president and five directors, a majority of whom, with the president, shall be citizens of Philadelphia, and such other officers as may be deemed necessary and expedient; and in every election for officers each share of stock shall entitle the holder to one vote.

SECT. 6. That said company shall have power to raise on bonds any sum not exceeding one-half of their capital stock, for the purpose of carrying out the true intent of this act: *Provided*, That no bond shall be issued for a less sum than one hundred dollars, and at a rate of interest not exceeding seven per centum.

SECT. 7. That the said company shall annually pay into

3. Act of April 6, 1859, Sec. 3, P. L. 390.
4. Act of April 6, 1859, Sec. 4, P. L. 390.
5. Act of April 6, 1859, Sec. 5, P. L. 391.
6. Act of April 6, 1859, Sec. 6, P. L. 391.
7. Act of April 6, 1859, Sec. 7, P. L. 391.

the treasury of the City of Philadelphia, for the use of said City, whenever the dividends shall exceed the sum of six per centum on the capital stock, the sum of six per centum on said dividends thus declared.

SECT. 8. That if it shall be found necessary in extending the track along the plank road and Fortieth street, or such other street or streets as may be convenient to Haverford street, to enter upon private property, damages for the same, if any, shall be assessed and paid for according to the Act of Assembly, approved the nineteenth day of February, Anno Domini one thousand eight hundred and forty-nine: *And provided further*, That before the said company shall use and occupy said bridge, the consent of councils of the City of Philadelphia shall be first obtained; and said councils may from time to time, by ordinance, establish such regulations in regard to said railway, as may be required for paving, re-paving, grading, culverting of, and laying gas and water pipes in and along said streets, and to prevent obstruction thereon.

SECT. 9. That said company, in constructing said road, shall conform to the grades now established or hereafter to be by law established, of the several streets traversed by said road, and keep said streets in perpetual good repair, at the proper expense of said company.

SECT. 10. That the said Hestonville, Mantua and Fairmount Passenger Railway Company is hereby authorized and empowered in constructing their passenger railway, to lay their track or tracks upon the line of the Merion plank road or the line of the Lancaster Turnpike Company: *Provided*, The consent of the stockholders of said company or companies be first obtained.

An Ordinance

To prohibit the Hestonville, Mantua and Fairmount Passenger Railway Company from using the Wire Bridge for Railway purposes.

SEC. 11. That the Select and Common Councils of the City of Philadelphia do hereby prohibit the said company

8. Act of April 8, 1859, Sec. 8, P. L. 391.
9. Act of April 9, 1859, Sec. 9, P. L. 391.
10. Act of April 10, 1859, Sec. 10, P. L. 391.
11. Ordinance May 4, 1859, page 237.

from laying any railway track upon said Wire Bridge, at Fairmount, or using it in any manner for railway purposes; and the City Solicitor is hereby directed to institute prompt equitable proceedings to enjoin said company from laying a track on said bridge, or using it for railway purposes, in case said company at any time commence or threaten to lay a railway track in the vicinity of said bridge; and any one placing a railway, or aiding in placing a railway on said bridge, shall be subject to a fine of five thousand dollars, which fine the mayor of said city is hereby authorized and directed to collect as other fines heretofore imposed are collected.

An Ordinance

Authorizing the Hestonville, Mantua, and Fairmount Passenger Railroad Company, to lay the rails of their road over the Wire Bridge.

SEC. 12. That the assent of the City of Philadelphia be, and is hereby given to the Hestonville, Mantua, and Fairmount Passenger Railroad Company to construct the railway of said company on the Wire Bridge, uuder the supervision and direction of the Chief Engineer and Surveyor: *Provided*, That the said company shall pay annually to the Treasurer of the City of Philadelphia, in the month of January of each year for the use of the City, twenty dollars toll for each car passing over said Wire Bridge, "which shall be in addition to such amount as is now required by ordinance to be paid, or which may hereafter be required to be paid by said company under ordinance hereafter to be enacted," and for each and every car passing over said bridge, before the time herein provided for paying the toll, a proportionate sum shall be paid until the succeeding January: *And provided also*, That the said company shall pay and satisfy all bills that may be incurred by the Commissioner of City Property in making any repairs to said bridge that he, the said Commissioner, may deem necessary and proper for its preservation and safe travel; said bills to be paid by the said company when presented by the said commissioner; and in default of the payment of toll for each car passing over said bridge as herein provided, or for the payment of

12. Ordinance September 28, 1859, page 312.

any bills for repairs made to said bridge as herein provided, the said commissioner shall have authority, when directed by councils, to remove the rails from said bridge: *And provided also*, That not more than two cars shall be upon the said bridge at the same time: *And provided further*, That the cars of said railroad company shall not stand on Callowhill street, to the east of said bridge.

SEC. 13. That in order and to the end that the City of Philadelphia may protect and save harmless the said bridge from its use and occupancy by the said company in the passage of the cars thereon, councils reserve the right at any time to order and direct the said company to remove their railway, and should they neglect or refuse to do so within five days after such notice, that then the said commissioner shall proceed without delay to remove the same. "*Provided*, Before said company shall proceed to lay their rails on said bridge, they shall enter into such agreement in writing as shall be deemed sufficient by the City Solicitor to secure the observance by them of this Ordinance, and all other ordinances which may hereafter be enacted in relation to passenger railways."

An Ordinance

Authorizing the Hestonville, Mantua, and Fairmount Passenger Railroad Company to lay the rails of their road over the Wire Bridge.

SEC. 14. That the assent of the City of Philadelphia be and is hereby given to the Hestonville, Mantua, and Fairmount Passenger Railway Company, to construct the railway of said company on the Wire Bridge, under the supervision and direction of the Chief Engineer and Surveyor: *Provided*, That the said company shall pay annually the sum of thirty dollars as is now required by ordinance to be paid by said company, or which may hereafter be required to be paid under ordinances hereafter to be enacted: *And provided also*, That the said company shall pay and satisfy all bills that may be incurred by the Commissioner of City Property in making any repairs to the roadway of said bridge, that he, the said commissioner may deem neces

13. Ordinance September 28, 1859, page 312.
14. Ordinance December 17, 1859, page 412.

sary and proper for its preservation and safe travel, said bills to be paid by the said company when presented by the said commissioner; in default of the payments being made as herein provided, the said commissioner shall have authority to remove the rails from the said bridge when directed by councils: *And provided also,* That not more than two cars shall be upon the said bridge at the same time: *And provided further,* That the cars of said railroad company shall not stand on Callowhill street to the east of said bridge: *And provided further,* Such permission to cross said bridge shall continue only during the pleasure of councils.

A Supplement

To an Act to Incorporate the Hestonville, Mantua and Fairmount Passenger Railroad Company, Approved April sixth, Anno Domini one thousand eight hundred and fifty-nine.

WHEREAS, It has been deemed for the present inexpedient that the Hestonville, Mantua and Fairmount Passenger Railroad Company avail themselves of that portion of their charter, which provides that the said company shall have the right to run their cars over any passenger railway now constructed, or which may hereafter be constructed, so as to give the said company a complete route from Hestonville to the eastern limit of the City of Philadelphia:

And whereas, The said company relying upon the express intention of the General Assembly to afford a through route to the inhabitants of that important part of the city through which said railroad is located, have expended a considerable sum of money in the laying of their tracks, the erection of depot, purchase of horses, cars, et cetera; therefore,

SEC. 15. That for the better carrying out the intention of the General Assembly, as expressed in the Act aforesaid, the Hestonville, Mantua and Fairmount Passenger Railroad Company are hereby authorized and empowered to lay out and construct their railway tracks from their present terminus, across the Schuylkill to Callowhill street, and along Callowhill street to Delaware avenue, and westwardly from Hestonville, and northwardly along Thirty-fifth street to such point or points as may be required, from time to time,

15. Act of March 8, 1860, page 123.

and to lay their tracks on and occupy such other street or streets as may be necessary, to reach Twenty-first or Twentieth and Callowhill streets, from their present terminus at Fairmount.

SEC. 16. That the said Hestonville, Mantua and Fairmount Passenger Railroad Company shall have the privilege of increasing their capital stock to an amount not exceeding five thousand shares.

An Ordinance

To authorize the Hestonville, Fairmount, and Mantua Railroad Company to continue their track along Front Street, in the City of Philadelphia.

SEC. 17. That the Hestonville, Fairmount, and Mantua Railroad Company be and they are hereby authorized to continue their track, as now laid along Front street, from the terminus of their road at Front and Callowhill streets to the north crossing at Front and Vine streets, and to use the same so far as the City of Philadelphia has the power to grant such license; and that any penalties incurred by said company in laying down such track, under an Ordinance passed February 28, 1860, entitled an Ordinance relating to the highways of the City of Philadelphia, or any section thereof, be and the same are hereby remitted.

16. Act of March 8, 1860, page 123.
17. Ordinance July 31, 1862, page 272.

Philadelphia and Darby Railroad Company.

SECTION 1. That Thomas Sparks, John W. Passmore, Morris Powers, Charles Lloyd, Robert Buist, Morris S. Wickersham, Isaac Leech, junior, Wm. A. Edwards, and Henry M. Philips, of the city of Philadelphia, James Andrews, Morgan Bunting, Albert Worrell, Pearson Serrill, Joseph B. Conover, and George M'Henry, of Delaware county, and their associates, and those who may hereafter become associated with them, be and hereby are incorporated and constituted a body politic, under the name and title of the Philadelphia and Darby Railroad Company, with all the rights and privileges, and subject to all the conditions and restrictions conferred or imposed by an Act to regulate railroad companies, approved the nineteenth day of February, Anno Domini one thousand eight hundred and forty-nine, and the supplements thereto.

SEC. 2. That the said Philadelphia and Darby Railroad Company are hereby authorized to construct a railroad from a point at or near the eighth mile stone on the Philadelphia and Chester post road to such a point in the city of Philadelphia, west of the river Schuylkill, as they deem fit: *Provided,* That the said road, so far as it may be in the county of Philadelphia, shall be located southeast of the said Philadelphia and Chester post road, and shall be subject to the tenth section of a supplement to the act consolidating the city of Philadelphia, approved the twenty-first day of April, Anno Domini one thousand eight hundred and fifty-five.

SEC. 3. That the capital stock of said company shall consist of ten thousand shares of twenty dollars each.

SEC. 4. That the proviso in the second section of an act to incorporate the Philadelphia and Darby Railroad Company, approved April eighteenth, one thousand eight hundred and fifty-seven, be and the same is hereby repealed,

SEC. 5. That the said Philadelphia and Darby railroad is hereby authorized, in constructing a passenger railroad, to lay the track or tracks upon the line of the Darby turnpike or plank road company: *Provided,* The consent of the stockholders of said company is first obtained.

1. Act of April 28, 1857, Sec. 1, P. L., 1858, page 551.
2. Act of April 28, 1857, Sec. 2, P. L., 1858, page 551.
3. Act of April 28, 1857, Sec. 3, P. L., 1858, page 551.
4. Act of April 21, 1858, Sec. 1, P. L., page 391.
5. Act of April 21, 1858, Sec. 2, P L., page 391.

West Philadelphia Passenger Railway.

SECTION 1. That Constant M. Eakin, James Miller, Samuel A. Harrison, John R. Vogdes, J. Sidney Keen, James M'Ilvain, Richard Simpson, Isaac Leech, J. Alexander Simpson, C. K. Landis, J. Francis Knorr, Thomas Allibone, L. H. Twaddell, Augustus C. Jones, Edward B. Twaddell, Joseph Fareira, Frederick Server, Robert L. Martin, Edward Wartman, John A. Houseman, John F. Gross, William Shriver, William Keichline, Thomas Gillespie, Joseph S. Silver, Jeremiah Bonsal, John Todd, Abram R. Paul, James Cochran, Robert Hutchinson, Jonathan Bonsall, John Alexander, Robert Neely, Samuel Hutchinson, Charles Hartshore, Wm. H. Evans and Edward H. Bonsall, and their associates, who may become stockholders in the company hereby incorporated, be and are hereby constituted a body politic and corporate, by the name, style and title of the West Philadelphia Passenger Railway Company, and as such shall have power to lay out and construct a passenger railway, and carry passengers over the same, along such route and street as hereinafter provided, and for such rate or toll as may from time to time be established; and the said company shall have the right to equip said road, and to purchase and hold such real estate, and to erect thereon such buildings and improvements as may be deemed expedient and neces sary for the purposes of said company.

SEC. 2. That the capital stock of said company shall consist of five thousand shares of fifty dollars each, with the privilege of increasing the same from time to time as required, to ten thousand shares.

SEC. 3. That the said company shall be authorized to lay a double or single track of railway, to be used exclusively with horse-power and passenger travel, from the intersection of Till and Washington streets, in the Twenty-fourth Ward of the City of Philadelphia, and extending eastwards across the river Schuylkill by the Market Street Bridge, and along said Washington and Market streets to Delaware Third street, with the privilege of connecting with and using such parts of the West Chester and Philadelphia Railroad, the Columbia

1. Act of May 14, 1857, Sec. 1, P. L., 1858, page 585.
2. Act of May 14, 1857, Sec. 2, P. L., 1858, page 585.
3. Act of May 14, 1857, Sec. 3, P. L., 1858, page 585.

Railroad, and the said City Railroad, or either of them, so far as may be necessary or convenient for the purpose of completing the said route for passenger railway travel between said points; and said railroad shall conform, as far as practicable, to the grades of the streets of said city, as they now are, or as the same may be altered from time to time; and the iron rail, used in said road, shall be of such pattern and so laid as not to obstruct ordinary travel upon said streets: *Provided*, That the said West Philadelphia Railway shall not connect with or use any part of the said West Chester and Philadelphia Railroad, without the consent in writing of the directors of said company; nor shall it connect with or use any part of the said Columbia and Philadelphia Railroad, without first having the consent in writing of the board of canal commissioners.

SEC. 4. That the councils of said city may prescribe the tolls, not exceeding those charged in other cases, which the said company shall pay for the use of such portions of the City Railroad as may be necessary to complete the circuit of travel on said passenger railway, and to establish such regulations as shall be required for the convenience and safety of travel, and to prevent obstructions from freight trains, or otherwise, over the same.

SEC. 5. That the parties hereinbefore named, or a majority of them, may proceed to organize said company and obtain subscriptions to the capital stock thereof, and after two thousand shares shall have been subscribed by not less than twenty persons, and at least ten per cent. paid in on said subscriptions, they shall provide by advertisement at least twice a week for two weeks, in two or more newspapers published in said city, for the election of a board of nine directors, who shall serve until the first Tuesday of November next, and until their successors shall be duly elected; and annually thereafter upon the first Tuesday in November, the stockholders shall elect a similar board of directors to serve in like manner for one year, and until their successors shall be duly elected; and if for any reason any of said elections shall not be held at the time appointed, another time shall be appointed according to the by-laws of said company for said purpose, not more than two months later than said date; and the said directors shall supply all vacancies in their board by death, resignation, or otherwise, until the next

4. Act of May 14, 1857, Sec. 4, P. L., 1858, page 586.
5. Act of May 14, 1857, Sec. 5, P. L., 1858, page 586.

annual election; but no person shall be elected a director who shall not be at the time a stockholder in said company.

SEC. 6. That the said directors shall have power to elect a president, treasurer, and such other officers, being citizens of Pennsylvania, as may be deemed necessary and expedient; and in every election for directors each stockholder shall be entitled to one vote for each share of stock, not exceeding ten shares, and one vote for every five shares exceeding that number; but no stockholder, whether original subscriber or assignee, shall be entitled to vote at any election or meeting of said company, unless the whole sum due and payable on the share or shares by him or her held at the time, shall have been fully paid and discharged.

SEC. 7. That the said company shall have power to make and have a common seal, the same to alter and renew at pleasure; and also, to establish and execute such by-laws and regulations as shall appear to be necessary and convenient for the government of said corporation, and not being contrary to the constitution and laws of the United States, or of this State, and generally to do and perform all and singular the matters and things which to them it shall lawfully appertain to do for the well-being of said corporation, and the proper management of the affairs thereof.

SEC. 8. That the dividends of so much of the profits of said company as shall appear advisable to the directors, shall be declared in the months of January and July in each and every year, and be paid at the office of said company, any time after ten days from the time of declaring the same, but said dividends shall in no case exceed the amount of the net profits of said company, so that the capital stock thereof shall be impaired thereby; and if said directors shall make any dividend impairing the capital stock of said company, the directors consenting thereto shall be liable in their individual capacities to said company for the excess so divided; and each director present when such dividend shall be declared shall be considered as consenting thereto, unless he or they enter their protest upon the minutes of the board, and give public notice of the same; and the said company shall annually pay into the treasury of the City of Philadelphia, for the use of said city, whenever the dividends shall exceed six per centum per annum on the cap-

6. Act of May 14, 1857, Sec. 6, P. L., 1858, page 586.
7. Act of May 14, 1857, Sec. 7, P. L., 1858, page 586.
8. Act of May 14, 1857, Sec. 8, P. L., 1858, page 587.

ital stock, the sum of six per centum on the said dividends thus declared.

SEC. 9. That said company shall have power to extend their said road from Till and Washington streets to Blockley avenue, or Sixty-fifth street, by way of Logan street, Haverford road and Vine street: *Provided*, That no plank road or turnpike shall be occupied, except in crossing, without the consent of the company owning the same.

SEC. 10. That said company, for the purpose of making a proper connection with the Columbia Railroad, near the line of the West Chester and Philadelphia Railroad, shall have the power to take such land as may be necessary, in the same manner, and subject to the same conditions as provided in the act to incorporate the West Chester and Philadelphia Railroad company, approved the eleventh day of April, Anno Domini one thousand eight hundred and forty-eight.

SEC. 11. That the road herein authorized shall be commenced within one year, and finished within two years from the date hereof.

SEC. 12. That before the said company shall use and occupy the said streets, the consent of the councils of the City of Philadelphia shall be first given; and said consent shall be taken and deemed to be given, if the said councils shall not, within thirty days after the passage of this act, by ordinance duly passed, signify their disapproval thereof; and said councils may from time to time, by ordinance, establish such regulations in regard to said railway, as may be required for the paving, repaving, grading, culverting and laying of water and gas pipes in and along said streets, and to prevent obstructions thereon; and the said company, before commencing to run their cars upon the said street, shall purchase at the option of the owner of the line of omnibuses now licensed as the Market Street Line, the stock of horses, omnibuses, owned and used in said line at the time of the completion of said road, at a price to be assessed in the following manner, to wit:—The said owners shall choose one disinterested person, and the said company shall choose a second person, and the two thus chosen shall select a third, or if they shall fail or refuse to act, then the Court of Common Pleas of said city and county, upon the application of

9. Act of May 14, 1857, Sec. 9, P. L., 1858, page 587.
10. Act of May 14, 1857, Sec. 10, P. L., 1858, page 587.
11. Act of May 14, 1857, Sec. 11, P. L., 1858, page 587.
12. Act of May 14, 1857, Sec. 12, P. L., 1858, page 587.

either party, and notice to the other party, shall appoint the third, and the three together thus chosen or appointed, shall appraise such stock, and the valuation thus arrived at shall be binding and final.

SEC. 13. *Provided*, That the privileges hereby granted shall continue for the period of twenty years, and no longer, unless extended or renewed by the Legislature.

A Supplement

To an Act to incorporate the West Philadelphia Passenger Railway Company, approved the fourteenth day of May, Anno Domini one thousand eight hundred and fifty-seven.

SEC. 14. That the West Philadelphia Passenger Railway Company be and the same is hereby authorized to borrow any sum or sums of money for the purpose of constructing and equipping their road, not exceeding the sum of one hundred thousand dollars, and to issue their bonds therefor in such sums and for such rates of interest, not exceeding seven per cent., and payable at such times as the president and directors of the said road may deem expedient; and to secure the payment of said loan, the said company is authorized to mortgage all or any of its property, real or personal: *Provided*, That no bond shall be issued for a less sum than one thousand dollars.

SEC. 15. That the said company is hereby authorized to extend their said road to any part of the Twenty-fourth Ward, in the City of Philadelphia, along any of the public streets or highways thereof: *Provided however*, That said company shall first present to the councils of said city a plan and statement, exhibiting the route of any such proposed extension; and if councils shall not within sixty days thereafter, by ordinance disapprove thereof, the consent of councils shall be deemed to be given thereto: *And provided further*, That nothing herein contained shall authorize the change of any part of the route of the said road in the Twenty-fourth ward, as located in the act to which this is a supplement; and that the said company, before commencing to run their cars upon any of the said streets, shall purchase, at the option of the

13. Act of May 14, 1857, Sec. 13, P. L., 1858, page 588.
14. Act of April 8, 1858, Sec. 1, P. L., page 226.
15. Act of April 8, 1858, Sec. 2, P. L., page 226.

owners of the lines of omnibuses licensed to run on said streets, the stock of horses, omnibuses, sleighs and harness owned and used in the said lines, upon the terms and conditions prescribed by the twelfth section of the act to which this a supplement, in respect to the Market street line.

Resolution

Dissenting from the application of the West Philadelphia Passenger Railway Company for permission to extend their road on Woodland and other streets in the Twenty-fourth Ward.

SEC. 16. *Resolved*, That in pursuance of the power vested in the councils of the city by an act of assembly, approved April 8th, 1858, entitled "a Supplement to an Act to Incorporate the West Philadelphia Passenger Railway Company," approved the 14th day of May, A. D. 1857, they hereby declare their disapproval of the plans submitted by the said West Philadelphia Passenger Railway Company, for the extension of their road over parts of Woodland, Chestnut and William streets, to Woodland Cemetry, in the Twenty-fourth Ward.

A Supplement

To an Act to incorporate the West Philadelphia Railway Company.

SEC. 17. That it is hereby declared to be the true intent and meaning of the first section of a supplement to an act to in corporate the West Philadelphia Passenger Railway Company, approved the fourteenth day of May, one thousand eight hundred and fifty-seven, and its true and legal effect shall be, that in all cases where said railway company has issued, or may hereafter issue bonds, certificates of loan or evidences of indebtedness, executed by this company, and has disposed, or may hereafter dispose of the same, at less than their par value, such transactions shall not be deemed usurious, or in violation of any law of this Commonwealth prohibiting the taking of more than six per cent. interest.

16. Resolution, November 5, 1858, page 427.
17. Act of April 11, 1859, Sec. 1, P. L., page 455.

A Further Supplement

To the Act to incorporate the West Philadelphia Passenger Railway Company.

SEC. 18. That from and after the passage of this act, the West Philadelphia Passenger Railway Company shall have power and authority to extend their road along Market street, from the present terminus of their road at Third street, to Front street, to be constructed and used in conformity with the provisions of the act to which this is a supplement.

SEC. 19. That at all elections for directors, after the passage of this act, each and every share of the stock of said company shall entitle the holder or holders thereof to one vote.

SEC. 20. That the said the West Philadelphia Passenger Railway Company shall annually pay into the treasury of the city of Philadelphia, for the use of the said city, whenever the dividends, declared by said company, shall exceed six per cent. per annum on the capital stock thereof, a tax of six per centum on such excess over six per centum thus declared.

SEC. 21. That so much of the act incorporating this company, as may be altered or supplied by this act, or which may be inconsistent herewith, be and the same is hereby repealed: *Provided,* That nothing herein contained shall authorize the change of any part of the route of the said road, in the Twenty-fourth ward, as located by the act incorporating said company.

An Ordinance

Authorizing the West Philadelphia Passenger Railway Company to lay the rails of their road over the Market Street Bridge.

SEC. 22. That the assent of the City of Philadelphia be, and is hereby given to the West Philadelphia Passenger Railway Company to construct the railway of said company on the Market street Bridge, under the supervision and direc-

18. Act of May 16, 1861, Sec, 1, P. L., page 697.
19. Act of May 16, 1861, Sec. 2, P. L., page 697.
20. Act of May 16, 1861, Sec. 3, P. L., page 697.
21. Act of May 16, 1861, Sec. 4, P. L., page 697.
22. Ordinance of March 3, 1859, Sec. 1, page 122.

tion of the Highway Department: *Provided* the said com. shall, within ten days from the passage of this ordinance, file in the office of the city Solicitor a written obligation, sufficient in law to bind such company to observe and be subject to all the restrictions, limitations, terms and conditions of an ordinance of said city, entitled "An Ordinance to regulate Passenger Railways," approved July 7th, 1857, and to all other ordinances of said city, in relation to passenger railways, which may be in force at the time of the execution of said obligation, and all such as may thereafter be passed ; and provided, also, that the said company shall pay annually to the city, twenty dollars toll for each car passing over said bridge, (as provided for by the act of the General Assembly, authorizing the construction of the railway of said company on said bridge :) *And provided, also,* That said company shall keep the southern roadway of the bridge occupied by them in good order and repair : *And provided, also,* That in laying their tracks through Market street, they shall not interfere with the use of the City Railroad, nor of private turn-outs constructed in connection with the City Railroad ; and provided further, that the provisions of the second section of an ordinance approved April 16th, 1858, entitled "An Ordinance relating to certain Passenger Railway Companies," shall apply to all railways to which conditional assent of councils has heretofore been granted, in lieu of any other like provision, so as to make the same conform to the regulations respecting the railway companies mentioned in the said recited ordinance, and all ordinances or parts of ordinances, inconsistent herewith, be and the same is hereby repealed.

An Ordinance

To grant permission to the West Philadelphia Passenger Railway Company to extend their Track.

SEC. 23. That the West Philadelphia Passenger Railroad Company have the consent and permission of councils to construct a double track of railway on Market street, commencing at the terminus of their road (Third and Market streets) and extending along the south side of Market street to Front street, and thence along Front street to the north side of Market street, and thence along the north side of

23. Ordinance of April 27, 1860, Sec. 1, page 210.

Market to Third and Market streets, the place of beginning; to the end that they may be enabled to run their passenger cars to Front street and return, for the better accommodation of parties doing business along the eastern portion of the city.

SEC. 24. *Resolved*, That the West Philadelphia Passenger Railway Company are hereby authorized to lay an additional railway track on Market, east of Eighth street, as near the middle of said street as shall be directed by the Chief Engineer and Surveyor of the City. *Provided*, that the said railway company shall first give full and sufficient security, to be approved by the City Solicitor, that they will, so soon as the said additional track is completed and ready for use, remove all the track and turnouts now used by them between Eighth and Third streets, and will repave the space from which the said track and turnouts shall be removed, in such manner and to such extent as may be directed by the Department of Highways.

24. 4th Resolution, July 18, 1860, page 328.

Philadelphia City Passenger Railway.

SECTION 1. That George Boldin, Conrad S. Grove, Harry Connelly, Charles Wister, John Ely, B. R. Petrikin, Joseph Singerly, William Juvenal, William D. Kelley, Lewis Scout, Charles Harlan and William Millward, or two-thirds of them, be and they are hereby constituted and appointed commissioners to open books, receive subscriptions and organize a company, by the name, style and title of the Philadelphia City Passenger Railway Company, with power and authority to lay out and construct a city passenger railway, commencing on Front street, at or near Walnut street; thence up the said Front street with a single track to Chestnut street; thence up said Chestnut street with a single track to Twenty-second street; thence down the said Twenty-second street with a single track to Walnut street; thence down the said Walnut street with a single track to Front street aforesaid, in the city of Philadelphia, and to extend the same on the west side of the Schuylkill river, along Chestnut or Walnut streets to Sixty-fifth street, by either single or double track, at such time, or from time to time, as the company may deem it expedient, subject to all the provisions and restrictions of an act regulating railroad companies, approved the nineteenth day of February, Anno Domini one thousand eight hundred and forty-nine, and the several supplements thereto, so far as the same are not altered or supplied by this act; and also an ordinance of city councils, entitled "An Ordinance to regulate Passenger Railways within the City of Philadelphia," approved the seventh day of July, Anno Domini one thousand eight hundred and fifty-seven: *Provided*, That no freight or burden trains or locomotives shall be permitted to pass along the same.

SEC. 2. The capital stock of said company shall consist of ten thousand shares of fifty dollars each, and the said company may from time to time, by a vote of the stockholders, at a meeting called for that purpose, of which meeting thirty days' notice shall be given, in two or more papers in the city of Philadelphia, increase the capital stock to an amount not exceeding fifteen thousand shares of fifty dollars each.

1. Act of March 26, 1859, Sec. 1, P. L., p. 243.
2. Act of March 26, 1859, Sec. 2, P. L., p. 243.

SEC. 3. That the said company shall have the power to borrow money in any sum not exceeding in amount one-half of its capital stock, at a rate of interest not exceeding seven per cent. per annum, and to secure the re-payment of the same and the interest thereon, to issue bonds, (the principal moneys secured by which shall be made payable at such date as the board of directors of said company may deem advisable,) and which bonds shall be further secured by a mortgage of and on the said railway, and the corporate rights and franchises thereof granted by this act; and such bonds and mortgage may contain a provision that it shall be optional with the holder of any such bond, at any time within five years from the date of the maturity thereof, to convert the same into the capital stock of the said company, at par: *Provided*, That no bond shall be issued of a less denomination than one hundred dollars.

SEC. 4. That whenever the councils of the City of Philadelphia shall proceed to build a free bridge across the river Schuylkill, at either Chestnut or Walnut street, the said the Philadelphia City Passenger Railway Company shall pay into the treasury of the said city, one half the cost of said bridge: *Provided*, The sum so paid by said Philadelphia City Passenger Railway Company, shall not exceed one hundred thousand dollars; said payment to be made in the first mortgage bonds of the said company, secured as aforesaid, towards the cost of construction of said bridge: *Provided*, That the said railway company shall have the exclusive right and authority to use the said bridge for passenger railway purposes and to lay tracks thereon.

SEC. 5. That the said councils may, from time to time by ordinance, establish such regulations in regard to said railway, as may be required for the paving, re-paving, grading, culverting, and the laying of gas and water pipes in and along said streets, and avenues, and to prevent obstructions thereon.

SEC. 6. That the said company, in constructing said road, shall conform to the grades now established or hereafter to be by law established, of the several streets or avenues traversed by said road, and to keep such streets or avenues in perpetual good repair, at the proper expense of said company.

3. Act of March 26, 1859, Sec. 3, P. L., p. 243.
4. Act of March 26, 1859, Sec. 4, P. L., p. 244.
5. Act of March 26, 1859, Sec. 5, P. L., p. 244.
6. Act of March 26, 1859, Sec. 6, P. L., p. 244.

SEC. 7. That the said company shall make and have a common seal and the same to alter and amend or renew at pleasure, and also to ordain, establish and put in execution such by-laws, ordinances and regulations as shall appear necessary or convenient for the government of said company, and not being contrary to the constitution and laws of the United States or of this commonwealth, and generally to do all and singular the matters and things which to them it shall lawfully appertain to do, for the well being of said company and due ordering and managing of the affairs thereof; and an act, entitled "An Act to incorporate the Central Passenger Railway Company," approved the twenty-first April, A. D. one thousand eight hundred and fifty-eight, and all other laws or parts of laws heretofore enacted, inconsistent with the rights and powers granted by the several sections of this act, are hereby repealed.

SEC. 8. That the said company shall have power to elect or appoint a president and six directors, a majority of whom, with the president, shall be citizens of Philadelphia, and such other officers as may be deemed necessary or expedient; and in every election for officers each share of stock shall entitle the holder thereof to one vote.

SEC. 9. That the said railway company shall have the right to connect with any other passenger railway company, for the purpose of completing a route or making a circuit, upon such terms and conditions as may be agreed upon by such other company or companies and the said the Philadelphia City Passenger Railway Company; and in case the said companies cannot agree, then upon such terms and conditions as may be prescribed by the councils of the city of Philadelphia; and the said the Philadelphia City Passenger Railway Company is hereby authorized to connect their road with that of the West Philadelphia Passenger Railway Company, by a single track on Twenty-second or Twenty-third street.

SEC. 10. That dividends of so much of the profits of said company, as shall appear advisable to the directors, shall be declared in the months of July and January in each and every year, and be paid at the office of the company at any time after the expiration of ten days from the time of declaring the same; but said dividends shall in no case

7. Act of March 26, 1859, Sec. 7, P. L., p. 244.
8. Act of March 26, 1859, Sec. 8, P. L., p. 244.
9. Act of March 26, 1859, Sec. 9, P. L., p. 244.
10. Act of March 26, 1859, Sec. 10, P. L., p. 255.

exceed the amount of the net profits of said company, sc that the capital stock shall never be impaired thereby; and if the said directors shall make any dividend impairing the capital stock of said company, the directors consenting thereto shall be liable, in their individual capacities, to said company for the amount so divided; and each director present when such dividends shall be declared, shall be considered as consenting thereto, unless he or they enter protest upon the minutes of the board, and give public notice of the same; and whenever the dividends shall exceed in amount six per cent. per annum on the capital stock, such excess of dividend over six per cent, thus declared, shall be subject to a tax of six per cent., which tax shall be paid into the treasury of the city of Philadelphia, for the use of said city.

Supplement

To an Act to incorporate the Philadelphia City Passenger Railway Company, passed the twenty-sixth day of March, A. D. one thousand eight hundred and fifty-nine.

SEC. 1. That the provision in the first section of an act regulating railroad companies, approved the nineteenth day of February, A. D. one thousand eight hundred and forty-nine, which requires the commissioners named in any special act incorporating any passenger railroad company to give at least twenty days' notice, in one or more newspapers, of the time and place for opening books for receiving subscriptions to the capital stock of such company, is hereby declared not to extend or apply to the act, entitled "An Act to incorporate the Philadelphia City Passenger Railway Company," passed the twenty-sixth day of March, A. D. one thousand eight hundred and fifty nine, to which this is a supplement; and the commissioners named in the said act, or two-thirds of them, are hereby authorized and empowered to open books for the purpose of making and receiving subscriptions to the capital stock of the said passenger railway company, and to make and receive such subscriptions after giving three or more days' notice, as the said commissioners shall determine, of the time and place of opening such books in at least two daily newspapers in the City of Philadelphia.

11. Act of March 31, 1859, Sec. 1, P. L., p. 325.

SEC. 12. That the said company shall have the exclusive right to use and occupy the streets named in the act to which this is a supplement for railway purposes, and is hereby authorized and directed to commence and lay their said railway upon the said streets, substantially, with the form and gauge of rail, and in the mode and manner of laying the same as are now used by the Frankford and Southwark Passenger Railway Company; and they shall conform in all respects to the grades and regulations of said streets, as they now are, under the directions of the chief engineer of said city. And so much of any law or ordinance as requires the proposed plan, courses, styles of rail, and manner of laying the same, to be approved by the board of surveys and regulations of said city; and all laws conflicting or inconsistent with this supplement be, and are hereby repealed.

An Ordinance

Relating to the Contract for the Construction of a Bridge over the Schuylkill, at Chestnut Street.

Whereas, By an ordinance approved July 3d, 1860, it is provided that the contractor or contractors for the con struction of the bridge, over the Schuylkill at Chestnut street, shall accept first mortgage bonds of the Philadelphia City Passenger Railway Company, not exceeding in amount the sum of one hundred thousand dollars, as so much cash, paid by the City of Philadelphia, on the cost of said work, and a difference of opinion exists between the City Solicitor and the counsel of the said Railway Company concerning the time when the interest on the said bonds shall commence, and it is important that this question should be settled before proceeding to advertise for proposals for building said bridge; therefore,

SEC. 13. That contemporaneously with the execution of the contract by the City of Philadelphia with the contractor for the building of the bridge over the Schuylkill river at Chestnut street, the Philadelphia City Passenger Railway Company shall deposit their first mortgage bonds, to the amount of one hundred thousand dollars, in bonds of five

12. Act of March 31, 1859, Sec. 2, P. L., p. 325.
13. Ordinance March 27, 1861, Sec. 1, p 125

hundred dollars each, with the Treasurer of the City of Philadelphia, to be held by him, in trust, for the purposes hereinafter mentioned.

SEC. 14. That the contract so entered into between the City of Philadelphia and said contractor shall contain a provision that the said Philadelphia City Passenger Railway Company shall, on the fulfilment of his contract and the completion of the said bridge, with the approval and acceptance of the Chief Engineer and Surveyor of the City of Philadelphia, as thereby provided, be paid and delivered to him for and on account of the sum by the said contract provided to be paid. But that the said bonds, so deposited, shall be held as and for the reserved per centage to be detained by the said city, until the full and final completion of the said contract to the satisfaction of the Chief Engineer of the said city, as thereby provided, and to secure the same. And the said contract shall contain a provision, that the said bonds so to be reserved, shall be forfeited to the said city if the said contractor shall not well and faithfully comply with each and all the provisions of said contract.

SEC. 15. That the said bonds, so delivered to the Treasurer of the City of Philadelphia, shall be held by him, in trust, for the said Philadelphia City Passenger Railway Company, and the same shall not be in any wise sold, used, or appropriated for any other purpose whatsoever, until the full and final completion of the said bridge, and shall then only be delivered to the said contractor upon the completion thereof, and contemporaneously with the execution and delivery to the said Philadelphia City Passenger Railway Company of a written contract, which the Mayor of the said city, under the seal thereof, is then, hereby authorized and directed to execute and deliver, covenanting and agreeing, on behalf of said city, that they, the said Philadelphia City Passenger Railway Company, their successors and assigns, shall have the immediate and exclusive right to use the said bridge for passenger railway purposes, in accordance with the charter of said company: *Provided, however*, That said city shall only be liable for damages for any breach of said contract arising from her own act or procurement and not otherwise.

SEC. 16. That the said bonds, so to be deposited, shall

14. Ordinance March 27, 1861, Sec. 2, p. 126.
15. Ordinance March 27, 1861, Sec. 3, p. 126.
16. Ordinance March 27, 1861, Sec. 4, p. 127.

bear an interest at the rate of six per centum per annum, with coupons attached, payable semi-annually on the first day of January and July. But at the time of the delivery of the said bonds to the said contractor as aforesaid, all the coupons which have matured antecedent to the time of such delivery shall be cut therefrom, cancelled and delivered to the said Philadelphia City Passenger Railway Company, and the coupon current at the time of said delivery shall be so altered by the Treasurer of the City of Philadelphia, for the time being, trustee as aforesaid, as to make the interest thereon payable at the then next period of payment, such sum only as shall be the amount of the interest upon said bonds respectively, from the date of such delivery to the said next period of payment then maturing.

SEC. 17. That all ordinances, or parts thereof, and all resolutions altered or supplied herein, be and the same are hereby repealed.

17. Ordinance March 27, 1861, Sec. 5, p. 127.

Richmond and Schuylkill Passenger Railway.

SECT. 1. That Samuel Overn, William Eckfelt, George F. Keyser, Samuel Ogden, Charles S. Wayne, James S. Pringle, George B. Enochs, Townsend Yearsley, Henry Neil, Joseph R. Flanigen, Wm. B. Mann, Thomas Ellis, Byard Robison, Jas. H. Billington, D. D. Jones, George A. Coffey, Stephen P. Hill, Alexander Cummings, Peter C. Ellmaker, Jos. M. Cowell, Edward Gratz, John M. Riley, Edmund Dingee, and Joseph Wood, or a majority of them, are hereby appointed commissioners to open books, receive subscriptions, and organize a company under the name and title of the Richmond and Schuylkill Passenger Railway Company, and as such shall have power to lay out and construct, or cause to be constructed, a railway in the city of Philadelphia, beginning at or near the eastern end of Franklin Avenue, at or near Richmond; thence along the said Franklin avenue and Girard avenue with a double track, until it reaches South College avenue, south of Girard College, thence by single track along said South College avenue until it shall strike Poplar street; thence along Poplar street to the West College avenue, or Twenty-fifth street; thence northwardly along West College avenue to North College avenue; thence eastwardly along North College avenue to Ridge avenue; thence along said Ridge avenue to connect with the double track at Girard avenue; also, to connect said single track at Girard avenue and West College avenue, or Twenty-fifth street, with a double track westwardly along Girard avenue to the Girard avenue bridge, at the river Schuylkill. This company shall, at any future time, have the privilege of crossing the river Schuylkill by the Girard Avenue Bridge, and of extending the said road to Lancaster avenue; and the said Richmond and Schuylkill Railway Company shall have the right to cross at grade and connect with any other road now built, or that may hereafter be built in the City of Philadelphia; and the said Richmond and Schuylkill Railway Company shall have the right to purchase real estate, and to erect thereon such buildings and improvements as may be deemed expedient and necessary for the purposes of said company.

SEC. 2 That the capital stock of the said company shall

1. Act of March 26, 1859, Section 1, P. L., 241.
2. Act of March 26, 1859, Section 2, P. L., 241.

consist of two thousand shares of fifty dollars each, and that the said company may, from time to time, by a vote of the stockholders at a meeting called for that purpose, of which meeting thirty days' notice shall be given in two or more papers in the City of Philadelphia, increase the capital stock to an amount sufficient to carry out the true intent and meaning of this act; and for the purpose of completing and equipping the said railway, the said company shall have the power to raise on bonds any sum of money not exceeding one hundred thousand dollars, at no greater rate of interest than seven per centum per annum; *Provided*, That no bond shall be issued for a less amount than one hundred dollars, nor for fractions of dollars.

SEC. 3. That dividends of so much of the profits of said company as shall appear advisable to the directors shall be declared semi-annually, in the months of January and July, in each and every year, and be paid at the office of said company at any time after ten days from the declaring of the same; but the said dividends shall in no case exceed the amount of the net profits, so that the capital stock shall never be impaired thereby.

SEC. 4. That said company shall have power to elect seven directors, a majority of whom shall be citizens of the city of Philadelphia; and said directors, at their first meeting after their election, shall elect one of their number as president of the said company, and elect or appoint such other officers as may be deemed necessary or expedient. In every election by the stockholders of this railway company, each share of stock shall entitle the holder to one vote.

SEC. 5. That the said company shall make and have a common seal, and the same to alter and renew at pleasure; also, shall ordain, establish, and put in execution such by-laws, ordinances, and regulations as shall appear necessary or convenient for the government of said corporation, and not contrary to the constitution and laws of the United States, or of this Commonwealth.

SEC. 6. That the said company shall be subject to the provisions of all ordinances heretofore, or that may be hereafter passed by the councils of the City of Philadelphia, regulating city passenger railways in said city.

3. Act of March 26, 1859, Section 3, P. L., 242.
4. Act of March 26, 1859, Section 4, P. L., 242.
5. Act of March 26, 1859, Section 5, P. L., 242.
6. Act of March 26, 1859, Section 6, P. L., 242.

A SUPPLEMENT.

To the Act incorporating the Richmond and Schuylkill Railway Company.

SEC. 7. That the par value of the shares of the Richmond and Schuylkill Passenger Railway Company be reduced to twenty dollars per share, and the number of shares shall be and is hereby increased to five thousand shares, of the par value of twenty dollars each, instead of two thousand shares, at fifty dollars as heretofore.

SEC. 8. That it shall be lawful for said railway company to lay a second track on South College avenue, from Corinthian avenue to West College avenue, and lay a return track on Twenty-ninth street, from Girard avenue to Poplar street, and along Poplar street to West College avenue, as aforesaid.

7. Act of April 27, 1861, Section 1, P. L. 1862, p. 567.
8. Act of April 27, 1861, Section 2, P. L. 1862, p. 567.

Ridge Avenue and Manayunk Passenger Railway.

SEC. 1. That John Lambert, Joseph Ripka, Charles T. Jones, James F. Nicholas, Charles E. Graeffe, Jacob Esher, Nathan L. Jones, Daniel Arbuckle, John F. Preston, John Bouker, Doctor William M. Uhler, Robert F. Taylor, Henry Croskey, Joseph A. Clay, John S. Nicholas, Robert Hutchinson, John Anspach, Junior, Samuel Gorgas, H. R. Coggshall, William O Kline, William P. Hacker, Joseph Evans, John Welsh, John Billington, and Frederick Stœver, or a majority of them, are hereby appointed commissioners to open books, receive subscriptions and organize a company under the provisions of the general railroad law of one thousand eight hundred and forty-nine, and the supplements thereto, by the name, style and title of the Ridge Avenue and Manayunk Passenger Railroad Company, and as such shall have power to lay out and construct a railway in the City of Philadelphia, from or near Girard College, by the Ridge Avenue and Manayunk turnpikes or Shur's lane, to Manayunk and Roxborough, with the right to construct a double or single track on said turnpike road, and shall have power to convey passengers over the same; and the said company shall have the right to purchase real estate and to erect thereon such buildings and improvements as may be deemed expedient and necessary for the purposes of said company, and also to purchase the necessary equipments for said railway; and no freight or burden trains or locomotives shall be permitted to pass over the same: *Provided*, That the said company before commencing to build the said road, shall purchase of the said Ridge Turnpike Company and Manayunk Turnpike Company, the right of way over their respective turnpike roads, at a price to be assessed and determined as follows: The said turnpike companies shall together choose one disinterested person as referee, and the said railway company another disinterested person as referee, who shall fix upon the said price for such respective rights of way; and the two thus chosen, in case of difference of opinion, shall choose a third person as umpire, and the price so fixed by the said two referees, or by a majority of the said referees and umpire, in case of dif-

1. Act of March 28, 1859, Sec. 1, P. L., p. 264.

ference of opinion as aforesaid, shall be final, conclusive and binding upon the said turnpike companies and the said railway company; and the said turnpike companies are hereby authorized, directed and empowered to appoint such referee under resolutions of meetings of the respective stockholders, to be convened for such purpose: *And, provided further*, That the said companies respectively are hereby authorized and empowered to such right of way to the said railway company, in fee, before the payment of the said prices respectively; which conveyance and payment of price may be enforced by any court of the City and County of Philadelphia, having the power of a court of equity, upon a bill to be filed for that purpose.

SEC. 2. That the capital stock of said company shall consist of five thousand shares of fifty dollars each: *Provided*, That said company may, from time to time, by a vote of the stockholders, at a meeting convened for that purpose, increase the capital stock as much as may in their opinion be necessary to complete said railway or railways, and to carry out the true intent and meaning of this act: *Provided*, That the whole number of shares shall not exceed ten thousand.

SEC. 3. That dividends of so much of the profits of said company as shall appear advisable to the directors, shall be declared in the months of January and July in each year, and be paid at the office of said company any time after ten days from the time of declaring the same; but said dividends shall at no time exceed the amount of the net profits of said company, so that the capital stock shall never be impaired thereby; and if said directors shall make any dividend impairing the capital stock of said company, the directors consenting thereto shall be liable in their individual capacities to said company for the amount so divided; and each director present when such dividend shall be declared, shall be considered as consenting thereto, unless he or they enter protest upon the minutes of the board and give public notice of the same.

SEC. 4. That the said companies shall make and have a common seal, and the same to alter and renew at pleasure, and also to ordain and put in execution such by-laws, ordinances and regulations, as shall appear necessary or convenient for the government of said corporation, and not being contrary to the constitution and laws of the United States or

2. Act of March 28, 1859, Sec. 2, P. L., p. 265.
3. Act of March 28, 1859, Sec. 3, P. L., p. 265.
4. Act of March 28, 1859, Sec. 4, P. L., p. 266.

of this Commonwealth, and, generally to do all and singular the matters and things which to them it shall lawfully appertain to do for the well being of said corporation and the due ordering and managing of the affairs thereof.

SEC. 5. That the said company shall have power to elect or appoint a president and five directors, a majority of whom, with the president, shall be citizens of Philadelphia, and such other officers as may be deemed necessary or expedient; and in every election for officers each share of stock shall entitle the holder to one vote.

SEC. 6. That the said company shall have power to raise on bonds any sum not exceeding one-half of their capital stock, for the purpose of carrying out the true intent of this act: *Provided*, That no bond shall be issued for a less amount than one hundred dollars.

SEC. 7. That said railway company shall not connect with any railroad other than for passenger purposes, and of the same gauge, under a penalty of the forfeiture of their charter; and the said company shall annually pay into the treasury of the City of Philadelphia, for the use of said city whenever the dividends shall exceed six per centum per annum on the capital stock, the sum of six per centum on the said dividends thus declared: *And provided further*, That the City Councils may, from time to time, by ordinance, establish such regulations in relation to said railway, as may be required for the paving and the laying of gas and water pipes in and along said streets, and to prevent obstructions thereon.

SEC. 8. That said company in constructing said road, shall conform to the grades now established, or hereafter to be by law established, of the several streets and avenues traversed by said road, and keep said roads and avenues in perpetual good repair, at the proper expense of said company; and shall moreover be subject to all ordinances of the City Councils heretofore or hereafter to be passed regulating city passenger railways.

5. Act of March 28, 1859, Sec. 5, P. L., p. 266.
6 Act of March 28, 1859, Sec. 6, P. L., p. 266.
7. Act of March 28, 1859, Sec. 7, P. L., p. 266.
8. Act of March 28, 1859, Sec. 8, P. L., p 266.

Seventeenth and Nineteenth Street Passenger Railway.

SECTION 1. That G. B. Hutchins, J. Bickel, James H, Billington, Bayard Robinson, P. C. Ellmaker, John Welsh. Warwick M. Oglesby, Thomas Ellis Benjamin R. Munson, George F. Gordon, James Harper, Samuel Miller, John M. Pomeroy, J. Alexander Simpson, James Johnson, Charles Vanhorn, Walter Allison, Thomas Fagen, R. P. M'Dowell, Thomas Potter, William Bell, Charles Hatheway, Simon P. Kase, James Bond, Henry Y. Smith, James M. Raybold, Samuel Kilpatrick, and Thomas C. Steel, or any ten of them, are hereby appointed commissioners to open books, receive subscriptions and organize a company by the name, style and title of the Seventeenth and Nineteenth Street Passenger Railway Company of Philadelphia, with power to lay out and construct a railway from or near the intersection of Nineteenth and Master streets; thence south along said Nineteenth street to Federal street, passing around Logan and Rittenhouse Squares, on the west side thereof; thence east along said Federal street to Seventeenth street; thence north along said Seventeenth street to Francis street; along said Francis street to Ridge avenue; thence along said Ridge avenue to said Seventeenth street; thence north along said Seventeenth street to Master street; thence along said Master street to the place of beginning; and also with power to construct a railway along Seventeenth street from Francis street to the Ridge avenue, whenever said Seventeenth street shall be open for public use.

SEC. 2. That the said company shall have the right to purchase such real estate, and erect such suildings and improvements thereon, and purchase such necessary equipments, as horses, cars and other vehicles and appendages for the conveyance of passengers on and over said railway, as may be deemed necessary and convenient for the accommodation and purposes of said company: *Provided*, That no freight or burden trains or locomotives shall be permitted ss over said railway.

1. Act of April 12, 1859, Sec. 1, P. L., 711.
2. Act of April 12, 1859, Sec. 2, P. L., 712.

SEC. 3. That the capital stock of said company shall consist of six thousand shares of fifty dollars each, with the power to increase the same to the number of ten thousand shares, whenever the stockholders, at a meeting convened for that purpose, shall deem the same necessary to complete said railway and to carry out the full and true intent and meaning of this act.

SEC. 4. That said company shall elect or appoint a president and five directors, a majority of whom, with the president, shall be citizens of Philadelphia, and such other officers as may be deemed necessary or expedient; and in every election for officers each share of stock shall entitle the holder to one vote.

SEC. 5. That dividends of so much of the profits of said company as shall appear advisable to the directors, shall be declared semi-annually in each and every year, and be paid at the office of the company any time after ten days from the time of declaring the same; said dividends shall in no case exceed the amount of the net profits of the company, and if the directors shall make any dividend impairing the capital stock, those consenting thereto shall be liable in their individual capacities to said company for the amount so divided; and each director present when such dividend shall be declared, shall be considered as consenting thereto, unless he or they enter his or their written protest on the minutes of the board and give public notice of the same; and the said company shall annually pay into the city treasury, for the use of said city, six per centum upon all dividends that shall exceed six per centum per annum on their capital stock.

SEC. 6. That said company shall have power to raise on their bonds, or other securities, any sum of money not exceeding one-half of the capital stock herein authorized; no bonds shall be issued or obligation incurred, until the whole captial stock of six thousand shares be paid in full, nor shall any bond or certificate of loan be issued for a fractional part of one hundred dollars.

SEC. 7. That before said company shall commence to use the said streets, the consent of the Councils of the City of Philadelphia shall be obtained, and said consent shall be

3. Act of April 12, 1859, Sec. 3, P. L., 712.
4. Act of April 12, 1859, Sec. 4, P. L., 712.
5. Act of April 12, 1859, Sec. 5, P. L., 712.
6. Act of April 12, 1859, Sec. 6, P. L., 712.
7. Act of April 12, 1859, Sec. 7, P. L., 713.

deemed and taken to have been given, if said councils shall not within thirty days after the passage of this act, signify their disapprobation by ordinance duly passed; and said councils may from time to time by ordinance, establish such regulations in regard to said railway as may be required for the purpose of paving, re-paving, grading, culverting and laying gas and water pipes in and along said streets, and to prevent obstructions thereon; and that the said company in constructing said road shall conform to the grades established by councils of the several streets and avenues traversed by said railway, and said company shall keep such streets and avenues in good order and repair at their own proper expense.

Thirteenth and Fifteenth Streets Passenger Railway.

SECTION 1. That John Anspach, Junior, George M. Stroud, John Lambert, Edward Gratz, Morton M'Michael, Henry Haines, Stacy B. Barcroft, Peter C. Ellmaker, Philip R. Freas, Joseph Wood, Thomas S. Cromberger, Alfred C. Harmer, Michael Bouvoir, John Welsh, William Deal, E. C. Kromer, George Williams, Bayard Robinson, Thomas Watson, James Benners, H. W. Fitzgerald, J. M. Bickel, George Magee, George W. Simons, George M. Hill, Samuel Lindsay, John Baird, John P. Verree, Robert Armstrong, Coffin Colket, E. C. Pechin, W. A. Edwards, E. T. Chase, J. M. Riley, Thomas C. Steele, James Harper, David M'Clain, John W. Forney, J. J. M'Elhone, James B. Sheridan, Samuel Williams, Dendy Sharwood, John H. Shryock, H. R. Coggshall, George A. Coffey, William D. Kelley, D. D. Jones, Stephen P. Hill, John Steele and James H. Walton, or a majority of them, are hereby appointed commissioners to open books, receive subscriptions, and organize a company by the name, style and title of the Thirteenth and Fifteenth Streets Passenger Railway Company of the City of Philadelphia, with power to lay out and construct a railway from the intersection of Carpenter and Thirteenth streets; thence north along said Thirteenth street to Columbia avenue; thence west along said Columbia avenue to Fifteenth street; thence south along said Fifteenth street to Carpenter street; thence east along the said Carpenter street to the place of beginning; and with power also to lay out and construct a railway from the intersection of Fifteenth street and Columbia Avenue to Ridge Avenue, and from Ridge avenue along Master street to Fifteenth street, for the purpose of making connection with any company now authorized or that may be hereafter authorized to construct a railway on said Ridge avenue.

SEC. 2. That the said company shall have the right to purchase such real estate and erect such buildings and im

1. Act of April 8, 1859, Sec. 1, P. L. 429.
2. Act of April 8, 1859, Sec. 1, P. L. 429.

provements thereon, and purchase such necessary equipments, as horses, cars and other vehicles and appendages for the conveyance of passengers on and over said railway, as may be deemed necessary and convenient for the accommodation and purposes of said company: *Provided*, That no freight or burden trains or locomotives shall be permitted to pass over said railway.

SEC. 3. That the capital stock of said company shall consist of six thousand shares of fifty dollars each, with the power of increasing the same by a vote of the stockholders, at a meeting convened for that purpose, to such an amount as may be deemed necessary to complete the said railway and carry out the full and true intent and meaning of this act: *Provided*, That in no event shall the capital stock of said company exceed the number of ten thousand shares.

SEC. 4. That dividends of so much of the profits of said company as shall appear advisable to the directors, shall be declared semi-annually in each and every year, and be paid at the office of said company, any time after ten days from the time of declaring the same; but said dividend shall in no case exceed the amount of the net profits of said company, so that the capital stock shall never be impaired thereby; and if said directors shall make any dividend impairing the capital stock of said company, the directors consenting thereto shall be liable in their individual capacities to said company, for the amount so divided; and each director present when such dividend shall be declared, shall be considered as consenting thereto, unless he or they enter his or their written protest upon the minutes of the board, and give public notice of the same.

SEC. 5. That the said company shall make and have a common seal, and the same to alter and renew at pleasure; and also shall have power to ordain, establish, and put in execution, such by-laws, ordinances and regulations as shall appear necessary or convenient for the government of said corporation, and not being contrary to the constitution and laws of the United States, or of this commonwealth; and generally to do all and singular the matters and things which to them shall lawfully appertain, for the well being of said corporation, and the proper order and management of the affairs thereof.

3. Act of April 8, 1859, Sec. 3, P. L. 429.
4. Act of April 8, 1869, Sec. 4, P. L. 430.
5. Act of April 8, 1359, Sec. 5, P. L. 430.

SEC. 6. That said company shall have power to elect or appoint a president and five directors, a majority of whom, with the president, shall be citizens of Philadelphia, and such other officers as may be deemed necessary or expedient, and in every election for officers, each share of stock shall entitle the holder to one vote.

SEC. 7. That said company shall have power to raise on their bonds, or other securities, any sum of money not exceeding one-half of the capital stock thus authorized, for the purpose of carrying out and perfecting the true intent and meaning of this act: *Provided*, That no bonds shall be issued or obligation incurred, until the whole capital stock of six thousand shares be paid in full: *And provided further*, That no bond or certificate of loan, shall be issued for a less sum than one hundred dollars.

SEC. 8. That the said railroad company shall not connect with any railroad other than for passenger purposes, and of the same gauge, under a penalty of a forfeiture of their charter; and the said company shall annually pay into the treasury of the City of Philadelphia, for the use of said city, whenever the dividends shall exceed six per centum per annum on the capital stock, the sum of six per centum on the said dividend thus declared.

SEC. 9. That the councils of the City of Philadelphia may from time to time, by ordinance, establish such regulations in regard to said railway, as may be required for the purposes of paving, re-paving, grading, culverting and laying gas and water pipes in and along said streets, and to prevent obstructions thereon; and that the said company in constructing said road shall conform to the grades established by councils of the several streets and avenues traversed by said railway: *Provided*, That the streets thus occupied by said company, shall be by them kept in good order and repair at their own proper expense.

SEC. 10. That for the purpose of completing their circuit, it shall be lawful for any other passenger railway company, within the City of Philadelphia, using the same motive power as is or may be hereafter used upon the road of the company hereby incorporated, to connect with the road of

6. Act of April 8, 1859, Sec. 6, P. L. 430.
7. Act of April 8, 1859, Sec. 7, P. L 430.
8. Act of April 8, 1859, Sec. 8, P. L. 430.
9. Act of April 8, 1859, Sec. 9, P. L. 430.
10. Act of April 8, 1859, Sec. 10, P. L. 341.

said company, and run their cars upon the same, or any portion thereof, upon terms to be agreed upon by said parties interested; and if the said parties cannot agree, then the District Court of the City of Philadelphia shall, upon petition presented by either party, appoint three persons, who shall fix the amount to be paid to the parties owning said road: *And provided,* That for the purpose of completing their circuit on the route hereby authorized, and on no other route, the said company hereby incorporated shall have the right to run their cars on any other passenger railway now incorporated or that may be hereafter incorporated in said City of Philadelphia, upon such terms as are above provided for in the case of any other passenger railway company using the road of the company hereby incorporated.

Lombard and South Street Passenger Railway.

SECTION 1. That James S. Kerr, Charles A. Rubicam, Edward S. Lawrence, Robert Harmer, Samuel M'Manemy, Joseph W. Souder, Andrew Morrow, John Wilson, William B. Mann, Francis M'Ilwain, and John M'Carty, are hereby appointed commissioners to open books, receive subscriptions, and organize a company, and that they and their associates and successors be and they are hereby constituted a body politic and corporate by the name, style and title of the Lombard and South Street Passenger Railway Company; and as such they shall have power to lay and construct a railway in the City of Philadelphia, and carry passengers along such routes and streets as are hereinafter provided for; and they shall have the right to charge such rate of fare as the directors of said company may from time to time determine upon, and to equip said road, to purchase, hold and convey such real estate, and to erect thereon such buildings and improvements as they may deem necessary for the purposes of said company.

SEC. 2. That the capital stock of said company shall consist of two thousand shares of fifty dollars each, with the privilege of increasing the same to twenty-five hundred shares; said increase, before being made, shall be approved of by the stockholders of said company at a meeting called for that purpose.

SEC. 3. That the said company is hereby authorized to lay a single track of railway, commencing at or near the intersection of Front and South streets, extending west along South street to Chippewa street; thence north along said Chippewa street to Lombard street; thence east along said Lombard to said Front street; thence south along said Front street to the place of beginning; and further, that they shall have the right to make such sidings and turnouts as may be necessary to carry on the business of the company; and if the directors of said company shall deem proper, they shall have the right to lay a double track along Sutherland avenue, commencing at South street, extending to any point at or near the Pennsylvania railroad bridge now in the course of construction. Said company shall have the privilege of laying a single track south-west along

1. Act of May 16, 1861. Sec. 1, P. L. 704.
2. Act of May 16, 1861. Sec. 2, P. L. 704.
3. Act of May 16, 1861. Sec. 3, P. L. 705.

Passyunk road to the banks of the river Schuylkill; thence south along the banks of the river Schuylkill to Beggar's lane; thence east along said lane to Rope Ferry road; thence northwardly along said Rope Ferry road to the said Passyunk road, with the right to lay such sidings on Passyunk road, between South street and said Rope Ferry road, as said company shall determine and deem necessary.

SEC. 4. That whenever a bridge shall be constructed over the river Schuylkill by the City of Philadelphia, at Lombard, South, or any street south of Locust street, or whenever any such bridge over the river Schuylkill, within the limits named, shall come into the possession of the said city, then the said Lombard and South Street Passenger Railway Company shall have the right and privilege to extend their railway, by single or double track, to and over said bridge, upon such terms as may be agreed upon between the said company and the councils of the said city; and further, to continue their railway tracks to and along said Lombard and South streets, on the west side of the said river Schuylkill, in like manner as they are herein authorized on the east side of said river; and further, to lay out a railway on any two streets they may deem advisable, running north and south on the west side of said river, between said Lombard and South streets, for the purpose of making their circuit complete. Whenever the said bridge at South street shall be completed, the Philadelphia and Darby Railroad Company shall have the right to connect with the said Lombard and South street railway, and to use the tracks of the same by running all their cars, which make the full trip to and from Darby, over said tracks, for which use the said Philadelphia and Darby Railroad Company shall pay a fair compensation, to be mutually agreed upon; and in case the said companies cannot agree upon such terms, then the Court of Common Pleas of the City of Philadelphia shall, upon petition presented by either party, appoint three disinterested persons, who shall fix the amount to be paid for the said use of tracks of said Lombard and South Streets Railway Company, and the decision of any two of whom in the premises, when confirmed by the said court, shall be final and conclusive: *Provided*, That the persons so appointed shall be duly sworn or affirmed before entering upon the discharge of their duties; and shall file their report in the prothonotary's office, in said court, within thirty days after their appointment as aforesaid.

4. Act of May 16, 1861. Sec. 4, P. L. 705.

SEC. 5. That the parties hereinbefore named, or a majority of them, may proceed to organize said company and obtain subscriptions to the capital stock thereof and after one thousand shares have been subscribed for, and ten per centum paid thereon, then the subscribers shall proceed to elect a board of five directors who shall serve until the first Tuesday in November following, or until their successors are elected; and the stockholders shall, annually thereafter, on the first Tuesday in November, elect a similar board of five directors, to serve for one year, or until their successors are elected; and if, for any reason, said election shall not be held at the time indicated, then another time shall be appointed by the directors, after public notice of two weeks has been given in one daily newspaper published in the City of Philadelphia; and the directors shall have power to fill all vacancies in their board, whether from death, resignation, or otherwise; but no person shall act as a director who is not a stockholder.

SEC. 6. That the said directors shall have the power to appoint a president, treasurer, and such other officers as they may deem necessary; and in all elections for directors and at other meetings of stockholders, each share shall entitle the holder thereof to one vote; but no stockholder or assignee shall vote upon any share of stock upon which an instalment is due and unpaid.

SEC. 7. That the said company shall have the power to make and have a common seal, and the same to alter and renew at pleasure; and also to establish and execute such by-laws and regulations as appear to be necessary for the government of said corporation, the same not being inconsistent with the Constitution of the United States and of this state; and they shall generally do and perform all and singular the matters and things which to them it shall lawfully appertain to do, for the well being of said corporation and proper management of the affairs thereof.

SEC. 8. That the said company shall have the power to borrow money, in any sum not exceeding in amount one-half of its authorized capital stock, at a rate of interest not exceeding seven per centum per annum; and for the purpose of securing the re-payment of the same, and the interest thereon, to issue bonds; the principal sum shall be made payable at such time as the directors may deem advisable

5. Act of May 16, 1861. Sec. 5, P. L. 706.
6. Act of May 16, 1861. Sec. 6, P. L. 706.
7. Act of May 16, 1861. Sec. 7, P. L. 706.
8. Act of May 16, 1861. Sec. 8, P. L. 706.

and the said bond shall be further secured by a mortgage of and on the said railway so constructed, and the corporate rights and franchises granted by this act: *Provided*, No bonds shall be issued for a sum less than one hundred dollars; and they shall have the right to create a sinking fund for the redemption of said bonds.

SEC. 9. That dividends of so much of the profits of the said company as shall appear desirable to the directors, shall be declared, from time to time, and shall be paid after ten days notice to the stockholders, at the office of the company; but said dividends shall, in no case, exceed the net earnings of the company.

SEC. 10. That the company shall be subject to all the ordinances of the councils of the said city, and shall be subject to pay such taxes as are now imposed by the said councils, not exceeding, in rate or amount, that paid by any other passenger railway company in the said city; and further, shall be subject to all the provisions of an act regulating railroad companies, approved nineteenth day of February, A. D. one thousand eight hundred and forty-nine, so 'ar as the same are not altered and supplied by this act.

Supplement.

To an act, entitled "An Act to incorporate the Lombard and South Street Passenger Railway Company."

SECTION 1. That the Lombard and South Street Passenger Railway Company shall have authority to increase the number of shares of their capital stock to ten thousand, and to reduce the par value of such shares to twenty-five dollars each.

SEC. 2. That the said company shall have authority to extend their railway, either by a double or a single track, with sidlings, from the intersection of Front and Lombard streets, along said Front street to Dock street, and along said Dock street to Delaware avenue.

SEC. 3. That the said railway company are hereby authorized and empowered to construct, and lay the said railway, without obtaining the consent of the city councils of said city thereto, anything in the act to which this is a supplement to the contrary thereto notwithstanding.

9. Act of May 16, 1861. Sec. 9, P. L. 706.
10. Act of May 16, 1861. Sec. 10, P. L. 707.
1. Act of April 14, 1863, Sec. 1, P. L. 353.
2. Act of April 14, 1863, Sec. 2, P. L. 353.
3. Act of April 14, 1863, Sec. 3, P. L. 353.

An Ordinance.

Relating to the Lombard and South Street Passenger Railway Company.

SEC. 1. The Select and Common Councils of the City of Philadelphia do ordain, That the consent of the said Councils is hereby given to the Lombard and South Street Passenger Railway Company to lay a track across Naudain street, west of Twenty-fifth street, at right angles with said street, so as to connect their real estate on the north and south side of said Naudain street

4. An Ordinance, June 15, 1863, Sec. 1, page 181.

Navy Yard, Broad St. and Fairmount Railway.

SECTION 1. That George H. Thomson, Robert Calcleugh, M. E. Rogers, Allen Robinett, Samuel S. Moon, Watson Malone, Jackson M'Abee, Henry W. Andrews, William T. Morrison, Robert O. Lowry, John A. Clark, Samuel Simes, Samuel Williams, and their associates and successors, be and they are hereby constituted a body politic and corporate, by the name, style and title of the Navy Yard, Broad Street and Fairmount Railway Company, and as such they shall have the right to lay out and construct a railway over the same, along such routes and streets as are hereafter provided for, to equip said road, and to purchase, hold and convey such real estate, and to erect thereon such buildings and improvements as they may deem necessary for the purposes of said corporation.

SEC. 2. That the capital stock of said company shall consist of ten thousand shares of fifty dollars each.

SEC. 3. That the said company are hereby authorized to lay out and construct, in such manner as railways are now constructed in the city of Philadelphia, a single or double track, commencing with a single track at or near the intersection of Broad street and Federal street, extending east along Federal street to Front street; thence south along Front street to Wharton street; thence west along Wharton street to Broad street; thence north with a double track along Broad street to Spring Garden street; thence west with a double track along Spring Garden street to Fairmount; and they shall have the right to connect their single track with their double track at Broad and Wharton streets, at Broad and Federal streets, and to make such turn-outs, connections and sidelings as may be necessary for the prosecution of the business of the company; and they shall have the right to cross at grade any other railroad, and by agreement to connect with and run over any other railroad now constructed, or which may hereafter be constructed in the city of Philadelphia; and further, shall have the right to extend their railway by single or double track, from Broad and Wharton streets southwardly, and from Broad and Spring Garden streets northwardly, at such times as the company may determine that the convenience of the

1. An Act of May 16, 1861. Sec. 1, P. L. 691.
2. An Act of May 16, 1861. Sec. 2, P. L. 692.
3. An Act of May 16, 1861. Sec. 3, P. L. 692.

public requires such extension or extensions; and they shall enjoy all and singular the same privileges that are now or hereafter may be extended to any other railway company.

SEC. 4. That the parties hereinbefore named, or a majority of them, may proceed to organize said company and obtain subscriptions to the capital stock thereof; and after five thousand shares have been subscribed for, and ten per cent. paid on said subscriptions, then the subscribers shall proceed to elect a board of five directors, who shall serve until the first Tuesday in November following, and until their successors are elected; and the stockholders shall annually thereafter, on the first Tuesday in November, elect a similar board of five directors, to serve for one year and until their successors are elected; and if for any reason the said election shall not be held at the time appointed, then another time shall be appointed by the directors, after public notice of two weeks, in two daily newspapers, has been given; and said directors shall have power to fill all vacancies which may occur in the Board, from death, resignation or otherwise; but no person shall act as a director, who is not a stockholder in said company.

SEC. 5. That the said directors shall have the power to appoint a president, treasurer, and such other officers as they may deem necessary and expedient; and in all elections for directors, and at all meetings of stockholders, each share represented, either in person by the owner, or by proxy, shall entitle the holder to one vote; but no stockholder or assignee shall vote upon any share of stock on which an instalment is due and unpaid.

SEC. 6. That the directors of said company shall have the power to make and have a common seal, and the same to alter and renew at pleasure, and also to establish such by-laws and regulations as may seem to them necessary to the good government of said corporation, the same not being inconsistent with the constitution and laws of the United States, or of this State; and they shall generally do and perform all and singular the matters and things which to them it shall lawfully appertain to do for the well-being of the said corporation and the proper management of the affairs thereof.

SEC. 7. That the said company shall have the power to borrow money in any sum not exceeding in amount one-

4. An Act of May 16, 1161. Sec. 4, P. L. 692.
5. An Act of May 16, 1861. Sec. 5, P. L. 693.
6. An Act of May 16, 1861. Sec. 6, P. L. 693.
7. An Act of May 16, 1861. Sec. 7, P. L. 693.

half of its authorized capital stock, at a rate of interest not exceeding seven per centum per annum, and for the purpose of securing repayment of the same, and the interest thereon, to issue bonds; and the said bonds shall be further secured by a mortgage of and on said railway so constructed or to be constructed, and the corporate rights and franchises granted by this act; the principal sum so borrowed, shall be made payable at such time as the directors may deem advisable; but no bond shall be issued for a sum less than one hundred dollars.

SEC. 8. That dividends of so much of the profits of the said company as shall appear desirable to the directors, shall be declared from time to time, and shall be paid after ten days notice, to the stockholders, at the office of the company; but said dividends shall in no case exceed the net profits of the company earned at the time of the declaring of said dividend.

SEC. 9. That when the Pennsylvania railroad company shall complete their connection with the Philadelphia, Wilmington and Baltimore railroad, and the councils of the city of Philadelphia shall direct the removal of the rails now laid in Broad street, from South street to Chestnut street, the Navy Yard, Broad street and Fairmount railway company shall, with the appurtenances and materials thus removed, be required to place said Broad street from South to Chestnut street, in such condition, as far as the paving, curbing and macadamizing is concerned, as will accord with any plan which may be adopted for the improvement of said street, by the councils of said city.

SEC. 10. That the said company shall be compelled to keep in constant repair that portion of the street which they use and occupy, and be subject to such ordinances of councils as relate thereto, not inconsistent with this act, and shall pay such taxes and tolls as are now or may hereafter be imposed by the councils of the said city, not exceeding in rate or amount that paid by any other railway company in the said city; and further, they shall be subject to all the provisions and restrictions of an act regulating railroad companies, approved the nineteenth day of February, Anno Domini one thousand eight hundred and forty-nine, in so far as the same is not altered, interfered with, or supplied by this act.

8. An Act of May 16, 1861. Sec. 8, P. L. 693.
9. An Act of May 16, 1861. Sec. 9, P. L. 693.
10. An Act of May 16, 1861. Sec. 10, P. L. 693.

Philadelphia and Olney Railroad.

SECTION 1. That Samuel C. Ford, John P. Verree, John Landall, John Turner, Charles Robbins, John Roberts, Joseph T. Ford, Thomas Drake, Charles Camblos, Thomas E. Potter, James Lynd, Henry Simons, Isaac Norris, Samuel Wright, Joshua Lippincott, George P. Evans, James N. Dickson, John Houghton, M. D., are hereby appointed commissioners to open books, sell stock, and organize a corporation, to be called the Philadelphia and Olney Railroad Company, with all the rights and privileges, and subject to all the conditions and restrictions conferred or imposed by an act to regulate railroad companies, approved the nineteenth day of February, Anno Domini one thousand eight hundred and forty-nine, and the supplements thereto, and with all the rights and privileges enjoyed by any railroad now incorporated, or which may hereafter be incorporated, located in the city of Philadelphia: *Provided,* That this company shall not alter the grade of any road or street over which the same shall be constructed, unless authorized to do so by the board of surveys of the city of Philadelphia.

SECT. 2. That the said Philadelphia and Olney Railroad Company are hereby authorized and empowered to construct a railway, of the same gauge as the present passenger railways in the city of Philadelphia, of one or more tracks, from Lehigh avenue to the village of Olney, in the Twenty-second Ward of the city of Philadelphia, with the right to extend the same to the village of Fox-chase, in the Twenty-third Ward of said city, either on, over and upon the line of the Kensington and Oxford Turnpike Road, or any part thereof, or by, along or over any route between said road and Seventh street, and to connect their said railroad either with the Second and Third Street Railroad, or the Frankford and Southwark City Passenger Railroad, and for that purpose to use any street or streets of the said city of Philadelphia, in manner and form as provided by the fourth section of an act entitled "An Act to incorporate the Second and Third Street Passenger Railway Company," approved the tenth day of April, Anno Domini one thousand eight hundred and fifty-eight: *Provided, however,* That

1. Act of April 1, 1859, Sec. 1, P. L.
2. Act of April 1, 1859, Sec. 2, P. L.

before the said railroad company shall take possession of, or occupy the whole or any portion of the said turnpike road, the consent of a majority of the stockholders thereof shall be first had and obtained thereto.

SECT. 3. That the capital stock of said company shall consist of two thousand shares, of the par value of twenty-five dollars each: *Provided,* That the said company may from time to time, by a vote of the stockholders at any general or special meeting, increase the capital stock to an amount not exceeding four thousand shares, if it should be deemed necessary for the purpose of completing and equipping the said railroad; and the said company shall have the power to borrow any sum of money, not exceeding in amount the one-half of their capital stock, at a rate of interest not exceeding seven per centum per annum, and to secure the payment of the same by the execution of a bond and mortgage of the said railroad, together with the corporate rights and franchises granted by this act, and to annex to the said bond and mortgage, the privilege of converting the same into the capital stock of said company, at par, at the option of the holders, if they shall signify their election so to do at any time previous to one year before its maturity, and to issue certificates of loan of a denomination not less than one hundred dollars, secured by said bond and mortgage.

SECT. 4. That when the said railroad, or any part or parts thereof, shall have been constructed and completed, the said company shall be authorized to charge and receive as tolls for the carriage of passengers, not more than ten cents for each passenger conveyed three miles, or any distance under three miles, and for any distance beyond three miles, at the rate of not more than three cents per mile, all fractional parts of a mile being considered and charged as one mile.

A Supplement

To an Act entitled " An Act to incorporate the Philadelphia and Olney Railroad Company."

SECT. 5. That the said the Philadelphia and Olney Railroad Company is hereby authorized to commence the con-

3. Act of April 1, 1859, Sec. 3, P. L.
4. Act of April 1, 1859, Sec. 4, P. L.
5. Act of May 16, 1861, Sec. 1, P. L. 696.

struction of their road at Sixth and Diamond streets, and from time to time, as their means will permit, to construct and use the same northward of said point, with the privilege of ten years from the passage of this Act to complete their said railroad northward and southward to the respective termini mentioned in the Act to which this is a Supplement: *Provided,* That until Fifth street is opened and in public use, from Nicetown lane to Wyoming avenue, the said company may occupy and use said Nicetown lane and Woodpecker lane to the intersection of the latter with Second street: *And provided further,* That nothing herein contained shall be so construed as to authorize the said company to exceed the limits of the route allowed them by the Act to which this act is a supplement.

A Supplement

To an Act to incorporate the Philadelphia and Olney Railroad Company.

Sec. 6. That the said, the Philadelphia and Olney Railroad Company, is hereby authorized to commence the construction of their road at any time within two years from the passage of this act, and finish and use the same, and exercise and enjoy their corporate franchises as fully as if the said road had been commenced within the time limited by the nineteenth section of the Act of Assembly, approved the nineteenth day of February, in the year of our Lord one thousand eight hundred and forty-nine.

6. Act of March 30, 1864, Sec. 1, P. L. 141.

Frankford and Philadelphia Railway Company of the City of Philadelphia.

SECTION 1. That Thomas Wriggins, John G. Whelan John E. Wootten, George W. Geisse, Francis S. Buckius Edwin T. Duffield, Samuel D. Harper, Jonathan Brooke Samuel D. Sidebotham, Hiram Stanhope, James Burns Samuel Wakeling, Ephraim F. Leake, William J. Fries, Thomas S. Foulkrod, William Baldwin, Rudolph Adams, William P. Cooper, Joseph H. Comly, Charles Williams and Simon R. Snyder, or a majority, or any five of them, be and they are hereby constituted and appointed commissioners to open books, receive subscriptions and organize a company, by the name, style and title of the Frankford and Philadelphia Passenger Railway Company of the City of Philadelphia, with power and authority to lay out and construct a railroad, with a single or double track, upon such portions of the hereinafter described route as the said company shall deem proper; beginning at the terminus of the Second and Third streets railway, at or near Frankford road and Lehigh avenue, in the Nineteenth Ward of the City of Philadelphia; thence extending northwardly along said Frankford road and the Frankford and Bristol turnpike road to Mill street, in the late borough of Frankford; thence eastwardly along said Mill street to Paul street; thence northwardly along said Paul street to Frankford street, or the Frankford and Bristol turnpike road; thence northwardly along said Frankford street, or the Frankford and Bristol turnpike road, to Harrison street; and thence southwardly down the said Frankford street and the Frankford and Bristol turnpike road, through the late borough of Frankford to the place of beginning: *Provided*, That horse locomotion shall be used exclusively for the purpose of transporting cars over said road.

SEC. 2. That the capital stock of the said company shall consist of one thousand shares, of fifty dollars each, providing that the said company may from time to time, by a vote of the stockholders, at a meeting called for that purpose, increase the capital stock, if it should be deemed

1. Act of April 10, 1862, Sec. 1, P. L., 393.
2. Act of April 10, 1862, Sec. 2, P L., 393.

necessary, to an amount not exceeding two thousand shares, for the purpose of completing, equipping and extending said railroad; the said company shall have the power of borrowing any sum of money, not exceeding in amount one half of their capital stock, at a rate of interest, not exceeding seven per centum per annum, and to secure the payment of the same by the issue of the bonds and mortgages of the said railroad, together with the corporate rights and franchises granted by this act, and to annex to the said bonds and mortgages the privilege of converting the same into the capital stock of the said company, at par, at the option of the holders, if they shall signify their election one year before their maturity: *Provided,* That the said company shall issue no certificate of loan of a less denomination than one hundred dollars.

SEC. 3. That whenever the said company shall declare dividends exceeding the rate of six per centum per annum, in addition to the tax imposed upon them by the general laws of their capital stock, they shall pay into the treasury of the City of Philadelphia, for the use of the said city, a tax of six per centum of the excess of dividends above the said rate of six per centum.

SEC. 4. That the said company, in constructing said railroad, shall conform to the grades, established by Councils, of the several streets and avenues traversed by said railroad, and to keep the same in good repair, at the proper expense of the said company, excepting such portions of the Frankford and Bristol turnpike road as are not now graded; and that the said railroad company shall have the privilege of laying their tracks in the present bed of the said turnpike road, until such time as the same shall be graded and paved by the said City of Philadelphia; and as to damages which may be claimed by the said Frankford and Bristol turnpike company, for or by reason of laying the said railroad along the said turnpike road, if the said companies cannot agree upon satisfactory terms and conditions, such damages shall be assessed by three disinterested persons, neither of whom shall be stockholders in either of the said companies, and who shall be appointed by the Court of Common Pleas of the City of Philadelphia for that purpose, subject to an appeal by either party to said Court.

3. Act of April 10, 1862, Sec. 3, P. L., 394.
4. Act of April 10, 1862, Sec. 4, P. L., 394.

SEC. 5. That the said railway company shall have the right to cross, at grade, any railroad that is now, or that hereafter may be built within the limits of the City of Philadelphia, and to connect with any passenger railway within the said city.

SEC. 6. That the said railway, on the route described, shall be subject to the use of any part or parts thereof by any passenger railway company, for the purpose of completing a route or circuit, upon such conditions as may be agreed upon by such other railway company and the said Frankford and Philadelphia Passenger Railroad Company; and the said Frankford and Philadelphia Passenger Railway Company shall have the right and privilege of using the tracks of any railway in the City of Philadelphia, for the purpose of completing a route or circuit upon such terms and conditions as may be agreed upon by the said Frankford and Philadelphia Railroad Company and such other railway companies; and in case said companies cannot agree upon such terms and conditions as aforesaid, then upon the payment of one half the value of such portions as may be used by them, and one half the expense of keeping the same in repair, the same to be assessed by three disinterested persons, neither of whom shall be stockholders in either of the said companies, and who shall be appointed by the Court of Common Pleas of the City of Philadelphia, for that purpose, subject to an appeal by either party to said Court.

SEC. 7. That the officers of the said company shall consist of a president and eight directors, to be elected annually, on the first Monday of January, to serve for a term of one year, in accordance with the provisions of the general railroad laws.

5. Act of April 10, 1862, Sec. 5, P. L., 394.
6. Act of April 10, 1862, Sec. 6, P. L., 394.
7. Act of April 10, 1862, Sec. 7, P. L., 395.

Frankford and Holmesburg Railroad.

SECTION 1. That George Clark, John B. William, William E. Evans, William Raphael, John Clark, Maxwell Rowland, Benjamin F. Crispin, Prestley Blackiston, Andreas Hartel, George S. Bethell, Lewis Shallcross, Ephraim Leak, George J. Hoff, J. T. Way, Thomas Shallcross, John Soley, Robert Patterson, Samuel C. Willet, John Farnham, Richard Garside, Nathan Hillis, James K. Davis, or any five of them, be and they are hereby appointed commissioners, to open books, receive subscriptions and organize a company by the name, style and title of the Frankford and Holmesburg Railroad Company, with all the powers, and subject to all the provisions and restrictions prescribed by an act, entitled "An Act regulating railroad companies," approved February nineteenth, Anno Domini one thousand eight hundred and forty-nine.

SEC. 2. That the capital stock of said company shall consist of one thousand shares, of fifty dollars each: *Provided*, That said company may, from time to time, by vote of the stockholders, at a meeting called for that purpose, increase the capital stock of said company, if it should be deemed necessary so to do, to an amount not exceeding one thousand shares.

SEC. 3. That the said company shall have the right to build and construct a railroad, from the village of Holmesburg, in the Twenty-third ward, of the city of Philadelphia, to the late borough of Frankford, within said ward, and at such point as may be within, or near to, said borough of Frankford, as may connect with any railroad built and constructed, or to be built and constructed, by the Frankford and Philadelphia Railway Company, of the City of Philadelphia, or with any other railroad, built and constructed, or to be built and constructed by any other railroad company located, or to be located, within the limits of said borough of Frankford, or in the vicinity thereof: *Provided*, That the officers and directors of any of said railroad companies, or their agents, duly authorized, can and do agree with the said, the Frankford and Holmesburg Railroad

1. Act of July 18, 1863, Sec. 1, P. L. 1115.
2. Act of July 18, 1863, Sec. 2, P. L. 1115.
. Act of July 18, 1863, Sec. 3, P . L. 1115.

Company, so to do, if such connection be considered to the greater benefit of said company, and of those using said railroad.

SEC. 4. That the said Frankford and Homlesburg Railroad company, if deemed expedient, may extend said railroad from Holmesburg to Bustleton, within said Twenty-third ward, of the City of Philadelphia.

SEC. 5. That said company shall, within three years from the passage of this act, commence the construction of said railroad; and unless the same shall be completed, within five years thereafter, this act shall be null and void.

SEC. 6. That the said Frankford and Holmesburg Railroad Company shall have power to borrow money, in any sum, or sums, not exceeding fifty thousand dollars, at a rate of interest, not exceeding seven per centum per annum, and for the purpose of securing the repayment of the same, and the interest thereon, to issue bonds; the principal sum shall be made payable at such time as the directors may deem advisable, and the said bonds shall be further secured by a mortgage of, and on, the said railroad, and the corporate rights, and franchises, granted by the act to which this is a supplement: *Provided*, That no bonds shall be issued for a sum less than fifty dollars, and that the said company shall have the right to create a sinking fund for the redemption of said bonds.

SEC. 7. That said railroad company shall have the right to extend their road, to connect with any city passenger railroad, leading from the City of Philadelphia, in the direction of Holmesburg.

4. Act of July 18, 1863, Sec. 4, P. L. 1115.
5. Act of July 18, 1863, Sec. 5, P. L. 1115.
6. Act of March 30, 1864, Sec. 1. P. L. 124.
7. Act of March 30, 1864, Sec. 2, P. L. 124.

Union Passenger Railway.

SECTION 1. That Robert P. King, William Elliott, Charles Welsh, William H. Kemble, Willott H. Ridgeway, William J. Pollock, John Miller, John. M. Melloy, and their associates, and successors, be and they are hereby constituted a body politic, and corporate, by the name, style, and title of the Union Passenger Railway Company of Philadelphia; and as such, they they shall have the right to lay out and construct, or cause to be laid out, and constructed, a railway, in the City of Philadelphia, along such routes, and streets, as are hereinafter provided for, namely: beginning at, or near, the intersection of Wharton and Front Streets; thence, with a single track, and such turn-outs as may be necessary, along Wharton to Ninth street; thence along Ninth street to Spring Garden street: thence along Spring Garden street to Seventh street; thence along Seventh street to Master street; thence along Master street fo Frankford road; thence along Frankford road to Belgrade street; thence along Belgrade street to Marlborough street; thence along Marlborough street to Thompson street; thence along Thompson street to York street; thence along York street to Edgmont street; thence along Edgmont street to Lehigh avenue; thence along Lehigh avenue to Memphis street; thence along Memphis street to York street; thence along York street to Emerald street; thence along Emerald street to Susquehanna avenue; thence along Susquehanna avenue to Fourth street; thence along Fourth street to Oxford street, with the privilege of using Cadwalader street, until Fourth street shall be opened to Oxford street; thence along Oxford street to Franklin street; thence along Franklin street to Race street; thence along Race street to Seventh street; thence along Seventh street to Walnut street; thence along Walnut street, and around Washington square, along the westwardly and southwardly side thereof, to Seventh street; thence along Seventh street to Federal street; thence along Federal Street to Front street; thence along Front street to the place of beginning; and the said company shall have the right to use York street from Thompson street to Memphis street, for the purpose of making a circuit; and, also, the right to use Seventh street from

1. Act of April 8, 1864, Sec. 1, P. L. 297.

Master street to Oxford street, for the purpose of making a circuit; and, also, the right of making a circuit on Locust street, from Washington square to Ninth street; and the said company shall have power, and authority, to extend their road, by single track, from Seventh street along Spring Garden street to Twenty-third street; thence along Twenty-third street to Parrish street; thence along Parrish street to Twenty-fourth street; thence along Twenty-fourth street to Poplar street; thence along Poplar street to Twenty-ninth street; thence along Twenty-ninth street and Pennsylvania avenue, to Brown street; thence along Brown street to Twenty-third street; thence along Twenty-third street to Wallace street; thence along Wallace street to Seventh street, with the right to use Brown Street, west of Twenty-third street, to Pennsylvania avenue, with a double track, or such sidelings as may be necessary, and, also, with the right, and privilege, to use Poplar street, with a single track, from Seventh street to Twenty-fourth street; and the said company shall have the right, in order to complete their route, and to make such circuits as they may deem necessary, to use, in lieu of Wharton and Federal streets, any other two streets south of Catharine street; and the said company shall first lay out, and construct, that part of their road extending from Wharton street to Oxford street, and afterwards, from time to time, as they may deem advantageous to the public, shall lay out, and complete, their road, on the routes and streets herein designated.

SEC. 2. The capital stock of said company shall consist of twenty thousand shares, of fifty dollars each.

SEC. 3. The said company shall have power, and authority to borrow money in any sum or sums, not exceeding in amount one-half of the par value of the capital stock, at a rate of interest, not exceeding seven per centum per annum; and to secure the re-payment of the same, and the interest thereon, to give bonds, secured by a mortgage of, and on the said railway, and the corporate rights and franchises, guarantied by this act; which principal moneys shall be payable, at such dates, and times, as the board of directors may deem advisable.

SEC. 4. The said company shall have the right to purchase such real estate, and erect, or cause to be erected,

2. Act of April 8, 1864, Sec. 2, P. L. 297.
3. Act of April 8, 1864, Sec. 3, P. L. 297.
4. Act of April 8, 1864, Sec. 4, P. L. 297.

such buildings, and improvements, thereon, from time to time, and use, and hold, the same; and further, to have the right to purchase all necessary equipments, such as horses, cars, and other vehicles, and all needful appendages, for the conveyance of passengers on and over said railway, as may be deemed necessary, or convenient, for the accommodation, and purposes, of said company: *Provided*, That said railway shall conform, in gauge, to the passenger railways now laid in the City of Philadelphia; and no freight, or burthen trains, or locomotives, shall be permitted to pass over said railway.

SEC. 5. That dividends, of so much of the profits of said company, as shall appear to be advisable to the directors, shall be declared, semi-annually, in each and every year, and be paid at the office of the said company, at any time after ten days, after declaring the same; but said dividends shall, in no case, exceed the amount of the net profits of said company, so that the capital stock, thereof, shall at no time be impaired thereby; and if said directors shall make, and declare, any dividend, impairing the capital stock of said company, the directors, consenting thereto, shall be liable, in their individual capacities, to said company, for the amount so divided; and each director present, when such dividend shall be declared, shall be considered as consenting thereto, unless he or they shall, at the time thereof, enter his or their written protest against the same, and shall cause the said protest to be entered upon the minutes of the board, and give public notice of the same.

SEC. 6. The said company shall make, have, and use, a common seal, and alter and renew the same at pleasure; and, also, shall have the power to ordain, establish, and put in execution, such by-laws, ordinances, and regulations as shall appear necessary or convenient for the government of the said corporation, and not being contrary to the constitution of the United States, or of this commonwealth; and generally to do all and singular the matters and things which to them shall lawfully appertain, for the well-being of said corporation, and the proper order and management thereof.

SEC. 7. That the persons herein named, or a majority of them, may proceed to organize said company, and obtain

5. Act of April 8, 1864, Sec. 5, P. L. 297.
6. Act of April 8, 1864, Sec. 6, P. L. 297.
7. Act of April 8, 1864, Sec. 7, P. L. 297.

subscriptions to the capital stock thereof; and said company shall have power to elect a president, vice president, and five directors, a majority of whom shall be citizens of Philadelphia, and, also, such other officers as may be deemed expedient; and at all elections, each share of stock represented, either in person, or by proxy, shall entitle the holder to one vote.

SEC. 8. The said company shall be subject to all the provisions and restrictions of an act regulating railroad companies, approved the nineteenth day of February, one thousand eight hundred and forty-nine, and the several supplements thereto, so far as the same are not altered or supplied by this act: *Provided*, That the provision in the first section of said act, which requires the commissioners, named in any special act, incorporating any passenger railroad company, to give public notice of the time, and place, for opening books for receiving subscriptions to the capital stock of such company, is hereby declared not to extend, or apply to this act, or to the commissioners herein named; and the said company, in constructing their road, shall conform to the surveys, and grades, now established, or hereafter to be established, by law, of the several streets, or avenues, traversed by said road; and shall, at the cost and expense of said company, lay flag-stones or crossings along the line of the paved streets, upon which the rails are laid, at intervals, not exceeding two hundred and fifty feet, and shall be at the entire cost and expense of paving, repairing, and re-paving, that may be necessary, upon any street where the track of said company may be laid; and it shall not be lawful for the said company to run their cars at a greater rate of speed than six miles an hour; and the said company is hereby authorized and empowered to construct and lay the said railway, without obtaining the consent of the City Councils, of the City of Philadelphia; but whenever the said railway shall be laid and used by running passenger cars thereon, the said company shall be subject to the ordinances of the City of Philadelphia, regulating the running of passenger railway cars.

SEC. 9. The said company shall have the right to cross at grade any railroad that is now or may hereafter be built, within the limits of the City of Philadelphia; and, also, to connect their railway with that of any other pas-

8. Act of April 8, 1864, Sec. 8, P. L. 297.
9. Act of April 8, 1864, Sec. 9, P. L. 297.

senger railway company, for the purpose of completing a route, or making a circuit, and upon such terms, and conditions, as may be agreed upon by such other company or companies and the said Union Passenger Railway Company of Philadelphia, and in case said railway companies cannot agree thereupon, such terms as the District Court of Philadelphia may prescribe and enjoin.

SEC. 10. That the said company shall pay, annually, into the treasury of the City of Philadelphia, for the use of said city, whenever the dividends declared by said company, shall exceed six per cent. per annum, on the par value of the capital stock thereof, a tax of six per centum, on such excess over six per centum, on the par value thus declared; and the said company shall, also, pay such license for each car run by said company, as is now paid by other passenger railway companies, in the City of Philadelphia.

10. Act of April 8, 1864, Sec. 10, P. L. 297.

SESSION OF 1865.

A Supplement

To an act to incorporate the Frankford and Philadelphia Passenger Railway Company, of the city of Philadelphia, approved April tenth, Anno Domini one thousand eight hundred and sixty-two, authorizing an extension of the route, increase of capital, and agreements to be made with other companies.

Extension of road authorized.

SEC. 1. That the said Frankford and Philadelphia Passenger Railway Company be and they are hereby authorized and empowered to extend and continue their railway, with single, or double, track, upon such portions of the hereinafter described route, and lateral roads and turn-outs, as said company shall deem proper, beginning at, or near, the terminus of said railway, on the Frankford road; thence extending along Lehigh avenue to Sepviva street; thence southwardly, along Sepviva street to Vienna street; thence along Vienna street and the Frankford road, to Thomson street; thence along Thomson street to Front street; thence along Front street (and make a connection with the Union Passenger railway: *Provided*, That no connection be made, south of Master street, without their consent thereto;) thence north along Front street to Coral street, and along Coral street to the place of beginning; along Huntingdon street, from Sepviva street to Coral street, and along Amber street, from Huntingdon street to Lehigh avenue; also, to continue their railway from Harrison street to Cedar Hill cemetery; thence along Bridge to Bridesburg; thence returning along Bridge street to Tacony road; thence along Tacony road, to the Frankford road, and along Orthodox street, to Frankford street, and to make a connection with the depot, or station of the Philadelphia and Trenton Railroad Company, should they, at any time hereafter remove their passenger depot north of the present location: *Provided*, That the consent of the said Philadelphia and Trenton Railroad Company, to have such aforesaid connection made, shall have been first had and obtained; and the said company are further authorized and empowered to construct such lateral railways and turn-outs, into and

May connect with the Philadelphia and Trenton railroad depot.

Proviso.

Authorized to construct lateral railways and turn-outs.

along any other street or streets, on either side of the line of said railways, at such places as are now occupied by other railways, and at such other places as said company shall deem necessary, and return again to the main line, in order to complete the circuit, or route of said company: *Provided*,

Proviso That in no case shall any lateral railway be constructed, by said company, at a greater distance than two squares, or streets, east or west, of the main line of

Proviso. said railway: *And Provided also*, That in no case shall any lateral railway, or turnout, be made or constructed, in, or upon, any depot, station, land or other property, belonging to the Philadelphia and Trenton Railroad Company, without the consent of the said Philadelphia

Capital stock may be increased and Trenton Railroad Company thereto, being first had and obtained; and for the purpose of extending, completing and equipping said railway, said company shall have power to increase their capital stock to an amount not exceeding six thousand shares, of

Subject to. fifty dollars each, including the previous capital of said company, subject to all the restrictions and provisions and with all the powers, rights, privileges and immunities, contained in the original act of incorporation of said

Proviso. company: *Provided further*, That said company may, from time to time, by a vote of the stockholders, at a meeting called for that purpose, increase their capital stock as much as, in their opinion, shall be necessary to complete said railway, and carry out the true intent and meaning of this act; that in all cases where a connection is authorized to be made, with any other railway, the right to construct the connecting link, and complete the circuit along any street or streets, is hereby granted.

Certain contracts may be made with other companies, &c. SEC. 2. That the said Frankford and Philadelphia Passenger Railway Company, and the President, Managers and Company of the Frankford and Bristol Turnpike Road, are hereby respectfully authorized to make and enter into any contracts, or agreements, they may think proper and expedient, with each other, in relation to the construction and maintenance of a passenger railway, on the bed of the road of said turnpike company, or any part, or parts, thereof; and all covenants, contracts, or agreements, made by and between either of said companies, with any other incorporated company, may be assigned, or transferred, by either of said corporations, to the other, and held and enjoyed by them, or either of them, to all intents and purposes, as if they, the holders thereof, had been one of the original contracting parties; that if the said railway company shall, at any time, agree with the Frankford and Holmesburg Railroad Company, or with any other steam railroad company, to purchase, lease, or merge, their road, with the said Frankford and Philadelphia Passenger Railway, then, and in that case, the passenger railway company are hereby authorized and empowered to continue their railway as far as shall be necessary, along the said Frankford and Bristol turnpike road, or any other street, or streets, that said company shall deem necessary and convenient, in order to connect the road, thus purchased, leased or merged, with the said passenger railway; anything in this act, or the act to which this is a supplement, to the contrary thereto notwithstanding: *Provided*, That steam shall not be used on any part of the aforesaid route, as a motive power, and no connection shall be made with any other road, other than for passenger purposes: *Provided*, That the said Frankford and Philadelphia Passenger Railway Company, shall charge the same rate of fare to persons, for riding in from Frankford to Master street, and from Master street to Frankford, as from Frankford to Lehigh avenue, and from Lehigh avenue to Frankford: *And provided further*, That if the said Frankford and Philadelphia Passenger Railway Company shall sell, exchange, or commutation, tickets, with the Union Passenger Railway Company, they shall make the same arrangements with the Second and Third Street Passenger Railway Company, and *vice versa: And provided further*, That if the railway of the said Frankford and Philadelphia Passenger Railway Company shall, at any time, be leased, or let, to any person, or persons, or to any Railway, or other company, or companies, the parties to such lease shall be bound by this act. —March 21, 1865.—P. L. 499.

Prohibition.

Rates to fare, relative to.

Parties leasing railway, to be bound by this act.

A Further Supplement

To the act to incorporate the West Philadelphia Passenger Railway Company, approved May fourteenth, one thousand eight hundred and fifty-seven.

SEC. 1. That the thirteenth section of an act, approved May fourteenth, one thousand eight hundred and fifty-seven, entitled "An Act to incorporate the West Philadelphia Passenger Railway Company," which provides, that the privileges granted the said company shall continue for the period of twenty years, and no longer, be and the same is hereby repealed; and that

Repeal of provision limiting term of charter.

all the privileges, granted by the said act of incorporation, to the West Philadelphia Passenger Railway Company, and its supplements, shall be held to have been granted, as if the restrictions and proviso, in the said thirteenth section, had never formed a part thereof.

Requirements as to running cars between certain streets

SEC. 2. That said company shall hereafter maintain, in good order, that portion of their road between Forty-first and Sixty-fifth streets, and shall run cars upon the same, at least one every half hour, from Forty-first to Sixty-fifth streets, and at least one every half hour, from Sixty-fifth to Forty-first streets, commencing every day except Sunday, at not later than half past six o'clock, A. M., and continuing until eight o'clock, P. M., inclusive, and after eight o'clock P. M., they shall run at least three trips up, and three trips down, at intervals of one hour each.—March 10, 1865.—P. L. 313.

A Further Supplement

To an act entitled "An Act to incorporate the Citizens' Passenger Railway Company of Philadelphia."

SEC. 1. That the Citizens' Passenger Railway Company of Philadelphia be and they are hereby authorized, whenever, and at such times as the public convenience may require, to extend their road northwardly, on Tenth and Eleventh streets, between Montgomery street and the Germantown road, with the right to connect the same, on any street between these two points, subject to all the limitations and restrictions, and with all the privileges, granted to the said company, under their act of incorporation.—March 22, 1865.—P. L. 568.

An Act

To incorporate the Broad Street and Island Road Company.

Commissioners.

SEC. 1. That Jacob Alburger, Charles Lloyd, D. B. Kershaw, Pearson Serrill, Thomas A. Scott, Mathew Baird, F. J. Dreer, George Rush Smith, George Cadwalader, D. K. Houtz, H. E. Wallace, William Millward, F. M'Ilvaine, W. W. Colkett, James C. Kelch, Robert Armstrong, Thomas A. Barlow, James Harper, D. K. Jackman, George Bokius, Thomas Daly, S. Kilpatrick, Charles F. Lex, John

L. Passmore, John H. Jones, B. J. Williams, S. D. Sagers, J. E. Black, Joseph Fuller, James Blaylock, William G. M'Michael, Q. C. Brown, John Kessler, C. Bastion, P. H. Kloshe, Charles Darragh, Thomas Dallas, Wm. J. Pollock, Charles Mink, Samuel Peak, R. Beaty, and John D. Look are hereby appointed commissioners, to open books, to receive subscriptions, and organize a company, by the name of Broad Street and Island Road Company, with power to construct a stone, or gravel, turnpike road, from a point, commencing at Broad street and its intersection with Passyunk road, and thence, along the said road, to Penrose ferry road, and thence, along the Penrose ferry road, and Island Road, to the terminus, or intersection of the Island road with the Darby road, subject to all the provisions and restrictions of an act regulating turnpike and plank road companies, passed the twenty-sixth day of January, one thousand eight hundred and forty-nine, and the supplements thereto, excepting that in lieu of erecting toll gates, and collecting toll, whenever five miles of road shall be finished, as provided in the twelfth section of said act, it shall be lawful for the company, hereby incorporated, to erect toll gates, and collect tolls, whenever one mile of such road is finished: *Pr vided*, That no toll shall be charged to persons going to or returning from funerals.

Name.

Construction of road authorized Route.

Subject to.

When tolls may be collected.

Proviso.

SEC. 2. That the capital stock of the said company shall consist of two thousand shares, at twenty-five dollars each.

Capital stock.

SEC. 3. That the said company shall have power to borrow any sum, not exceeding twenty thousand dollars, on their bonds, secured by a mortgage on their road, property and franchises of the company.

May borrow money.

SEC. 4. That no railroad shall ever be constructed on, or over, said road, or any part thereof, by said company, or others.

Prohibition.

SEC. 5 That if said company shall not commence the construction of said road, within two years from the passage of this act, and complete the same, within five years thereafter, then this act shall be null and void, except so far as the same may be necessary to settle up the affairs, and pay the debts of the company.—April 4, 1865.—P. L. 516.

When road to be commenced and completed.

A Further Supplement

To an act, entitled "An Act to incorporate the Lombard and South Street Railway Company," passed May sixteenth, one thousand eight hundred and sixty-one, to authorize said company to extend said road, and to create a ferry, across the river Schuylkill, at South street.

Authorized to extend their road.

SEC. 1. That the Lombard and South Street Passenger Railway Company are hereby authorized and empowered to extend their said railway north, by Front or Water street to Walnut street; thence down said Walnut street to Delaware avenue; thence along said Delaware avenue to Dock street.

Further extension may be made

SEC. 2. And furthermore, that the said Lombard and South Street Passenger Railway Company are hereby authorized to extend their said railway, by single, or double, track, from the wharf opposite South street, on the almshouse property, of the city of Philadelphia, west to the Darby road, at, or near, the Woodlands cemetery, by such route as the engineers of the said company may select, but in such manner as to avoid passing through any building of said almshouse; and further, to continue said railway, from the said Darby road, westward, along such streets, and by such roads, opened, or to be opened, for public use, as the said engineers may select, to Fiftieth street, or any point east of said Fiftieth street, as the said company may determine, with power to use any street, or streets, running north, or south, for the purpose of making a circuit.

May establish a public ferry across the Schuylkill, at South street.

SEC. 3. And that the said Lombard and South Street Passenger Railway Company are hereby authorized to establish a public ferry, across the Schuylkill river, by steamboats, or other conveyance, from South street wharf, opposite, on the almshouse property; but in no manner to interfere with the free navigation of the said river, or the right of the city of Philadelphia to construct a bridge, across the river Schuylkill, at South street; and to charge and receive such tolls as are customary, and are allowed, by law; and furthermore, are hereby authorized and empowered, to make an additional railway track, on Passyunk road, thereby making a double tract on said road; and that the said Lombard and South Street Passenger Railway Company can make a circuit, on any streets, west of Sixteenth, from Lombard to South street.—May 18, 1865.—P. L. 844.

Double track on Passyunk road, authorized, &c.

General Railroad Law.

SECTION 1. That whenever a special Act of the General Assembly shall hereafter be passed, authorizing the incorporation of a company for the construction of a railroad within this commonwealth, the commissioners named in such Act, or any five of them, shall have power to open books for receiving subscriptions to the capital stock of such company, at such time or times, and at such place or places, as they may deem expedient, after having given at least twenty days' notice, in one or more newspapers, published in the county where books of subscription are to be opened; and at the times and places so designated and named in the public notices to be given as aforesaid, the said commissioners, or any two of them, shall attend and furnish to all persons duly qualified, who shall offer to subscribe, an opportunity of so doing; and it shall be lawful for all such persons, and for all firms and co-partnerships, by themselves or by persons duly authorized, to subscribe for shares in said stock; and the said books shall be kept open at least six hours in every day, for the term of three juridical days, or until there shall have been subscribed the whole number of shares authorized by the special Act; and if at the expiration of three days, the books aforesaid shall not have the number of shares therein subscribed, the said commissioners may adjourn from time to time, and to such places as they may deem proper, until the whole number of shares authorized, as aforesaid, shall be subscribed, of which adjournment the commissioners aforesaid shall give such public notice as the occasion may require; and when the whole number of shares shall be subscribed, the books shall be closed: *Provided always*, That no subscription for such stock shall be valid unless the party or parties making the same shall, at the time of subscribing, pay to the said commissioners five dollars on each and every share subscribed, for the use of the company.

SEC. 2. That when ten per centum on the capital stock, as provided by any special Act of Incorporation, shall have been subscribed, and five dollars paid on each and

1. Act of February 19, 1849, Sec. 1, P. L. 79.
2. Act of February 19, 1849, Sec. 2, P. L. 80.

every share, as aforesaid, the said commissioners, or such of them as shall have acted, shall certify to the governor, under their hands and seals, the names of the subscribers, and the number of shares subscribed by each, and that five dollars on each share have been paid, whereupon the governor shall, by letters patent, under his hand and the seal of the commonwealth, create and constitute the subscribers, and if the subscription be not full at the time, those who shall thereafter subscribe to the number of shares aforesaid, their successors and assigns, into a body politic and corporate, in deed and in law, by the name, style and title designated by the special act of assembly; and by the said name, style and title, the said subscribers shall have perpetual succession, with all the privileges, franchises and immunities incident to a corporation, and be able to sue and be sued, plead and be impleaded, in all courts of record and elsewhere, and to purchase, receive, have, hold, use, and enjoy to them and their successors, goods, chattels, and estate, real and personal, of what kind and nature soever, and the same from time to time, to sell, exchange, mortgage, grant, alien, or otherwise dispose of, and to make dividends of such portion of the profits as they may deem proper; and also to make and have a common seal, and the same to alter and renew at pleasure, and also to ordain, establish, and put in execution such by-laws, ordinances, and regulations as shall appear necessary or convenient for the government of said corporation, not being contrary to the Constitution and laws of the United States, or of this commonwealth, and generally to do all and singular the matters and things which to them it shall lawfully appertain to do for the well being of said corporation, and the due ordering and management of the affairs thereof: *Provided*, That nothing herein contained shall be construed as in any way giving to such corporation any banking privileges whatever, or any other liberties, privileges, or franchises but such as may be necessary or convenient to the procuring, owning, making, maintaining regulating, and using their railroad, the locomotives, machinery, cars, and other appendages thereof, and the conveyance of passengers, the transportation of goods, merchandise, and other commodities thereon: *And provided further*, That such company shall not purchase or hold any real estate, except such as may be necessary or convenient for the making and constructing of their railroad, or for the furnishing of materials therefor, and for the accommedation of depots, offices, warehouses, machine shops, toll-houses, engine and water stations, and other appropriate appurtenances, and for the persons and things employed, or used in and about the same.

SEC. 3. That the commissioners named as aforesaid, or such of them as shall have acted, shall, as soon as conveniently may be after the said letters patent shall be obtained, appoint a time and place for the subscribers to meet, to organize the company, and shall give at least two weeks' notice thereof in the manner provided for in the first section of this act; and the said subscribers, when met, shall elect, by a majority of the votes present, to be given in person or by proxy, a president and twelve directors, the president and a majority of whom shall be resident citizens of this Commonwealth, and shall be owners respectively of at least three shares in the stock of such company; and the said president and directors shall conduct and manage the affairs and business of said company, until the second Monday in January then next ensuing, and until others are chosen; and may make, ordain and establish such by-laws, rules, orders and regulations, and perform such other matters and things as are by this act authorized: *Provided,* That in case of the resignation, death, or removal of the president, the directors shall, by a majority of votes, supply the vacancy until the next annual election.

SEC. 4. That the stockholders of such company shall meet on the second Monday in January in every year, at such place as may be fixed on by the by-laws, of which notice shall be given at least two weeks previously by the secretary, in the manner before mentioned, and choose, by a majority of the votes present, a president and twelve directors, qualified as aforesaid, for the ensuing year, who shall continue in office until the next annual election, and until others are chosen; at which annual meeting the said stockholders shall have full power and authority to make, alter or repeal, by a majority of votes given, any or all such by-laws, rules, orders and regulations as aforesaid, and do and perform every other corporate act authorized by their charter; the stockholders may meet at such other times and places as they be summoned by the president and directors, in such manner and form, and giving such notice as may be prescribed by the by-laws· and the

3. Act of February 19, 1849, Sec. 3, P. L. 80.
4. Act of February 19, 1849, Sec. 4, P. L. 81.

president, on the request, in writing, of any number of stockholders, representing not less than one-tenth in interest, shall call a special meeting, giving the like notice, and stating specifically the objects of the meeting; and the objects stated in such notice, and no other, shall be acted on at such special meeting.

SEC. 5. The elections for directors provided for in this Act, shall be conducted as follows, to wit: At the first election the commissioners shall appoint three stockholders to be judges of the said election, and to hold the same; and at every succeeding election the directors, for the time being, shall appoint three stockholders for the like purpose; and the persons so appointed by said commissioners and directors, shall not be eligible to an election as a director at said election, and shall respectively take and subscribe an oath or affirmation, before an alderman or justice of the peace, well and truly and according to law, to conduct such election to the best of their knowledge and ability; and the said judges shall decide upon the qualifications of voters, and when the election is closed, shall count the votes, and declare who have been elected; and if at any time it shall happen that an election of directors shall not be made at the specified time, the corporation shall not for that reason be dissolved; but it shall be lawful to hold and make such election of directors, on any day within three months thereafter, by giving at least ten days' previous notice of the time and place of holding said election in the manner aforesaid; and the directors of the preceding year shall in that case continue in office, and be invested with all powers belonging to them as such, until others are elected in their stead: in case of the death or resignation of a director, or a failure to elect in case of a tie vote, the vacancy may be filled by the board of directors: at all general meetings or elections by the stockholders, each share of stock shall entitle the holder thereof to one vote, and each ballot shall have endorsed thereon the number of shares thereby represented; but no share or shares transferred within sixty days next preceding any election, or general meeting of the stockholders, shall entitle the holder or holders thereof to vote at any such election or general meeting; nor shall any proxy be received, or entitle the holder to vote, unless the same shall bear date, and have been duly executed within the three months next preceding such election or general meeting.

5. Act of February 19, 1849, Sec. 5, P. L. 81.

SEC. 6. That the president and directors of such company, for the time being, are hereby authorized and empowered to exercise all the powers granted to the corporation; they shall meet at such times and places as shall be by them deemed most convenient for the transaction of their business, and when met, seven shall be a quorum to do business; the president, if present, shall preside at all meetings of the board, and when absent, the board shall appoint a president *pro tem.;* they shall keep minutes of their proceedings fairly entered in a suitable book to be kept for that purpose; they shall choose a secretary and treasurer, and may appoint or employ all such officers, engineers, agents, superintendents, artizans, workmen or other persons, as in their opinions may be necessary or proper in the management of the affairs and business of said corporation, at such times, in such manner, and under such regulations as they may from time to time determine; they shall fix the amount of the salaries and wages of such officers and persons employed by them, and they may require bond, with security in such amounts as they may deem necessary, of each or any of said officers or other persons by them appointed and employed, for the faithful discharge of their duties, and generally to do all such other acts, matters and things as by this act and the by-laws and regulations of the said company, they may be authorized to do.

SEC. 7. That the president and directors of such company first chosen, shall procure certificates or evidences of stock for all the shares of such company, and shall deliver one or more certificates or evidences, signed by the president, countersigned by the treasurer, and sealed with the common seal of the corporation, to such person or party entitled to receive the same, according to the number of shares by him, her, or them respectively subscribed or held; which certificates or evidences of stock shall be transferable at the pleasure of the holder, in a suitable book or books to be kept by the company for that purpose, in person or by attorney duly authorized, in the presence of the president or treasurer, subject, however, to all payments due or to become due thereon; and the assignee or party to whom the same shall have been so transferred, shall thereupon be a member of said corporation, and have and enjoy all the immunities, privileges

6. Act of February 19, 1849, Sec. 6, P. L. 81.
7. Act of February 19, 1849, Sec. 7, P. L. 82.

and franchises, and be subject to all the liabilities, conditions and penalties incident thereto, in the same manner as the original subscriber would have been: *Provided*, That no certificate shall be transferred so long as the holder thereof is indebted to said company, unless the board of directors shall consent thereto: *And provided*, That no such transfer of stock shall have the effect of discharging any liabilities or penalties theretofore incurred by the owner thereof.

SEC. 8. The capital stock of such company shall be divided into shares of fifty dollars each, and shall be called in and paid at such times and places, and in such proportions and instalments, not, however, exceeding five dollars per share in any period of thirty days, as the directors shall require, of which public notice shall be given for at least two weeks next preceding the time or times appointed for that purpose, in the manner above mentioned; and if any stockholder shall neglect to pay such proportion or instalment so called for at the time and place appointed, he, she, or they shall be liable to pay, in addition to the proportion or instalment so called for, at the rate of one per cent. per month for the delay of such payment; and if the same and the additional penalty, or any part thereof, shall remain unpaid for the period of six months, he, she or they shall, at the discretion of the directors, forfeit to the use of the company, all right, title and interest in and to every and all share or shares, on account of which such default in payment may be made as aforesaid, or the directors may, at their option, cause suit to be brought before any competent tribunal, for the recovery of the amount due on such shares, together with the penalty of one per cent. per month as aforesaid; and in the event of a forfeiture, the share or shares so forfeited may be disposed of at the discretion of the president and directors, under such rules and regulations as may be prescribed by the by-laws. No stockholder shall be entitled to vote at any election, nor at any general or special meeting of the company, on whose share or shares any instalment or arrearages may be due more than thirty days next preceding said election or meeting: *Provided*, That no forfeiture of stock shall release or discharge the owner thereof from any liabilities or penalties incurred prior to the time of such forfeiture.

SEC. 9. That the dividends of so much of the profits of

8. Act of February 19, 1849, Sec. 7, P. L. 82.
9. Act of February 19, 1849, Sec. 9, P. L. 83.

such company as shall appear advisable to the directors, shall be declared in the months of July and January in each and every year, and be paid to the stockholders or their legal representatives, on application at the office of such company, at any time after the expiration of ten days from the time of declaring the same; but the said dividends shall in no case exceed the amount of the net profits actually acquired by the company, so that the capital stock shall never be impaired thereby; and if the said directors shall make any dividend which shall impair the capital stock of the company, the directors consenting thereto shall be liable, in their individual capacities, to such company for the amount of the capital stock so divided, recoverable by action of debt as in other cases; and each director present when such dividend shall be declared, shall be considered as consenting thereto, unless he forthwith enter his protest on the minutes of the board, and give public notice to the stockholders of the declaring of such dividend.

SEC. 10. That the president and directors of such company shall have power and authority by themselves, their engineers, superintendents, agents, artizans and workmen, to survey, ascertain, locate, fix, mark, and determine such route for a railroad as they may deem expedient, not, however, passing through any burying-ground or place of public worship, or any dwelling-house in the occupancy of the owner or owners thereof, without his, her, or their consent, and not except in the neighborhood of deep cuttings, or high embankments, or places selected for sidelings, turnouts, depots, engine or water stations, to exceed sixty feet in width, and thereon to lay down, erect, construct and establish a railroad, with one or more tracks, with such branches or lateral roads as may be especially authorized, and with such bridges, viaducts, turnouts, sidelings, or other devices as they may deem necessary or useful between the points named in the special act incorporating such company, commencing at or within, and extending to or into, any town, city or village named as the place of beginning or terminus of such road; and in like manner, by themselves, or other persons by them appointed or employed as aforesaid, to enter upon and into, and occupy all land on which the said railroad or depots, warehouses, offices, toll-houses, engine and water stations, other buildings or appurtenances hereinbefore

10. Act of February 19, 1849, Sec. 10, P. L. 83.

mentioned may be located, or which may be necessary or convenient for the erection of the same, or for any purpose necessary or useful in the construction, maintenance or repairs of said railroad, and therein and thereon to dig, excavate and embank, make, grade, and lay down and construct the same; and it shall in like manner be lawful for such company, their officers, agents, engineers, contractors or workmen, with their implements and beasts of draught or burden, to enter upon any lands adjoining or in the neighborhood of their railroad, so to be constructed, and to quarry, dig, cut, take and carry away therefrom, any stone, gravel, clay, sand, earth, wood, or other suitable material necessary or proper for the construction of any bridges, viaduct or other buildings, which may be required for the use, maintenance or repairs of said railroad: *Provided,* That before such company shall enter upon or take possession of any such lands or materials, they shall make ample compensation to the owner or owners thereof, or tender adequate security therefor: *Provided further,* That the timber used in the construction or repair of such railroad shall be obtained from the owner thereof only by agreement or purchase: *And provided further,* That whenever any company shall locate its road in and upon any street or alley, in any city or borough, ample compensation shall be made to the owners of lots fronting upon such street or alley, for any damages they may sustain, by reason of any excavation or embankment made in the construction of such road, to be ascertained as other damages are authorized to be ascertained by this act.

SEC. 11. That when the said company cannot agree with the owner or owners of any lands or materials, for the compensation proper for the damage done or likely to be done to, or sustained by, any such owner or owners of such lands or materials, which such company may enter upon, use or take away, in pursuance of the authority hereinbefore given, or by reason of the absence or legal incapacity of any such owner or owners, no such compensation can be agreed upon, the Court of Common Pleas of the proper county, on application thereto by petition, either by said company or owner or owners, or any one in behalf of either, shall appoint seven discreet and disinterested freeholders of said county, neither of whom shall be residents or owners of property upon or adjoining the line of such railroad, and appoint a time, not less than twenty nor more

11. Act of February 19, 1849, Sec. 11, P. L. 84.

than thirty days thereafter, for said viewers to meet at or upon the premises where the damages are alleged to be sustained, of which time and place ten days' notice shall be given by the petitioner to the said viewers and the other party; and the said viewers, or any five of them, having been first duly sworn or affirmed, faithfully, justly and impartially to decide, and true report to make concerning all matters and things to be submitted to them, and in relation to which they are authorized to inquire in pursuance of the provisions of this act, and having viewed the premises, they shall estimate and determine the quantity, quality and value of said lands so taken or occupied, or to be so taken or occupied, or the materials so used or taken away, as the case may be, and having a due regard to, and making just allowance for, the advantages which may have resulted, or which may seem likely to result, to the owner or owners of said land or materials, in consequence of the making or opening of said railroad, and of the construction of works connected therewith; and after having made a fair and just comparison of said advantages and disadvantages, they shall estimate and determine whether any, and if any, what amount of damages has been or may be sustained, and to whom payable, and make report thereof to the said Court; and if any damages be awarded, and the report be confirmed by the said Court, judgment shall be entered thereon; and if the amount thereof be not paid within thirty days after the entry of such judgment, execution may then issue thereon as in other cases of debt, for the sum so awarded, and the costs and expenses incurred shall be defrayed by the said railroad company; and each of said viewers shall be entitled to one dollar and fifty cents per day for every day necessarily employed in the performance of the duties herein prescribed, to be paid by such railroad company.

SEC. 12. That whenever, in the construction of such road or roads, it shall be necessary to cross or intersect any established road or way, it shall be the duty of the president and directors of the said company so to construct the said road across such established road or way as not to impede the passage or transportation of persons or property along the same; and that, for the accommodation of all persons owning or possessing land through which the said railroad may pass, it shall be the duty of such company to make, or cause to be made, a good and sufficient

12. Act of February 19, 1849, Sec. 12, P. L. 84.

causeway or causeways, whenever the same may be necessary to enable the occupant or occupants of said lands to cross or pass over the same, with wagons, carts and implements of husbandry, as occasion may require; and the said causeway or causeways, when so made, shall be maintained and kept in good repair by such company; and if the said company shall neglect or refuse, on request, to make such causeway or causeways, or when made, to keep the same in good order, the said company shall be liable to pay any person aggrieved thereby all damages sustained by such person in consequence of such neglect or refusal; such damages to be assessed and ascertained in the same manner as provided in the last section for the assessment of damages: *Provided*, That the said company shall, in no case, be required to make, or cause to be made, more than one causeway through each plantation or lot of land, for the accommodation of any one person owning or possessing land through which the said railroad may pass; and where any public road shall cross such railroad, the person owning or possessing land through which the said public road may pass, shall not be entitled to require the company to erect or keep in repair any causeway or bridge for the accommodation of the occupant of said land.

SEC. 13. That if any such railroad company shall find it necessary to change the site of any portion of any turnpike or public road, they shall cause the same to be re-constructed forthwith at their own proper expense, on the most favorable location, and in as perfect a manner as the original road: *Provided*, That the damages incurred in changing the location of any road authorized by this section, shall be ascertained and paid by such company, in the same manner as is provided for in regard to the location and construction of their own road.

SEC. 14. That in all suits or actions against such company, the service of process on the president, secretary, treasurer, engineer, agent, or any director of the same, shall be good and available in law; but no suit or action shall be prosecuted by any person or persons for any penalties incurred under this act, unless such suit or action shall be commenced within two years next after the offence committed or cause of action accrued; and the defendants in such suit or action may plead the general issue, and give this act and the special matter in evidence, and that the same was done in pursuance and by authority of this act.

13. Act of February 19, 1849, Sec. 13, P. L. 85.
14. Act of February 19, 1849, Sec. 14, P. L. 85.

SEC. 15. That if any person or persons shall wilfully and knowingly break, injure or destroy any railroad authorized by special act of assembly, or any part thereof, or any edifice, device, property or work, or any part thereof, or any machinery, engine, car, implement or utensil, erected, owned or used by such company, in pursuance of this act, he, she or they so offending shall forfeit and pay to such company three times the actual damage so sustained, to be sued for and recovered with full costs, before any tribunal having cognizance thereof, by action in the name and for the use of the company.

SEC. 16. That if any person or persons shall wilfully and maliciously remove or destroy any part of the road, property, buildings, or other works belonging to such company, or place, designedly and with evil intent, any obstruction on the line of such railroad, so as to jeopard the safety or endanger the lives of persons traveling on or over the same, such person or persons so offending shall be deemed guilty of a misdemeanor, and shall, on conviction, be imprisoned in the county jail or penitentiary, at the discretion of the court, for a term not more than three years: *Provided.* That nothing herein contained shall prevent the company from pursuing any other appropriate remedy at law in such cases.

SEC. 17. That at each annual meeting of the stockholders of any such company, the president and managers of the preceding year shall exhibit to them a full and complete statement of the affairs and proceedings of the company for such year, with all such matters as shall be necessary to convey to the stockholders a full knowledge of the condition and affairs of said company; and the said president and directors of every such company shall, whenever required, furnish to the legislature, or either branch thereof, a full and authentic report of their affairs and transactions, or such information relating thereto as may be demanded of them.

SEC. 18. That upon the completion of any railroad authorized as aforesaid, the same shall be esteemed a public highway for the conveyance of passengers and the transportation of freight, subject to such rules and regulations in relation to the same, and to the size and construction of wheels, cars and carriages, the weight of loads, and all

15. Act of February 19, 1849, Sec. 15, P. L. 85.
16. Act of February 19, 1849, Sec. 16, L. L. 85.
17. Act of February 19, 1849, Sec. 17, P. L. 86.
18. Act of February 19, 1848, Sec. 18, P. L. 86.

other matters and things connected with the use of said railroad, as the president and directors may prescribe and direct: *Provided*, That the said company shall have the exclusive control of the motive power, and may, from time to time, establish, demand and receive such rates of toll, or other compensation, for the use of such road and of said motive power, and for the conveyance of passengers, the transportation of merchandise and commodities, and the cars or other vehicles containing the same, or otherwise passing over or on the said railroad, as to the president and directors shall seem reasonable: *Provided, however, nevertheless*, That said rates of toll and motive power charges so to be established, demanded or received, when the cars used for such conveyance or transportation are owned or furnished by others, shall not exceed two and one-half cents per mile for each passenger, three cents per mile for each ton of two thousand pounds of freight, three cents per mile for each passenger or baggage car, and two cents per mile for each burden or freight car, every four wheels being computed a car; and in the transportation of passengers, no charge shall be made to exceed three cents per mile for through passengers, and three and a-half cents per mile for way passengers.

SEC. 19. That if any company incorporated as aforesaid shall not commence the construction of their proposed railroad within three years, and complete and open the same for use, with at least one track, within the term prescribed by the special act authorizing the same, or if, after completion, the said railroad shall be suffered to go into decay, and be impassable for the term of two years, then their charter shall be null and void, except so far as to compel the said company to make reparation for damages.

SEC. 20. That if any company incorporated as aforesaid, shall at any time misuse or abuse any of the privileges granted by this act, or by the special act of incorporation, the legislature may revoke all and singular the rights and privileges so granted to such company; and the legislature hereby reserves the power to resume, alter or amend any charter granted under this act, and take for public use any road constructed in pursuance of such charter: *Provided*, That in resuming, altering, or amending said charters, no injustice shall be done to the corporators; and that in taking such roads for public use, full compensation shall be made to the stockholders.

19. Act of February 19, 1849, Sec. 19, P. L. 86.
20. Act of February 19, 1849, Sec. 20, P. L. 86.

A Supplement

To an Act entitled, "An Act regulating Railroad Companies," approved the nineteenth day of February, Anno Domini 1849.

WHEREAS, Some doubts and difficulties have arisen in regard to the intention and proper construction of the first section of a certain act approved the twenty-seventh day of April, Anno Domini one thousand eight hundred and fifty-five, entitled "An act extending the right of trial by jury to certain cases:" Now, for the removal of said doubts and difficulties, and for certainty in the premises,

SECTION 1. That the true intent and meaning of the said act was, that it should apply to and embrace cases pending at the time of the passage of said act.

SECT. 2. That hereafter in all cases where the parties cannot agree upon the amount of damages claimed, or by reason of the absence or legal incapacity of such owner or owners no such agreement can be made, either for lands, water, water rights, or materials, the company shall tender a bond, with at least two sufficient sureties, to the party claiming or entitled to any damages, or to the attorney or agent of any person absent, or to the guardian or committee of any one under legal incapacity, the condition of which shall be, that the company will pay or cause to be paid such amount of damages as the party shall be entitled to receive, after the same shall have been agreed upon by the parties, or assessed in the manner provided for by this and the act to which it is a supplement: *Provided*, That in case the party or parties claiming damages refuse, or do not accept the bond as tendered, the said company shall then give the party a written notice of the time when the same will be presented for filing in court; and thereafter the said company may present said bond to the Court of Common Pleas of the county where the lands, water, or materials are, and if the bond and sureties are approved, the bond shall be filed in said court for the benefit of those interested; and recovery may be had thereon for the amount of damages assessed, if the same be not paid or cannot be made by execution on the judgment in the issue formed to try the question.

1. Act of April 9, 1856, Sec. 1, P. L. 288.
2. Act of April 9, 1856, Sec. 2, P. L. 288.

SECT. 3. That the viewers provided for in the thirteenth section of the act to which this is a supplement, may be appointed before or after the entry for constructing said road, or taking materials therefor, and upon the report of said viewers, or any four of them, being filed in said court, either party within thirty days thereafter, may file his, her, or their appeal from said report to the said court; after such an appeal, either party may put the cause at issue in the form directed by said court, and the same shall then be tried by said court and a jury; and after final judgment, either party may have a writ of error thereto from the Supreme Court, in the manner prescribed in other cases. The said court shall have power to order what notices shall be given connected with any part of the proceedings, and may make all such orders connected with the same as may be deemed requisite. If any exceptions be filed with any appeal to the proceedings, they shall be speedily disposed of; and if allowed, a new view shall be ordered; and if disallowed, the appeal shall proceed as before provided.

An Act

For the better security of the holders of the bonds of Passenger Railways in the City of Philadelphia.

SECTION 1. That every act of Assembly authorizing any passenger railway company in the city of Philadelphia to issue bonds, shall be construed to authorize such company to mortgage their road and franchises to secure such bonds.

3. Act of April 9, 1856, Sec. 3, P. L. 289.
1. Act of April 2, 1860, Sec. 1, P. L. 562.

General Ordinances relative to Passenger Railways.

SECTION 1. That all Passenger Railroad Companies within the City of Philadelphia shall be subject to the restrictions, limitations, terms and conditions hereinafter provided; and any such company, before entering upon any road, street, avenue or alley, with the limits of said city, shall be understood and deemed to be subject thereto, upon the conditions hereinafter prescribed.

SEC. 2. That it shall be the duties of said companies, or any of them, to conform to the surveys, regulations and gradients as they are now or may hereafter be established by law. They shall submit all proposed plans, courses, styles of rails, and the manner of laying the same, to the Board of Surveys and Regulations, for their approval and sanction, which shall be obtained before they proceed to break the ground or occupy any of the highways as aforesaid; and they shall be further required to lay flag-stones or crossings along the line of the paved streets upon which the rails are laid, at intervals not exceeding two hundred and fifty feet; and any neglect, omission or refusal to do so on the part of any such company, shall be punished by a fine of not less than fifty dollars, for each and every offence, recoverable before any alderman of the City of Philadelphia, and payable into the city treasury.

SEC. 3. That all Railroad Companies as aforesaid, shall be at the entire cost and expense of maintaining, paving, repairing and repaving that may be necessary upon any road, street, avenue or alley, occupied by them. That for the convenience of the public, it shall also be the duty of such companies to clear the streets, or other public highways that they may occupy, of snow, or any obstructions placed therein by such companies, when the same impedes the travel upon said highways, and for any neglect on their part to do so for a period of five days, they shall be punishable by a fine of twenty dollars for each square that may be so impeded, recoverable before any alderman of the City of Philadelphia, and payable into the city trea

1. Ordinance of July 7, 1857, Sec. 1, p. 248.
2. Ordinance of July 7, 1857, Sec. 2, p. 248.
3. Ordinance of July 7, 1857, Sec. 3, p. 248.

sury, upon complaint of five citizens residing therein, upon oath or affirmation: *Provided, nevertheless,* That whenever any such company shall deem it inexpedient to use their said road during the continuance of the snow, they shall provide comfortable sleighs, or other vehicles for the transportation of passengers along the route of their railway, at the usual rates as aforesaid, then, and in that case, no such penalty shall be recoverable.

SEC. 4. That it shall be the duty of any company as aforesaid, when requested so to do by the Chief Commisssioner of Highways, to remove any obstruction, mend or repair their road, pave or repave the highways as hereinbefore provided, and should they refuse or neglect to do so for thirty days from the date of such notice, then and in such case, the Councils may forbid the running of any car or cars upon said road until the same is fully complied with; and the city reserves the right in all such cases to repair or repave such streets, and the expense thereof shall be a judgment upon the road, stock and effects of such company, recoverable as such judgments are now recoverable by the City of Philadelphia.

SECT. 5. It shall be the duty of said company or companies to employ careful, sober and prudent agents, conductors or drivers, to take charge of their car or cars when upon the road, and for the violation of any act of Assembly or ordinance of the city, on the part of any such officer or officers, or employees upon said road, the company shall be liable for all fines, forfeitures or damages arising therefrom: *Provided, however,* That this act shall not be taken to excuse or free any such officer or employee from the penalties or responsibilties of any such violation or other acts by them committed.

SEC. 6. The running speed of the cars upon any City Passenger Railroad shall not at any time be at a greater rate than six miles an hour in the paved and built-up portion of the city, nor shall they incommode the crossings, nor stop at the corners of any street or elsewhere, to solicit passengers. It shall also be the duty of conductors and drivers of the cars to give ample notice to drivers of vehicles and pedestrians of their approach, and also to afford all reasonable opportunity for them or either of them to avoid collision or accident, and any neglect by

4. Ordinance of July 7, 1857, Sec. 4, p. 249.
5. Ordinance of July 7, 1857, Sec. 5, p. 249.
6. Ordinance of July 7, 1857, Sec. 6, p. 250.

them to comply with the provisions of this section, shall be punishable by a fine of five dollars, to be recovered before any alderman of the city, and paid into the city treasury, and the Mayor of the city is in such cases empowered to revoke the license of such car or cars, and they shall not be permitted to be again placed on the road until such license is renewed.

SEC. 7. It shall be incumbent on all railroad companies, as aforesaid, before placing cars upon their road, to pay into the office of the Chief Commissioner of Highways, and annually thereafter, for the use of the city, the sum of five dollars for each car intended to be run on the same. They shall also have the number painted in some conspicuous place upon each car; and any omission or neglect to comply with either of these provisions, shall be punishable by a fine of ten dollars, to be recovered on complaint before any alderman of the city, who shall pay the same forthwith into the city treasury.

SEC. 8. The Directors of any such company or companies shall immediately after the completion of any passenger railroad in the city, file in the office of the City Solicitor a detailed statement, under the seal of the company, and certified under oath or affirmation by the president and secretary of the entire cost of the same; and the City of Philadelphia reserves the right at any time to purchase the same, by paying the original costs of said road or roads and cars, at a fair valuation. And any such company or companies, refusing to consent to such purchase, shall thereby forfeit all privileges, rights and immunities they may have acquired in the use or possession of any of the highways as aforesaid; or should any such company or corporation neglect to run cars upon their road or roads for the accommodation of the public, for the space of three consecutive months, the Councils reserve the right to rent the same to any other person or persons, company or companies, who will be willing to run cars on the same; or in the event of the Councils as aforesaid being unable to rent said road, or place cars upon the same for one year after the same shall have been abandoned, as aforesaid, by the company constructing or owning the same, then and in such case, the Councils reserve the right to cause the said road to be removed from the highways, and to sell or dispose of the materials thereof, and after paying all expenses

7. Ordinance of July 7, 1857, Sec. 7, p. 250.
8. Ordinance of July 7, 1857, Sec. 8, p. 251.

arising therefrom, pay the balance, if any, to the legal representatives of the said defaulting company.

SEC. 9. Any Passenger Railroad Company, which is now or may hereafter be incorporated in the City of Philadelphia, shall, by their proper officer or officers, who shall sign the same, file in the office of the City Solicitor a written obligation to comply with the provisions of this ordinance: *Provided*, That no railroad company now incorporated shall be authorized to commence work upon any of the highways of the city until this section has been complied with; and a failure to do so for ten days, shall be taken and deemed as a refusal on the part of said company; and in case the Philadelphia and Delaware River Railroad Company should fail to comply with the provisions of this section, on or before the 8th day of July, proximo, the City Councils hereby express their disapproval of an Act entitled "A Supplement to an Act to incorporate the Philadelphia and Delaware River Railroad Company," approved June 9, 1857, which provides for the construction of a Passenger Railway by a private corporation, over Fifth and Sixth streets, in the City of Philadelphia.

An Ordinance.

Supplementary to an Ordinance entitled "An Ordinance to regulate Passenger Railways," approved July 7th, 1857.

SECTION 1. That all passenger railroad companies, within the limits of the city of Philadelphia, shall, in addition to the restrictions, limitations, terms, and conditions contained in an Ordinance, entitled "An Ordinance to regulate Passenger Railways," approved July 7, 1857, be subject to all the restrictions, limitations, terms and conditions hereinafter provided for, to wit:—

First. They shall be required to lay flag-stones or crossings of not less than two feet in width, across the entire width of all paved streets occupied by them, at each and every public lane, street, or alley opening upon any street or highway upon which the rails are laid, and where no such street, lane or alley opens thereon, then the said flagging shall be at distances of not exceeding two hundred and fifty feet.

Second. That all streets or highways which are unpaved at the time of laying the rails, shall be kept in good trav-

9. Ordinance of July 7, 1857, Sec. 9, p. 251.
1. Ordinance of April 1, 1859, Sec. 1, p. 138.

elling order by the railroad company, until the same shall be paved by the owners of property thereon, after which they shall be repaved, repaired and kept in good order, at the proper cost of the railroad company occupying the same.

Third. That each and every passenger railway company shall pay into the office of the Chief Commissioner of Highways, in the month of January of each year, for the use of the city, the sum of thirty dollars for each car intended to be run upon any road; and for each and every car placed upon any road before the time herein provided for paying the license, a proportionate sum shall be paid until the succeeding January, and that no car shall be placed or run upon any road or street, until it shall be regularly licensed, and a certificate duly numbered, hung in a conspicuous place in said car.

Fourth. That no connection shall be made by one company with the road of any other company, without the special authority of city councils, except when otherwise provided for by their charter.

Fifth. That no passenger railway shall, at any time, be used for any other purpose than passenger travel.

Sixth. That whenever and wherever it may be found necessary for any company to lay iron plates or any other material across any gutter along the line of any railroad, the same shall be laid from curbstone to curbstone, and under direction and supervision of the Chief Commissioner of Highways, and the company laying the same, or whose road passes over such crossings, shall be required to keep the said gutters, at all times, open and free from all obstructions, whether by dirt, ice, or from any other cause; and they shall be required to keep a passage way for carts and vehicles clear of snow in the winter season on each side of their track or railway.

SEC. 2. That all persons driving vehicles on any passenger railway in the city, in the direction that the cars travel on said roads, shall have the right to the railway track when meeting any other vehicle going in the opposite direction; and the driver of the vehicle going in the opposite direction shall be compelled to turn entirely off the track, under a penalty of five dollars, to be recovered before any alderman, in any suit or action brought to recover the same, which penalty shall be paid into the city treasury for the use of the city: *Provided*, That the rail-

2. Ordinance of April 1, 1859, Sec. 2, p. 140.

road company shall in all cases have the first right of way, subject to like penalty.

SEC. 3. That whenever it shall be found necessary for the city of Philadelphia to occupy all or any portion of any street or highway, whereupon a passenger railroad now is, or hereafter may be constructed, for the purpose of making improvements thereon, such as culverts, laying of water or gas pipes, or any other alteration or improvement that may from time to time be found necessary, the said city shall have full and entire power and authority to make such alteration or improvement, without recourse on the part of any railroad company against the said city, for any obstruction or embarrassment that the said railroad Company may meet with, consequent upon such alteration or improvement: *Provided, however*, That on the occasion of any alteration or improvement as hereinbefore recited, directed to be done, or performed by the authority of councils, no unnecessary delay shall be made or caused in any manner that shall work prejudicial to the interest of the railroad company.

SEC. 4. That any city passenger railway company now incorporated, or that may be hereafter incorporated, shall, after notice has been given to said company by the Chief Commissioner of Highways, repave or repair from curb-stone to curb-stone any street over and along which the tracks or rails of said company may pass; the said paving and repairing shall be done according to the grade now established, or that may be hereafter established by law, and shall replace the grade of said street so far as the same may be altered by said company and shall repave any street used by said company as aforesaid, within the time fixed by the Chief Commissioner of Highways in said notice. They shall also remove any gravel, dirt, materials or other obstructions placed by said company on any street within forty-eight hours after notice shall have been given to said company by the Chief Commissioner of Highways, and if said company shall fail to comply with the provisions of this section according to the term of notice served upon it, the Chief Commissioner of Highways shall pave, repave and repair the streets, replace the grades thereof, and remove such gravel, dirt, materials, or other obstructions, the cost of which shall be collected of and from said company by the city of Philadelphia.

3. Ordinance of April 1, 1859, Sec. 3, p. 140.
4. Ordinance of April 1, 1859, Sec. 4, p. 141.

SEC. 5. That for each and every violation of the provisions of this ordinance, such railroad company shall pay a penalty of fifty dollars; and for every continued violation of any of the provisions thereof after notice by the Commissioner of Highways, the penalty shall be five dollars for each and every day the violation continues; and the Chief Commissioner of Highways shall have authority, when directed by councils, to stop the running of all cars upon any road whose company refuses to pay the penalty as provided herein.

SEC. 6. That so much of the 3d Section of the Ordinance approved July 7, 1857, to which this is a Supplement, as provides that the railroad companies shall pave any street that has not heretofore been paved, be and the same is hereby repealed.

An Ordinance.

Supplementary to an Ordinance approved the Seventh day of July 1857, *entitled an Ordinance to regulate Passenger Railways.*

SECTION 1. The Select and Common Councils of the City of Philadelphia, do ordain, That whenever any Passenger Railway shall hereafter be made or laid down in the City of Philadelphia, or whenever any part or portion of any such Railway now laid down shall be relaid, the sides thereof shall be paved with cubical blocks or granite laid on each side of the rail to the extent of the lines of said Railway so laid or relaid within the limits of the City.

5. Ordinance of April 1, 1859, Sec. 5, p. 141.
6. Ordinance of April 1, 1859, Sec. 6, p. 141.
1. Ordinance of October 16, 1860, Sec. 1, page 362.

A Supplement.

To an Ordinance entitled "An Ordinance to regulate Passenger Railways," approved the 7th day of July, A. D. 1857.

SECTION 1. That if any passenger railway company required by law to maintain and keep in repair the roads, streets, avenues or alleys occupied by them, shall suffer any such road, street, avenue or alley, or any part thereof, to be and remain out of repair, it shall be the duty of the Chief Commissioner of Highways to give such company a notice in writing forthwith to put the same in good repair, and if, at the expiration of ten days from the service of such notice, the said road, street, avenue or alley, or part thereof, mentioned in such notice, shall not have been repaired by the said company, such company shall forfeit and pay a fine of twenty-five dollars for each and every day such road, street, avenue or alley, or part thereof, shall be suffered thereafter to remain out of repair, to be recovered, with costs of suit, as debts of like amount are by law recoverable. And if, at the expiration of a further period of fifteen days thereafter, such street, road, avenue or alley, or part thereof, shall still remain unrepaired by such company, it shall be the duty of the Chief Commissioner of Highways forthwith to repair the same, and thereupon the City Solicitor shall bring suit against such offending company to recover as well the several penalties incurred for such offence, as also for the amount expended by the Chief Commissioner in the repairing of such road, street, avenue or alley

1. Ordinance of October 5, 1863, Sec. 1, page. 283.

www.ingramcontent.com/pod-product-compliance
Lightning Source LLC
LaVergne TN
LVHW010134110826
845151LV00002B/351

* 9 7 8 1 4 2 5 5 4 0 3 1 9 *